# T. B. PETERSON AND BROTHERS'

COMPLETE AND ILLUSTRATED EDITIONS OF

# CHARLES DICKENS' WORKS.

☞ GREAT REDUCTION IN THEIR PRICES. ☜

## PEOPLE'S DUODECIMO EDITION. ILLUSTRATED.

*Reduced in price from* **$2.50** *to* **$1.50** *a volume.*

*This edition is printed on fine paper, from large, clear type, leaded, Long Primer in size, that all can read, and each book is complete in one large duodecimo volume.*

| | | | |
|---|---|---|---|
| Our Mutual Friend,......Cloth, | $1.50 | Little Dorrit,...............Cloth, | $1.50 |
| Pickwick Papers,..........Cloth, | 1.50 | Dombey and Son,.........Cloth, | 1.50 |
| Nicholas Nickleby,.......Cloth, | 1.50 | Christmas Stories,........Cloth, | 1.50 |
| Great Expectations,......Cloth, | 1.50 | Sketches by "Boz,".......Cloth, | 1.50 |
| Lamplighter's Story,.....Cloth, | 1.50 | Barnaby Rudge,...........Cloth, | 1.50 |
| David Copperfield,........Cloth, | 1.50 | Martin Chuzzlewit,.......Cloth, | 1.50 |
| Oliver Twist,...............Cloth, | 1.50 | Old Curiosity Shop,......Cloth, | 1.50 |
| Bleak House,...............Cloth, | 1.50 | Message from the Sea,...Cloth, | 1.50 |
| A Tale of Two Cities,....Cloth, | 1.50 | Dickens' New Stories,....Cloth, | 1.50 |

| | |
|---|---|
| Price of a set, in Black cloth, in eighteen volumes...................... | $27.00 |
| " " Full sheep, Library style,.............................. | 36.00 |
| " " Half calf, sprinkled edges,............................ | 45.00 |
| " " Half calf, marbled edges,.............................. | 50.00 |
| " " Half calf, antique,........................................ | 55.00 |
| " " Half calf, full gilt backs, etc.......................... | 55.00 |

## ILLUSTRATED OCTAVO EDITION.

*Reduced in price from* **$2.50** *to* **$2.00** *a volume.*

*This edition is printed from large type, double column, octavo page, each book being complete in one volume, the whole containing near Six Hundred Illustrations, by Cruikshank, Phiz, Browne, Maclise, McLenan, and other eminent artists.*

| | | | |
|---|---|---|---|
| Our Mutual Friend,.....Cloth, | $2.00 | David Copperfield,.......Cloth, | $2.00 |
| Pickwick Papers,.........Cloth, | 2.00 | Barnaby Rudge,..........Cloth, | 2.00 |
| Nicholas Nickleby,.......Cloth, | 2.00 | Martin Chuzzlewit,......Cloth, | 2.00 |
| Great Expectations,......Cloth, | 2.00 | Old Curiosity Shop,......Cloth, | 2.00 |
| Lamplighter's Story,....Cloth, | 2.00 | Christmas Stories,.......Cloth, | 2.00 |
| Oliver Twist,..............Cloth, | 2.00 | Dickens' New Stories,...Cloth, | 2.00 |
| Bleak House,..............Cloth, | 2.00 | A Tale of Two Cities,...Cloth, | 2.00 |
| Little Dorrit,..............Cloth, | 2.00 | American Notes and | |
| Dombey and Son,........Cloth, | 2.00 | Pic-Nic Papers,........Cloth, | 2.00 |
| Sketches by "Boz,".....Cloth, | 2.00 | | |

| | |
|---|---|
| Price of a set, in Black cloth, in eighteen volumes...................... | $36.00 |
| " " Full sheep, Library style.................................. | 45.00 |
| " " Half calf, sprinkled edges................................ | 55.00 |
| " " Half calf, marbled edges.................................. | 62.00 |
| " ' Half calf, antique.......................................... | 70.00 |
| " " Half calf, full gilt backs, etc............................ | 70.00 |

☞ Books sent, postage paid, on receipt of the Retail Price, by T. B. Peterson & Brothers, Philadelphia, Pa.

(1)

# CHARLES DICKENS' WORKS.

## ILLUSTRATED DUODECIMO EDITION.

*Reduced in price from $2.00 to $1.50 a volume.*

*This edition is printed on the finest paper, from large, clear type, leaded, Long Primer in size, that all can read, the whole containing near Six Hundred full page Illustrations, printed on tinted paper, from designs by Cruikshank, Phiz, Browne, Maclise, McLenan, and other artists. The following books are each contained in two volumes.*

| | | | |
|---|---|---|---|
| Our Mutual Friend,......Cloth, | $3.00 | Bleak House,..............Cloth, | $3.00 |
| Pickwick Papers..........Cloth, | 3.00 | Sketches by "Boz,"......Cloth, | 3.00 |
| Tale of Two Cities,.......Cloth, | 3.00 | Barnaby Rudge,..........Cloth, | 3.00 |
| Nicholas Nickleby,......Cloth, | 3.00 | Martin Chuzzlewit, ......Cloth, | 3.00 |
| David Copperfield,.......Cloth, | 3.00 | Old Curiosity Shop,......Cloth, | 3.00 |
| Oliver Twist,...............Cloth, | 3.00 | Little Dorrit,...............Cloth, | 3.00 |
| Christmas Stories,........Cloth, | 3.00 | Dombey and Son,.........Cloth, | 3.00 |

*The following are each complete in one volume, and are reduced in price from $2.50 to $1.50 a volume.*

| | | | |
|---|---|---|---|
| Great Expectations,......Cloth, | $1.50 | Dickens' New Stories,...Cloth, | $1.50 |
| Lamplighter's Story,.....Cloth, | 1.50 | Message from the Sea,..Cloth, | 1.50 |

| | |
|---|---|
| Price of a set, in thirty-two volumes, bound in cloth,.................. | $48.00 |
| " " Full sheep, Library style,.............................. | 64.00 |
| " " Half calf, antique,........................................ | 96.00 |
| " " Half calf, full gilt backs, etc........................... | 96.00 |

## THE "NEW NATIONAL EDITION."

This is the cheapest complete edition of the works of Charles Dickens, "Boz," published in the world, all his writings being contained in *seven large octavo volumes*, with a portrait of Charles Dickens, and other illustrations, the whole making nearly *six thousand very large double columned pages*, in large, clear type, and handsomely printed on fine white paper, and bound in the strongest and most substantial manner.

| | |
|---|---|
| Price of a set, in Black cloth, in seven volumes,...................... | $20.00 |
| " " Full sheep, Library style,............................ | 25.00 |
| " " Half calf, antique,.................................... | 30.00 |
| " " Half calf, full gilt backs, etc....................... | 30.00 |

## BUFF PAPER COVER EDITION.

*Each book being complete in one large octavo volume.*

| | | | |
|---|---|---|---|
| Our Mutual Friend,................ | $1.00 | Sketches by "Boz,"................ | 75 |
| Great Expectations,................ | 75 | Oliver Twist,.......................... | 75 |
| Lamplighter's Story,............... | 75 | Little Dorrit,.......................... | 75 |
| David Copperfield,.................. | 75 | Tale of Two Cities,.................. | 75 |
| Dombey and Son,.................... | 75 | New Years' Stories,................. | 75 |
| Nicholas Nickleby,................. | 75 | Dickens' Short Stories,............ | 75 |
| Pickwick Papers,.................... | 75 | Message from the Sea,............ | 75 |
| Christmas Stories,.................. | 75 | Holiday Stories,...................... | 75 |
| Martin Chuzzlewit,................. | 75 | American Notes,..................... | 75 |
| Old Curiosity Shop,................ | 75 | Pic Nic Papers,........................ | 75 |
| Barnaby Rudge,...................... | 75 | Somebody's Luggage,.............. | 25 |
| Dickens' New Stories,............. | 75 | Tom Tiddler's Ground,............ | 25 |
| Bleak House,.......................... | 75 | The Haunted House,............... | 25 |
| Joseph Grimaldi,.................... | 75 | | |

☞ **Books sent, postage paid, on receipt of the Retail Price, by**
**T. B. Peterson & Brothers, Philadelphia, Pa.**

# AMERICAN NOTES;

AND

# THE UNCOMMERCIAL TRAVELER.

BY CHARLES DICKENS.

PEOPLE'S EDITION.

PHILADELPHIA:
T. B. PETERSON & BROTHERS;
306 CHESTNUT STREET.

# CONTENTS.

# AMERICAN NOTES.

# PREFACE.

My readers have opportunities of judging for themselves whether the influences and tendencies which I distrusted in America, had any existence but in my imagination. They can examine for themselves whether there has been anything in the public career of that country since, at home or abroad, which suggests that those influences and tendencies really did exist. As they find the fact, they will judge me. If they discern any evidences of wrong-going, in any direction that I have indicated, they will acknowledge that I had reason in what I wrote. If they discern no such thing, they will consider me altogether mistaken—but not wilfully.

Prejudiced, I am not, and never have been, otherwise than in favor of the United States. I have many friends in America, I feel a grateful interest in the country, I hope and believe it will successfully work out a problem of the highest importance to the whole human race. To represent me as viewing America with ill-nature, coldness, or animosity, is merely to do a very foolish thing, which is always a very easy one.

# CONTENTS.

# AMERICAN NOTES.

## CHAPTER I.

### GOING AWAY.

I SHALL never forget the one-fourth serious and three-fourths comical astonishment with which, on the morning of the third of January eighteen-hundred-and-forty-two, I opened the door of, and put my head into, a "state room" on board the Britannia steam-packet, twelve hundred tons burthen per register, bound for Halifax and Boston, and carrying Her Majesty's mails.

That this state-room had been specially engaged for "Charles Dickens, Esquire, and Lady," was rendered sufficiently clear even to my scared intellect by a very small manuscript, announcing the fact, which was pinned on a very flat quilt, covering a very thin mattress, spread like a surgical plaster on a most inaccessible shelf. But that this was the state-room concerning which Charles Dickens, Esquire, and Lady, had held daily and nightly conferences for at least four months preceding: that this could by any possibility be that small snug chamber of the imagination, which Charles Dickens, Esquire, with the spirit of prophecy strong upon him, had always foretold would contain at least one little sofa, and which his lady, with a modest yet most magnificent sense of its limited dimensions, had from the first opined would not hold more than two enormous portmanteaus in some odd corner out of sight (portmanteaus which could now no more be got in at the door, not to stay stowed away, than a giraffe could be persuaded or forced into a flower-pot): that this utterly impracticable, thoroughly hopeless, and profoundly preposterous box had the remotest reference to, or connection with, those chaste and pretty, not to say gorgeous little bowers, sketched by a masterly hand in the highly varnished lithographic plan hanging up in the agent's counting-house in the city of London: that this room of state, in short, could be anything but a pleasant fiction and cheerful jest of the captain's, invented and put in practice for the better relish and enjoyment of the real state-room presently to be disclosed:—these were the truths which I really could not, for the moment, bring my mind at all to bear upon or comprehend. And I sat down upon a kind of horsehair slab, or perch, of which there were two within; and looked, without any expression of countenance whatever, at some friends who had come on board with us, and who were crushing their faces into all manner of shapes by endeavoring to squeeze them through the small doorway.

We had experienced a pretty smart shock before coming below, which, but that we were the most sanguine people living, might have prepared us for the worst. The imaginative artist to whom I have already made allusion, has depicted in the same great work, a chamber of almost interminable perspective, furnished, as Mr. Robins would say, in a style of more than Eastern splendor, and filled (but not inconveniently so) with groups of ladies and gentlemen, in the very highest state of enjoyment and vivacity. Before descending into the bowels of the ship, we had passed from the deck into a long narrow apartment, not unlike a gigantic hearse with windows in the sides; having at the upper end a melancholy stove, at which three or four chilly stewards were warming their hands; while on either side, extending down its whole dreary length, was a long, long table, over each of which a rack, fixed to the low roof, and stuck full of drinking-glasses and cruet-stands, hinted dismally at rolling seas, and heavy weather. I had not at that time seen the ideal presentment of this chamber which has since gratified me so much, but I observed that one of our friends who had made the arrangements for our voyage, turned pale on entering, retreated on the friend behind him, smote his forehead involuntarily, and said below his breath, "Impossible! it cannot be!" or words to that effect. He recovered himself however by a great effort, and after a preparatory cough or two, cried, with a ghastly smile which is still before me, looking at the same time round the walls, "Ha! the breakfast-room, steward—eh?" We all foresaw what the answer must be: we knew the agony he suffered. He had often spoken of *the saloon;* had taken in and lived upon the pictorial idea; had usually given us to understand, at home, that to form a just conception of it, it would be necessary to multiply the size and furniture of an ordinary drawing-room by seven, and then fall short of the reality. When the man in reply avowed the truth; the blunt, remorseless, naked truth; "This is the saloon, sir"—he actually reeled beneath the blow.

In persons who were so soon to part, and interpose between their else daily communication the formidable barrier of many thousand miles of stormy space, and who were for that reason anxious to cast no other cloud, not even the passing shadow of a moment's disappointment or discomfiture, upon the short interval of happy companionship that yet remained to them—in persons so situated, the natural transition from these first surprises was obviously into peals of hearty laughter; and I can report that I, for one, being still seated upon the slab or perch before-mentioned, roared outright until the vessel rang again. Thus, in less than two minutes after coming upon it for the first time, we all by common consent agreed that this state-room was the pleasantest and most facetious and capital contrivance possible; and that to have had it one inch larger, would have been quite a disagreeable and deplorable state of things. And with this; and with showing how,—by very nearly closing the door, and twining in and out like serpents, and by counting the little washing slab as standing-room,—we could manage to insinuate four people into it, all at one time; and entreating each other to observe how very airy it was (in dock), and how there was a beautiful port-hole which could be kept open all day (weather permitting), and how there was quite a large bull's eye just over the looking-glass which would render shaving a perfectly easy and delightful process (when the ship didn't roll too much); we arrived, at last, at the unanimous conclusion that it was rather spacious though I do verily believe that, deducting the two berths, one above the other, than which nothing smaller for sleeping in was ever made except coffins, it was no bigger than one of those hackney cabriolets which have the door behind, and shoot their fares out, like sacks of coals upon the pavement.

Having settled this point to the perfect satisfaction of all parties, concerned and unconcerned, we sat down round the fire in the ladies' cabin—just to try the effect. It was rather dark, certainly; but somebody said, "of course it would be light at sea," a proposition to which we all assented; echoing "of course, of course;" though it would be exceedingly difficult to say why we thought so. I remember, too, when we had discovered and exhausted another topic of consolation in the circumstance of this ladies' cabin adjoining our state-room, and the consequently immense feasibility of sitting there at all times and seasons, and had fallen into a momentary silence, leaning our faces on our hands and looking at the fire, one of our party said, with the solemn air of a man who had made a discovery, "What a relish mulled claret will have down here!" which appeared to strike us all most forcibly; as though there were something spicy and high-flavored in cabins, which essentially improved that composition, and rendered it quite incapable of perfection anywhere else.

There was a stewardess, too, actively engaged in producing clean sheets and tablecloths from the very entrails of the sofas, and from unexpected lockers, of such artful mechanism that it made one's head ache to see them opened one after another, and rendered it quite a distracting circumstance to follow her proceedings, and to find that every nook and corner and individual piece of furniture was something else besides what it pretended to be, and was a mere trap and deception and place of secret stowage, whose ostensible purpose was its least useful one.

God bless that stewardess for her piously fraudulent account of January voyages! God bless her for her clear recollection of the companion passage of last year, when nobody was ill, and every body danced from morning to night, and it was "a run" of twelve days, and a piece of the purest frolic, and delight, and jollity! All happiness be with her for her bright face and her pleasant Scotch tongue, which had sounds of old Home in it for my fellow traveller; and for her predictions of fair winds and fine weather (all wrong, or I shouldn't be half so fond of her); and for the ten thousand small fragments of genuine womanly tact, by which, without piecing them elaborately together, and patching them up into shape and form and case and pointed application, she nevertheless did plainly show that all young mothers on one side of the Atlantic were near and close at hand to their little children left upon the other; and that what seemed to the uniniated a serious journey, was, to those who were in the secret, a mere frolic, to be sung about and whistled at! Light be her heart, and gay her merry eyes, for years.

The state-room had grown pretty fast; but by this time it had expanded into something quite bulky, and almost boasted a bay-window to view the sea from. So we went upon deck again in high spirits; and there, everything was in such a state of bustle and active preparation, that the blood quickened its pace, and whirled through one's veins on that clear frosty morning with involuntary mirthfulness. For every gallant ship was riding slowly up and down, and every little boat was plashing noisily in the water; and knots of people stood upon the wharf, gazing with a kind of "dread delight" on the far-famed fast American steamer; and one party of men were "taking in the milk," or, in other words, getting the cow on board; and another were filling the icehouses to the very throat with fresh provisions; with butcher's-meat and garden-stuff, pale sucking-pigs, calves' heads in scores, beef, veal, and pork, and poultry out of all proportion; and others were coiling ropes, and busy with oakum yarns; and others, were lowering heavy packages into the hold; and the purser's head was barely visible as it loomed in a state of exquisite perplexity from the midst of a vast pile of pasengers' luggage; and there seemed to be nothing going on anywhere, or uppermost in the mind of anybody, but preparations for this mighty voyage. This, with the bright cold sun, the bracing air, the crisply-curling water, the thin white crust of morning ice upon the decks which crackled with a sharp and cheerful sound beneath the lightest tread, was irresistible. And when, again upon the shore, we turned and saw from the vessel's mast her name signalled in flags of joyous colors, and fluttering by their side the beautiful American banner with its stars and stripes,—the long three thousand miles and more, and, longer still, the six whole months of absence, so dwindled and faded, that the ship had gone out and come home again, and it was broad spring already in the Coburg Dock at Liverpool.

I have not inquired among my medical acquaintance, whether Turtle, and cold Punch, with Hock, Champagne, and Claret, and all the slight et cetera usually included in an unlimited order for a good dinner—especially when it is left to the liberal construction of my faultless friend, Mr. Radley of the Adelphi Hotel—are peculiarly calculated to suffer a sea-change; or whether a plain mutton-chop, and a glass or two of sherry, would be less likely of conversion into foreign and disconcerting material. My own opinion is, that whether one is discreet or indiscreet in these particulars, on the eve of a sea-voyage, is a matter of little consequence; and that, to use a common phrase, "it comes to very much the same thing in the end." Be this as it may, I know that the dinner of that day was undeniably perfect; that it comprehended all these items, and a great many more; and that we all did ample justice to it. And I know too, that, bating a certain tacit avoidance of any allusion to to-morrow; such as may be supposed to prevail between delicate-minded turnkeys, and a sensitive prisoner who is to be hanged next morning; we got on very well, and, all things considered, were merry enough.

When the morning—*the* morning—came, and we met at breakfast, it was curious to see how eager we all were to prevent a moment's pause in the conversation, and how astoundingly gay everybody was: the forced spirits of each member of the little party having as much likeness to his natural mirth, as hot-house peas at five guineas the quart, resemble in flavor the growth of the dews, and air, and rain of Heaven. But as one o'clock, the hour for going aboard, drew near, this volubility dwindled away by little and little, despite the most persevering efforts to the contrary, until at last, the matter being now quite desperate, we threw off all disguise; openly speculated upon where we should be this time to-morrow, this time next day, and so forth; and entrusted a vast number of messages to those who intended returning to town that night, which were to be delivered at home and elsewhere without fail, within the very shortest possible space of time after the arrival of the railway train at Euston Square. And commissions and remembrances do so crowd upon one at such a time, that we were still busied with this employment when we found ourselves fused, as it were, into a dense conglomeration of passengers and passengers' friends, and passengers' luggage, all jumbled together on the deck of a small steamboat, and panting and snorting off to the packet, which had worked out of dock yesterday afternoon and was now lying at her moorings in the river.

And there she is! all eyes are turned to where she lies, dimly discernible through the gathering fog of the early winter afternoon; every finger is pointed in the same direction; and murmurs of interest and admiration—as "How beautiful she looks!" "How trim she is!"—are heard on every side. Even the lazy gentleman with his hat on one side and his hands in his pockets, who has dispensed so much consolation by inquiring with a yawn of another gentleman whether he is "going across"—as if it were a ferry—even he condescends to look that way, and nod his head, as who should say, "No mistake about *that:*" and not even the sage Lord Burleigh in his nod, included half so much as this lazy gentleman of might who has made the passage (as everybody on board has found out already; it's impossible to say how) thirteen times without a single accident! There is another passenger very much wrapped-up, who has been frowned down by the rest, and morally trampled upon and crushed, for presuming to inquire with a timid interest how long it is since the poor President went down. He is standing close to the lazy gentleman, and says with a faint smile that he believes She is a very strong Ship; to which the lazy gentleman looking first in his questioner's eye and then very hard in the wind's, answers unexpectedly and ominously, that She need be. Upon this the lazy gentleman instantly falls very low in the popular estimation, and the passengers, with looks of defiance, whisper to each other that he is an ass, and an impostor, and clearly don't know anything at all about it.

But we are made fast alongside the packet, whose huge red funnel is smoking bravely, giving rich promise of serious intentions. Packing-cases, portmanteaus, carpet-bags, and boxes, are already passed from hand to hand, and hauled on board with breathless rapidity. The officers, smartly dressed, are at the gangway handing the passengers up the side, and hurrying the men. In five minutes' time, the little steamer is utterly deserted, and the packet is beset and over-run by its late freight, who instantly pervade the whole ship, and are to be met with by the dozen in every nook and corner: swarming down below with their own baggage, and stumbling over other people's; disposing themselves comfortably in wrong cabins, and creating a most horrible confusion by having to turn out again; madly bent upon opening locked doors, and on forcing a passage into all kinds of out-of-the way places where there is no thoroughfare; sending wild stewards, with elfin hair, to and fro upon the breezy decks on unintelligible errands, impossible of execution: and in short, creating the most extraordinary and bewildering tumult. In the midst of all this, the lazy gentleman, who seems to have no luggage of any kind—not so much as a friend, even—lounges up and down the hurricane-deck, coolly puffing a cigar; and, as this unconcerned demeanor again exalts him in the opinion of those who have leisure to observe his proceedings, every time he looks up at the masts, or down at the decks, or over the side, they look there too, as wondering whether he sees anything wrong anywhere, and hoping that, in case he should, he will have the goodness to mention it.

What have we here? The captain's boat! and yonder the captain himself. Now, by all our hopes and wishes, the very man he ought to be! A well-made, tight-built, dapper little fellow; with a ruddy face, which is a letter of invitation to shake him by both hands at once; and with a clear, blue honest eye, that it does one good to see one's sparkling image in. "Ring the bell!" "Ding, ding, ding!" the very bell is in a hurry. "Now for the shore—who's for the shore?"

—"These gentlemen, I am sorry to say." They are away, and never said, Good b'ye. Ah! now they wave it from the little boat. "Good b'ye! Good b'ye!" Three cheers from them; three more from us; three more from them; and they are gone.

"To and fro, to and fro, to and fro again a hundred times! This waiting for the latest mail-bags is worse than all. If we could have gone off in the midst of that last burst, we should have started triumphantly: but to lie here, two hours and more, in the damp fog, neither staying at home nor going abroad, is letting one gradually down into the very depths of dullness and low spirits. A speck in the mist, at last! That's something. It is the boat we wait for! That's more to the purpose. The captain appears on the paddle-box with his speaking-trumpet; the officers take their stations; all hands are on the alert; the flagging hopes of the passengers revive; the cooks pause in their savory work, and look out with faces full of interest. The boat comes alongside; the bags are dragged in anyhow, and flung down for the moment anywhere. Three cheers more: and as the first one rings upon our ears, the vessel throbs like a strong giant that has just received the breath of life; the two great wheels turn fiercely round for the first time; and the noble ship, with wind and tide astern, breaks proudly through the lashed and foaming water.

## CHAPTER II.

### THE PASSAGE OUT.

We all dined together that day; and a rather formidable party we were: no fewer than eighty-six strong. The vessel being pretty deep in the water, with all her coals on board and so many passengers, and the weather being calm and quiet, there was but little motion; so that before the dinner was half over, even those passengers who were most distrustful of themselves plucked up amazingly; and those who in the morning had returned to the universal question, "Are you a good sailor?" a very decided negative, now either parried the inquiry with the evasive reply, "Oh! I suppose I'm no worse than anybody else;" or, reckless of all moral obligations, answered boldly "Yes:" and with some irritation too, as though they would add, "I should like to know what you see in *me*, sir, particularly, to justify suspicion!"

Notwithstanding this high tone of courage and confidence, I could not but observe that very few remained long over their wine; and that every body had an unusual love of the open air; and that the favorite and most coveted seats were invariably those nearest to the door. The tea-table, too, was by no means as well attended as the dinner-table; and there was less whist-playing than might have been expected. Still, with the exception of one lady, who had retired with some precipitation at dinner-time, immediately after being assisted to the finest cut of a very yellow boiled leg of mutton with very green capers, there were no invalids as yet; and walking, and smoking, and drinking of brandy-and-water (but always in the open air,) went on with unabated spirit, until eleven o'clock or thereabouts, when "turning in"—no sailor of seven hours' experience talks of going to bed—became the order of the night. The perpetual tramp of boot-heels on the decks gave place to a heavy silence, and the whole human freight was stowed away below, excepting a very few stragglers, like myself, who were probably, like me, afraid to go there.

To one unaccustomed to such scenes, this is a very striking

time on shipboard. Afterwards, and when its novelty had long worn off, it never ceased to have a peculiar interest and charm for me. The gloom through which the great black mass holds its direct and certain course; the rushing water, plainly heard, but dimly seen; the broad, white, glistening track, that follows in the vessel's wake; the men on the look-out forward, who would be scarcely visible against the dark sky, but for their blotting out some score of glistening stars; the helmsman at the wheel, with the illuminated card before him, shining, a speck of light amidst the darkness, like something sentient and of Divine intelligence; the melancholy sighing of the wind through block, and rope, and chain; the gleaming forth of light from every crevice, nook, and tiny piece of glass about the decks, as though the ship were filled with fire in hiding, ready to burst through any outlet, wild with its resistless power of death and ruin. At first, too, and even when the hour, and all the objects it exalts, have come to be familiar, it is difficult, alone and thoughtful, to hold them to their proper shapes and forms. They change with the wandering fancy; assume the semblance of things left far away; put on the well-remembered aspect of favorite places dearly loved; and even people them with shadows. Streets, houses, rooms; figures so like their usual occupants, that they have startled me by their reality, which far exceeded, as it seemed to me, all power of mine to conjure up the absent; have, many and many a time, at such an hour, grown suddenly out of objects with whose real look, and use, and purpose, I was as well acquainted as with my own two hands.

My own two hands, and feet likewise, being very cold, however, on this particular occasion, I crept below at midnight. It was not exactly comfortable below. It was decidedly close; and it was impossible to be unconscious of the presence of that extraordinary compound of strange smells, which is to be found nowhere but on board ship, and which is such a subtle perfume that it seems to enter at every pore of the skin, and whisper of the hold. Two passengers' wives (one of them my own) lay already in silent agonies on the sofa; and one lady's maid (*my* lady's) was a mere bundle on the floor, execrating her destiny, and pounding her curl-papers among the stray boxes. Everything sloped the wrong way: which in itself was an aggravation scarcely to be borne. I had left the door open, a moment before, in the bosom of a gentle declivity and, when I turned to shut it, it was on the summit of a lofty eminence. Now every plank and timber creaked, as if the ship were made of wicker-work; and now crackled, like an enormous fire of the driest possible twigs. There was nothing for it but bed; so I went to bed.

It was pretty much the same for the next two days, with a tolerably fair wind and dry weather. I read in bed (but to this hour I don't know what) a good deal; and reeled on deck a little; drank cold brandy-and-water with an unspeakable disgust, and ate hard biscuit perseveringly: not ill but going to be.

It is the third morning. I am awakened out of my sleep, by a dismal shriek from my wife, who demands to know whether there's any danger. I rouse myself, and look out of bed. The water-jug is plunging and leaping like a lively dolphin; all the smaller articles are afloat, except my shoes, which are stranded on a carpet-bag, high and dry, like a couple of coal-barges. Suddenly I see them spring into the air, and behold the looking-glass, which is nailed to the wall, sticking fast upon the ceiling. At the same time the door entirely disappears, and a new one is opened in the floor. Then I begin to comprehend that the state-room is standing on its head.

Before it is possible to make any arrangement at all compatible with this novel state of things, the ship rights. Before one can say, "Thank Heaven!" she wrongs again. Before one can cry she *is* wrong, she seems to have started forward, and to be a creature actively running of its own accord, with broken knees and failing legs, through every variety of hole and pitfall, and stumbling constantly. Before one can so much as wonder, she takes a high leap into the air. Before she has well done that, she takes a deep dive into the water. Before she has gained the surface, she throws a summerset. The instant she is on her legs, she rushes backward. And so she goes on staggering, heaving, wrestling, leaping, diving, jumping, pitching, throbbing, rolling, and rocking: and going through all these movements, sometimes by turns, and sometimes all together: until one feels disposed to roar for mercy.

A steward passes. "Steward!" "Sir?" "What *is* the matter? what *do* you call this?" "Rather a heavy sea on, sir, and a head-wind."

A head-wind! Imagine a human face upon the vessel's prow, with fifteen thousand Samsons in one bent upon driving her back, and hitting her exactly between the eyes whenever she attempts to advance an inch. Imagine the ship herself, with every pulse and artery of her huge body swoln and bursting under this maltreatment, sworn to go on or die. Imagine the wind howling, the sea roaring, the rain beating: all in furious array against her. Picture the sky both dark and wild, and the clouds, in fearful sympathy with the waves, making another ocean in the air. Add to all this, the clattering on deck and down below; the tread of hurried feet; the loud hoarse shouts of seamen; the gurgling in and out of water through the scuppers; with, every now and then, the striking of a heavy sea upon the planks above, with the deep, dead, heavy sound of thunder heard within a vault;—and there is the head-wind of that January morning.

I say nothing of what may be called the domestic noises of the ship: such as the breaking of glass and crockery, the tumbling down of stewards, the gambols, overhead, of loose casks and truant dozens of bottled porter, and the very remarkable and far from exhilarating sounds raised in their various state-rooms by the seventy passengers who were too ill to get up to breakfast. I say nothing of them; for although I lay listening to this concert for three or four days, I don't think I heard it for more than a quarter of a minute, at the expiration of which term, I lay down again, excessively sea-sick.

Not sea-sick, be it understood, in the ordinary acceptation of the term: I wish I had been: but in a form which I have never seen or heard described, though I have no doubt it is very common. I lay there, all the day long, quite coolly and contentedly; with no sense of weariness, with no desire to get up, or get better, or take the air; with no curiosity, or care, or regret, of any sort or degree, saving that I think I can remember, in this universal indifference, having a kind of lazy joy — of fiendish delight, if anything so lethargic can be dignified with the title—in the fact of my wife being too ill to talk to me. If I may be allowed to illustrate my state of mind by such an example, I should say that I was exactly in the condition of the elder Mr. Willet, after the incursion of the rioters into his bar at Chigwell. Nothing would have surprised me. If, in the momentary illumination of any ray of intelligence that may have come upon me in the way of thoughts of Home, a goblin postman, with a scarlet coat and bell, had come into that little kennel before me, broad awake in broad day, and, apologizing for being damp through walking in the sea, had handed me a letter, directed to myself, in familiar characters, I am certain I should not have felt one atom of astonishment: I should have been perfectly satisfied. If Neptune himself had walked in, with a toasted shark on his trident, I should have looked upon the event as one of the very commonest everyday occurrences.

Once—once—I found myself on deck. I don't know how I got there, or what possessed me to go there, but there I was; and completely dressed too, with a huge pea-coat on, and a pair of boots such as no weak man in his senses could ever have got into. I found myself standing, when a gleam of consciousness came upon me, holding on to something. I don't know what. I think it was the boatswain: or it may have been the pump: or possibly the cow. I can't say how long I had been there; whether a day or a minute. I recollect trying to think about something (about anything in the whole wide world, I was not particular) without the smallest effect. I could not even make out which was the sea, and which the sky; for the horizon seemed drunk, and was flying wildly about in all directions. Even in that incapable state however, I recognized the lazy gentleman standing before me: nautically clad in a suit of shaggy blue, with an oilskin hat. But I was too imbecile, although I knew it to be he, to separate him from his dress; and tried to call him, I remember, *Pilot.* After another interval of total unconsciousness, I found he had gone, and recognized another figure in its place. It seemed to wave and fluctuate before me as though I saw it reflected in an unsteady looking-glass; but I knew it for the captain; and such was the cheerful influence of his face, that I tried to smile: yes, even then I tried to smile. I saw by his gestures that he addressed me; but it was a long time before I could make out that he remonstrated against my standing up to my knees in water—as I was; of course I don't know why. I tried to thank him, but couldn't. I could only point to my boots—or wherever I supposed my boots to be—and say in a plaintive voice, "Cork soles:" at the same time endeavoring, I am told, to sit down in the pool. Finding that I was quite insensible, and for the time a maniac, he humanely conducted me below.

There I remained until I got better: suffering, whenever I was recommended to eat anything, an amount of anguish only second to that which is said to be endured by the apparently drowned, in the process of restoration to life. One gentleman on board had a letter of introduction to me from a mutual friend in London. He sent it below with his card, on the morning of the head-wind; and I was long troubled with the idea that he might be up, and well, and a hundred times a-day expecting me to call upon him in the saloon. I imagined him one of those cast-iron images—I will not call them men—who ask, with red faces and lusty voices, what sea-sickness means, and whether it really is as bad as it is represented to be. This was very torturing indeed; and I don't think I ever felt such perfect gratification and gratitude of heart, as I did when I heard from the ship's doctor that he had been obliged to put a large mustard poultice on this very gentleman's stomach. I date my recovery from the receipt of that intelligence. It was materially assisted though, I have no doubt, by a heavy gale of wind, which came slowly up at sunset, when we were about ten days out, and raged with gradually increasing fury until morning, saving that it lulled for an hour a little before midnight. There was something in the unnatural repose of that hour, and in the after gathering of the storm, so inconceivably awful and tremendous, that its bursting into full violence was almost a relief.

The laboring of the ship in the troubled sea on this night I shall never forget. "Will it ever be worse than this?" was a question I had often heard asked, when everything was sliding and bumping about, and when it certainly did seem difficult to comprehend the possibility of anything afloat being more disturbed, without toppling over and going down. But what the agitation of a steam-vessel is, on a bad winter's night in the wild Atlantic, it is impossible for the most vivid imagination to conceive. To say that she is flung down on her side in the waves, with her masts dipping into them, and that, springing up again, she rolls over on the other side, until a heavy sea strikes her with the noise of a hundred great guns, and hurls her back—that she stops, and staggers, and shivers, as though stunned, and then, with a violent throbbing at her heart, darts onward like a monster goaded into madness, to be beaten down, and battered, and crushed, and leaped on by the angry sea—that thunder, lightning, hail, and rain, and wind, are all in fierce contention for the mastery—that every plank has its groan, every nail its shriek, and every drop of water in the great ocean its howling voice—is nothing. To say that all is grand, and all appalling and horrible in the last degree, is nothing. Words cannot express it. Thoughts cannot convey it. Only a dream can call it up again in all its fury, rage, and passion.

And yet, in the very midst of these terrors, I was placed in a situation so exquisitely ridiculous, that even then I had as strong a sense of its absurdity as I have now: and could no more help laughing than I can at any other comical incident, happening under circumstances the most favorable to its enjoyment. About midnight we shipped a sea, which forced its way through the skylights, burst open the doors above, and came raging and roaring down into the ladies' cabin, to the unspeakable consternation of my wife and a little Scotch lady—who, by the way, had previously sent a message to the captain by the stewardess, requesting him, with her compliments, to have a steel conductor immediately attached to the top of every mast, and to the chimney, in order that the ship might not be struck by lightning. They, and the handmaid before-mentioned, being in such ecstacies of fear that I scarcely knew what to do with them, I naturally bethought myself of some restorative or comfortable cordial; and nothing better occurring to me, at the moment, than hot brandy-and-water, I procured a tumbler-full without delay. It being impossible to stand or sit without holding on, they were all heaped together in one corner of a long sofa—a fixture, extending entirely across the cabin—where they clung to each other in momentary expectation of being drowned. When I approached this place with my specific, and was about to administer it, with many consolatory expressions, to the nearest sufferer, what was my dismay to see them all roll slowly down to the other end! And when I staggered to that end, and held out the glass once more, how immensely baffled were my good intentions by the ship giving another lurch, and their all rolling back again! I suppose I dodged them up and down this sofa, for at least a quarter of an hour, without reaching them once; and by the time I did catch them, the brandy-and-water was diminished, by constant spilling, to a tea-spoonful. To complete the group, it is necessary to recognize in this disconcerted dodger, an individual very pale from sea-sickness, who had shaved his beard and brushed his hair, last, at Liverpool: and whose only articles of dress (linen not included) were a pair of dreadnought trousers; a blue jacket, formerly admired upon the Thames at Richmond; no stockings; and one slipper.

Of the outrageous antics performed by that ship next morning; which made bed a practical joke, and getting up, by any process short of falling out, an impossibility; I say nothing. But anything like the utter dreariness and desolation that met my eyes when I literally "tumbled up" on deck at noon, I never saw. Ocean and sky were all of one dull, heavy, uniform lead color. There was no extent of prospect even over the dreary waste that lay around us, for the sea ran high, and the horizon encompassed us like a large black hoop. Viewed from the air, or some tall bluff on shore, it would have been imposing and stupendous, no doubt; but seen from the wet and rolling decks, it only impressed one giddily and painfully. In the gale of last night the life-boat had been crushed by one blow of the sea like a walnut-shell; and there it hung dangling in the air: a mere faggot of crazy boards. The planking of the paddle-boxes had been torn sheer away. The wheels were exposed and bare; and they whirled and dashed their spray about the decks at random. Chimney, white with crusted salt; topmasts struck; stormsails set; rigging all knotted, tangled, wet, and drooping: a gloomier picture it would be hard to look upon.

I was now comfortably established by courtesy in the ladies' cabin, where, besides ourselves, there were only four other passengers. First, the little Scotch lady before-mentioned, on her way to join her husband at New York, who had settled there three years before. Secondly and thirdly, an honest young Yorkshireman, connected with some American house; domiciled in that same city, and carrying thither his beautiful young wife, to whom he had been married but a fortnight, and who was the fairest specimen of a comely English country girl I have ever seen. Fourthly, fifthly, and lastly, another couple: newly married too, if one might judge from the endearments they frequently interchanged: of whom I know no more than that they were rather a mysterious, run-away kind of couple; that the lady had great personal attractions also; and that the gentleman carried more guns with him than Robinson Crusoe, wore a shooting-coat, and had two great dogs on board. On further consideration, I remember that he tried hot roast pig and bottled ale as a cure for sea-sickness; and that he took these remedies (usually in bed) day after day, with astonishing perseverance. I may add, for the information of the curious, that they decidedly failed.

The weather continuing obstinately and almost unprecedentedly bad, we usually straggled into this cabin, more or less faint and miserable, about an hour before noon, and lay down on the sofas, to recover; during which interval, the captain would look in to communicate the state of the wind, the moral certainty of its changing to-morrow, (the weather is always going to improve to-morrow, at sea), the vessel's rate of sailing, and so forth. Observations there were none to tell us of, for there was no sun to take them by. But a description of one day will serve for all the rest. Here it is.

The captain being gone, we compose ourselves to read, if the place be light enough; and if not, we doze and talk alternately. At one, a bell rings, and the stewardess comes down with a steaming dish of baked potatoes, and another of roasted apples; and plates of pig's face, cold ham, salt beef; or perhaps a smoking mess of rare hot collops. We fall-to upon these dainties; eat as much as we can (we have great appetites now); and are as long as possible about it. If the fire will burn (it *will* sometimes) we are pretty cheerful. If it won't, we all remark to each other that it's very cold, rub our hands, cover ourselves with coats and cloaks, and lie down again to doze, talk, and read (provided as aforesaid), until dinner time. At five, another bell rings, and the stewardess re-appears with another dish of potatoes—boiled this time—and store of hot meat of various kinds: not forgetting the roast pig, to be taken medicinally. We sit down at table again (rather more cheerfully than before); prolong the meal with a rather mouldy dessert of apples, grapes, and oranges; and drink our wine and brandy-and-water. The bottles and glasses are still upon the table, and the oranges and so forth are rolling about according to their fancy and the ship's way, when the doctor comes down, by special nightly invitation, to join our evening rubber: immediately on whose arrival we make a party at whist, and as it is a rough night and the cards will not lie on the cloth, we put the tricks in our pockets as we take them. At whist we remain with exemplary gravity (deducting a short time for tea and toast) until eleven o'clock, or thereabouts; when the captain comes down again, in a sou'-wester hat tied under his chin, and a pilot-coat: making the ground wet where he stands. By this time the card-playing is over, and after an hour's pleasant conversation about the ship, the passengers, and things in general, the captain (who never goes to bed, and is never out of humor) turns up his coat collar for the deck again; shakes hands all round;

and goes laughing out into the weather as merrily as to a birth-day party.

As to daily news, there is no dearth of that commodity. This passenger is reported to have lost fourteen pounds at Vingt-et-un in the saloon yesterday; and that passenger drinks his bottle of champagne every day, and how he does it (being only a clerk), nobody knows. The head engineer has distinctly said that there never was such times—meaning weather—and four good hands are ill, and have given in, dead beat. Several berths are full of water, and all the cabins are leaky. The ship's cook, secretly swigging damaged whiskey, has been found drunk; and has been played upon by the fire-engine until quite sober. All the stewards have fallen down-stairs at various dinner-times, and go about with plasters in various places. The baker is ill, and so is the pastry-cook. A new man, horribly indisposed, has been required to fill the place of the latter officer; and has been propped and jammed up with empty casks in a little house upon deck, and commanded to roll out pie-crusts, which he protests (being highly bilious) it is death to him to look at. News! A dozen murders on shore would lack the interest of these slight incidents at sea.

Divided between our rubber and such topics as these, we were running (as we thought) into Halifax Harbor, on the fifteenth night, with little wind and a bright moon—indeed, we had made the Light at its outer entrance, and put the pilot in charge—when suddenly the ship struck upon a bank of mud. An immediate rush on deck took place of course; the sides were crowded in an instant; and for a few minutes we were in as lively a state of confusion as the greatest lover of disorder would desire to see. The passengers, and guns, and water-casks, and other heavy matters, being all huddled together aft, however, to lighten her in the head, she was soon got off; and after some driving on towards an uncomfortable line of objects (whose vicinity had been announced very early in the disaster by a loud cry of "Breakers a-head!") and much backing of paddles, and heaving of the lead into a constantly decreasing depth of water, we dropped anchor in a strange outlandish-looking nook which nobody on board could recognize, although there was land all about us and, so close that we could plainly see the waving branches of the trees.

It was strange enough, in the silence of midnight, and the dead stillness that seemed to be created by the sudden and unexpected stoppage of the engine which had been clanking and blasting in our ears incessantly for so many days, to watch the look of blank astonishment expressed in every face: beginning with the officers, tracing it through all the passengers, and descending to the very stokers and furnace-men, who emerged from below, one by one, and clustered together in a smoky group about the hatchway of the engine-room, comparing notes in whispers. After throwing up a few rockets and firing signal-guns in the hope of being hailed from the land, or at least of seeing a light—but without any other sight or sound presenting itself—it was determined to send a boat on shore. It was amusing to observe how very kind some of the passengers were, in volunteering to go ashore in this same boat; for the general good, of course: not by any means because they thought the ship in an unsafe position, or contemplated the possibility of her heeling over in case the tide were running out. Nor was it less amusing to remark how desperately unpopular the poor pilot became in one short minute. He had had his passage out from Liverpool, and during the whole voyage had been quite a notorious character, as a teller of anecdotes and cracker of jokes. Yet here were the very men who had laughed the loudest at his jests, now flourishing their fists in his face, loading him with imprecations, and defying him to his teeth as a villain!

The boat soon shoved off, with a lantern and sundry blue lights on board; and in less than an hour returned; the officer in command bringing with him a tolerably tall young tree, which he had plucked up by the roots, to satisfy certain distrustful passengers whose minds misgave them that they were to be imposed upon and shipwrecked, and who would on no other terms believe that he had been ashore, or had done anything but fraudulently row a little way into the mist, specially to deceive them and compass their deaths. Our captain had foreseen from the first that we must be in a place called the Eastern passage; and so we were. It was about the last place in the world in which we had any business or reason to be, but a sudden fog, and some error on the pilot's part were the cause. We were surrounded by banks, and rocks, and shoals of all kinds, but had happily drifted, it seemed, upon the only safe speck that was to be found thereabouts. Eased by this report, and by the assurance that the tide was past the ebb, we turned in at three o'clock in the morning.

I was dressing about half-past nine next day, when the noise above hurried me on deck. When I had left it overnight, it was dark, foggy, and damp, and there were bleak hills all round us. Now, we were gliding down a smooth, broad stream, at the rate of eleven miles an hour: our colors flying gaily; our crew rigged out in their smartest clothes; our officers in uniform again; the sun shining as on a brilliant April day in England; the land stretched out on either side, streaked with light patches of snow; white wooden houses; people at their doors; telegraphs working; flags hoisted; wharves appearing; ships; quays crowded with people; distant noises; shouts; men and boys running down steep places towards the pier: all more bright and gay and fresh to our unused eyes than words can paint them. We came to a wharf, paved with uplifted faces; got alongside, and were made fast, after some shouting and straining of cables; darted, a score of us along the gangway, almost as soon as it was thrust out to meet us, and before it had reached the ship—and leaped upon the firm glad earth again!

I suppose this Halifax would have appeared an Elysium, though it had been a curiosity of ugly dullness. But I carried away with me a most pleasant impression of the town and its inhabitants, and have preserved it to this hour. Nor was it without regret that I came home, without having found an opportunity of returning thither, and once more shaking hands with the friends I made that day.

It happened to be the opening of the Legislative Council and General Assembly, at which Ceremonial the forms observed on the commencement of a new Session of Parliament in England was so clearly copied, and so gravely presented on a small scale, that it was like looking at Westminster through the wrong end of a telescope. The governor, as her Majesty's representative, delivered what may be called the Speech from the Throne. He said what he had to say manfully and well. The military band outside the building struck up "God save the Queen" with great vigor before his Excellency had quite finished; the people shouted; the ins rubbed their hands; the outs shook their heads; the Government party said there never was such a good speech; the opposition declared there never was such a bad one; the Speaker and members of the House of Assembly withdrew from the bar to say a great deal among themselves and do a little: and in short, everything went on, and promised to go on, just as it does at home upon the like occasions.

The town is built on the side of a hill, the highest point being commanded by a strong fortress, not yet quite finished. Several streets of good breadth and appearance extend from its summit to the water-side, and are intersected by cross streets running parallel with the river. The houses are chiefly of wood. The market is abundantly supplied: and provisions are exceedingly cheap. The weather being unusually mild at that time for the season of the year, there was no sleighing: but there were plenty of those vehicles in yards and bye-places, and some of them, from the gorgeous quality of their decorations, might have "gone on" without alteration as triumphal cars in a melodrama at Astley's. The day was uncommonly fine; the air bracing and healthful; the whole aspect of the town cheerful, thriving, and industrious.

We lay there seven hours, to deliver and exchange the mails. At length, having collected all our bags and all our passengers (including two or three choice spirits, who, having indulged too freely in oysters and champagne, were found lying insensible on their backs in unfrequented streets), the engines were again put in motion, and we stood off for Boston.

Encountering squally weather again in the Bay of Fundy,

we tumbled and rolled about as usual all that night and all next day. On the next afternoon, that is to say, on Saturday, the twenty-second of January, an American pilot-boat came alongside, and soon afterwards the Britannia steam-packet from Liverpool, eighteen days out, was telegraphed at Boston.

The indescribable interest with which I strained my eyes, as the first patches of American soil peeped like molehills from the green sea, and followed them, as they swelled, by slow and almost imperceptible degrees, into a continuous line of coast, can hardly be exaggerated. A sharp keen wind blew dead against us; a hard frost prevailed on shore; and the cold was most severe. Yet the air was so intensely clear, and dry, and bright, that the temperature was not only endurable, but delicious.

How I remained on deck, staring about me, until we came alongside the dock, and how, though I had had as many eyes as Argus, I should have had them all wide open, and all employed on new objects—are topics which I will not prolong this chapter to discuss. Neither will I more than hint at my foreigner-like mistake, in supposing that a party of most active persons, who scrambled on board at the peril of their lives as we approached the wharf, were newsmen, answering to that industrious class at home; whereas, despite the leathern wallets of news slung about the necks of some, and the broad sheets in the hands of all, they were Editors, who boarded ships in person (as one gentleman in a worsted comforter informed me), "because they liked the excitement of it." Suffice it in this place to say, that one of these invaders, with a ready courtesy for which I thank him here most gratefully, went on before to order rooms at the hotel; and that when I followed, as I soon did, I found myself rolling through the long passages with an involuntary imitation of the gait of Mr. T. P. Cooke, in a new nautical melo-drama.

"Dinner, if you please," said I to the waiter.

"When?" said the waiter.

"As quick as possible," said I.

"Right away?" said the waiter.

After a moment's hesitation, I answered, "No," at hazard.

"*Not* right away?" cried the waiter, with an amount of surprise that made me start.

I looked at him doubtfully, and returned, "No; I would rather have it in this private room. I like it very much."

At this, I really thought the waiter must have gone out of his mind; as I believe he would have done, but for the interposition of another man, who whispered in his ear, "Directly."

"Well! and that's a fact!" said the waiter, looking helplessly at me: "Right away."

I saw now that "Right away" and "Directly" were one and the same thing. So I reversed my previous answer, and sat down to dinner in ten minutes afterwards; and a capital dinner it was.

The hotel (a very excellent one), is called the Tremont House. It has more galleries, colonnades, piazzas, and passages than I can remember, or the reader would believe.

## CHAPTER III.

### BOSTON.

In all the public establishments of America, the utmost courtesy prevails. Most of our Departments are susceptible of considerable improvement in this respect, but the Custom-house above all others would do well to take example from the United States, and render itself somewhat less odious and offensive to foreigners. The servile rapacity of the French officials is sufficiently contemptible; but there is a surly boorish incivility about our men, alike disgusting to all persons who fall into their hands, and discreditable to the nation that keeps such ill-conditioned curs snarling about its gates.

When I landed in America, I could not help being strongly impressed with the contrast their Custom-house presented, and the attention, politeness and good humor with which its officers discharged their duty.

As we did not land at Boston, in consequence of some detention at the wharf, until after dark, I received my first impressions of the city in walking down to the Custom-house on the morning after our arrival, which was Sunday. I am afraid to say, by the way, how many offers of pews and seats in church for that morning were made to us, by formal note of invitation, before we had half finished our first dinner in America, but if I may be allowed to make a moderate guess, without going into nicer calculation, I should say that at least as many sittings were proffered us, as would have accommodated a score or two of grown-up families. The number of creeds and forms of religion to which the pleasure of our company was requested, was in very fair proportion.

Not being able, in the absence of any change of clothes, to go to church that day, we were compelled to decline these kindnesses, one and all; and I was reluctantly obliged to forego the delight of hearing Dr. Channing, who happened to preach that morning for the first time in a very long interval. I mention the name of this distinguished and accomplished man (with whom I soon afterwards had the pleasure of becoming personally acquainted), that I may have the gratification of recording my humble tribute of admiration and respect for his high abilities and character; and for the bold philanthropy with which he has ever opposed himself to that most hideous blot and foul disgrace—Slavery.

To return to Boston. When I got into the streets upon this Sunday morning, the air was so clear, the houses were so bright and gay; the signboards were painted in such gaudy colors; the gilded letters were so very golden; the bricks were so very red, the stone was so very white, the blinds and area railings were so very green, the knobs and plates upon the street doors so marvellously bright and twinkling; and all so slight and unsubstantial in appearance—that every thoroughfare in the city looked exactly like a scene in a pantomime. It rarely happens in the business streets that a tradesman—if I may venture to call anybody a tradesman, where everybody is a merchant—resides above his store; so that many occupations are often carried on in one house, and the whole front is covered with boards and inscriptions. As I walked along, I kept glancing up at these boards, confidently expecting to see a few of them change into something; and I never turned a corner suddenly without looking out for the clown and pantaloon, who, I had no doubt, were hiding in a doorway or behind some pillar close at hand. As to Harlequin and Columbine, I discovered immediately that they lodged (they are always looking after lodgings in a pantomime) at a very small clock-maker's, one story high, near the hotel; which, in addition to various symbols and devices, almost covering the whole front, had a great dial hanging out—to be jumped through, of course.

The suburbs are, if possible, even more unsubstantial-looking than the city. The white wooden houses (so white that it makes one wink to look at them), with their green jalousie blinds, are so sprinkled and dropped about in all directions, without seeming to have any root at all in the ground; and the small churches and chapels are so prim, and bright, and highly varnished; that I almost believed the whole affair could be taken up piecemeal like a child's toy, and crammed into a little box.

The city is a beautiful one, and cannot fail, I should imagine, to impress all strangers very favorably. The private dwelling-houses are, for the most part, large and elegant; the shops extremely good; and the public buildings handsome. The State House is built upon the summit of a hill, which rises gradually at first, and afterwards by a steep ascent, almost from the water's edge. In front is a green inclosure, called the Common. The site is beautiful: and from the top there is a charming panoramic view of the whole town and neighborhood. In addition to a variety of commodious offices, it contains two handsome chambers: in one the House of Representatives of the State hold their meetings: in the other, the Senate. Such proceedings as I saw here, were conducted with perfect gravity and decorum; and were certainly calculated to inspire attention and respect.

There is no doubt that much of the intellectual refinement and superiority of Boston, is referable to the quiet influence of the University of Cambridge, which is within three or four miles of the city. The resident professors at the university are gentlemen of learning and varied attainments; and are, without one exception that I can call to mind, men who would shed a grace upon, and do honor to, any society in the civilized world. Many of the resident gentry in Boston and its neighborhood, and I think I am not mistaken in adding, a large majority of those who are attached to the liberal professions there, have been educated at this same school. Whatever the defects of American universities may be, they disseminate no prejudices; rear no bigots; dig up the buried ashes of no old superstitions; and never interpose between the people and their improvement; exclude no man because of his religious opinions; above all, in their whole course of study and instruction, recognize a world, and a broad one too, lying beyond the college walls.

It was a source of inexpressible pleasure to me to observe the almost imperceptible, but not less certain effect, wrought by this institution among the small community of Boston; and note every turn the humanizing tastes and desires it has engendered; the affectionate friendships to which it has given rise; the amount of vanity and prejudice it has dispelled. The golden calf they worship at Boston is a pigmy compared with the giant effigies set up in other parts of that vast counting-house which lies beyond the Atlantic; and the almighty dollar sinks into something comparatively insignificant amidst a whole Pantheon of better gods.

Above all, I sincerely believe that the public institutions and charities of this capital of Massachusetts are as nearly perfect, as the most considerate wisdom, benevolence, and humanity, can make them. I never in my life was more affected by the contemplation of happiness, under circumstances of privation and bereavement, than in my visits to these establishments.

It is a great and pleasant feature of all such institutions in America, that they are either supported by the State or assisted by the State; or (in the event of their not needing its helping hand) that they act in concert with it, and are emphatically the people's. I cannot but think, with a view to the principle and its tendency to elevate or depress the character of the industrious classes, that a Public Charity is immeasurably better than a Private Foundation, no matter how munificently the latter may be endowed. In our own country, where it has not, until within these latter days, been a very popular fashion with governments to display any extraordinary regard for the great mass of the people, or to recognize their existence as improvable creatures, private charities, unexampled in the history of the earth, have arisen, to do an incalculable amount of good among the destitute and afflicted. But the government of the country, having neither act nor part in them, is not in the receipt of any portion of the gratitude they inspire; and, offering very little shelter or relief beyond that which is to be found in the workhouse and the jail, has come, not unnaturally, to be looked upon by the poor rather as a stern master, quick to correct and punish, than a kind protector, merciful and vigilant in their hour of need.

The maxim that out of evil cometh good, is strongly illustrated by these establishments at home; as the records of the Prerogative Office in Doctors' Commons can abundantly prove. Some immensely rich old gentleman or lady, surrounded by needy relatives, makes, upon a low average, a will a-week. The old gentleman or lady, never very remarkable in the best of times for good temper, is full of aches and pains from head to foot; full of fancies and caprices; full of spleen, distrust, suspicion, and dislike. To cancel old wills, and invent new ones, is at last the sole business of such a testator's existence; and relations and friends (some of whom have been bred up distinctly to inherit a large share of the property, and have been, from their cradles, specially disqualified from devoting themselves to any useful pursuit, on that account) are so often and so unexpectedly and summarily cut off, and re-instated, and cut off again, that the whole family, down to the remotest cousin, is kept in a perpetual fever. At length it becomes plain that the old lady or gentleman has not long to live; and the plainer this becomes, the more clearly the old lady or gentleman perceives that everybody is in a conspiracy against their poor old dying relative; wherefore the old lady or gentleman makes another last will—positively the last this time—conceals the same in a china tea-pot, and expires next day. Then it turns out, that the whole of the real and personal estate is divided between half-a-dozen charities; and that the dead and gone testator has in pure spite helped to do a great deal of good, at the cost of an immense amount of evil passion and misery.

The Perkins Institution and Massachusetts Asylum for the Blind, at Boston, is superintended by a body of trustees who make an annual report to the corporation. The indigent blind of that state are admitted gratuitously. Those from the adjoining state of Connecticut, or from the states of Maine, Vermont, or New Hampshire, are admitted by a warrant from the state to which they respectively belong; or, failing that, must find security among their friends, for the payment of about twenty pounds English for their first year's board and instruction, and ten for the second. "After the first year," say the trustees, "an account current will be opened with each pupil; he will be charged with the actual cost of his board, which will not exceed two dollars per week;" a trifle more than eight shillings English; "and he will be credited with the amount paid for him by the state, or by his friends; also with his earnings over and above the cost of the stock which he uses; so that all his earnings over one dollar per week will be his own. By the third year it will be known whether his earnings will more than pay the actual cost of his board; if they should, he will have it at his option to remain and receive his earnings, or not. Those who prove unable to earn their own livelihood will not be retained; as it is not desirable to convert the establishment into an almshouse, or to retain any but working bees in the hive. Those who by physical or mental imbecility are disqualified for work, are thereby disqualified from being members of an industrious community; and they can be better provided for in establishments fitted for the infirm."

I went to see this place one very fine winter morning: an Italian sky above, and the air so clear and bright on every side, that even my eyes, which are none of the best, could follow the minute lines and scraps of tracery in distant buildings. Like most other public institutions in America, of the same class, it stands a mile or two without the town, in a cheerful healthy spot; and is an airy, spacious, handsome edifice. It is built upon a height, commanding the harbor. When I paused for a moment at the door, and marked how fresh and free the whole scene was—what sparkling bubbles glanced upon the waves, and welled up every moment to the surface, as though the world below, like that above, were radiant with the bright day, and gushing over in its fulness of light: when I gazed from sail to sail away upon a ship at sea, a tiny speck of shining white, the only cloud upon the still, deep, distant blue—and, turning, saw a blind boy with his sightless face addressed that way, as though he too had some sense within him of the glorious distance: I felt a kind of sorrow that the place should be so very light, and a strange wish that for his sake it were darker. It was but momentary, of course, and a mere fancy, but I felt it keenly for all that.

The children were at their daily tasks in different rooms, except a few who were already dismissed, and were at play. Here, as in many institutions, no uniform is worn; and I was very glad of it, for two reasons. Firstly, because I am sure that nothing but senseless custom and want of thought would reconcile us to the liveries and badges we are so fond of at home. Secondly, because the absence of these things presents each child to the visitor in his or her own proper character, with its individuality unimpaired; not lost in a dull, ugly, monotonous repetition of the same unmeaning garb: which is really an important consideration. The wisdom of encouraging a little harmless pride in personal appearance even among the blind, or the whimsical absurdity of considering charity and leather breeches inseparable companions, as we do, requires no comment.

Good order, cleanliness, and comfort, pervaded every corner of the building. The various classes, who were gathered round their teachers, answered the questions put to them with readiness and intelligence, and in a spirit of cheerful contest for precedence which pleased me very much. Those who were at play, were gleesome and noisy as other children. More spiritual and affectionate friendships appeared to exist among them, than would be found among other young persons suffering under no deprivation; but this I expected and was prepared to find. It is a part of the great scheme of Heaven's merciful consideration for the afflicted.

In a portion of the building, set apart for that purpose, are workshops for blind persons whose education is finished, and who have acquired a trade, but who cannot pursue it in an ordinary manufactory because of their deprivation. Several people were at work here; making brushes, mattresses, and so forth; and the cheerfulness, industry, and good order discernible in every other part of the building, extended to this department also.

On the ringing of a bell, the pupils all repaired, without any guide or leader, to a spacious music-hall, where they took their seats in an orchestra erected for that purpose, and listened with manifest delight to a voluntary on the organ, played by one of themselves. At its conclusion, the performer, a boy of nineteen or twenty, gave place to a girl; and to her accompaniment they all sang a hymn, and afterwards a sort of chorus. It was very sad to look upon and hear them, happy though their condition unquestionably was; and I saw that one blind girl, who (being for the time deprived of the use of her limbs, by illness) sat close beside me with her face towards them, wept silently the while she listened.

It is strange to watch the faces of the blind, and see how free they are from all concealment of what is passing in their thoughts; observing which, a man with eyes may blush to contemplate the mask he wears. Allowing for one shade of anxious expression which is never absent from their countenances, and the like of which we may readily detect in our own faces if we try to feel our way in the dark, every idea, as it rises within them, is expressed with the lightning's speed, and nature's truth. If the company at a rout, or drawing-room at a court, could only for one time be as unconscious of the eyes upon them as blind men and women are, what secrets would come out, and what a worker of hypocrisy this sight, the loss of which we so much pity, would appear to be!

The thought occurred to me as I sat down in another room, before a girl, blind, deaf, and dumb; destitute of smell; and nearly so, of taste: before a fair young creature with every human faculty, and hope, and power of goodness and affection, inclosed within her delicate frame, and but one outward sense —the sense of touch. There she was, before me; built up, as it were, in a marble cell, impervious to any ray of light, or particle of sound; with her poor white hand peeping through a chink in the wall, beckoning to some good man for help, that an Immortal soul might be awakened.

Long before I looked upon her, the help had come. Her face was radiant with intelligence and pleasure. Her hair, braided by her own hands, was bound about a head, whose intellectual capacity and development were beautifully expressed in its graceful outline, and its broad open brow; her dress, arranged by herself, was a pattern of neatness and simplicity; the work she had knitted, lay beside her; her writing-book was on the desk she leaned upon. From the mournful ruin of such bereavement, there had slowly risen up this gentle, tender, guileless, grateful-hearted being.

Like other inmates of that house, she had a green ribbon bound round her eyelids. A doll she had dressed lay near upon the ground. I took it up, and saw that she had made a green fillet such as she wore herself, and fastened it about its mimic eyes.

She was seated in a little enclosure, made by school-desks and forms, writing her daily journal. But soon finishing this pursuit, she engaged in an animated communication with a teacher who sat beside her. This was a favorite mistress with the poor pupil. If she could see the face of her fair instructress, she would not love her less, I am sure.

I have extracted a few disjointed fragments of her history, from an account, written by that one man who has made her what she is. It is a very beautiful and touching narrative; and I wish I could present it entire.

Her name is Laura Bridgman. "She was born in Hanover, New Hampshire, on the twenty-first of December, 1829. She is described as having been a very sprightly and pretty infant, with bright blue eyes. She was, however, so puny and feeble until she was a year and a-half old, that her parents hardly hoped to rear her. She was subject to severe fits, which seemed to rack her frame almost beyond her power of endurance: and life was held by the feeblest tenure: but when a year and a-half old, she seemed to rally; the dangerous symptoms subsided; and at twenty months old, she was perfectly well.

"Then her mental powers, hitherto stinted in their growth, rapidly developed themselves; and during the four months of health which she enjoyed, she appears (making due allowance for a fond mother's account) to have displayed a considerable degree of intelligence.

"But suddenly she sickened again; her disease raged with great violence during five weeks, when her eyes and ears were inflamed, suppurated, and their contents were discharged. But though sight and hearing were gone for ever, the poor child's sufferings were not ended. The fever raged during seven weeks; for five months she was kept in bed in a darkened room; it was a year before she could walk unsupported, and two years before she could sit up all day. It was now observed that her sense of smell was almost entirely destroyed; and, consequently, that her taste was much blunted.

"It was not until four years of age that the poor child's bodily health seemed restored, and she was able to enter upon her apprenticeship of life and the world.

"But what a situation was hers! The darkness and the silence of the tomb were around her: no mother's smile called forth her answering smile, no father's voice taught her to imitate his sounds:—they, brothers and sisters, were but forms of matter which resisted her touch, but which differed not from the furniture of the house, save in warmth, and in the power of locomotion; and not even in these respects from the dog and the cat.

"But the immortal spirit which had been implanted within

her could not die, nor be maimed nor mutilated; and though most of its avenues of communication with the world were cut off, it began to manifest itself through the others. As soon as she could walk, she began to explore the room, and then the house; she became familiar with the form, density, weight, and heat, of every article she could lay her hands upon. She followed her mother, and felt her hands and arms, as she was occupied about the house; and her disposition to imitate, led her to repeat everything herself. She even learned to sew a little, and to knit."

The reader will scarcely need to be told, however, that the opportunities of communicating with her, were very, very limited; and that the moral effects of her wretched state soon began to appear. Those who cannot be enlightened by reason, can only be controlled by force; and this, coupled with her great privations, must soon have reduced her to a worse condition than that of the beasts that perish, but for timely and unhoped-for aid.

"At this time, I was so fortunate as to hear of the child, and immediately hastened to Hanover to see her. I found her with a well-formed figure; a strongly-marked, nervous-sanguine temperament; a large and beautifully-shaped head; and the whole system in healthy action. The parents were easily induced to consent to her coming to Boston, and on the 4th of October, 1837, they brought her to the Institution.

"For a while, she was much bewildered; and after waiting about two weeks, until she became acquainted with her new locality, and somewhat familiar with the inmates, the attempt was made to give her knowledge of arbitrary signs, by which she could interchange thoughts with others.

"There was one or two ways to be adopted: either to go on to build up a language of signs on the basis of the natural language which she had already commenced herself, or to teach her the purely arbitrary language in common use: that is, to give her a sign for every individual thing, or to give her a knowledge of letters by combination of which she might express her idea of the existence, and the mode and condition of existence, of any thing. The former would have been easy, but very ineffectual; the latter seemed very difficult, but, if accomplished, very effectual. I determined therefore to try the latter.

"The first experiments were made by taking articles in common use, such as knives, forks, spoons, keys, &c., and pasting upon them labels with their names printed in raised letters. These she felt very carefully, and soon, of course, distinguished that the crooked lines *s p o o n*, differed as much from the crooked lines *k e y*, as the spoon differed from the key in form.

"Then small detached labels, with the same words printed upon them, were put into her hands; and she soon observed that they were similar to the ones pasted on the articles. She showed her perception of this similarity by laying the label *k e y* upon the key, and the label *s p o o n* upon the spoon. She was encouraged here by the natural sign of approbation, patting on the head.

"The same process was then repeated with all the articles which she could handle; and she very easily learned to place the proper labels upon them. It was evident, however, that the only intellectual exercise was that of imitation and memory. She recollected that the label *b o o k* was placed upon a book, and she repeated the process first from imitation, next from memory, with only the motive of love of approbation, but apparently without the intellectual perception of any relation between the things.

"After a while, instead of labels, the individual letters were given to her on detached bits of paper: they were arranged side by side so as to spell *b o o k*, *k e y*, &c.; then they were mixed up in a heap, and a sign was made for her to arrange them herself, so as to express the words *b o o k*, *k e y*, &c.; and she did so.

"Hitherto, the process had been mechanical, and the success about as great as teaching a very knowing dog a variety of tricks. The poor child had sat in mute amazement, and patiently imitated everything her teacher did; but now the truth began to flash upon her: her intellect began to work: she perceived that here was a way by which she could herself make up a sign of anything that was in her own mind, and show it to another mind; and at once her countenance lighted up with a human expression: it was no longer a dog, or parrot: it was an immortal spirit, eagerly seizing upon a new link of union with other spirits! I could almost fix upon the moment when this truth dawned upon her mind, and spread its light to her countenance; I saw that the great obstacle was overcome; and that henceforward nothing but patient and persevering, but plain and straightforward, efforts were to be used.

"The result, thus far, is quickly related, and easily conceived; but not so was the process; for many weeks of apparently unprofitable labor were passed before it was effected.

"When it was said above, that a sign was made, it was intended to say that the action was performed by her teacher, she feeling his hands, and then imitating the motion.

"The next step was to procure a set of metal types, with the different letters of the alphabet cast upon their ends; also a board, in which were square holes, into which holes she could set the types; so that the letters on their ends could alone be felt above the surface.

"Then, on any article being handed to her,—for instance, a pencil, or a watch,—she would select the component letters, and arrange them on her board, and read them with apparent pleasure.

"She was exercised for several weeks in this way, until her vocabulary became extensive; and then the important step was taken of teaching her how to represent the different letters by the position of her fingers, instead of the cumbrous apparatus of the board and types. She accomplished this speedily and easily, for her intellect had begun to work in aid of her teacher, and her progress was rapid.

"This was the period, about three months after she had commenced, that the first report of her case was made, in which it is stated that 'she has just learned the manual alphabet, as used by the deaf mutes, and it is a subject of delight and wonder to see how rapidly, correctly, and eagerly, she goes on with her labors. Her teacher gives her a new object,—for instance, a pencil,—first lets her examine it, and get an idea of its use, then teaches her how to spell it by making the signs for the letters with her own fingers: the child grasps her hand, and feels her fingers, as the different letters are formed; she turns her head a little on one side, like a person listening closely; her lips are apart; she seems scarcely to breathe; and her countenance, at first anxious, gradually changes to a smile, as she comprehends the lesson. She then holds up her tiny fingers, and spells the word in the manual alphabet; next, she takes her types and arranges her letters; and last, to make sure that she is right, she takes the whole of the types composing the word, and places them upon or in contact with the pencil, or whatever the object may be.'

"The whole of the succeeding year was passed in gratifying her eager inquiries for the names of every object which she could possibly handle; in exercising her in the use of the manual alphabet; in extending in every possible way her knowledge of the physical relations of things; and in proper care of her heath.

"At the end of the year a report of her case was made, from which the following is an extract.

"'It has been ascertained beyond the possibility of doubt, that she cannot see a ray of light, cannot hear the least sound, and never exercises her sense of smell, if she have any. Thus her mind dwells in darkness and stillness, as profound as that of a closed tomb at midnight. Of beautiful sights, and sweet sounds, and pleasant odors, she has no conception; nevertheless, she seems as happy and playful as a bird or a lamb; and the employment of her intellectual faculties, or the acquirement of a new idea, gives her a vivid pleasure, which is plainly marked in her expressive features. She never seems to repine, but has all the buoyancy and gaiety of childhood. She is fond of fun and frolic, and when playing with the rest of the children, her shrill laugh sounds loudest of the group.

"'When left alone, she seems very happy if she have her knitting or sewing, and will busy herself for hours: if she have no occupation, she evidently amuses herself by imaginary dialogues, or by recalling past impressions; she counts with her fingers, or spells out names of things which she has recently learned, in the manual alphabet of the deaf mutes. In this lonely self-communion she seems to reason, reflect, and argue: if she spell a word wrong with the fingers of her right hand, she instantly strikes it with her left, as her teacher does, in sign of disapprobation; if right, then she pats herself upon the head and looks pleased. She sometimes purposely spells a word wrong with the left hand, looks roguish for a moment and laughs, and then with the right hand strikes the left, as if to correct it.

"'During the year she has attained great dexterity in the use of the manual alphabet of the deaf mutes; and she spells out the words and sentences which she knows, so fast and so deftly, that only those accustomed to this language can follow with the eye the rapid motions of her fingers.

"But wonderful as is the rapidity with which she writes her thoughts upon the air, still more so is the ease and accuracy with which she reads the words thus written by another; grasping their hands in hers, and following every movement of their fingers, as letter after letter conveys their meaning to her mind. It is in this way that she converses with her blind playmates, and nothing can more forcibly show the power of mind in forcing matter to its purpose than a meeting between them. For if great talent and skill are necessary for two pantomimes to paint their thoughts and feelings by the movements of the body, and the expression of the countenance, how much greater the difficulty when darkness shrouds them both, and the one can hear no sound!

"'When Laura is walking through a passage-way, with her hands spread before her, she knows instantly every one she meets, and passes them with a sign of recognition: but if it be a girl of her own age, and especially if it be one of her favorites, there is instantly a bright smile of recognition, and a twining of arms, a grasping of hands, and a swift telegraphing upon the tiny fingers; whose rapid evolutions convey the thoughts and feelings from the outposts of one mind to those of the other. There are questions and answers, exchanges of joy or sorrow, there are kissings and partings, just as between little children with all their senses!'

"During this year, and six months after she had left home, her mother came to visit her, and the scene of their meeting was an interesting one.

"The mother stood some time, gazing with overflowing eyes upon her unfortunate child, who, all unconscious of her presence, was playing about the room. Presently Laura ran against her, and at once began feeling her hands, examining her dress, and trying to find out if she knew her; but not succeeding in this, she turned away as from a stranger, and the poor woman could not conceal the pang she felt, at finding that her beloved child did not know her.

"She then gave Laura a string of beads which she used to wear at home, which were recognized by the child at once, who, with much joy, put them around her neck, and sought me eagerly to say she understood the string was from her home.

"The mother now tried to caress her, but poor Laura repelled her, preferring to be with her acquaintances.

"Another article from home was now given her, and she began to look much interested; she examined the stranger much closer, and gave me to understand that she knew she came from Hanover; she even endured her caresses, but would leave her with indifference at the slightest signal. The distress of the mother was now painful to behold; for, although she had feared that she should not be recognized, the painful reality of being treated with cold indifference by a darling child, was too much for woman's nature to bear.

"After a while, on the mother taking hold of her again, a vague idea seemed to flit across Laura's mind, that this could not be a stranger; she therefore felt her hands very eagerly, while her countenance assumed an expression of intense interest; she became very pale, and then suddenly red; hope seemed struggling with doubt and anxiety, and never were contending emotions more strongly painted upon the human face: at this moment of painful uncertainty, the mother drew her close to her side, and kissed her fondly, when at once the truth flashed upon the child, and all mistrust and anxiety disappeared from her face, as with an expression of exceeding joy she eagerly nestled to the bosom of her parent, and yielded herself to her fond embraces.

"After this, the beads were all unheeded; the playthings which were offered to her were utterly disregarded; her playmates, for whom but a moment before she gladly left the stranger, now vainly strove to pull her from her mother; and though she yielded her usual instantaneous obedience to my signal to follow me, it was evidently with painful reluctance. She clung close to me, as if bewildered and fearful; and when, after a moment, I took her to her mother, she sprang to her arms, and clung to her with eager joy.

"The subsequent parting between them, showed alike the affection, the intelligence, and the resolution of the child.

"Laura accompanied her mother to the door, clinging close to her all the way, until they arrived at the threshold, where she paused, and felt around to ascertain who was near her. Perceiving the matron, of whom she is very fond, she grasped her with one hand, holding on convulsively to her mother with the other; and thus she stood for a moment: then she dropped her mother's hand; put her handkerchief to her eyes; and turning round, clung sobbing to the matron; while her mother departed, with emotions as deep as those of her child.

* * * * *

"It has been remarked in former reports, that she can distinguish different degrees of intellect in others, and that she soon regarded almost with contempt, a new comer, when, after a few days, she discovered her weakness of mind. This unamiable part of her character has been more strongly developed during the past year.

"She chooses for her friends and companions, those children who are intelligent, and can talk best with her; and she evidently dislikes to be with those who are deficient in intellect, unless, indeed, she can make them serve her purposes, which she is evidently inclined to do. She takes advantage of them, and makes them wait upon her, in a manner that she knows she could not exact of others; and in various ways she shows her Saxon blood.

"She is fond of having other children noticed and caressed by the teachers, and those whom she respects; but this must not be carried too far, or she becomes jealous. She wants to have her share, which, if not the lion's, is the greater part; and if she does not get it, she says, '*My mother will love me.*'

"Her tendency to imitation is so strong, that it leads her to actions which must be entirely incomprehensible to her, and which can give her no other pleasure than the gratification of an internal faculty. She has been known to sit for half an hour, holding a book before her sightless eyes, and moving her lips, as she had observed seeing people do when reading.

"She one day pretended that her doll was sick; and went through all the motions of tending it, and giving it medicine; she then put it carefully to bed, and placed a bottle of hot water to its feet, laughing all the time most heartily. When I came home, she insisted upon my going to see it, and feel its pulse; and when I told her to put a blister on its back, she seemed to enjoy it amazingly, and almost screamed with delight.

"Her social feelings, and her affections, are very strong; and when she is sitting at work, or at her studies, by the side of one of her little friends, she will break off from her task every few moments, to hug and kiss them with an earnestness and warmth that is touching to behold.

"When left alone, she occupies and apparently amuses herself, and seems quite contented; and so strong seems to be the natural tendency of thought to put on the garb of language, that she often soliloquizes in the *finger language*, slow and tedious as it is. But it is only when alone, that she is quiet: for if she becomes sensible of the presence of any one near her, she is restless until she can sit close beside them, hold their hand, and converse with them by signs.

"In her intellectual character it is pleasing to observe an insatiable thirst for knowledge, and a quick perception of the relations of things. In her moral character, it is beautiful to behold her continual gladness, her keen enjoyment of existence her expansive love, her unhesitating confidence, her sympathy with suffering, her conscientiousness, truthfulness, and hopefulness."

Such are a few fragments from the simple but most interesting and instructive history of Laura Bridgman. The name of her great benefactor and friend, who writes it, is Doctor Howe. There are not many persons, I hope and believe, who, after reading these passages, can ever hear that name with indifference.

A further account has been published by Dr. Howe, since the report from which I have just quoted. It describes her rapid mental growth and improvement during twelve months more, and brings her little history down to the end of last year. It is very remarkable, that as we dream in words, and carry on imaginary conversation, in which we speak both for ourselves and for the shadows who appear to us in those visions of the night, so she, having no words, uses her finger alphabet in her sleep. And it has been ascertained that when her slumber is broken, and is much disturbed by dreams, she expresses her thoughts in an irregular and confused manner on her fingers: just as we should murmur and mutter them indistinctly, in the like circumstances.

I turned over the leaves of her Diary, and found it written in a fair legible square hand, and expressed in terms which were quite intelligible without an explanation. On my saying that I should like to see her write again, the teacher who sat beside her, bade her, in their language, sign her name upon a slip of paper, twice or thrice. In doing so, I observed that she kept her left hand always touching, and following up, her right, in which of course, she held her pen. No line was indicated by any contrivance, but she wrote straight and freely.

She had, until now, been quite unconscious of the presence of visitors; but, having her hand placed in that of the gentleman who accompanied me, she immediately expressed his name upon her teacher's palm. Indeed her sense of touch is now so exquisite, that having been acquainted with a person once, she can recognize him or her after almost any interval. This gentleman had been in her company, I believe, but very seldom, and certainly had not seen her for many months. My hand she rejected at once, as she does that of any man who is a stranger to her. But she retained my wife's with evident pleasure, kissed her, and examined her dress with a girl's curiosity and interest.

She was merry and cheerful, and showed much innocent playfulness in her intercourse with her teacher. Her delight on recognizing a favorite playfellow and companion—herself a blind girl—who silently, and with an equal enjoyment of the coming surprise, took a seat beside her, was beautiful to witness. It elicited from her at first, as other slight circumstances did twice or thrice during my visit, an uncouth noise which was rather painful to hear. But on her teacher touching her lips, she immediately desisted, and embraced her laughingly and affectionately.

I had previously been into another chamber, where a number of blind boys were swinging, and climbing, and engaged in various sports. They all clamored, as we entered, to the assistant-master, who accompanied us, "Look at me, Mr. Hart! Please, Mr. Hart, look at me!" evincing, I thought even in this, an anxiety peculiar to their condition, that their little feats of agility should be *seen*. Among them was a small laughing fellow, who stood aloof, entertaining himself with a gymnastic exercise for bringing the arm and chest into play; which he enjoyed mightily; especially when, in thrusting out his right arm, he brought it into contact with another boy. Like Laura Bridgman, this young child was deaf, and dumb, and blind.

Dr. Howe's account of this pupil's first instruction is so very striking, and so intimately connected with Laura herself, that I cannot refrain from a short extract. I may premise that the poor boy's name is Oliver Caswell; that he is thirteen years of age; and that he was in full possession of all his faculties, until three years and four months old. He was then attacked by scarlet fever: in four weeks became deaf; in a few weeks more, blind; in six months, dumb. He showed his anxious sense of this last deprivation, by often feeling the lips of other persons when they were talking, and then putting his hand upon his own, as if to assure himself that he had them in the right position.

"His thirst for knowledge," says Dr. Howe, "proclaimed itself as soon as he entered the house, by his eager examination of everything he could feel or smell in his new location. For instance, treading upon the register of a furnace, he instantly stooped down, and began to feel it, and soon discovered the way in which the upper plate moved upon the lower one; but this was not enough for him, so lying down upon his face, he applied his tongue first to one then to the other, and seemed to discover that they were of different kinds of metal.

"His signs were expressive: and the strictly natural language, laughing, crying, sighing, kissing, embracing, &c., was perfect.

"Some of the analogical signs which (guided by his faculty of imitation) he had contrived, were comprehensible; such as the waving motion of his hand for the motion of a boat, the circular one for a wheel, &c.

"The first object was to break up the use of these signs and to substitute for them the use of purely arbitrary ones.

"Profiting by the experience I had gained in the other cases, I omitted several steps of the process before employed, and commenced at once with the finger language. Taking therefore, several articles having short names, such as key, cup, mug, &c., and with Laura for an auxiliary, I sat down, and taking his hand, placed it upon one of them, and then with my own, made the letters *k e y*. He felt my hands eagerly with both of his, and on my repeating the process, he evidently tried to imitate the motions of my fingers. In a few minutes he contrived to feel the motions of my fingers with one hand, and holding out the other he tried to imitate them, laughing most heartily when he succeeded. Laura was by, interested even to agitation; and the two presented a singular sight: her face was flushed and anxious, and her fingers twined in among ours so closely as to follow every motion, but so lightly as not to embarrass them; while Oliver stood attentive, his head a little aside, his face turned up, his left hand grasping mine, and his right held out: at every motion of my fingers his countenance betokened keen attention; there was an expression of anxiety as he tried to imitate the motions; then a smile came stealing out as he thought he could do so, and spread into a joyous laugh the moment he succeeded, and felt me pat his head, and Laura clap him heartily upon the back, and jump up and down in her joy.

"He learned more than a half dozen letters in half an hour, and seemed delighted with his success, at least in gaining approbation. His attention then began to flag, and I commenced playing with him. It was evident that in all this he had merely been imitating the motions of my fingers, and placing his hand upon the key, cup, &c., as part of the process, without any perception of the relation between the sign and the object.

"When he was tired with play I took him back to the table, and he was quite ready to begin again his process of imitation. He soon learned to make the letters for *key*, *pen*, *pin*; and by having the object repeatedly placed in his hand, he at last perceived the relation I wished to establish between them. This was evident, because, when I made the letters *p i n*, or *p e n*, or *c u p*, he would select the article.

"The perception of this relation was not accompanied by that radiant flash of intelligence, and that glow of joy, which marked the delightful moment when Laura first perceived it. I then placed all the articles on the table, and going away a little distance with the children, placed Oliver's fingers in the positions to spell *key*, on which Laura went and brought the article: the little fellow seemed to be much amused by this, and looked very attentive and smiling. I then caused him to make the letters *b r e a d*, and in an instant Laura went and brought him a piece: he smelled at it; put it to his lips; cocked up his head with a most knowing look; seemed to reflect a moment; and then laughed outright, as much as to say, 'Aha! I understand now how something may be made out of this.'

"It was now clear that he had the capacity and inclination to learn, that he was a proper subject for instruction, and needed only persevering attention. I therefore put him in the hands of an intelligent teacher, nothing doubting of his rapid progress."

Well may this gentleman call that a delightful moment, in which some distant promise of her present state first gleamed upon the darkened mind of Laura Bridgman. Throughout his life, the recollection of that moment will be to him a source of pure, unfading happiness; nor will it shine least brightly on the evening of his days of Noble Usefulness.

The affection that exists between these two—the master and the pupil—is as far removed from all ordinary care and regard, as the circumstances in which it has had its growth, are apart from the common occurrences of life. He is occupied now, in devising means of imparting to her higher knowledge, and of conveying to her some adequate idea of the Great Creator of that universe in which, dark and silent and scentless though it be to her, she has such deep delight and glad enjoyment.

Ye who have eyes and see not, and have ears and hear not; ye who are as the hypocrites of sad countenances, and disfigure your faces that ye may seem unto men to fast; learn healthy cheerfulness, and mild contentment, from the deaf, and dumb, and blind! Self-elected saints with gloomy brows, this sightless, earless, voiceless child may teach you lessons you will do well to follow. Let that poor hand of hers lie gently on your hearts; for there may be something in its healing touch akin to that of the Great Master whose precepts you misconstrue, whose lessons you pervert, of whose charity and sympathy with all the world, not one among you in his daily practice knows as much as many of the worst among those fallen sinners, to whom you are liberal in nothing but the preachment of perdition!

As I rose to quit the room, a pretty little child of one of the attendants came running in to greet its father. For the moment, a child with eyes, among the sightless crowd, impressed me almost as painfully as the blind boy in the porch had done, two hours ago. Ah! how much brighter and more deeply blue, glowing and rich though it had been before, was the scene without, contrasting with the darkness of so many youthful lives within!

At South Boston, as it is called, in a situation excellently adapted for the purpose, several charitable institutions are clustered together. One of these, is the State Hospital for the insane; admirably conducted on those enlightened principles of conciliation and kindness, which twenty years ago would have been worse than heretical, and which have been acted upon with so much success in our own pauper asylum at Hanwell. "Evince a desire to show some confidence, and repose some trust, even in mad people,"—said the resident physician, as he walked along the galleries, his patients flocking round us unrestrained. Of those who deny or doubt the wisdom of this maxim after witnessing its effects, if there be such people still alive, I can only say that I hope I may never be summoned as a Juryman on a Commission of Lunacy whereof they are the subjects; for I should certainly find them out of their senses, on such evidence alone.

Each ward in this institution is shaped like a long gallery or hall, with the dormitories of the patients opening from it on either hand. Here they work, read, play at skittles, and other games; and when the weather does not admit of their taking exercise out of doors, pass the day together. In one of these rooms, seated, calmly, and quite as a matter of course, among a throng of madwomen, black and white, were the physician's wife and another lady, with a couple of children. These ladies were graceful and handsome; and it was not difficult to perceive at a glance that even their presence there, had a highly beneficial influence on the patients who were grouped about them.

Leaning her head against the chimney-piece, with a great assumption of dignity and refinement of manner, sat an elderly female, in as many scraps of finery as Madge Wildfire herself. Her head in particular was so strewn with scraps of gauze and cotton and bits of paper, and had so many queer odds and ends stuck all about it, that it looked like a bird's-nest. She was radiant with imaginary jewels; wore a rich pair of undoubted gold spectacles; and gracefully dropped upon her lap, as we approached, a very old greasy newspaper, in which I dare say she had been reading an account of her own presentation at some Foreign Court.

I have been thus particular in describing her, because she will serve to exemplify the physician's manner of acquiring and retaining the confidence of his patients.

"This," he said aloud, taking me by the hand, and advancing to the fantastic figure with great politeness—not raising her suspicions by the slightest look or whisper, or any kind of aside, to me: "this lady is the hostess of this mansion, sir. It belongs to her. Nobody else has anything whatever to do with it. It is a large establishment, as you see, and requires a great number of attendants. She lives, you observe, in the very first style. She is kind enough to receive my visits, and to permit my wife and family to reside here; for which it is hardly necessary to say, we are much indebted to her. She is exceedingly courteous, you perceive," on this hint she bowed condescendingly, "and will permit me to have the pleasure of introducing you; a gentleman from England, Ma'am: newly arrived from England, after a very tempestuous passage: Mr. Dickens—the lady of the house!"

We exchanged the most dignified salutations with profound gravity and respect, and so went on. The rest of the mad-women seemed to understand the joke perfectly (not only in this case, but in all the others, except their own), and to be highly amused by it. The nature of their several kinds of insanity was made known to me in the same way, and we left each of them in high good humor. Not only is a thorough confidence established, by these means, between physician and patient, in respect of the nature and extent of their hallucinations, but it is easy to understand that opportunities are afforded for seizing any moment of reason, to startle them by placing their own delusion before them in its most incongruous and ridiculous light.

Every patient in this asylum sits down to dinner every day with a knife and fork; and in the midst of them sits the gentleman, whose manner of dealing with his charges, I have just described. At every meal, moral influence alone restrains the more violent among them from cutting the throats of the rest; but the effect of that influence is reduced to an absolute certainty, and is found, even as a means of restraint, to say nothing of it as a means of cure, a hundred times more efficacious than all the strait-waistcoats, fetters, and hand-cuffs, that ignorance, prejudice, and cruelty have manufactured since the creation of the world.

In the labor department, every patient is as freely trusted with the tools of his trade as if he were a sane man. In the garden, and on the farm, they work with spades, rakes, and hoes. For amusement, they walk, run, fish, paint, read, and ride out to take the air in carriages provided for the purpose. They have among themselves a sewing society to make clothes for the poor, which holds meetings, passes resolutions, never comes to fisty cuffs or bowie-knives as sane assemblies have been known to do elsewhere; and conducts all its proceedings with the greatest decorum. The irritability, which would otherwise be expended on their own flesh, clothes, and furniture, is dissipated in these pursuits. They are cheerful, tranquil, and healthy.

Once a week they have a ball, in which the Doctor and his family, with all the nurses and attendants, take an active part. Dances and marches are performed alternately, to the enlivening strains of a piano; and now and then some gentleman or lady (whose proficiency has been previously ascertained) obliges the company with a song; nor does it ever degenerate, at a tender crisis, into a screech or howl; wherein, I must confess, I should have thought the danger lay. At an early hour they all meet together for these festive purposes; at eight o'clock refreshments are served; and at nine they separate.

Immense politeness and good-breeding are observed throughout. They all take their tone from the Doctor; and he moves a very Chesterfield among the company. Like other assemblies, these entertainments afford a frightful topic of conversation among the ladies for some days; and the gentlemen are so anxious to shine on the occasions, that they have been sometimes found "practising their steps" in private, to cut a more distinguished figure in the dance.

It is obvious that one great feature of this system, is the inculcation and encouragement, even among such unhappy persons, of a decent self-respect. Something of the same spirit pervades all the Institutions at South Boston.

There is the House of Industry. In that branch of it, which is devoted to the reception of old or otherwise helpless paupers, these words are painted on the walls: "WORTHY OF NOTICE. SELF-GOVERNMENT, QUIETUDE, AND PEACE, ARE BLESSINGS." It is not assumed and taken for granted that being there they must be evil-disposed and wicked people, before whose vicious eyes it is necessary to flourish threats and harsh restraints. They are met at the very threshold with this mild appeal. All within-doors is very plain and simple, as it ought to be, but arranged with a view to peace and comfort. It costs no more than any other plan of arrangement, but it bespeaks an amount of consideration for those who are reduced to seek shelter there, which puts them at once upon their gratitude and good behavior. Instead of being parcelled out in great, long, rambling wards, where a certain amount of weazen life may mope, and pine, and shiver, all day long, the building is divided into separate rooms, each with its share of light and air. In these, the better kind of paupers live. They have a motive for exertion and becoming pride, in the desire to make these little chambers comfortable and decent. I do not remember one but it was clean and neat, and had its plant or two upon the window-sill, or row of crockery upon the shelf, or small display of colored prints upon the white-washed wall, or, perhaps, its wooden clock behind the door.

The orphans and young children are in an adjoining building; separate from this, but a part of the same Institution. Some are such little creatures, that the stairs are of lilliputian measurement, fitted to their tiny strides. The same consideration for their years and weakness is expressed in their very seats, which are perfect curiosities, and look like articles of furniture for a pauper doll's-house. I can imagine the glee of our Poor Law Commissioners at the notion of these seats having arms and backs; but small spines being of older date than their occupation of the Board-room at Somerset House, I thought even this provision very merciful and kind.

Here again, I was greatly pleased with the inscriptions on

the wall, which were scraps of plain morality, easily remembered and understood: such as "Love one another"—"God remembers the smallest creature in his creation:" and straightforward advice of that nature. The books and tasks of these smallest of scholars, were adapted, in the same judicious manner, to their childish powers. When we had examined these lessons, four morsels of girls (of whom one was blind) sang a little song, about the merry month of May, which I thought (being extremely dismal) would have suited an English November better. That done, we went to see their sleeping-rooms on the floor above, in which the arrangements were no less excellent and gentle than those we had seen below. And after observing that the teachers were of a class and character well suited to the spirit of the place, I took leave of the infants with a lighter heart than ever I have taken leave of pauper infants yet.

Connected with the House of Industry, there is also an Hospital, which was in the best order, and had, I am glad to say, many beds unoccupied. It had one fault, however, which is common to all American interiors: the presence of the eternal, accursed, suffocating, red-hot demon of a stove, whose breath would blight the purest air under Heaven.

There are two establishments for boys in this same neighborhood. One is called the Boylston school, and is an asylum for neglected and indigent boys who have committed no crime, but who in the ordinary course of things would very soon be purged of that distinction if they were not taken from the hungry streets and sent here. The other is a House of Reformation for Juvenile Offenders. They are both under the same roof, but the two classes of boys never come in contact.

The Boylston boys, as may be readily supposed, have very much the advantage of the others in point of personal appearance. They were in their school-room when I came upon them, and answered correctly, without book, such questions as where was England; how far was it; what was its population; its capital city; its form of government; and so forth. They sang a song too, about a farmer sowing his seed: with corresponding action at such parts as "'tis thus he sows," "he turns him round," "he claps his hands;" which gave it greater interest for them, and accustomed them to act together, in an orderly manner. They appeared exceedingly well taught, and not better taught than fed; for a more chubby-looking full-waistcoated set of boys, I never saw.

The juvenile offenders had not such pleasant faces by a great deal, and in this establishment there were many boys of color. I saw them first at their work (basket-making, and the manufacture of palm-leaf hats), afterwards in their schools, where they sang a chorus in praise of Liberty: an odd, and, one would think, rather aggravating, theme for prisoners. These boys were divided into four classes, each denoted by a numeral, worn on a badge upon the arm. On the arrival of a new comer, he is put into the fourth or lowest class, and left, by good behavior, to work his way up into the first. The design and object of this Institution is to reclaim the youthful criminal by firm but kind and judicious treatment; to make his prison a place of purification and improvement, not of demoralization and corruption; to impress upon him that there is but one path, and that one sober industry, which can ever lead him to happiness; to teach him how it may be trodden, if his footsteps have never yet been led that way; and to lure him back to it if they have strayed: in a word, to snatch him from destruction, and restore him to society a penitent and useful member. The importance of such an establishment, in every point of view, and with reference to every consideration of humanity and social policy, requires no comment.

One other establishment closes the catalogue. It is the House of Correction for the State, in which silence is strictly maintained, but where the prisoners have the comfort and mental relief of seeing each other, and of working together. This is the improved system of Prison Discipline which we have imported into England, and which has been in successful operation among us for some years past.

America, as a new and not over-populated country, has in all her prisons, the one great advantage, of being enabled to find useful and profitable work for the inmates: whereas, with us, the prejudice against prison labor is naturally very strong, and almost insurmountable, when honest men, who have not offended against the laws, are frequently doomed to seek employment in vain. Even in the United States, the principle of bringing convict labor and free labor into a competition which must obviously be to the disadvantage of the latter, has already found many opponents, whose number is not likely to diminish with access of years.

For this very reason though, our best prisons would seem at the first glance to be better conducted than those of America. The treadmill is accompanied with little or no noise; five hundred men may pick oakum in the same room, without a sound: and both kinds of labor admit of such keen and vigilant superintendence, as will render even a word of personal communication among the prisoners almost impossible. On the other hand, the noise of the loom, the forge, the carpenter's hammer, or the stone-mason's saw, greatly favor those opportunities of intercourse—hurried and brief no doubt, but opportunities still—which these several kinds of work, by rendering it necessary for men to be employed very near to each other, and often side by side, without any barrier or partition between them, in their very nature present. A visitor, too, requires to reason and reflect a little, before the sight of a number of men engaged in ordinary labor, such as he is accustomed to out of doors, will impress him half as strongly as the contemplation of the same persons in the same place and garb would, if they were occupied in some task, marked and degraded everywhere as belonging only to felons in jails. In an American state prison or house of correction, I found it difficult at first to persuade myself that I was really in a jail: a place of ignominious punishment and endurance. And to this hour I very much question whether the humane boast that it is not like one, has its root in the true wisdom or philosophy of the matter.

I hope I may not be misunderrtood on this subject, for it is one in which I take a strong and deep interest. I incline as little to the sickly feeling which makes every canting lie or maudlin speech of a notorious criminal a subject of newspaper report and general sympathy, as I do to those good old customs of the good old times which made England, even so recently as in the reign of the Third King George, in respect of her criminal code and her prison regulations, one of the most bloody-minded and barbarous countries on the earth. If I thought it would do any good to the rising generation, I would cheerfully give my consent to the disinterment of the bones of any genteel highwayman (the more genteel, the more cheerfully,) and to their exposure, piece-meal, on any sign-post, gate, or gibbet, that might be deemed a good elevation for the purpose. My reason is as well convinced that these gentry were utterly worthless and debauched villains, as it is that the laws and jails hardened them in their evil courses, or that their wonderful escapes were effected by the prison-turnkeys who, in those admirable days, had always been felons themselves, and were, to the last, their bosom-friends and pet-companions. At the same time I know, as all men do or should, that the subject of Prison Discipline is one of the highest importance to any community; and that in her sweeping reform and bright example to other countries on this head, America has shown great wisdom, great benevolence and exalted policy. In contrasting her system with that which we have modelled upon it, I merely seek to show that with all its drawbacks, ours has some advantages of its own.*

The House of Correction which has led to these remarks, is not walled, like other prisons, but is palisaded round about with tall rough stakes, something after the manner of an enclosure for keeping elephants in, as we see it represented in Eastern prints and pictures. The prisoners wear a parti-

* Apart from profit made by the useful labor of prisoners which we can never hope to realize to any great extent, and which it is perhaps not expedient for us to try to gain, there are two prisons in London, in all respects equal, and in some decidedly superior, to any I saw or have ever heard or read of in America. One is the Tothill Fields Bridewell, conducted by Lieutentant A. F. Tracy, R. N.; the other the Middlesex House of Correction, superintended by Mr. Chesterton. This gentleman also holds an appointment in the Public Service. Both are enlightened and superior men: and it would be as difficult to find persons better qualified for the functions they discharge with firmness, zeal, intelligence, and humanity, as it would be to exceed the perfect order and arrangement of the institutions they govern.

colored dress; and those who are sentenced to hard labor work at nail-making or stone-cutting. When I was there, the latter class of laborers were employed upon the stone for a new custom-house in course of erection at Boston. They appeared to shape it skillfully and with expedition, though there were very few among them (if any) who had not acquired the art within the prison gates.

The women, all in one large room, were employed in making light clothing, for New Orleans and the Southern States. They did their work in silence, like the men; and like them, were overlooked by the person contracting for their labor, or by some agent of his appointment. In addition to this, they are every moment liable to be visited by the prison officers appointed for that purpose.

The arrangements for cooking, washing of clothes, and so forth, are much upon the plan of those I have seen at home. Their mode of bestowing the prisoners at night (which is of general adoption) differs from ours, and is both simple and effective. In the centre of a lofty area, lighted by windows in the four walls, are five tiers of cells, one above the other; each tier having before it a light iron gallery, attainable by stairs of the same construction and material: excepting the lower one, which is on the ground. Behind these, back to back with them and facing the opposite wall, are five corresponding rows of cells, accessible by similar means: so that supposing the prisoners locked up in their cells, an officer stationed on the ground, with his back to the wall, has half their number under his eye at once; the remaining half being equally under the observation of another officer on the opposite side; and all in one great apartment. Unless this watch be corrupted or sleeping on his post, it is impossible for a man to escape; for even in the event of his forcing the iron door of his cell without noise (which is exceedingly improbable), the moment he appears outside, and steps into that one of the five galleries on which it is situated, he must be plainly and fully visible to the officer below. Each of these cells holds a small truckle-bed, in which one prisoner sleeps; never more. It is small, of course; and the door being not solid, but grated, and without blind or curtain, the prisoner within is at all times exposed to the observation and inspection of any guard who may pass along that tier at any hour or minute of the night. Every day, the prisoners receive their dinner, singly, through a trap in the kitchen wall; and each man carries his to his sleeping cell to eat it, where he is locked up, alone, for that purpose, one hour. The whole of this arrangement struck me as being admirable; and I hope that the next new prison we erect in England may be built on this plan.

I was given to understand that in this prison no swords or fire-arms, or even cudgels, are kept; nor is it probable that, so long as its present excellent management continues, any weapon, offensive or defensive, will ever be required within its bounds.

Such are the Institutions at South Boston! In all of them, the unfortunate or degenerate citizens of the State are carefully instructed in their duties both to God and man; are surrounded by all reasonable means of comfort and happiness that their condition will admit of; are appealed to, as members of the great human family, however afflicted, indigent, or fallen; are ruled by the strong Heart, and not by the strong (though immeasurably weaker) Hand. I have described them at some length: firstly, because their worth demanded it; and secondly, because I mean to take them for a model, and to content myself with saying of others we may come to, whose design and purpose are the same, that in this or that respect they practically fail, or differ.

I wish by this account of them, imperfect in its execution, but, in its just intention, honest, I could hope to convey to my readers one hundredth part of the gratification, the sights I have described afforded me.

To an Englishman, accustomed to the paraphernalia of Westminster Hall, an American Court of Law is as odd a sight as, I suppose, an English Court of Law would be to an American. Except in the Supreme Court at Washington (where the judges wear a plain black robe), there is no such thing as a wig or gown connected with the administration of justice. The gentlemen of the bar being barristers and attorneys too (for there is no division of those functions as in England) are no more removed from their clients than attorneys in our Court for the Relief of Insolvent Debtors are from theirs. The jury are quite at home, and make themselves as comfortable as circumstances will permit. The witness is so little elevated above, or put aloof from, the crowd in the court, that a stranger entering during a pause in the proceedings would find it difficult to pick him out from the rest. And if it chanced to be a criminal trial, his eyes, in nine cases out of ten, would wander to the dock in search of the prisoner in vain; for that gentleman would most likely be lounging among the most distinguished ornaments of the legal profession, whispering suggestions in his counsel's ear, or making a toothpick out of an old quill with his penknife.

I could not but notice these differences when I visited the courts at Boston. I was much surprised at first, too, to observe that the counsel who interrogated the witness under examination at the time did so *sitting*. But seeing that he was also occupied in writing down the answers, and remembering that he was alone and had no "junior," I quickly consoled myself with the reflection that law was not quite so expensive an article here as at home; and that the absence of sundry formalities which we regard as indispensable, had doubtless a very favorable influence upon the bill of costs.

In every court ample and commodious provision is made for the accommodation of the citizens. This is the case all through America. In every Public Institution, the right of the people to attend, and to have an interest in the proceedings, is most fully and distinctly recognized. There are no grim door-keepers to dole out their tardy civility by the sixpennyworth; nor is there, I sincerely believe, any insolence of office of any kind. Nothing national is exhibited for money; and no public officer is a showman. We have begun of late years to imitate this good example. I hope we shall continue to do so; and that, in the fullness of time, even deans and chapters may be converted.

In the civil court an action was trying for damages sustained in some accident upon a railway. The witnesses had been examined, and counsel was addressing the jury. The learned gentleman (like a few of his English brethren) was desperately long-winded, and had a remarkable capacity of saying the same thing over and over again. His great theme was "Warren the ĕn*gine* driver," whom he pressed into the service of every sentence he uttered. I listened to him for about a quarter of an hour; and, coming out of court at the expiration of that time, without the faintest ray of enlightenment as to the merits of the case, felt as if I were at home again.

In the prisoners' cell, waiting to be examined by the magistrate on a charge of theft, was a boy. This lad, instead of being committed to a common jail, would be sent to the asylum at South Boston, and there taught a trade; and in the course of time he would be bound apprentice to some respectable master. Thus his detection in this offence, instead of being the prelude to a life of infamy and a miserable death, would lead, there was a reasonable hope, to his being reclaimed from vice, and becoming a worthy member of society.

I am by no means a wholesale admirer of our legal solemnities, many of which impress me as being exceedingly ludicrous. Strange as it may seem, too, there is undoubtedly a degree of protection in the wig and gown—a dismissal of individual responsibility in dressing for the part—which encourages that insolent bearing and language, and that gross perversion of the office of a pleader for The Truth, so frequent in our courts of law. Still, I cannot help doubting whether America, in her desire to shake off the absurdities and abuses of the old system, may not have gone too far into the opposite extreme; and whether it is not desirable, especially in the small community of a city like this, where each man knows the other, to surround the administration of justice with some artificial barriers against the "Hail, fellow, well met" deportment of every-day life. All the aid it can have in the very high character and ability of the Bench, not only here but elsewhere, it has, and well deserves to have; but it may need something more: not to impress the thoughtful and well-informed, but the ignorant and heedless; a class which includes some prisoners and many witnesses. These institutions were established, no doubt, upon the principle that those who had so large a share in making the laws, would certainly respect them. But experience has proved this hope to be fallacious; for no men know better than the judges of America, that on the occasion of any great popular excitement the law is powerless, and cannot, for the time, assert its own supremacy.

The tone of society in Boston is one of perfect politeness, courtesy, and good breeding. The ladies are unquestionably very beautiful—in face: but there I am compelled to stop. Their education is much as with us; neither better nor worse. I had heard some very marvellous stories in this respect; but not believing them, was not disappointed. Blue ladies there are, in Boston; but like philosophers of that color and sex in most other latitudes, they rather desire to be thought superior than to be so. Evangelical ladies there are, likewise, whose attachment to forms of religion, and horror of theatrical entertainments, are most exemplary. Ladies who have a passion for attending lectures are to be found among all classes and all conditions. In the kind of provincial life which preails in cities such as this, the Pulpit has great influence. The peculiar province of the Pulpit in New England (always excepting the Unitarian ministry) would appear to be the denouncement of all innocent and rational amusements. The church, the chapel, and the lecture-room, are the only means of excitement excepted; and to the church, the chapel, and the lecture-room, the ladies resort in crowds.

Wherever religion is resorted to, as a strong drink, and as an escape from the dull monotonous round of home, those of its ministers who pepper the highest will be the surest to please. They who strew the Eternal Path with the greatest amount of brimstone, and who most ruthlessly tread down the flowers and leaves that grow by the way-side, will be voted the most righteous; and they who enlarge with the greatest pertinacity on the difficulty of getting into heaven, will be considered by all true believers certain of going there: though it would be hard to say by what process of reasoning this conclusion is arrived at. It is so at home, and so abroad. With regard to the other means of excitement, the Lecture, it has at least the merit of being always new. One lecture treads so quickly on the heels of another, that none are remembered; and the course of this month may be safely repeated next, with its charm of novelty unbroken, and its interest unabated.

The fruits of the earth have their growth in corruption. Out of the rottenness of these things, there has sprung up in Boston a sect of philosophers known as Transcendentalists. On inquiring what this appellation might be supposed to signify, I was given to understand that whatever was unintelligible would be certainly transcendental. Not deriving much comfort from its elucidation, I pursued the inquiry still further, and found that Transcendentalists are followers of my friend Mr. Carlyle, or I should rather say a follower of his, Mr. Ralph Waldo Emerson. This gentleman has written a volume of Essays, in which, among much that is dreamy and fanciful (if he will pardon me for saying so) there is much more that is true and manly, honest and bold. Transcendentalism has its occasional vagaries (what school has not?) but it has good healthful qualities in spite of them; not least among the number a hearty disgust of Cant, and an aptitude to detect her in all the million varieties of her everlasting wardrobe. And therefore if I were a Bostonian, I think I would be a Transcendentalist.

The only preacher I heard in Boston was Mr. Taylor, who addressed himself peculiarly to seamen, and who was once a mariner himself. I found his chapel down among the shipping, in one of the narrow, old, water-side streets, with a gay blue flag waving freely from its roof. In the gallery opposite to the pulpit were a little choir of male and female singers, a violoncello, and a violin. The preacher already sat in the pulpit, which was raised on pillars, and ornamented behind him with painted drapery of a lively and somewhat theatrical appearance. He looked a weather-beaten hard-featured man, of about six or eight and fifty; with deep lines graven as it were into his face, dark hair, and a stern, keen eye. Yet the general character of his countenance was pleasant and agreeable.

The service commenced with a hymn, to which succeeded an extemporary prayer. It had the fault of frequent repetition, incidental to all such prayers; but it was plain and comprehensive in its doctrines, and breathed a tone of general sympathy and charity, which is not so commonly a characteristic of this form of address to the Deity as it might be. That done he opened his discourse, taking for his text a passage from the Song of Solomon, laid upon the desk before the commencement of the service by some unknown member of the congregation: "Who is this coming up from the wilderness, leaning on the arm of her beloved!"

He handled his text in all kinds of ways, and twisted it into all manner of shapes; but always ingeniously, and with a rude eloquence, well-adapted to the comprehension of his hearers. Indeed if I be not mistaken, he studied their sympathies and understandings much more than the display of his own powers. His imagery was all drawn from the sea, and from the incidents of a seaman's life; and was often remarkably good. He spoke to them of "that glorious man, Lord Nelson," and of Collingwood; and drew nothing in, as the saying is, by the head and shoulders, but brought it to bear upon his purpose, naturally, and with a sharp mind to its effect. Sometimes, when much excited with his subject, he had an odd way—compounded of John Bunyan, and Balfour of Burley—of taking his great quarto bible under his arm and pacing up and down the pulpit with it; looking steadily down, meantime, into the midst of the congregation. Thus, when he applied his text to the first assemblage of his hearers, and pictured the wonder of the church at their presumption in forming a congregation among themselves, he stopped short with his bible under his arm in the manner I have described, and pursued his discourse after this manner:

"Who are these—who are they—who are these fellows? where do they come from? Where are they going to?—Come from! What's the answer?"—leaning out of the pulpit, and pointing downward with his right hand: "From below!"—starting back again, and looking at the sailors before him: "From below, my brethren. From under the hatches of sin, battened down above you by the evil one. That's where you came from!"—a walk up and down the pulpit: "and where are you going"—stopping abruptly: "where are you going? Aloft!"—very softly, and pointing upward: "Aloft!"—louder: "aloft!"—louder still: "That's where you are going—with a fair wind,—all taut and trim, steering direct for Heaven in its glory, where there are no storms or foul weather, and where the wicked cease from troubling, and the weary are at rest."—Another walk: "That's where you're going to, my friends. That's it. That's the place. That's the port. That's the haven. It's a blessed harbor—still water there, in all changes of the winds and tides; no driving ashore upon the rocks, or slipping your cables and running out to sea, there: Peace—Peace—Peace—all peace!"—Another walk, and patting the bible under his left arm: "What! These fellows are coming from the wilderness, are they? Yes. From the dreary, blighted wilderness of Iniquity, whose only crop is Death. But do they lean upon anything—do they lean upon nothing, these poor seamen?"—Three raps upon the bible: "Oh yes.—Yes.—They lean upon the arm of their Beloved"—three more raps: "upon the arm of their Beloved"—three more, and a walk: "Pilot, guiding-star, and compass, all in one, to all hands—here it is"—three more: "Here it is. They can do their seaman's duty manfully, and be easy in their minds in the utmost peril and danger, with this"—two more: "They can come, even these poor fellows can come, from the wilderness leaning on the arm of their Beloved, and go up—up—up!"—raising his hand higher, and higher, at every repetition of the word, so that he stood with it at last stretched above his head, regarding them in a strange, rapt manner, and pressing the book triumphantly to his breast, until he gradually subsided into some other portion of his discourse.

I have cited this, rather as an instance of the preacher's eccentricities than his merits, though taken in connection with his look and manner, and the character of his audience, even this was striking. It is possible, however, that my favorable impression of him may have been greatly influenced and strengthened, firstly, by his impressing upon his hearers that the true observance of religion was not inconsistent with a cheerful deportment and an exact discharge of the duties of their station, which, indeed, it scrupulously required of them; and secondly, by his cautioning them not to set up any monopoly in Paradise and its mercies. I never heard these two points so wisely touched (if indeed I have ever heard them touched at all), by any preacher of that kind, before.

Having passed the time I spent in Boston, in making myself acquainted with these things, in settling the course I should take in my future travels, and in mixing constantly with its society, I am not aware that I have any occasion to prolong this chapter. Such of its social customs as I have not mentioned, however, may be told in a very few words.

The usual dinner-hour is two o'clock. A dinner party takes place at five; and at an evening party, they seldom sup later than eleven; so that it goes hard but one gets home, even from a rout, by midnight. I never could find out any difference between a party at Boston and a party in London, saving that at the former place all assemblies are held at more rational hours; that the conversation may possibly be a little louder and more cheerful; that a guest is usually expected to ascend to the very top of the house to take his cloak off; that he is certain to see, at every dinner, an unusual amount of poultry on the table; and at every supper, at least two mighty bowls of hot stewed oysters, in any one of which a half-grown Duke of Clarence might be smothered easily.

There are two theatres in Boston, of good size and construction, but sadly in want of patronage. The few ladies who resort to them, sit, as of right, in the front rows of the boxes.

The bar is a large room with a stone floor, and there people stand and smoke, and lounge about, all the evening: dropping in and out as the humor takes them. There too the stranger is initiated into the mysteries of Gin-sling, Cocktail, Sangaree, Mint Julep, Sherry-cobbler, Timber Doodle, and other rare drinks. The House is full of boarders, both married and single, many of whom sleep upon the premises, and contract by the week for their board and lodging: the charge for which diminishes as they go nearer the sky to roost. A public table is laid in a very handsome hall for breakfast, and for dinner, and for supper. The party sitting down together to these meals will vary in number from one to two hundred: sometimes more. The advent of each of these epochs in the day is proclaimed by an awful gong, which shakes the very window frames as it reverberates through the house, and horribly disturbs nervous foreigners. There is an ordinary for ladies, and an ordinary for gentlemen.

In our private room the cloth could not, for any earthly consideration, have been laid for dinner without a huge glass dish of cranberries in the middle of the table; and breakfast would have been no breakfast unless the principal dish were a deformed beef-steak with a great flat bone in the centre, swimming in hot butter, and sprinkled with the very blackest of all possible pepper. Our bedroom was spacious and airy, but (like every bedroom on this side of the Atlantic) very bare of furniture, having no curtains to the French bedstead or to the window. It had one unusual luxury, however, in the shape of a wardrobe of painted wood, something smaller than an English watch-box: or if this comparison should be insufficient to convey a just idea of its dimensions, they may be estimated from the fact of my having lived for fourteen days and nights in the firm belief that it was a shower-bath.

## CHAPTER IV.

### AN AMERICAN RAILROAD. LOWELL AND ITS FACTORY SYSTEM.

Before leaving Boston, I devoted one day to an excursion to Lowell. I assign a separate chapter to this visit; not because I am about to describe it at any great length, but because I remember it as a thing by itself, and am desirous that my readers should do the same.

I made acquaintance with an American railroad on this occasion, for the first time. As these works are pretty much alike all through the States, their general characteristics are easily described.

There are no first and second class carriages as with us; but there is a gentleman's car and a ladies' car: the main distinction between which is that in the first, everybody smokes; and in the second, nobody does. As a black man never travels with a white one, there is also a negro car; which is a great blundering clumsy chest, such as Gulliver put to sea in, from the kingdom of Brobdingnag. There is a great deal of jolting, a great deal of noise, a great deal of wall, not much window, a locomotive engine, a shriek, and a bell.

The cars are like shabby omnibuses, but larger: holding thirty, forty, fifty, people. The seats, instead of stretching from end to end, are placed crosswise. Each seat holds two persons. There is a long row of them on each side of the caravan, a narrow passage up the middle, and a door at both ends. In the centre of the carriage there is usually a stove, fed with charcoal or anthracite coal; which is for the most part red-hot. It is insufferably close; and you see the hot air fluttering between yourself and any other object you may happen to look at, like the ghost of smoke.

In the ladies' car, there are a great many gentlemen who have ladies with them. There are also a great many ladies who have nobody with them: for any lady may travel alone, from one end of the United States to the other, and be certain of the most courteous and considerate treatment everywhere. The conductor or check-taker, or guard, or whatever he may be, wears no uniform. He walks up and down the car, and in an out of it, as his fancy dictates; leans against the door with his hands in his pockets and stares at you, if you chance to be a stranger; or enters into conversation with the passengers about him. A great many newspapers are pulled out, and a few of them are read. Everybody talks to you, or to anybody else who hits his fancy. If you are an Englishman, he expects that that railroad is pretty much like an English railroad. If you say "No," he says "Yes?" (interrogatively), and asks in what respect they differ. You enumerate the heads of difference, one by one, and he says "Yes?" (still interrogatively) to each. Then he guesses that you don't travel faster in England; and on your replying that you do, says "Yes?" again (still interrogatively), and, it is quite evident, don't believe it. After a long pause he remarks, partly to you, and partly to the knob on the top of his stick, that "Yankees are reckoned to be considerable of a go-ahead people too;" upon which *you* say "Yes," and then *he* says "Yes" again (affirmatively this time); and upon your looking out of window, tells you that behind that hill, and some three miles from the next station, there is a clever town in a smart lo-ca-tion, where he expects you have con-cluded to stop. Your answer in the negative naturally leads to more questions in reference to your intended route (always pronounced rout); and wherever you are going, you invariably learn that you can't get there without immense difficulty and danger, and that all the great sights are somewhere else.

If a lady take a fancy to any male passenger's seat, the gentleman who accompanies her gives him notice of the fact, and he immediately vacates it with great politeness. Politics are much discussed, so are banks, so is cotton. Quiet people avoid the question of the Presidency, for there will be a new election in three years and a half, and party feeling runs very high: the great constitutional feature of this institution being, that directly the acrimony of the last election is over, the acrimony of the next one begins; which is an unspeakable comfort to all strong politicians and true lovers of their country: that is to say, to ninety-nine men and boys out of every ninety-nine and a quarter.

Except when a branch road joins the main one, there is seldom more than one track of rails; so that the road is very narrow, and the view, where there is a deep cutting, by no means extensive. When there is not, the character of the scenery is always the same. Mile after mile of stunted trees: some hewn down by the axe, some blown down by the wind, some half fallen and resting on their neighbors, many mere logs half hidden in the swamp, others mouldered away to spongy chips. The very soil of the earth is made up of minute fragments such as these; each pool of stagnant water has its crust of vegetable rottenness; on every side there are the boughs, and trunks, and stumps of trees, in every possible stage of decay, decomposition, and neglect. Now you emerge for a few brief minutes on an open country, glittering with some bright lake or pool, broad as many an English river, but so small here that it scarcely has a name; now catch hasty glimpses of a distant town, with its clean white houses and their cool piazzas, its prim New England church and schoolhouse; when whir-r-r-r! almost before you have seen them, comes the same dark screen: the stunted trees, the stumps, the logs, the stagnant water—all so like the last that you seem to have been transported back again by magic.

The train calls at stations in the woods, were the wild impossibility of anybody having the smallest reason to get out, is only to be equalled by the apparently desperate hopelessness of there being anybody to get in. It rushes across the turnpike road, where there is no gate, no policeman, no signal: nothing but a rough wooden arch, on which is painted "WHEN THE BELL RINGS, LOOK OUT FOR THE LOCOMOTIVE." On it whirls headlong, dives through the woods again, emerges in the light, clatters over frail arches, rumbles upon the heavy ground, shoots beneath a wooden bridge which intercepts the light for a second like a wink, suddenly awakens all the slumbering echoes in the main street of a large town, and dashes on haphazard, pell-mell, neck or nothing, down the middle of the road. There—with mechanics working at their trades, and people leaning from their doors and windows, and boys flying kites and playing marbles, and men smoking, and women talking, and children crawling, and pigs burrowing, and unaccustomed horses plunging and rearing, close to the very rails—there—on, on, on—tears the mad dragon of an engine with its train of cars; scattering in all directions a shower of burning sparks from its wood fire; screeching, hissing, yelling, panting; until at last the thirsty monster stops beneath a covered way to drink, the people cluster round, and you have time to breathe again.

I was met at the station at Lowell by a gentleman intimately connected with the management of the factories there; and gladly putting myself under his guidance, drove off at once to that quarter of the town in which the works, the object of my visit, were situated. Although only just of age —for if my recollection serve me, it has been a manufacturing town barely one-and-twenty years—Lowell is a large, populous, thriving place. Those indications of its youth which first attract the eye, give it a quaintness and oddity of character which, to a visitor from the old country, is amusing enough. It was a very dirty winter's day, and nothing in the whole town looked old to me, except the mud, which in some parts was almost knee-deep, and might have been deposited there, on the subsiding of the waters after the Deluge. In one place, there was a new wooden church, which, having no steeple, and being yet unpainted, looked like an enormous packing-case without any direction upon it. In another there was a large hotel, whose walls and colonnades were so crisp, and thin, and slight, that it had exactly the appearance of being built with cards. I was careful not to draw my breath as we passed, and trembled when I saw a workman come out upon the roof, lest with one thoughtless stamp of his foot he should crush the structure beneath him, and bring it rattling down. The very river that moves the machinery in the mills (for they are all worked by water power,) seems to acquire a new character from the fresh buildings of bright red brick and painted wood among which it takes its course; and to be as light-headed, thoughtless, and brisk a young river, in its murmurings and tumblings, as one would desire to see. One would swear that every "Bakery," "Grocery," and "Bookbindery," and other kind of store, took its shutters down for the first time, and started in business yesterday. The golden pestles and mortars fixed as signs upon the sun-blind frames outside the Druggists', appear to have been just turned out of the United States Mint; and when I saw a baby of some week or ten days old in a woman's arms at a street corner, I found myself unconsciously wondering where it came from: never supposing that it could have been born in such a young town as that.

There are several factories in Lowell, each of which belongs to what we should term a Company of Proprietors, but what they call in America a Corporation. I went over several of these; such as a woolen factory, a carpet factory, and a cotton factory: examined them in every part; and saw them in their ordinary working aspect, with no preparation of any kind, or departure from their ordinary every-day proceedings. I may add that I am well acquainted with our manufacturing towns in England, and have visited many mills in Manchester and elsewhere in the same manner.

I happened to arrive at the first factory just as the dinner hour was over, and the girls were returning to their work; indeed the stairs of the mill were thronged with them as I ascended. They were all well-dressed, but not to my thinking above their condition: for I like to see the humbler classes of society careful of their dress and appearance, and even, if they please, decorated with such little trinkets as come within the compass of their means. Supposing it confined within reasonable limits, I would always encourage this kind of pride, as a worthy element of self-respect, in any person I employed; and should no more be deterred from doing so, because some wretched female referred her fall to a love of dress, than I would allow my construction of the real intent and meaning of the Sabbath to be influenced by any warning to the well-disposed, founded on his backslidings on that particular day, which might emanate from the rather doubtful authority of a murderer in Newgate.

These girls, as I have said, were all well dressed: and that phrase necessarily includes extreme cleanliness. They had serviceable bonnets, good warm cloaks and shawls; and were not above clogs and pattens. Moreover, there were places in the mill in which they could deposit these things without injury; and there were conveniences for washing. They were healthy in appearance, many of them remarkably so, and had the manners and deportment of young women; not of degraded brutes of burden. If I had seen in one of those mills (but I did not, though I looked for something of this kind with a sharp eye), the most lisping, mincing, affected, and ridiculous young creature that my imagination could suggest, I should have thought of the careless, moping, slatternly, degraded, dull reverse (I *have* seen that), and should have been still well pleased to look upon her.

The rooms in which they worked, were as well ordered as themselves. In the windows of some, there were green plants, which were trained to shade the glass; in all, there was as much fresh air, cleanliness, and comfort, as the nature of the occupation would possibly admit of. Out of so large a number of females, many of whom were only then just verging upon womanhood, it may be reasonably supposed that some were delicate and fragile in appearance: no doubt there were. But I solemnly declare, that from all the crowd I saw in the different factories that day, I cannot recall or separate one young face that gave me a painful impression; not one young girl whom, assuming it to be matter of necessity that she should gain her daily bread by the labor of her hands, I would have removed from those works if I had had the power.

They reside in various boarding-houses near at hand. The owners of the mills are particularly careful to allow no persons to enter upon the possession of these houses, whose characters have not undergone the most searching and thorough inquiry. Any complaint that is made against them, by the boarders, or by any one else, is fully investigated; and if good ground of complaint be shown to exist against them, they are removed, and their occupation is handed over to some more deserving person. There are a few children employed in these factories, but not many. The laws of the State forbid their working more than nine months in the year, and require that they be educated during the other three. For this purpose there are schools in Lowell; and there are churches and chapels of various persuasions, in which the young women may observe that form of worship in which they have been educated.

At some distance from the factories, and on the highest and

pleasantest ground in the neighborhood, stands their hospital, or boarding-house for the sick: it is the best house in those parts, and was built by an eminent merchant for his own residence. Like that institution at Boston, which I have before described, it is not parcelled out into wards, but is divided into convenient chambers, each of which has all the comforts of a very comfortable home. The principal medical attendant resides under the same roof; and were the patients members of his own family, they could not be better cared for, or attended with greater gentleness and consideration. The weekly charge in this establishment for each female patient is three dollars, or twelve shillings English; but no girl employed by any of the corporations is ever excluded for want of the means of payment. That they do not very often want the means, may be gathered from the fact, that in July, 1841, no fewer than nine hundred and seventy-eight of these girls were depositors in the Lowell Savings Bank: the amount of whose joint savings was estimated at one hundred thousand dollars, or twenty thousand English pounds.

I am now going to state three facts, which will startle a large class of readers on this side of the Atlantic, very much.

Firstly, there is a joint-stock piano in a great many of the boarding-houses. Secondly, nearly all these young ladies subscribe to circulating libraries. Thirdly, they have got up among themselves a periodical called THE LOWELL OFFERING, "A repository of original articles, written exclusively by females actively employed in the mills,"—which is duly printed, published, and sold; and whereof I brought away from Lowell four hundred good solid pages, which I have read from beginning to end.

The large class of readers, startled by these facts, will exclaim, with one voice, "How very preposterous!" On my deferentially inquiring why, they will answer, "These things are above their station." In reply to that objection, I would beg to ask what their station is.

It is their station to work. And they *do* work. They labor in these mills, upon an average, twelve hours a day, which is unquestionably work, and pretty tight work too.

Perhaps it is above their station to indulge in such amusements, on any terms. Are we quite sure that we in England have not formed our ideas of the "station" of working people, from accustoming ourselves to the contemplation of that class as they are, and not as they might be? I think that if we examine our own feelings, we shall find that the pianos, and the circulating libraries, and even the Lowell Offering, startle us by their novelty, and not by their bearing upon any abstract question of right or wrong.

For myself, I know no station in which, the occupation of to-day cheerfully done and the occupation of to-morrow cheerfully looked to, any one of these pursuits is not most humanizing and laudable. I know no station which is rendered more endurable to the person in it, or more safe to the person out of it, by having ignorance for its associate. I know no station which has a right to monopolize the means of mutual instruction, improvement, and rational entertainment; or which has ever continued to be a station very long, after seeking to do so.

Of the merits of the Lowell Offering as a literary production, I will only observe, putting entirely out of sight the fact of the articles having been written by these girls after the arduous labors of the day, that it will compare advantageously with a great many English Annuals. It is pleasant to find that many of its Tales are of the Mills and of those who work in them; that they inculcate habits of self-denial and contentment, and teach good doctrines of enlarged benevolence. A strong feeling for the beauties of nature, as displayed in the solitudes the writers have left at home, breathes through its pages like wholesome village air; and though a circulating library is a favorable school for the study of such topics, it has very scant allusion to fine clothes, fine marriages, fine houses, or fine life. Some persons might object to the papers being signed occasionally with rather fine names, but this is an American fashion. One of the provinces of the state legislature of Massachusetts is to alter ugly names into pretty ones, as the children improve upon the tastes of their parents. These changes costing little or nothing, scores of Mary Annes are solemnly converted into Bevelinas every session.

It is said that on the occasion of a visit from General Jackson or General Harrison to this town (I forget which, but it is not to the purpose), he walked through three miles and a half of these young ladies all dressed out with parasols and silk stockings. But as I am not aware that any worse consequence ensued, then a sudden looking-up of all the parasols and silk stockings in the market: and perhaps the Bankruptcy of some speculative New Englander who bought them all up at any price, in expectation of a demand that never came; I set no great store by the circumstance.

In this brief account of Lowell, and inadequate expression of the gratification it yielded me, and cannot fail to afford to any foreigner to whom the condition of such people at home is a subject of interest and anxious speculation, I have carefully abstained from drawing a comparison between these factories and those of our own land. Many of the circumstances whose strong influence has been at work for years in our manufacturing towns have not arisen here; and there is no manufacturing population in Lowell, so to speak: for these girls (often the daughters of small farmers) come from other States, remain a few years in the mills, and then go home for good.

The contrast would be a strong one, for it would be between the Good and Evil, the living light and deepest shadow. I abstain from it, because I deem it just to do so. But I only the more earnestly adjure all those whose eyes may rest on these pages, to pause and reflect upon the difference between this town and those great haunts of desperate misery: to call to mind, if they can in the midst of party strife and squabble, the efforts that must be made to purge them of their suffering and danger: and last, and foremost, to remember how the precious Time is rushing by.

I returned at night by the same railroad and in the same kind of car. One of the passengers being exceedingly anxious to expound at great length to my companion (not to me, of course) the true principles on which books of travel in America should be written by Englishmen, I feigned to fall asleep. But glancing all the way out at window from the corners of my eyes, I found abundance of entertainment for the rest of the ride in watching the effects of the wood fire, which had been invisible in the morning but were now brought out in full relief by the darkness: for we were travelling in a whirlwind of bright sparks, which showered about us like a storm of fiery snow.

---

## CHAPTER V.

WORCESTER. THE CONNETICUT RIVER. HARTFORD. NEW HAVEN. TO NEW YORK.

LEAVING Boston on the afternoon of Saturday the fifth of February, we proceeded by another railroad to Worcester: a pretty New England town, where we had arranged to remain under the hospitable roof of the Governor of the State, until Monday morning.

These towns and cities of New England (many of which would be villages in Old England), are as favorable specimens of rural America, as their people are of rural Americans. The well-trimmed lawns and green meadows of home are not there; and the grass, compared with our ornamental plots and pastures, is rank and rough, and wild: but delicate slopes of land, gently-swelling hills, wooded valleys, and slender streams abound. Every little colony of houses has its church and school-house peeping from among the white roofs and shady trees; every house is the whitest of the white; every Venetian blind the greenest of the green; every fine day's sky the bluest of the blue. A sharp dry wind and a slight frost had so hardened the roads when we alighted at Worcester, that their furrowed tracks were like ridges of granite. There was the usual aspect of newness on every object, of course. All the buildings looked as if they had been built and painted that morning, and could be taken down on Monday with very little trouble. In the keen evening air, every sharp outline looked a hundred times sharper than ever. The clean cardboard colonnades had no more perspective than a Chinese bridge on a tea-cup, and appeared equally well calculated for use. The razor-like edges of the detached cottages seemed to cut the very wind as it whistled against them, and to send it smarting on its way with a shriller cry than before. Those slightly-built wooden dwellings behind which the sun was setting with a brilliant lustre, could be so looked through and through, that the idea of any inhabitant being able to hide himself from the public gaze, or to have any secrets from the public eye, was not entertainable for a moment. Even where a blazing fire shone through the uncurtained windows of some distant house, it had the air of being newly-lighted, and of lacking warmth; and instead of awakening thoughts of a snug chamber, bright with faces that first saw the light round that same hearth, and ruddy with warm hangings, it came upon one suggestive of the smell of new mortar and damp walls.

So I thought, at least, that evening. Next morning when the sun was shining brightly, and the clear church bells were ringing, and sedate people in their best clothes enlivened the pathway near at hand and dotted the distant thread of road, there was a pleasant Sabbath peacefulness on everything, which it was good to feel. It would have been the better for an old church; better still for some old graves; but as it was, a wholesome repose and tranquillity pervaded the scene, which, after the restless ocean and the hurried city, had a doubly grateful influence on the spirits.

We went on next morning, still by railroad, to Springfield. From that place to Hartford, whither we were bound, is a distance of only five-and-twenty miles, but at that time of the year the roads were so bad that the journey would probably have occupied ten or twelve hours. Fortunately however, the winter having been unusually mild, the Connecticut River was "open," or, in other words, not frozen. The captain of a small steam-boat was going to make his first trip for the season that day (the second February trip, I believe, within the memory of man,) and only waited for us to go on board. Accordingly, we went on board, with as little delay as might be. He was as good as his word, and started directly.

It certainly was not called a small steam-boat without reason. I omitted to ask the question, but I should think it must have been of about a half pony power. Mr. Paap, the celebrated Dwarf, might have lived and died happily in the cabin, which was fitted with common sash-windows like an ordinary dwelling-house. These windows had bright red curtains, too, hung on slack strings across the lower panes; so that it looked like the parlor of a Lilliputian public-house, which had got afloat in a flood or some other water accident, and was drifting nobody knew where. But even in this chamber there was a rocking-chair. It would be impossible to get on anywhere, in America, without a rocking-chair.

I am afraid to tell how many feet short this vessel was, or how many feet narrow: to apply the words length and width to such measurement would be a contradiction in terms. But I may state that we all kept the middle of the deck, lest the boat should unexpectedly tip over; and that the machinery, by some surprising process of condensation, worked between it and the keel: the whole forming a warm sandwich, about three feet thick.

It rained all day as I once thought it never did rain anywhere, but in the Highlands of Scotland. The river was full of floating blocks of ice, which were constantly crunching and cracking under us; and the depth of water, in the course we took to avoid the larger masses, carried down the middle of the river by the current, did not exceed a few inches. Nevertheless, we moved onward, dexterously; and being well wrapped up, bade defiance to the weather, and enjoyed the journey. The Connecticut River is a fine stream; and the banks in summer-time are, I have no doubt, beautiful: at all events I was told so by a young lady in the cabin; and she should be a judge of beauty, if the possession of a quality include the appreciation of it, for a more beautiful creature I never looked upon.

After two hours and a half of this odd travelling (including a stoppage at a small town, where we were saluted by a gun considerably bigger than our own chimney), we reached Hartford, and straightway repaired to an extremely comfortable hotel: except, as usual, in the article of bed-rooms, which, in almost every place we visited, were very conducive to early rising.

We tarried here four days. The town is beautifully situated in a basin of green hills; the soil is rich, well-wooded, and carefully improved. It is the seat of the local legislature of Connecticut, which sage body enacted, in by-gone times, the renowned code of "Blue Laws," in virtue whereof, among other enlightened provisions, any citizen who could be proved to have kissed his wife on Sunday, was punishable, I believe, with the stocks. Too much of the old Puritan spirit exists in these parts to the present hour; but its influence has not tended, that I know, to make the people less hard in their bargains, or more equal in their dealings. As I never heard of its working that effect anywhere else, I infer that it never will, here. Indeed, I am accustomed, with reference to great professions and severe faces, to judge of the goods of the other world pretty much as I judge of the goods of this; and whenever I see a dealer in such commodities with too great a display of them in his window, I doubt the quality of the article within.

In Hartford stands the famous oak in which the charter of King Charles was hidden. It is now enclosed in a gentleman's garden. In the State-house is the charter itself. I found the courts of law here, just the same as at Boston; the public Institutions almost as good. The Insane Asylum is admirably conducted, and so is the Institution for the Deaf and Dumb.

I very much questioned within myself, as I walked through the Insane Asylum, whether I should have known the attendants from the patients, but for the few words which passed between the former, and the Doctor, in reference to the persons under their charge. Of course I limit this remark merely to their looks; for the conversation of the mad people was mad enough.

There was one little prim old lady, of very smiling and

good-humored appearance, who came sidling up to me from the end of a long passage, and with a curtsey of inexpressible condescension, propounded this unaccountable inquiry:

"Does Pontefract still flourish, sir, upon the soil of England?"

"He does, ma'am," I rejoined.

"When you last saw him, sir, he was—"

"Well, ma'am," said I, "extremely well. He begged me to present his compliments. I never saw him looking better."

At this, the old lady was very much delighted. After glancing at me for a moment, as if to be quite sure that I was serious in my respectful air, she sidled back some paces; sidled forward again; made a sudden skip (at which I precipitately retreated a step or two); and said:

"*I* am an antediluvian, sir."

I thought the best thing to say was, that I had suspected as much from the first. Therefore I said so.

"It is an extremely proud and pleasant thing, sir, to be an antediluvian," said the old lady.

"I should think it was, ma'am," I rejoined.

The old lady kissed her hand, gave another skip, smirked and sidled down the gallery in a most extraordinary manner, and ambled gracefully into her own bed-chamber.

In another part of the building, there was a male patient in bed; very much flushed and heated.

"Well!" said he, starting up, and pulling off his night-cap: "It's all settled, at last. I have arranged it with Queen Victoria."

"Arranged what?" asked the Doctor.

"Why, that business," passing his hand wearily across his forehead, "about the siege of New York."

"Oh!" said I, like a man suddenly enlightened. For he looked at me for an answer.

"Yes. Every house without a signal will be fired upon by the British troops. No harm will be done to the others. No harm at all. Those that want to be safe, must hoist flags. That's all they'll have to do. They must hoist flags."

Even while he was speaking he seemed, I thought, to have

some faint idea that his talk was incoherent. Directly he had said these words, he lay down again; gave a kind of a groan, and covered his hot head with the blankets.

There was another: a young man, whose madness was love and music. After playing on the accordion a march he had composed, he was very anxious that I should walk into his chamber, which I immediately did.

By way of being very knowing, and humoring him to the top of his bent, I went to the window, which commanded a beautiful prospect, and remarked, with an address upon which I greatly plumed myself:

"What a delicious country you have about these lodgings of yours."

"Poh!" said he, moving his fingers carelessly over the notes of his instrument: "*Well enough for such an Institution as this!*"

I don't think I was ever so taken aback in all my life.

"I come here just for a whim," he said coolly. "That's all."

"Oh! That's all!" said I.

"Yes. That's all. The Doctor's a smart man. He quite enters into it. It's a joke of mine. I like it for a time. You needn't mention it, but I think I shall go out next Tuesday!"

I assured him that I would consider our interview perfectly confidential; and rejoined the Doctor. As we were passing through a gallery on our way out, a well-dressed lady, of quiet and composed manners, came up, and proffering a slip of paper and a pen, begged that I would oblige her with an autograph. I complied, and we parted.

"I think I remember having had a few interviews like that, with ladies out of doors. I hope *she* is not mad?"

"Yes."

"On what subject? Autographs?"

"No. She hears voices in the air."

"Well!" thought I, "it would be well if we could shut up a few false prophets of these later times, who have professed to do the same; and I should like to try the experiment on a Mormanist or two to begin with."

In this place, there is the best Jail for untried offenders in the world. There is also a very well-ordered State prison, arranged upon the same plan as that at Boston, except that here, there is always a sentry on the wall with a loaded gun. It contained at that time about two hundred prisoners. A spot was shown me in the sleeping ward, where a watchman was murdered some years since in the dead of night, in a desperate attempt to escape, made by a prisoner who had broken from his cell. A woman, too, was pointed out to me, who, for the murder of her husband, had been a close prisoner for sixteen years.

"Do you think," I asked of my conductor, "that after so very long an imprisonment, she has any thought or hope of ever regaining her liberty?"

"Oh dear yes," he answered. "To be sure she has."

"She has no chance of obtaining it, I suppose?"

"Well I don't know:" which, by the bye, is a national answer. "Her friends mistrust her."

"What have *they* to do with it?" I naturally inquired.

"Well, they won't petition.

"But if they did, they couldn't get her out, I suppose?"

"Well, not the first time, perhaps, nor yet the second, but tiring and wearying for a few years might do it."

"Does that ever do it?"

"Why yes, that'll do it sometimes. Political friends'll do it sometimes. It's pretty often done, one way or another."

I shall always entertain a very pleasant and grateful recollection of Hartford. It is a lovely place, and I had many friends there, whom I can never remember with indifference. We left it with no little regret on the evening of Friday the 11th, and travelled that night by railroad to New Haven. Upon the way, the guard and I were formally introduced to each other (as we usually were on such occasions), and exchanged a variety of small-talk. We reached New Haven at about eight o'clock, after a journey of three hours, and put up for the night at the best inn.

New Haven, known also as the City of Elms, is a fine town. Many of its streets (as its *alias* sufficiently imports) are planted with rows of grand old elm-trees; and the same natural, ornaments surround Yale College, an establishment of considerable eminence and reputation. The various departments of this Institution are erected in a kind of park or common in the middle of the town, where they are dimly visible among the shadowing trees. The effect is very like that of an old cathedral yard in England; and when their branches are in full leaf must be extremely picturesque. Even in the winter time, these groups of well-grown trees, clustering among the busy streets and houses of a thriving city, have a very quaint appearance: seeming to bring about a kind of compromise between town and country; as if each had met the other halfway, and shaken hands upon it; which is at once novel and pleasant.

After a night's rest, we rose early, and in good time went down to the wharf, and on board the packet New York *for* New York. This was the first American steamboat of any size that I had seen; and certainly to an English eye it was infinitely less like a steamboat than a huge floating bath. I could hardly persuade myself, indeed, but that the bathing establishment off Westminster Bridge, which I left a baby, had suddenly grown to an enormous size; run away from home; and set up in foreign parts as a steamer. Being in America, too, which our vagabonds do so particularly favor, it seemed the more probable.

The great difference in appearance between these packets and ours, is, that there is so much of them out of the water: the main-deck being enclosed on all sides, and filled with casks and goods, like any second or third floor in a stack of warehouses; and the promenade or hurricane-deck being a-top of that again. A part of the machinery is always above this deck; where the connecting-rod, in a strong and lofty frame, is seen working away like an iron top-sawyer. There is seldom any mast or tackle: nothing aloft but two tall black chimneys. The man at the helm is shut up in a little house in the fore part of the boat (the wheel being connected with the rudder by iron chains, working the whole length of the deck); and the passengers unless the weather be very fine indeed, usually congregate below. Directly you have left the wharf, all the life, and stir, and bustle of a packet cease. You wonder for a long time how she goes on, for there seems to be nobody in charge of her and when another of these dull machines comes splashing by, you feel quite indignant with it, as a sullen, cumbrous, ungraceful, unshiplike leviathan: quite forgetting that the vessel you are on board of, is its very counterpart.

There is always a clerk's office on the lower deck, where you pay your fare; a ladies' cabin; baggage and stowage rooms; engineer's room; and in short a great variety of perplexities which render the discovery of the gentlemen's cabin, a matter of some difficulty. It often occupies the whole length of the boat (as it did in this case), and has three or four tiers of berths on each side. When I first descended into the cabin of the New York, it looked, in my unaccustomed eyes, about as long as the Burlington Arcade.

The sound which has to be crossed on this passage, is not always a very safe or pleasant navigation, and has been the scene of some unfortunate accidents. It was a wet morning, and very misty, and we soon lost sight of land. The day was calm, however, and brightened towards noon. After exhausting (with good help from a friend) the larder, and the stock of bottled beer, I lay down to sleep: being very much tired with the fatigues of yesterday. But I awoke from my nap in time to hurry up, and see Hell Gate, the Hog's Back, the Frying Pan, and other notorious localities, attractive to all readers of famous Diedrich Knickerbocker's History. We were now in a narrow channel, with sloping banks on either side, besprinkled with pleasant villas, and made refreshing to the sight by turf and trees. Soon we shot in quick succession, past a lighthouse; a madhouse (how the lunatics flung up their caps and roared in sympathy with the headlong engine and the driving tide!); a jail; and other buildings: and so emerged into a noble bay, whose waters sparkled in the now cloudless sunshine like Nature's eyes turned up to Heaven.

Then there lay stretched out before us, to the right, confused heaps of buildings, with here and there a spire or steeple, looking down upon the herd below; and here and there, again, a cloud of lazy smoke; and in the foreground a forest of ships' masts, cheery with flapping sails and waving flags. Crossing from among them to the opposite shore, were steam ferry-boats laden with people, coaches, horses, wagons, baskets, boxes: crossed and re-crossed by other ferry-boats all travelling to and fro: and never idle. Stately among these restless Insects, were two or three large ships, moving with slow majestic pace, as creatures of a prouder kind, disdainful of their puny journeys, and making for the broad sea. Beyond, were shining heights, and islands in the glancing river, and a distance scarcely less blue and bright than the sky it seemed to meet. The city's hum and buzz, the clinking of capstans, the ringing of bells, the barking of dogs, the clattering of wheels, tingled in the listening ear. All of which life and stir, coming across the stirring water, caught new life and animation from its free companionship; and, sympathizing with its buoyant spirits, glistened as it seemed in sport upon its surface, and hemmed the vessel round, and plashed the water high about her sides, and floating her gallantly into the dock, flew off again to welcome other comers, and speed before them to the busy port.

## CHAPTER VI.

### NEW YORK.

The beautiful metropolis of America is by no means so clean a city as Boston, but many of its streets have the same characteristics; except that the houses are not quite so fresh-colored, the sign-boards are not quite so gaudy, the gilded letters not quite so golden, the bricks not quite so red, the stone not quite so white, the blinds and area railings not quite so green, the knobs and plates upon the street doors, not quite so bright and twinkling. There are many bye-streets, almost as neutral in clean colors, and positive in dirty ones, as bye-streets in London; and there is one quarter, commonly called the Five Points, which, in respect of filth and wretchedness, may be safely backed against Seven Dials, or any other part of famed St. Giles's.

The great promenade and thoroughfares, as most people know, is Broadway; a wide and bustling street, which, from the Battery Gardens to its opposite termination in a country road, may be four miles long. Shall we sit down in an upper floor of the Carlton House Hotel (situated in the best part of this main artery of New York), and when we are tired of looking down upon the life below, sally forth arm-in-arm and mingle with the stream?

Warm weather! The sun strikes upon our heads at this open window, as though its rays were concentrated through a burning-glass; but the day is in its zenith, and the season an unusual one. Was there ever such a sunny street as this Broadway! The pavement stones are polished with the tread of feet until they shine again; the red bricks of the houses might be yet in the dry, hot kilns; and the roofs of those omnibuses look as though, if water were poured on them, they would hiss and smoke, and smell like half-quenched fires. No stint of omnibuses here! Half a dozen have gone by within as many minutes. Plenty of hackney cabs and coaches too; gigs, phaetons, large-wheeled tilburies, and private carriages — rather of a clumsy make, and not very different from the public vehicles, but built for the heavy roads beyond the city pavement. Negro coachmen and white; in straw hats, black hats, white hats, glazed caps, fur caps; in coats of drab, black, brown, green, blue, nankeen, striped jean and linen; and there, in that one instance (look while it passes, or it will be too late), in suits of livery. Some southern republican that, who puts his blacks in uniform, and swells with Sultan pomp and power. Yonder, where that phaeton with the well-clipped pair of grays has stopped—standing at their heads now—is a Yorkshire groom, who has not been very long in these parts, and looks sorrowfully round for a companion pair of top-boots, which he may traverse the city half a year without meeting. Heaven save the ladies, how they dress! We have seen more colors in these ten minutes, than we should have seen elsewhere, in as many days. What various parasols! what rainbow silks and satins! what pinking of thin stockings, and pinching of thin shoes, and fluttering of ribbons and silk tassels, and display of rich cloaks with gaudy hoods and linings! The young gentlemen are fond, you see, of turning down their shirt-collars and cultivating their whiskers, especially under the chin; but they cannot approach the ladies in their dress or bearing, being, to say the truth, humanity of quite another sort. Byrons of the desk and, counter, pass on, and let us see what kind of men those are behind ye: those two laborers in holiday clothes, of whom one carries in his hand a crumpled scrap of paper from which he tries to spell out a hard name, while the other looks about for it on all the doors and windows.

Irishmen both! You might know them, if they were masked, by their long-tailed blue coats and bright buttons, and their drab trowsers, which they wear like men well used to working dresses, who are easy in no others. It would be hard to keep your model republics going, without the countrymen and countrywomen of those two laborers. For who else would dig, and delve, and drudge, and do domestic work, and make canals and roads, and execute great lines of Internal Improvement!` Irishmen both, and sorely puzzled too, find out what they seek. Let us go down, and help them, for the love of home, and that spirit of liberty which admits of honest service to honest men, and honest work for honest bread, no matter what it be.

That's well! We have got at the right address at last, though it is written in strange characters truly, and might have been scrawled with the blunt handle of the spade the writer better knows the use of, than a pen. Their way lies yonder, but what business takes them there? They carry savings: to hoard up? No. They are brothers, those men. One crossed the sea alone, and working very hard for one half year, and living harder, saved funds enough to bring the other out. That done, they worked together side by side, contentedly sharing hard labor and hard living for another term, and then their sisters came, and then another brother, and lastly, their old mother. And what now? Why, the poor old crone is restless in a strange land, and yearns to lay her bones, she says, among her people in the old graveyard at home: and so they go to pay her passage back: and God help her and them, and every simple heart, and all who turn to the Jerusalem of their younger days, and have an altar-fire upon the cold hearth of their fathers.

This narrow thoroughfare, baking and blistering in the sun is Wall Street: the Stock Exchange and Lombard Street of New York. Many a rapid fortune has been made in this street, and many a no less rapid ruin. Some of these very merchants whom you see hanging about here now, have locked up money in their strong-boxes, like the man in the Arabian Nights, and opening them again, have found but withered leaves. Below, here by the water side, where the bowsprits of ships stretch across the footway, and almost thrusts themselves into the windows, lie the noble American vessels which have made their Packet Service the finest in the world. They have brought hither the foreigners who abound in all the streets: not perhaps, that there are more here, than in other commercial cities; but elsewhere, they have particular haunts, and you must find them out; here, they pervade the town.

We must cross Broadway again; gaining some refreshment from the heat, in the sight of the great blocks of clean ice which are being carried into shops and bar-rooms; and the pine-apples and water-melons profusely displayed for sale. Fine streets of spacious houses here, you see!—Wall Street has furnished and dismantled many of them very often—and here a deep green leafy square. Be sure that is a hospitable house with inmates to be affectionately remembered always, where they have the open door and pretty show of plants within, and where the child with laughing eyes is peeping out of window at the little dog below. You wonder what may be the use of this tall flagstaff in the bye-street, with something like Liberty's head-dress on its top: so do I. But there is a passion for tall flagstaffs hereabout, and you may see its twin brother in five minutes, if you have a mind.

Again across Broadway, and so—passing from the many-colored crowd and glittering shops—into another long main street, the Bowery. A rail-road yonder, see, where two stout horses trot along, drawing a score or two of people and a great wooden ark, with ease. The stores are poorer here; the passengers less gay. Clothes ready made, and meat ready-cooked, are to be bought in these parts; and the lively whirl of carriages is exchanged for the deep rumble of carts and wagons. These signs which are so plentiful, in shape like river buoys, or small balloons, hoisted by cords to poles, and dangling there, announce, as you may see by looking up, "OYSTERS IN EVERY STYLE." They tempt the hungry most at night, for then dull candles glimmering inside, illuminate these dainty words, and make the mouths of idlers water, as they read and linger.

What is this dismal-fronted pile of bastard Egyptian, like an enchanter's palace in a melodrama!—a famous prison, called The Tombs. Shall we go in?

So. A long narrow lofty building, stove-heated as usual, with four galleries, one above the other, going round it, and communicating by stairs. Between the two sides of each gallery, and in its centre, a bridge, for the greater convenience of crossing. On each of these bridges sits a man: dozing or reading, or talking to an idle companion. On each tier, are two opposite rows of small iron doors. They look like furnace doors, but are cold and black, as though the fires within had all gone out. Some two or three are open, and women, with drooping heads bent down, are talking to the inmates. The whole is lighted by a skylight, but it is fast closed; and from the roof there dangle, limp and drooping, two useless wind-sails.

A man with keys appears, to show us round. A good-looking fellow, and, in his way, civil and obliging.

"Are those black doors the cells?"

"Yes."

"Are they all full?"

"Well, they're pretty nigh full, and that's a fact, and no two ways about it."

"Those at the bottom are unwholesome, surely?"

"Why, we *do* only put colored people in em'. That's the truth."

"When do the prisoners take exercise?"

"Well, they do without it pretty much."

"Do they never walk in the yard?"

"Considerable seldom."

"Sometimes, I suppose?"

"Well, it's rare they do. They keep pretty bright without it."

"But suppose a man were here for a twelvemonth. I know this is only a prison for criminals who are charged with grave offences, while they are waiting their trial, or are under remand, but the law, here, affords criminals many means of delay. What with motions for new trial, and in arrest of judgment, and what not, a prisoner might be here for twelve months, I take it, might he not?"

"Well, I guess he might."

"Do you mean to say that in all that time he would never come out at that little iron door, for exercise?"

"He might walk some, perhaps—not much."

"Will you open one of the doors?"

"All, if you like."

The fastenings jar and rattle, and one of the doors turns slowly on its hinges. Let us look in. A small bare cell, into which the light enters through a high chink in the wall. There is a rude means of washing, a table, and a bedstead. Upon the latter, sits a man of sixty; reading. He looks up for a moment; gives an impatient dogged shake; and fixes his eyes upon his book again. As we withdrew our heads, the door closes on him, and is fastened as before. This man has murdered his wife, and will probably be hanged.

"How long has he been here?"

"A month."

"When will he be tried?"

"Next term."

"When is that?"

"Next month."

"In England, if a man be under sentence of death even, he has air and exercise at certain periods of the day."

"Possible?"

With what stupendous and untranslatable coolness he says this, and how loungingly he leads on to the women's side: making, as he goes, a kind of iron castanet of the key and the stair-rail!

Each cell door on this side has a square aperture in it. Some of the women peep anxiously through it at the sound of footsteps; others shrink away in shame.—For what offence can that lonely child, of ten or twelve years old, be shut up here? Oh! that boy? He is the son of the prisoner we saw just now; is a witness against his father; and is detained here for safe-keeping, until the trial; that's all.

But it is a dreadful place for the child to pass the long days and nights in. This is rather hard treatment for a young witness, is it not?—What says our conductor?

"Well, it an't a very rowdy life, and *that's* a fact!"

Again he clinks his metal castanet, and leads us leisurely away. I have a question to ask him as we go.

"Pray, why do they call this place The Tombs?"

"Well, it's the cant name."

"I know it is. Why?"

"Some suicides happened here, when it was first built. I expect it come about from that."

"I saw just now, that that man's clothes were scattered about the floor of his cell. Don't you oblige the prisoners to be orderly, and put such things away?"

"Where should they put 'em?"

"Not on the ground, surely. What do you say to hanging them up?"

He stops and looks round to emphasize his answer:

"Why, I say that's just it. When they had hooks they *would* hang themselves, so they're taken out of every cell, and there's only the marks left where they used to be!"

The prison-yard in which he pauses now, has been the

scene of terrible performances. Into this narrow, grave-like place, men are brought out to die. The wretched creature stands beneath the gibbet on the ground; the rope about his neck; and when the sign is given, a weight at its other end comes running down, and swings him up into the air—a corpse.

The law requires that there be present at this dismal spectacle, the judge, the jury, and citizens to the amount of twenty-five. From the community it is hidden. To the dissolute and bad, the thing remains a frightful mystery. Between the criminal and them, the prison-wall is interposed as a thick gloomy veil. It is the curtain to his bed of death, his winding sheet, and grave. From him it shuts out life, and all the motives to unrepenting hardihood in that last hour, which its mere sight and presence is often all-sufficient to sustain. There are no bold eyes to make him bold; no ruffians to uphold a ruffian's name before. All beyond the pitiless stone wall, is unknown space.

Let us go forth again into the cheerful streets.

Once more in Broadway! Here are the same ladies in bright colors, walking to and fro, in pairs and singly; yonder the very same light blue parasol which passed and repassed the hotel-window twenty times while we were sitting there. We are going to cross here. Take care of the pigs. Two portly sows are trotting up behind this carriage, and a select party of half-a-dozen gentleman hogs have just now turned the corner.

Here is a solitary swine lounging homeward by himself. He has only one ear; having parted with the other to vagrant-dogs in the course of his city rambles. But he gets on very well without it; and leads a roving, gentlemanly, vagabond kind of life, somewhat answering to that of our club-men at home. He leaves his lodgings every morning at a certain hour, throws himself upon the town, gets through his day in some manner quite satisfactory to himself, and regularly appears at the door of his own house again at night, like the mysterious master of Gil Blas. He is a free-and-easy, careless, indifferent kind of pig, having a very large acquaintance among other pigs of the same character, whom he rather knows by sight than conversation, as he seldom troubles himself to stop and exchange civilities, but goes grunting down the kennel, turning up the news and small-talk of the city in the shape of cabbage-stalks and offal, and bearing no tails but his own: which is a very short one, for his old enemies, the dogs, have been at that too, and have left him hardly enough to swear by. He is in every respect a republican pig, going wherever he pleases, and mingling with the best society, on an equal, if not superior footing, for every one makes way when he appears, and the haughtiest give him the wall, if he prefer it. He is a great philosopher, and seldom moved, unless by the dogs before mentioned. Sometimes, indeed, you may see his small eye twinkling on a slaughtered friend, whose carcase garnishes a butcher's door-post, but he grunts out "Such is life: all flesh is pork!" buries his nose in the mire again, and waddles down the gutter: comforting himself with the reflection that there is one snout the less to anticipate stray cabbage-stalks, at any rate.

They are the city scavengers, these pigs. Ugly brutes they are; having, for the most part, scanty, brown backs, like the lids of old horse-hair trunks: spotted with unwholesome black blotches. They have long, gaunt legs, too, and such peaked snouts, that if one of them could be persuaded to sit for his profile, nobody would recognize it for a pig's likeness. They are never attended upon, or fed, or driven, or caught, but are thrown upon their own resources in early life, and become preternaturally knowing in consequence. Every pig knows where he lives, much better than anybody could tell him. At this hour, just as evening is closing in, you will see them roaming towards bed by scores, eating their way to the last. Occasionally, some youth among them who has over-eaten himself, or has been much worried by dogs, trots shrinkingly homeward, like a prodigal son: but this is a rare case: perfect self-possession and self-reliance, and immovable composure, being their foremost attributes.

The streets and shops are lighted now; and as the eye

travels down the long thoroughfare, dotted with bright jets of gas, it is reminded of Oxford Street or Piccadilly. Here and there a flight of broad stone cellar-steps appears, and a painted lamp directs you to the Bowling Saloon, or Ten Pin alley: Ten-Pins being a game of mingled chance and skill, invented when the legislature passed an act forbidding Nine-Pins. At other downward flights of steps, are other lamps, marking the whereabouts of oyster-cellars—pleasant retreats, say I: not only by reason of their wonderful cookery of oysters, pretty nigh as large as chese-plates, (or for thy dear sake, heartiest of Greek Professors!) but because of all kinds of eaters of fish, or flesh, or fowl, in these latitudes, the swallowers of oysters alone are not gregarious; but subduing themselves, as it were, to the nature of what they work in, and copying the coyness of the thing they eat, do sit apart in curtained boxes, and consort by twos, not by two hundreds.

But how quiet the streets are! Are there no itinerant bands; no wind or stringed instruments? No, not one. By day, are there no Punches, Fantoccini, Dancing-dogs, Jugglers, Conjurors, Orchestrinas, or even Barrel-organs? No, not one. Yes, I remember one. One barrel-organ and a dancing-monkey—sportive by nature, but fast fading into a dull, lumpish monkey, of the Utilitarian school. Beyond that, nothing lively; no, not so much as a white mouse in a twirling cage.

Are there no amusements? Yes, there is a lecture-room across the way, from which that glare of light proceeds, and there may be evening service for the ladies thrice a week, or oftener. For the young gentlemen, there is the counting-house, the store, the bar-room: the latter, as you may see through these windows, pretty full. Hark! to the clinking sound of hammers breaking lumps of ice, and to the cool gurgling of the wounded bits, as, in the process of mixing, they are poured from glass to glass! No amusements? What are these suckers of cigars and swallowers of strong drinks, whose hats and legs we see in every possible variety of twist, doing, but amusing themselves? What are the fifty news-papers, which those precocious urchins are bawling down the street, and which are kept filed within, what are they but amusements? Not vapid waterish amusements, but good strong stuff; dealing in round abuse and blackguard names; pulling off the roofs of private houses, as the Halting Devil did in Spain; pimping and pandering for all degrees of vicious taste, and gorging with coined lies the most voracious maw; imputing to every man in public life the coarsest and the vilest motives; scaring away from the stabbed and prostrate body-politic, every Samaritan of clear conscience and good deeds; and setting on, with yell and whistle, and the clapping of foul hands, the vilest vermin and worst birds of prey.—No amusements!

Let us go on again; and passing this wilderness of an hotel with stores about its base, like some Continental theatre, or the London Opera House shorn of its colonnade, plunge into the Five Points. But it is needful, first, that we take as our escort these two heads of the police, whom you would know for sharp and well-trained officers if you met them in the Great Desert. So true it is, that certain pursuits, wherever carried on, will stamp men with the same character. These two might have been begotten, born, and bred, in Bow Street.

We have seen no beggars in the streets by night or day; but of other kinds of strollers, plenty. Poverty, wretchedness, and vice, are rife enough where we are going now.

This is the place, these narrow ways, diverging to the right and left, and reeking everywhere with dirt and filth. Such lives as are led here, bear the same fruits here as elsewhere. The coarse and bloated faces at the doors, have counterparts at home, and all the wide world over. Debauchery has made the very houses prematurely old. See how the rotten beams are tumbling down, and how the patched and broken windows seem to scowl dimly, like eyes that have been hurt in drunken frays. Many of those pigs live here. Do they ever wonder why their masters walk upright in lieu of going on all-fours? and why they talk instead of grunting?

So far, nearly every house is a low tavern; and on the bar-room walls, are colored prints of Washington, and Queen Victoria of England, and the American Eagle. Among the pigeon-holes that hold the bottles, are pieces of plate-glass and colored paper, for there is, in some sort, a taste for decoration, even here. And as seamen frequent these haunts, there are maritime pictures by the dozen: of partings between sailors and their lady-loves, portraits of William, of the ballad, and his Black-Eyed Susan; of Will Watch, the Bold Smuggler; of Paul Jones the Pirate, and the like: on which the painted eyes of Queen Victoria, and of Washington to boot, rest in as strange companionship, as on most of the scenes that are enacted in their wondering presence.

What place is this, to which the squalid street conducts us? A kind of square of leprous houses, some of which are attainable only by crazy wooden stairs without. What lies beyond this tottering flight of steps, that creak beneath our tread!—a miserable room, lighted by one dim candle, and destitute of all comfort, save that which may be hidden in a wretched bed. Beside it, sits a man: his elbows on his knees: his forehead hidden in his hands. "What ails that man?" asks the foremost officer. "Fever," he sullenly replies, without looking up. Conceive the fancies of a fevered brain, in such a place as this!

Ascend these pitch-dark stairs, heedful of a false footing on the trembling boards, and grope your way with me into this wolfish den, where neither ray of light nor breath of air appears to come. A negro lad, startled from his sleep by the officer's voice—he knows it well—but comforted by his assurance that he has not come on business, officiously bestirs himself to light a candle. The match flickers for a moment, and shows great mounds of dusky rags upon the ground; then dies away and leaves a denser darkness than before, if there can be degrees in such extremes. He stumbles down the stairs and presently comes back, shading a flaring taper with his hand. Then the mounds of rags are seen to be astir, and rise slowly up, and the floor is covered with heaps of negro women, waking from their sleep: their white teeth chattering, and their bright eyes glistening and winking on all sides with surprise and fear, like the countless repetition of one astonished African face in some strange mirror.

Mount up these other stairs with no less caution (there are traps and pitfalls here, for those who are not so well escorted as ourselves) into the housetop; where the bare beams and rafters meet over-head, and calm night looks down through the crevices in the roof. Open the door of one of these cramped hutches full of sleeping negroes. Pah! They have a charcoal fire within; there is a smell of singeing clothes, or flesh, so close they gather round the brazier; and vapors issue forth that blind and suffocate. From every corner, as you glance about you in these dark retreats, some figure crawls half-awakened, as if the judgment-hour were near at hand, and every obscene grave were giving up its dead. Where dogs would howl to lie, women, and men, and boys slink off to sleep, forcing the dislodged rats to move away in quest of better lodgings.

Here too are lanes and alleys, paved with mud knee-deep, under-ground chambers, where they dance and game; the walls bedecked with rough designs of ships, and forts, and flags, and American Eagles out of number: ruined houses, open to the street, whence, through wide gaps in the walls, other ruins loom upon the eye, as though the world of vice and misery had nothing else to show: hideous tenements which take their name from robbery and murder; all that is loathsome, drooping, and decayed is here.

Our leader has his hand upon the latch of "Almack's," and calls to us from the bottom of the steps; for the assembly-room of the Five-Point fashionables is approached by a descent." Shall we go in? It is but a moment.

Heyday! the landlady of Almack's thrives! A buxom fat mulatto woman, with sparkling eyes, whose head is daintily ornamented with a handkerchief of many colors. Nor is the landlord much behind her in his finery, being attired in a smart blue jacket, like a ship's steward, with a thick gold ring upon his little finger, and round his neck a gleaming golden watch-guard. How glad he is to see us! What will we please to call for? A dance? It shall be done directly, sir: a regular break-down."

The corpulent black fiddler, and his friend who plays the

tambourine, stamp upon the boarding of the small raised orchestra in which they sit, and play a lively measure. Five or six couple come upon the floor, marshalled by a lively young negro, who is the wit of the assembly, and the greatest dancer known. He never leaves off making queer faces, and is the delight of all the rest, who grin from ear to ear incessantly. Among the dancers are two young mulatto girls, with large, black, drooping eyes, and head-gear after the fashion of the hostess, who are as shy, or feign to be, as though they never danced before, and so look down before the visitors, that their partners can see nothing but the long fringed lashes.

But the dance commences. Every gentleman sets as long as he likes to the opposite lady, and the opposite lady to him, and all are so long about it that the sport begins to languish, when suddenly the lively hero dashes in to the rescue. Instantly the fiddler grins, and goes at it tooth and nail; there is new energy in the tambourine; new laughter in the dancers; new smiles in the landlady; new confidence in the landlord; new brightness in the very candles. Single shuffle, double shuffle, cut and cross-cut: snapping his fingers; rolling his eyes, turning in his knees, presenting the backs of his legs in front, spinning about on his toes and heels like nothing but the man's fingers on the tambourine; dancing with two left legs, two right legs, two wooden legs, two wire legs, two spring legs—all sorts of legs and no legs—what is this to him? And in what walk of life, or dance of life, does man ever get such stimulating applause as thunders about him, when, having danced his partner off her feet, and himself too, he finishes by leaping gloriously on the bar-counter, and calling for something to drink, with the chuckle of a million of counterfeit Jim Crows, in one inimitable sound!

The air, even in these distempered parts, is fresh after the stifling atmosphere of the houses; and now, as we emerge into a broader street, it blows upon us with a purer breath, and the stars look bright again. Here are The Tombs once more. The city watch-house is a part of the building. It follows naturally on the sights we have just left. Let us see that, and then to bed.

What! do you thrust your common offenders against the police discipline of the town, into such holes as these? Do men and women, against whom no crime is proved, lie here all night in perfect darkness, surrounded by the noisome vapors which encircle that flagging lamp you light us with, and breathing this filthy and offensive stench? Why, such indecent and disgusting dungeons as these cells, would bring disgrace upon the most despotic empire in the world! Look at them, man—you, who see them every night, and keep the keys. Do you see what they are? Do you know how drains are made below the streets, and wherein these human sewers differ, except in being always stagnant?

Well, he don't know. He has had five-and-twenty young women locked up in this very cell at one time, and you'd hardly realize what handsome faces there were among 'em.

In God's name! shut the door upon the wretched creature who is in it now, and put its screen before a place quite unsurpassed in all the vice, neglect, and devilry, of the worst old town in Europe.

Are people really left all night, untried, in those black sties?—Every night. The watch is set at seven in the evening. The magistrate opens his court at five in the morning. That is the earliest hour at which the first prisoner can be released; and if an officer appear against him, he is not taken out till nine o'clock or ten.—But if any one among them die in the interval, as one man did, not long ago? Then he is half-eaten by the rats in an hour's time; as that man was; and there an end.

What is this intolerable tolling of great bells, and crashing of wheels, and shouting in the distance? A fire. And what that deep red light in the opposite direction? Another fire. And what these charred and blackened walls we stand before? A dwelling where a fire has been. It was more than hinted, in an official report, not long ago, that some of these conflagrations were not wholly accidental, and that speculation and enterprise found a field of exertion, even in flames: but be this as it may, there was a fire last night, there are two to-night, and you may lay an even wager there will be at least one, to-morrow. So, carrying that with us for our comfort, let us say, Good night, and climb up-stairs to bed.

One day, during my stay in New York, I paid a visit to the different public institutions on Long Island, or Rhode Island: I forget which. One of them is a Lunatic Asylum. The building is handsome; and is remarkable for a spacious and elegant staircase. The whole structure is not yet finished, but it is already one of considerable size and extent, and is capable of accommodating a very large number of patients.

I cannot say that I derived much comfort from the inspection of this charity. The different wards might have been cleaner and better ordered; I saw nothing of that salutary system which had impressed me so favorably elsewhere; and everything had a lounging, listless, madhouse air, which was very painful. The moping idiot, cowering down with long dishevelled hair; the gibbering maniac, with his hideous laugh and pointed finger; the vacant eye, the fierce wild face, the gloomy picking of the hands and lips, and munching of the nails: there they were all, without disguise, in naked ugliness and horror. In the dining-room, a bare, dull, dreary place, with nothing for the eye to rest on but the empty walls, a woman was locked up alone. She was bent, they told me, on committing suicide. If anything could have strengthened her in her resolution, it would certainly have been the insupportable monotony of such an existence.

The terrible crowd with which these halls and galleries were filled, so shocked me, that I abridged my stay within the shortest limits, and declined to see that portion of the building in which the refractory and violent were under closer restraint. I have no doubt that the gentleman who presided over this establishment at the time I write of, was competent to manage it, and had done all in his power to promote its usefulness: but will it be believed that the miserable strife of Party feeling is carried even into this sad refuge of afflicted and degraded humanity? Will it be believed that the eyes which are to watch over and control the wanderings of minds on which the most dreadful visitation to which our nature is exposed has fallen, must wear the glasses of some wretched side in Politics? Will it be believed that the governor of such a house as this, is appointed, and deposed, and changed perpetually, as Parties fluctuate and vary, and as their despicable weathercocks are blown this way or that? A hundred times in every week, some new most paltry exhibition of that narrow-minded and injurious Party Spirit, which is the Simoon of America, sickening and blighting everything of wholsome life within its reach, was forced upon my notice; but I never turned my back upon it with feelings of such deep disgust and measureless contempt, as when I crossed the threshold of this madhouse.

At a short distance from this building is another called the Alms House, that is to say, the workhouse of New York. This is a large institution also: lodging, I believe, when I was there, nearly a thousand poor. It was badly ventilated, and badly lighted; was not too clean; and impressed me, on the whole, very uncomfortably. But it must be remembered that New York, as a great emporium of commerce, and as a place of general resort, not only from all parts of the States, but from most parts of the world, has always a large pauper population to provide for; and labors, therefore, under peculiar difficulties in this respect. Nor must it be forgotten that New York is a large town, and that in all large towns a vast amount of good and evil is intermixed and jumbled up together.

In the same neighborhood is the Farm, where young orphans are nursed and bred. I did not see it, but I believe it is well conducted; and I can the more easily credit it, from knowing how mindful they usually are, in America, of that beautiful passage in the Litany which remembers all sick persons and young children.

I was taken to these Institutions by water, in a boat belonging to the Island Jail, and rowed by a crew of prisoners, who were dressed in a striped uniform of black and buff, in which they looked like faded tigers. They took me, by the same conveyance, to the Jail itself.

It is an old prison, and quite a pioneer establishment, on the plan I have already described. I was glad to hear this, for it is unquestionably a very indifferent one. The most is made, however, of the means it possesses, and it is as well regulated as such a place can be.

The women worked in covered sheds erected for that purpose. If I remember right, there are no shops for the men, but be that as it may, the greater part of them labor in certain stone-quarries near at hand. The day being very wet indeed, this labor was suspended, and the prisoners were in their cells. Imagine these cells, some two or three hundred in number, and in every one a man locked up; this one at his door for air, with his hands thrust through the grate; this one in bed (in the middle of the day, remember); and this one flung down in a heap upon the ground, with his head against the bars, like a wild beast. Make the rain pour down, outside, in torrents. Put the everlasting stove in the midst; hot, and suffocating, and vaporous as a witch's cauldron. Add a collection of gentle odors, such as would arise from a thousand mildewed umbrellas, wet through, and a thousand buck-baskets, full of half-washed linen—and there is the prison, as it was that day.

The prison for the State at Sing Sing, is, on the other hand, a model jail. That, and Auburn, are, I believe, the largest and best examples of the silent system.

In another part of the city, is the Refuge for the Destitute: an Institution whose object is to reclaim youthful offenders, male and female, black and white, without distinction; to teach them useful trades, apprentice them to respectable masters, and make them worthy members of society. Its design, it will be seen, is similar to that at Boston; and it is a no less meritorious and admirable establishment. A suspicion crossed my mind during my inspection of this noble charity, whether the superintendent had quite sufficient knowledge of the world and worldly characters; and whether he did not commit a great mistake in treating some young girls, who were to all intents and purposes, by their years and their past lives, women, as though they were little children; which certainly had a ludicrous effect in my eyes, and, or I am much mistaken, in theirs also. As the Institution, however, is always under the vigilant examination of a body of gentlemen of great intelligence and experience, it cannot fail to be well conducted; and whether I am right or wrong in this slight particular, is unimportant to its deserts and character, which it would be difficult to estimate too highly.

In addition to these establishments, there are in New York, excellent hospitals and schools, literary institutions and libraries; an admirable fire department (as indeed it should be, having constant practice), and charities of every sort and kind. In the suburbs there is a spacious cemetery; unfinished yet, but every day improving. The saddest tomb I saw there was "The Strangers' Grave. Dedicated to the different hotels in this city."

There are three principal theatres. Two of them, the Park and the Bowery, are large, elegant, and handsome buildings, and are, I grieve to write it, generally deserted. The third, the Olympic, is a tiny show-box for vaudevilles and burlesques. It is singularly well conducted by Mr. Mitchell, a comic actor of great quiet humor and originality, who is well-remembered and esteemed by London play-goers. I am happy to report of this deserving gentleman, that his benches are usually well filled, and that his theatre rings with merriment every night. I had almost forgotten a small summer theatre, called Niblo's, with gardens and open air amusements attached; but I believe it is not exempt from the general depression under which Theatrical Property, or what is humorously called by that name, unfortunately labors.

The country round New York is surpassingly and exquisitely picturesque. The climate, as I have already intimated, is somewhat of the warmest. What it would be, without the sea breezes which come from its beautiful Bay in the evening time, I will not throw myself or my readers into a fever by inquiring.

The tone of the best society in this city, is like that of Boston; here and there, it may be, with a greater infusion of the mercantile spirit, but generally polished and refined, and always most hospitable. The houses and tables are elegant; the hours later and more rakish; and there is, perhaps, a greater spirit of contention in reference to appearances, and the display of wealth and costly living. The ladies are singularly beautiful.

Before I left New York I made arrangements for securing a passage home in the George Washington packet ship, which was advertised to sail in June: that being the month in which I had determined, if prevented by no accident in the course of my ramblings, to leave America.

I never thought that going back to England, returning to all who are dear to me, and to pursuits that have insensibly grown to be part of my nature, I could have felt so much sorrow as I endured, when I parted at last, on board this ship, with the friends who had accompanied me from this city. I never thought the name of any place, so far away, and so lately known, could ever associate itself in my mind with the crowd of affectionate remembrances that now cluster about it. There are those in this city who would brighten, to me, the darkest winter-day that ever glimmered and went out in Lapland; and before whose presence even Home grew dim, when they and I exchanged that painful word which mingles with our every thought and deed; which haunts our cradle-heads in infancy, and closes up the vista of our lives in age.

---

## CHAPTER VII.

### PHILADELPHIA, AND ITS SOLITARY PRISON.

The journey from New York to Philadelphia is made by railroad, and two ferries; and usually occupies between five and six hours. It was a fine evening when we were passengers in the train: and watching the bright sunset from a little window near the door by which we sat, my attention was attracted to a remarkable appearance issuing from the windows of the gentlemen's car immediately in front of us, which I supposed for some time was occasioned by a number of industrious persons inside, ripping open feather-beds, and giving the feathers to the wind. At length it occurred to me that they were only spitting, which was indeed the case; though how any number of passengers which it was possible for that car to contain, could have maintained such a playful and incessant shower of expectoration, I am still at a loss to understand: notwithstanding the experience in all salivatory phenomena which I afterwards acquired.

I made acquaintance, on this journey, with a mild and modest young quaker, who opened the discourse by informing me, in a grave whisper, that his grandfather was the inventor of cold-drawn castor oil. I mention the circumstance here, thinking it probable that this is the first occasion on which the valuable medicine in question was ever used as a conversational aperient.

We reached the city late that night. Looking out of my chamber window, before going to bed, I saw, on the opposite side of the way, a handsome building of white marble, which had a mournful ghost-like aspect, dreary to behold. I attributed this to the sombre influence of the night, and on rising in the morning looked out again, expecting to see its steps and portico thronged with groups of people passing in and out. The door was still tight shut, however; the same cold cheerless air prevailed; and the building looked as if the marble statue of Don Guzman could alone have any business to transact within it gloomy walls. I hastened to inquire its name and purpose, and then my surprise vanished. It was the Tomb of many fortunes; the Great Catacomb of investment; the memorable United States Bank.

The stoppage of this bank, with all its ruinous consequences, had cast (as I was told on every side) a gloom on Philadelphia, under the depressing effect of which it yet labored. It certainly did seem rather dull and out of spirits.

It is a handsome city, but distractingly regular. After walking about it for an hour or two, I felt that I would have given the world for a crooked street. The collar of my coat appeared to stiffen, and the brim of my hat to expand, beneath its quakerly influence. My hair shrunk into a sleek short crop, my hands folded themselves upon my breast of their own calm accord, and thoughts of taking lodgings in Mark Lane over against the Market Place, and of making a large fortune by speculations in corn came over me involuntarily.

Philadelphia is most bountifully provided with fresh water, which it showered and jerked about, and turned on, and poured off, everywhere. The Waterworks, which are on a height near the city, are no less ornamental than useful, being tastefully laid out as a public garden, and kept in the best and neatest order. The river is dammed at this point, and forced by its own power into certain high tanks or reservoirs, whence the whole city, to the top stories of the houses, is supplied at a very trifling expense.

There are various public institutions. Among them a most excellent Hospital—a quaker establishment, but not sectarian in the great benefits it confers; a quiet, quaint old Library, named after Franklin; a handsome Exchange and Post Office; and so forth. In connection with the quaker Hospital, there is a picture by West, which is exhibited for the benefit of the funds of the institution. The subject is, our Savior healing the sick, and it is, perhaps, as favorable a specimen of the master as can be seen anywhere. Whether this be high or low praise, depends upon the reader's taste.

In the same room, there is a very characteristic and life-like portrait by Mr. Sully, a distinguished American artist.

My stay in Philadelphia was very short, but what I saw of its society I greatly liked. Treating of its general characteristics, I should be disposed to say that it is more provincial than Boston or New York, and that there is afloat in the fair city, an assumption of taste and criticism, savoring rather of those genteel discussions upon the same themes, in connection with Shakspeare and the Musical Glasses, of which we read in the Vicar of Wakefield. Near the city, is a most splendid unfinished marble structure, for the Girard College, founded by a deceased gentleman of that name and of enormous wealth, which, if completed according to the original design, will be perhaps the richest edifice of modern times. But the bequest is involved in legal disputes, and pending them the work has stopped; so that like many other great undertakings in America, even this is rather going to be done one of these days, than doing now.

In the outskirts, stands a great prison, called the Eastern Penitentiary: conducted on a plan peculiar to the state of Pennsylvania. The system here, is rigid, strict, and hopeless solitary confinement. I believe it, in its effects, to be cruel and wrong.

In its intention, I am well convinced that it is kind, humane, and meant for reformation; but I am persuaded that those who devised this system of Prison Discipline, and those benevolent gentlemen who carry it into execution, do not know what it is they are doing. I believe that very few men are capable of estimating the immense amount of torture and agony which this dreadful punishment, prolonged for years, inflicts upon the sufferers; and in guessing at it myself, and in reasoning from what I have seen written upon their faces, and what to my certain knowledge they feel within, I am only the more convinced that there is a depth of terrible endurance in it which none but the sufferers themselves can fathom, and which no man has a right to inflict upon his fellow creature. I hold this slow and daily tampering with the mysteries of the brain, to be immeasurably worse than any torture of the body; and because its ghastly signs and tokens are not so palpable to the eye and sense of touch as scars upon the flesh; because its wounds are not upon the surface, and it extorts few cries that human ears can hear; therefore I the more denounce it, as a secret punishment which slumbering humanity is not roused up to stay. I hesitated once, debating with myself, whether, if I had the power of saying "Yes" or "No," I would allow it to be tried in certain cases, where the terms of imprisonment were short; but now, I solemnly declare, that with no rewards or honors could I walk a happy man beneath the open sky by day, or lie me down upon my bed at night, with the consciousness that one human creature, for any length of time, no matter what, lay suffering this unknown punishment in his silent cell, and I the cause, or I consenting to it in the least degree.

I was accompanied to this prison by two gentlemen, officially connected with its management, and passed the day in going from cell to cell, and talking with the inmates. Every facility was afforded me, that the utmost courtesy could suggest. Nothing was concealed or hidden from my view, and every piece of information that I sought, was openly and frankly given. The perfect order of the building cannot be praised too highly, and of the excellent motives of all who are immediately concerned in the administration of the system, there can be no kind of question.

Between the body of the prison and the outer wall, there is a spacious garden. Entering it, by a wicket in the massive gate, we pursued the path before us to its other termination, and passed into a large chamber, from which seven long passages radiate. On either side of each, is a long, long row of low cell doors, with a certain number over every one. Above, a gallery of cells like those below, except that they have no narrow yard attached (as those in the ground tier have), and are somewhat smaller. The possession of two of these, is supposed to compensate for the absence of so much air and exercise as can be had in the dull strip attached to each of the others, in an hour's time every day; and therefore every prisoner in this upper story has two cells, adjoining, and communicating with, each other.

Standing at the central point, and looking down these dreary passages, the dull repose and quiet that prevails, is awful. Occasionally there is a drowsy sound from some lone weaver's shuttle, or shoemaker's last, but it is stifled by the thick walls and heavy dungeon-door, and only serves to make the general stillness more profound. Over the head and face of every prisoner who comes into this melancholy house, a black hood is drawn; and in this dark shroud, an emblem of the curtain dropped between him and the living world, he is led to the cell from which he never again comes forth, un his whole term of imprisonment has expired. He never hears of wife or children; home or friends; the life or death of any single creature. He sees the prison-officers, but with that exception, he never looks upon a human countenance, or hears a human voice. He is a man buried alive; to be dug out in the slow round of years; and in the meantime dead to everything but torturing anxieties and horrible despair.

His name, and crime, and term of suffering, are unknown, even to the officer who delivers him his daily food. There is a number over his cell-door, and in a book of which the governor of the prison has one copy, and the moral instructor another: this is the index to his history. Beyond these pages the prison has no record of his existence: and though he live to be in the same cell ten weary years, he has no means of knowing, down to the very last hour, in what part of the building it is situated; what kind of men there are about him; whether in the long winter nights there are living people near, or he is in some lonely corner of the great jail, with walls, and passages, and iron doors between him and the nearest sharer in its solitary horrors.

Every cell has double doors; the outer one of sturdy oak, the other of grated iron, wherein there is a trap through which his food is handed. He has a Bible, and a slate and pencil, and, under certain restrictions, has sometimes other books, provided for the purpose, and pen and ink and paper. His razor, plate, and can, and basin, hang upon the wall, or shine upon the little shelf. Fresh water is laid on in every cell, and he can draw it at his pleasure. During the day, his bedstead turns up against the wall, and leaves more space for him to work in. His loom, or bench, or wheel, is there; and there he labors, sleeps and wakes, and counts the seasons as they change, and grows old.

The first man I saw was seated at his loom, at work. He had been there six years, and was to remain, I think, three more. He had been convicted as a receiver of stolen goods, but even after this long imprisonment denied his guilt, and said he had been hardly dealt by. It was his second offence.

He stopped his work when we went in, took off his spectacles, and answered freely everything that was said to him, but always with a strange kind of pause first, and in a low, thoughtful voice. He wore a paper hat of his own making, and was pleased to have it noticed and commended. He had very ingeniously manufactured a sort of Dutch clock from some disregarded odds and ends; and his vinegar-bottle served for the pendulum. Seeing me interested in this contrivance, he looked up at it with a great deal of pride, and said that he had been thinking of improving it, and that he hoped the hammer and a little piece of broken glass beside it "would play music before long." He had extracted some colors from the yarn with which he worked, and painted a few poor figures on the wall. One, of a female, over the door, he called "The Lady of the Lake."

He smiled as I looked at these contrivances to wile away the time; but, when I looked from them to him, I saw that his lip trembled, and could have counted the beating of his heart. I forgot how it came about, but some allusion was made to his having a wife. He shook his head at the word, turned aside, and covered his face with his hands.

"But you are resigned now!" said one of the gentlemen after a short pause, during which he had resumed his former manner. He answered with a sigh that seemed quite reckless in its hopelessness, "Oh yes, oh yes! I am resigned to it." "And you are a better man, you think?" "Well, I hope so: I'm sure I hope I may be." "And time goes pretty quickly?" "Time is very long, gentlemen, within these four walls!"

He gazed about him—Heaven only knows how wearily!—as he said these words; and in the act of doing so, fell into a strange stare as if he had forgotten something. A moment afterwards he sighed heavily, put on his spectacles, and went about his work again.

In another cell, there was a German, sentenced to five years' imprisonment for larceny, two of which had just expired. With colors procured in the same manner, he had painted every inch of the walls and ceiling quite beautifully. He had laid out the few feet of ground, behind, with exquisite neatness, and had made a little bed in the centre, that looked by the bye like a grave. The taste and ingenuity he had displayed in everything were most extraordinary; and yet a more dejected, heart-broken, wretched creature, it would be difficult to imagine. I never saw such a picture of forlorn affliction and distress of mind. My heart bled for him; and when the tears ran down his cheeks, and he took one of the visitors aside, to ask, with his trembling hands nervously clutching at his coat to detain him, whether there was no hope of his dismal sentence being commuted, the spectacle was really too painful to witness. I never saw or heard of any kind of misery that impressed me more than the wretchedness of this man.

In a third cell was a tall strong black, a burglar, working at his proper trade of making screws and the like. His time was nearly out. He was not only a very dextrous thief, but was notorious for his boldness and hardihood, and for the number of his previous convictions. He entertained us with a long account of his achievements, which he narrated with such infinite relish, that he seemed to lick his lips as he told us racy anecdotes of stolen plate, and of old ladies whom he had watched as they sat at windows in silver spectacles (he had plainly had an eye to their metal, even from the other side of the street) and had afterwards robbed. This fellow, upon the slightest encouragement, would have mingled with his professional recollections the most detestable cant; but I am very much mistaken if he could have surpassed the unmitigated hypocrisy with which he declared that he blessed the day on which he came into that prison, and that he never would commit another robbery as long as he lived.

There was one man who was allowed, as an indulgence, to keep rabbits. His room having rather a close smell in consequence, they called to him at the door to come out into the passage. He complied of course, and stood shading his haggard face in the unwonted sunlight of the great window, looking as wan and unearthly as if he had been summoned from the grave. He had a white rabbit in his breast; and when the little creature, getting down upon the ground, stole back into the cell, and he, being dismissed, crept timidly after it, I thought it would have been very hard to say in what respect the man was the nobler animal of the two.

There was an English thief, who had been there but a few

days out of seven years: a villanous, low-bred, thin-lipped fellow, with a white-face; who had as yet no relish for visitors, and who, but for the additional penalty, would have gladly stabbed me with his shoemaker's knife. There was another German who had entered the jail but yesterday, and who started from his bed when we looked in, and pleaded in his broken English, very hard for work. There was a poet, who after doing two days' work in every four-and-twenty hours, one for himself and one for the prison, wrote verses about ships (he was by trade a mariner), and the "maddening wine-cup," and his friends at home. There were very many of them. Some reddened at the sight of visitors, and some turned very pale. Some two or three had prisoner nurses with them, for, they were very sick, and one, a fat old negro, whose leg had been taken off within the jail, had for his attendant a classical scholar and an accomplished surgeon himself a prisoner likewise. Sitting upon the stairs, engaged in some slight work, was a pretty colored boy. "Is there no refuge for young criminals in Philadelphia, then?" said I. "Yes, but only for white children." Noble aristocracy in crime!

There was a sailor who had been there upwards of eleven years, and who in a few months' time would be free. Eleven years of solitary confinement!

"I am very glad to hear your time is nearly out." What does he say? Nothing. Why does he stare at his hands, and pick the flesh upon his fingers, and raise his eyes for an instant, every now and then, to those bare walls which have seen his head turn grey? It is a way he has sometimes.

Does he never look men in the face, and does he always pluck at those hands of his, as though he were bent on parting skin and bone? It is his humor: nothing more.

It is his humor, too, to say that he does not look forward to going out; that he is not glad the time is drawing near; that he did look forward to it once, but that was very long ago; that he has lost all care for everything. It is his humor to be a helpless, crushed, and broken man. And, Heaven be his witness that he has his humor thoroughly gratified!

There were three young women in adjoining cells, all con

victed at the same time of a conspiracy to rob their prosecutor. In the silence and solitude of their lives they had grown to be quite beautiful. Their looks were very sad, and might have moved the sternest visitor to tears, but not to that kind of sorrow which the contemplation of the men awakens. One was a young girl; not twenty, as I recollect; whose snow-white room was hung with the work of some former prisoner, and upon whose downcast face the sun in all its splendor shone down through the high chink in the wall, where one narrow strip of bright'blue sky was visible. She was very penitent and quiet; had come to be resigned, she said, and I believe her); and had a mind at peace. "In a word, you are happy here?" said one of my companions. She struggled—she did struggle very hard—to answer, Yes: but raising her eyes, and meeting that glimpse of freedom over-head, she burst into tears, and said, "She tried to be; she uttered no complaint; but it was natural that she should somtimes long to go out of that one cell: she could not help *that*," she sobbed, poor thing!

I went from cell to cell that day; and every face I saw, or word I heard, or incident I noted, is present to my mind in all its painfulness. But let me pass them by, for one, more pleasant, glance of a prison on the same plan which I afterwards saw at Pittsburgh.

When I had gone over that, in the same manner, I asked the Governor if he had any person in his charge who was shortly going out. He had one, he said, whose time was up next day; but he had only been a prisoner two years.

Two years! I looked back through two years in my own life—out of jail, prosperous, happy, surrounded by blessings, comforts, and good fortune—and thought how wide a gap it was, and how long those two years passed in solitary captivity would have been. I have the face of this man, who was going to be released next day, before me now. It is almost more memorable in its happiness than the other faces in their misery. How easy and how natural it was for him to say that the system was a good one; and that the time went "pretty quick—considering;" and that when a man once felt he had offended the law, and must satisfy it, "he got along, somehow;" and so forth!

"What did he call you back to say to you, in that strange flutter?" I asked of my conductor, when he had locked the door and joined me in the passage.

"Oh! That he was afraid the soles of his boots were not fit for walking, as they were a good deal worn when he came in; and that he would thank me very much to have them mended, ready."

Those boots had been taken off his feet, and put away with the rest of his clothes, two years before!

I took that opportunity of inquiring how they conducted themselves immediately before going out; adding that I presume they trembled very much.

"Well, it's not so much a trembling," was the answer—"though they do quiver—as a complete derangement of the nervous system. They can't sign their names to the book; sometimes can't even hold the pen; look about 'em without appearing to know why, or where they are; and sometimes get up and sit down again, twenty times in a minute. This is when they're in the office, where they are taken with the hood on, as they were brought in. When they get outside the gate, they stop, and look first one way and then the other: not knowing which to take. Sometimes they stagger as if they were drunk, and sometimes are forced to lean against the fence, they're so bad:—but they clear off in course of time."

As I walked among these solitary cells, and looked at the faces of the men within them, I tried to picture to myself the thoughts and feelings natural to their condition. I imagined the hood just taken off, and the scene of their captivity disclosed to them in all its dismal monotony.

At first the man is stunned. His confinement is a hideous vision; and his old life a reality. He throws himself upon his bed, and lies there abandoned to despair. By degrees the insupportable solitude and barrenness of the place rouses him from this stupor, and when the trap in his grated door is opened, he humbly begs and prays for work. "Give me some work to do, or I shall go raving mad!"

He has it; and by fits and starts applies himself to labor;

but every now and then there comes upon him a burning sense of the years that must be wasted in that stone coffin, and an agony so piercing in the recollection of those who are hidden from his view and knowledge, that he starts from his seat, and striding up and down the narrow room with both hands clasped on his uplifted head, hears spirits tempting him to beat his brains out on the wall.

Again he falls upon his bed, and lies there moaning. Suddenly he starts up, wondering whether any other man is near; whether there is another cell like that on either side of him; and listens keenly.

There is no sound, but other prisoners may be near for all that. He remembers to have heard once, when he little thought of coming here himself, that the cells were so constructed that the prisoners could not hear each other, though the officers could hear them. Where is the nearest man—upon the right, or on the left? or is there one in both directions? Where is he sitting now—with his face to the light? or is he walking to and fro? How is he dressed? Has he been here long? Is he much worn away? Is he very white and spectre-like? Does *he* think of his neighbor too?

Scarcely venturing to breathe, and listening while he thinks, he conjures up a figure with his back towards him, and imagines it moving about in his next cell. He has no idea of the face, but he is certain of the dark form of a stooping man. In the cell upon the other side, he puts another figure, whose face is hidden from him also. Day after day, and often when he wakes up in the middle of the night, he thinks of these two men until he is almost distracted. He never changes them. There they are always as he first imagined them—an old man on the right; a younger man upon the left—whose hidden features torture him to death, and have a mystery that makes him tremble.

The weary days pass on with solemn pace, like mourners at a funeral; and slowly he begins to feel that the white walls of the cell have something dreadful in them: that their color is horrible: that their smooth surface chills his blood: that there is one hateful corner which torments him. Every morning when he wakes, he hides his head beneath the coverlet, and shudders to see the ghastly ceiling looking down upon him. The blessed light of day itself peeps in, an ugly phantom face, through the unchangeable crevice which is his prison window.

By slow but sure degrees, the terrors of that hateful corner swell until they beset him at all times; invade his rest, make his dreams hideous, and his nights dreadful. At first, he took a strange dislike to it: feeling as though it gave birth in his brain to something of corresponding shape, which ought not to be there, and racked his head with pains. Then he began to fear it, then to dream of it, and of men whispering its name and pointing to it. Then he could not bear to look at it, nor yet to turn his back upon it. Now, it is every night the lurking-place of a ghost: a shadow:—a silent something, horrible to see, but whether bird, or beast, or muffled human shape, he cannot tell.

When he is in his cell by day, he fears the little yard without. When he is in the yard he dreads to re-enter the cell. When night comes, there stands the phantom in the corner. If he have the courage to stand in its place, and drive it out (he had once; being desperate), it broods upon his bed. In the twilight, and always at the same hour, a voice calls to him by name; as the darkness thickens, his Loom begins to live; and even that, his comfort, is a hideous figure, watching him till daybreak.

Again, by slow degrees, these horrible fancies depart from him one by one; returning sometimes, unexpectedly, but at longer intervals, and in less alarming shapes. He has talked upon religious matters with the gentleman who visits him, and has read his Bible, and has written a prayer upon his slate, and hung it up as a kind of protection, and an assurance of Heavenly companionship. He dreams now, sometimes, of his children or his wife, but is sure that they are dead, or have deserted him. He is easily moved to tears; is gentle, submissive, and broken-spirited. Occasionally the old agony comes back: a very little thing will revive it: even a familiar sound, or the scent of summer flowers in the air;

but it does not last long, now; for the world without, has come to be the vision, and this solitary life the sad reality.

If his term of imprisonment be short—I mean comparatively, for short it cannot be—the last half year is almost worse than all; for then he thinks the prison will take fire and he be burned in the ruins, or that he is doomed to die within the walls, or that he will be detained on some false charge and sentenced for another term: or that something, no matter what, must happen to prevent his going at large. And this is natural, and impossible to be reasoned against, because, after his long separation from human life, and his great suffering, any event will appear to him more probable in the contemplation, than the being restored to liberty and his fellow-creatures.

If his period of confinement have been very long, the prospect of release, bewilders and confuses him. His broken heart may flutter for a moment, when he thinks of the world outside, and what it might have been to him in all those lonely years, but that is all. The cell-door has been closed too long on all its hopes and cares. Better to have hanged him in the beginning than bring him to this pass, and send him forth to mingle with his kind, who are his kind no more.

On the haggard face of every man among these prisoners, the same expression sat. I know not what to liken it to. It had something of that strained attention which we see upon the faces of the blind and deaf, mingled with a kind of horror, as though they had all been secretly terrified. In every little chamber that I entered, and at every grate through which I looked, I seemed to see the same appalling countenance. It lives in my memory, with the fascination of a remarkable picture. Parade before my eyes, a hundred men, with one among them newly released from this solitary suffering, and I would point him out.

The faces of the women, as I have said, it humanizes and refines. Whether this be because of their better nature, which is elicited in solitude, or because of their being gentler creatures, of greater patience and longer suffering, I do not know; but so it is. That the punishment is nevertheless, to my thinking, fully as cruel and as wrong in their case, as in that of the men, I need scarcely add.

My firm conviction is that, independent of the mental anguish it occasions—an anguish so acute and tremendous, that all imagination of it must fall far short of the reality—it wears the mind into a morbid state, which renders it unfit for the rough contact and busy action of the world. It is my fixed opinion that those who have undergone this punishment, MUST pass into society again morally unhealthy and diseased. There are many instances on record, of men who have chosen, or have been condemned, to lives of perfect solitude, but I scarcely remember one, even among sages of strong and vigorous intellect, where its effect has not become apparent, in some disordered train of thought, or some gloomy hallucination. What monstrous phantoms, bred of despondency and doubt, and born and reared in solitude, have stalked upon the earth, making creation ugly, and darkening the face of Heaven!

Suicides are rare among these prisoners: are almost, indeed, unknown. But no argument in favor of the system, can reasonably be deduced from this circumstance, although it is very often urged. All men who have made diseases of the mind their study, know perfectly well that such extreme depression and despair as will change the whole character, and beat down all its powers of elasticity and self-resistance may be at work within a man, and yet stop short of self destruction. This is a common case.

That it makes the senses dull, and by degrees impairs the bodily faculties, I am quite sure. I remarked to those who were with me in this very establishment at Philadelphia, that the criminals who had been there long, were deaf. They, who were in the habit of seeing these men constantly, were perfectly amazed at the idea, which they regarded as groundless and fanciful. And yet the very first prisoner to whom they appealed—one of their own selection—confirmed my impression (which was unknown to him) instantly, and said, with a genuine air it was impossible to doubt, that he couldn't think how it happened, but he *was* growing very dull of hearing.

That it is a singularly unequal punishment, and affects the worst man least, there is no doubt. In its superior efficiency as a means of reformation, compared with that other code of regulations which allows the prisoners to work in company without communicating together, I have not the smallest faith. All the instances of reformation that were mentioned to me were of a kind that might have been—and I have no doubt whatever, in my own mind, would have been—equally well brought about by the Silent System. With regard to such men as the negro burglar and the English thief, even the most enthusiastic have scarcely any hope of their conversion.

It seems to me that the objection that nothing wholesome or good has ever had its growth in such unnatural solitude, and that even a dog or any of the more intelligent among beasts, would pine, and mope, and rust away, beneath its influence, would be in itself a sufficient argument against this system. But when we recollect, in addition, how very cruel and severe it is, and that a solitary life is always liable to peculiar and distinct objections of a most deplorable nature, which have arisen here, and call to mind, moreover, that the choice is not between this system, and a bad or ill-considered one, but between it and another which has worked well, and is, in its whole design and practice, excellent; there is surely more than sufficient reason for abandoning a mode of punishment attended by so little hope or promise, and fraught, beyond dispute, with such a host of evils.

As a relief to its contemplation, I will close this chapter with a curious story, arising out of the same theme, which was related to me, on the occasion of this visit, by some of the gentlemen concerned.

At one of the periodical meetings of the inspectors of this prison, a working man of Philadelphia presented himself before the Board, and earnestly requested to be placed in solitary confinement. On being asked what motive could possibly prompt him to make this strange demand, he answered that he had an irresistible propensity to get drunk; that he was constantly indulging it, to his great misery and ruin; that he had no power of resistance; that he wished to be put beyond the reach of temptation; and that he could think of no better way than this. It was pointed out to him, in reply, that the prison was for criminals who had been tried and sentenced by the law, and could not be made available for any such fanciful purposes; he was exhorted to abstain from intoxicating drinks, as he surely might if he would; and received other very good advice, with which he retired, exceedingly dissatisfied with the result of his application.

He came again, and again, and again, and was so very earnest and importunate, that at last they took counsel together, and said, "He will certainly qualify himself for admission, if we reject him any more. Let us shut him up. He will soon be glad to go away, and then we shall get rid of him." So they made him sign a statement which would prevent his ever sustaining an action for false imprisonment, to the effect that his incarceration was voluntary, and of his own seeking; they requested him to take notice that the officer in attendance had orders to release him at any hour of the day or night, when he might knock upon his door for that purpose; but desired him to understand, that once going out, he would not be admitted any more. These conditions agreed upon, and he still remaining in the same mind, he was conducted to the prison, and shut up in one of the cells.

In this cell, the man, who had not the firmness to leave a glass of liquor standing untasted on a table before him—in this cell, in solitary confinement, and working every day at his trade of shoemaking, that man remained nearly two years. His health beginning to fail at the expiration of this time, the surgeon recommended that he should work occasionally in the garden; and as he liked the notion very much, he went about this new occupation with great cheerfulness.

He was digging here, one summer day, very industriously, when the wicket in the outer gate chanced to be left open: showing, beyond, the well-remembered dusty road and sunburnt fields. The way was as free to him as to any man living, but he no sooner raised his head and caught sight of it, all shining in the light, than, with the involuntary instinct of a prisoner, he cast away his spade, scampered off as fast as his legs would carry him, and never once looked back.

## CHAPTER VIII.

### WASHINGTON. THE LEGISLATURE. AND THE PRESIDENT'S HOUSE.

We left Philadelphia by steamboat, at six o'clock one very cold morning, and turned our faces toward Washington.

In the course of this day's journey, as on subsequent occasions, we encountered some Englishmen (small farmers, perhaps, or country publicans at home) who were settled in America, and were travelling on their own affairs. Of all grades and kinds of men that jostle one in the public conveyances of the States, these are often the most intolerable and the most insufferable companions. United to every disagreeable characteristic that the worst kind of American travellers possess, these countrymen of ours display an amount of insolent conceit and cool assumption of superiority, quite monstrous to behold. In the coarse familiarity of their approach, and the effrontery of their inquisitiveness (which they are in great haste to assert as if they panted to revenge themselves upon the decent old restraints of home) they surpass any native specimens that came within my range of observation: and I often grew so patriotic when I saw and heard them, that I would cheerfully have submitted to a reasonable fine, if I could have given any other country in the whole world, the honor of claiming them for its children.

As Washington may be called the head-quarters of tobacco-tinctured saliva, the time is come when I must confess, without any disguise, that the prevalence of those two odious practices of chewing and expectorating began about this time to be anything but agreeable, and soon became most offensive and sickening. In all the public places of America, this filthy custom is recognized. In the courts of law, the judge has his spittoon, the crier his, the witness his, and the prisoner his; while the jurymen and spectators are provided for, as so many men who in the course of nature must desire to spit incessantly. In the hospitals, the students of medicine are requested, by notice upon the wall, to eject their tobacco juice into the boxes provided for that purpose, and not to discolor the stairs. In public buildings, visitors are implored, through the same agency, to squirt the essence of their quids, or "plugs," as I have heard them called by gentlemen learned in this kind of sweetmeat, into the national spittoons, and not about the bases of the marble columns. But in some parts, this custom is inseparably mixed up with every meal and morning call, and with all the transactions of social life. The stranger, who follows in the track I took myself, will find it in its full bloom and glory, luxuriant in all its alarming recklessness, at Washington. And let him not persuade himself (as I once did, to my shame,) that previous tourists have exaggerated its extent. The thing itself is an exaggeration of nastiness, which cannot be outdone.

On board this steamboat, there were two young gentlemen, with shirt-collars reversed as usual, and armed with very big walking-sticks; who planted two seats in the middle of the deck, at a distance of some four paces apart; took out their tobacco-boxes; and sat down opposite each other, to chew. In less than a quarter of an hour's time, these hopeful youths had shed about them on the clean boards, a copious shower of yellow rain; clearing, by that means, a kind of magic circle, within whose limits no intruders dared to come, and which they never failed to refresh and re-refresh before a spot was dry. This being before breakfast, rather disposed me, I confess, to nausea; but looking attentively at one of the expectorators, I plainly saw that he was young in chewing, and felt inwardly uneasy, himself. A glow of delight came over me at this discovery; and as I marked his face turn paler and paler, and saw the ball of tobacco in his left cheek, quiver with his suppressed agony, while yet he spat, and chewed, and spat again, in emulation of his older friend, I could have fallen on his neck and implored him to go on for hours.

We all sat down to a comfortable breakfast in the cabin below, where there was no more hurry or confusion than at such a meal in England, and where there was certainly greater politeness exhibited than at most of our stage-coach banquets. At about nine o'clock we arrived at the railroad station, and went on by the cars. At noon we turned out again, to cross a wide river in another steam boat; landed at a continuation of the railroad on the opposite shore; and went on by other cars; in which in the course of the next hour or so, we crossed by wooden bridges, each a mile in length, two creeks, called respectively Great and Little Gunpowder. The water in both was blackened with flights of canvas-backed ducks, which are most delicious eating, and abound hereabouts at that season of the year.

These bridges are of wood, have no parapet, and are only just wide enough for the passage of the trains; which, in the event of the smallest accident, would inevitably be plunged into the river. They are startling contrivances, and are most agreeable when passed.

We stopped to dine at Baltimore, and being now in Maryland, were waited on, for the first time, by slaves. The sensation of exacting any service from human creatures who are bought and sold, and being, for the time, a party as it were to their condition, is not an enviable one. The institution exists, perhaps, in its least repulsive and most mitigated form in such a town as this; but it *is* slavery; and though I was with respect to it, an innocent man, its presence filled me with a sense of shame and self-reproach.

After dinner we went down to the railroad again, and took our seats in the cars for Washington. Being rather early, those men and boys who happened to have nothing particular to do, and were curious in foreigners, came (according to custom) round the carriage in which I sat; let down all the windows; thrust in their heads and shoulders; hooked themselves on conveniently, by their elbows: and fell to comparing notes on the subject of my personal appearance, with as much indifference as if I were a stuffed figure. I never gained so much uncompromising information with reference to my own nose and eyes, the various impressions wrought by my mouth and chin on different minds, and how my head looks when it is viewed from behind, as on these occasions. Some gentlemen were only satisfied by exercising their sense of touch; and the boys (who are surprisingly precocious in America) were seldom satisfied, even by that, but would return to the charge over and over again. Many a budding president has walked into my room with his cap on his head and his hands in his pockets, and stared at me for two whole hours: occasionally refreshing himself with a tweak at his nose, or a draught from the water jug; or by walking to the windows and inviting other boys in the street below, to come up and do likewise: crying, "Here he is!" "Come on!" "Bring all your brothers!" with other hospitable entreaties of that nature.

We reached Washington at about half-past six that evening, and had upon the way a beautiful view of the Capitol, which is a fine building of the Corinthian order, placed upon a noble and commanding eminence. Arrived at the hotel; I saw no more of the place that night; being very tired, and glad to get to bed.

Breakfast over next morning, I walk about the streets for an hour or two, and, coming home, throw up the window in the front and back, and look out. Here is Washington, fresh in my mind and under my eye.

Take the worst parts of the City Road and Pentonville, or the straggling outskirts of Paris, where the houses are smallest, preserving all their oddities, but especially the small shops and dwellings, occupied in Pentonville (but not in Washington) by furniture-brokers, keepers of poor eating-houses, and fanciers of birds. Burn the whole down; build it up again in wood and plaster; widen it a little; throw in part of St. John's Wood; put green blinds outside all the private houses, with a red curtain and a white one in every window, plough up all the roads; plant a great deal of coarse turf in every place where it ought *not* to be; erect three handsome buildings in stone and marble, anywhere, but the more entirely out of everybody's way the better; call one the Post Office, one the Patent Office, and one the Treasury; make it scorching hot in the morning, and freezing cold in the afternoon, with an occasional tornado of wind and dust; leave a brickfield without the bricks, in all central places where a street may naturally be expected: and that's Washington.

The hotel in which we live is a long row of small houses fronting on the street, and opening at the back upon a common yard, in which hangs a great triangle. Whenever a servant is wanted, somebody beats on this triangle from one stroke up to seven, according to the number of the house in which his presence is required; and as all the servants are always being wanted, and none of them ever come, this enlivening engine is in full performance the whole day through. Clothes are drying in this same yard; female slaves, with cotton handkerchiefs twisted round their heads, are running to and fro on the hotel business; black waiters cross and recross with dishes in their hands; two great dogs are playing upon a mound of loose bricks in the centre of the little square; a pig is turning up his stomach to the sun, and grunting "that's comfortable!" and neither the men, nor the women, nor the dogs, nor the pig, nor any created creature takes the smallest notice of the triangle, which is tingling madly all the time.

I walk to the front window, and look across the road upon a long, straggling row of houses, one story high, terminating nearly opposite, but a little to the left, in a melancholy piece of waste ground with frowzy grass, which looks like a small piece of country that has taken to drinking, and has quite lost itself. Standing anyhow and all wrong, upon this open space like something meteoric that has fallen down from the moon, is an odd, lop-sided, one-eyed kind of wooden building, that looks like a church, with a flag-staff as long as itself sticking out of a steeple something larger than a tea-chest. Under the window, is a small stand of coaches, whose slave-drivers are sunning themselves on the steps of our door, and talking idly together. The three most obtrusive houses near at hand, are the three meanest. On one—a shop, which never has anything in the window, and never has a door open—is painted in large characters, "THE CITY LUNCH." At another, which looks like the back way to somewhere else, but is an independent building in itself, oysters are procurable in every style. At the third, which is a very, very little tailor's shop, pants are fixed to order; or, in other words, pantaloons are made to measure. And that is our street in Washington.

It is sometimes called the City of Magnificent Distances, but it might with greater propriety be termed the City of Magnificent Intentions; for it is only on taking a bird's-eye view of it from the top of the Capitol, that one can at all comprehend the vast designs of its projector, an aspiring Frenchman. Spacious avenues, that begin in nothing, and lead nowhere; streets, mile-long, that only want houses, roads, and inhabitants; public buildings that need but a public to be complete; and ornaments of great thoroughfares, which only lack great thoroughfares to ornament—are its leading features. One might fancy the season over, and most of the houses gone out of town forever with their masters. To the admirers of cities it is a Barmecide Feast; a pleasant field for the imagination to rove in; a monument raised to a deceased project, with not even a legible inscription to record its departed greatness.

Such as it is, it is likely to remain. It was originally chosen for the seat of Government, as a means of averting the conflicting jealousies and interests of the different states; and very probably, too, as being remote from mobs: a consideration not to be slighted, even in America. It has no trade or commerce of its own: having little or no population beyond the President and his establishment; the members of the legislature who reside there during the session; the Government clerks and officers employed in the various departments; the keepers of the hotels and boarding-houses; and the tradesmen who supply their tables. It is very unhealthy. Few people would live in Washington, I take it, who were not obliged to reside there; and the tides of emigration and speculation, those rapid and regardless currents, are little likely to flow at any time towards such dull and sluggish water.

The principal features of the Capitol, are, of course, the two Houses of Assembly. But there is, besides, in the centre of the building, a fine rotunda, ninety-six feet in diameter, and ninety-six high, whose circular wall is divided into compartments, ornamented by historical pictures. Four of these have for their subjects prominent events in the revolutionary struggle. They were painted by Colonel Trumbull, himself a member of Washington's staff at the time of their occurrence; from which circumstance they derive a peculiar interest of their own. In this same hall Mr. Greenough's large statue of Washington has been lately placed. It has great merits of course, but it struck me as being rather strained and violent for its subject. I could wish, however, to have seen it in a better light than it can ever be viewed in, where it stands.

There is a very pleasant and commodious library in the Capitol; and from a balcony in front, the bird's-eye view, of which I have just spoken, may be had, together with a beautiful prospect of the adjacent country. In one of the ornamented portions of the building, there is a figure of Justice; whereunto the Guide Book says, "the artist at first contemplated giving more of nudity, but he was warned that the public sentiment in this country would not admit of it, and in his caution he has gone, perhaps, into the opposite extreme." Poor Justice! she has been made to wear much stranger garments in America than those she pines in, in the Capitol. Let us hope that she has changed her dress-maker since they were fashioned, and that the public sentiment of the country did not cut out the clothes she hides her lovely figure in, just now.

The House of Representatives is a beautiful and spacious hall of semi-circular shape, supported by handsome pillars. One part of the gallery is appropriated to the ladies, and there they sit in front rows, and come in, and go out, as at a play or concert. The chair is canopied, and raised considerably above the floor of the House; and every member has an easy chair and a writing desk to himself; which is denounced by some people out of doors as a most unfortunate and injudicious arrangement, tending to long sittings and prosaic speeches. It is an elegant chamber to look at, but a singularly bad one for all purposes of hearing. The Senate, which is smaller, is free from this objection, and is exceedingly well adapted to the uses for which it is designed. The sittings, I need hardly add, take place in the day; and the parliamentary forms are modelled on those of the old country.

I was sometimes asked, in my progress through other

places, whether I had not been very much impressed by the *heads* of the lawmakers at Washington; meaning not their chiefs and leaders, but literally their individual and personal heads, whereon their hair grew, and whereby the phrenological character of each legislator was expressed: and I almost as often struck my questioner dumb with indignant consternation by answering "No, that I didn't remember being at all overcome." As I must, at whatever hazard, repeat the avowal here, I will follow it up by relating my impressions on this subject in as few words as possible.

In the first place—it may be from some imperfect development of my organ of veneration—I do not remember having ever fainted away, or having even been moved to tears of joyful pride, at sight of any legislative body. I have borne the House of Commons like a man, and have yielded to no weakness, but slumber, in the House of Lords. I have seen elections for borough and county, and have never been impelled (no matter which party won) to damage my hat by throwing it up into the air in triumph, or to crack my voice by shouting forth any reference to our Glorious Constitution, to the noble purity of our independent voters, or the unimpeachable integrity of our independent members. Having withstood such strong attacks upon my fortitude, it is possible that I may be of a cold and insensible temperament, amounting to iciness, in such matters; and therefore my impressions of the live pillars of the Capitol at Washington must be received with such grains of allowance as this free confession may seem to demand.

Did I see in this public body an assemblage of men, bound together in the sacred names of Liberty and Freedom, and so asserting the chaste dignity of those twin goddesses, in all their discussions, as to exalt at once the Eternal Principles to which their names are given, and their own character, and the character of their countrymen, in the admiring eyes of the whole world?

It was but a week, since an aged, grey-haired man, a lasting honor to the land that gave him birth, who has done good service to his country, as his forefathers did, and who will be remembered scores of years after the worms bred in its corruption are but so many grains of dust—it was but a week, since this old man had stood for days upon his trial before this very body, charged with having dared to assert the infamy of that traffic, which has for its accursed merchandise men and women, and their unborn children. Yes. And publicly exhibited in the same city all the while; gilded, framed and glazed; hung up for general admiration; shown to strangers not with shame, but pride; its face not turned towards the wall, itself not taken down and burned; is the Unanimous Declaration of The Thirteen United States of America, which solemnly declares that all Men are created Equal; and are endowed by their Creator with the Inalienable Rights of Life, Liberty, and the Pursuit of Happiness!

It was not a month since this same body had sat calmly by, and heard a man, one of themselves, with oaths which beggars in their drink reject, threaten to cut another's throat from ear to ear. There he sat, among them; not crushed by the general feeling of the assembly, but as good a man as any.

There was but a week to come, and another of that body, for doing his duty to those who sent him there; for claiming in a Republic the Liberty and Freedom of expressing their sentiments, and making known their prayer; would be tried, found guilty, and have strong censure passed upon him by the rest. His was a grave offence indeed; for years before, he had risen up and said, "A gang of male and female slaves for sale, warranted to breed like cattle, linked to each other by iron fetters, are passing now along the open street beneath the windows of your Temple of Equality! Look!" But there are many kinds of hunters engaged in the Pursuit of Happiness, and they go variously armed. It is the Inalienable Right of some among them, to take the field after *their* Happiness, equipped with cat and cartwhip, stocks, and iron collar, and to shout their view halloa! (always in praise of Liberty) to the music of clanking chains and bloody stripes.

Where sat the many legislators of coarse threats; of words and blows such as coalheavers deal upon each other, when they forget their breeding? On every side. Every session had its anecdotes of that kind, and the actors were all there.

Did I recognize in this assembly, a body of men, who applying themselves in a new world to correct some of the falsehoods and vices of the old, purified the avenues to Public Life, paved the dirty ways to Place and Power, debated and made laws for the Common Good, and had no party but their Country?

I saw in them, the wheels that move the meanest perversion of virtuous Political Machinery that the worst tools ever wrought. Despicable trickery at elections; under-handed tamperings with public officers; cowardly attacks upon opponents, with scurrilous newspapers for shields, and hired pens for daggers; shameful trucklings to mercenary knaves, whose claim to be considered, is, that every day and week they sow new crops of ruin with their venal types, which are the dragon's teeth of yore, in everything but sharpness; aidings and abettings of every bad inclination in the popular mind, and artful suppressions of all its good influences; such things as these, and in a word, Dishonest Faction in its most depraved and most unblushing form, stared out from every corner of the crowded hall.

Did I see among them, the intelligence and refinement: the true, honest, patriotic heart of America? Here and there, were drops of its blood and life, but they scarcely colored the stream of desperate adventurers which sets that way for profit and for pay. It is the game of these men, and of their profligate organs, to make the strife of politics so fierce and brutal, and so destructive of all self-respect in worthy men, that sensitive and delicate-minded persons shall be kept aloof, and they, and such as they, be left to battle out their selfish views unchecked. And thus this lowest of all scrambling fights goes on, and they who in other countries would, from their intelligence and station, most aspire to make the laws, do here recoil the farthest from that degradation.

That there are, among the representatives of the people in both Houses, and among all parties, some men of high character and great abilities, I need not say. The foremost among those politicians who are known in Europe, have been already described, and I see no reason to depart from the rule I have laid down for my guidance, of abstaining from all mention of individuals. It will be sufficient to add, that to the most favorable accounts that have been written of them, I more than fully and most heartily subscribe; and that personal intercourse and free communication have bred within me, not the result predicted in the very doubtful proverb, but increased admiration and respect. They are striking men to look at, hard to deceive, prompt to act, lions in energy, Crichtons in varied accomplishment, Indians in fire of eye and gesture, Americans in strong and generous impulse; and they as well represent the honor and wisdom of their country at home, as the distinguished gentleman who is now its minister at the British Court sustains its highest character abroad.

I visited both houses nearly every day, during my stay in Washington. On my initiatory visit to the House of Representatives, they divided against a decision of the chair; but the chair won. The second time I went, the member who was speaking, being interrupted by a laugh, mimicked it, as one child would in quarrelling with another, and added, "that he would make honorable gentlemen opposite, sing out a little more on the other side of their mouths presently." But interruptions are rare; the speaker being usually heard in silence. There are more quarrels than with us, and more threatenings than gentlemen are accustomed to exchange in any civilized society of which we have record: but farm-yard imitations have not as yet been imported from the Parliament of the United Kingdom. The feature in oratory which appears to be the most practised, and most relished, is the constant repetition of the same idea or shadow of an idea in fresh words; and the inquiry out of doors is not, "What did he say?" but, "How long did he speak?" These, however, are but enlargements of a principle which prevails elsewhere.

The Senate is a dignified and decorous body, and its proceedings are conducted with much gravity and order. Both houses are handsomely carpeted; but the state to which these carpets are reduced by the universal disregard of the spittoon with which every honorable member is accommodated, and the extraordinary improvements on the pattern which are squirted and dabbled upon it in every direction, do not admit of being described. I will merely observe that I strongly recommend all strangers not to look at the floor; and if they happen to drop anything, though it be their purse, not to pick it up with an ungloved hand on any account.

It is somewhat remarkable too, at first, to say the least, to see so many honorable members with swelled faces; and it is scarcely less remarkable to discover that this appearance is caused by the quantity of tobacco they contrive to stow within the hollow of the cheek. It is strange enough too, to see an honorable gentleman leaning back in his tilted chair with his legs on the desk before him, shaping a convenient "plug" with his penknife, and when it is quite ready for use, shooting the old one from his mouth, as from a pop-gun, and clapping the new one in its place.

I was surprised to observe that even steady old chewers of great experience, are not always good marksmen, which has rather inclined me to doubt that general proficiency with the rifle, of which we have heard so much in England. Several gentlemen called upon me who, in the course of conversation, frequently missed the spittoon at five paces; and one (but he was certainly short-sighted) mistook the closed sash for the open window, at three. On another occasion, when I dined out, and was sitting with two ladies and some gentlemen round a fire before dinner, one of the company fell short of the fire-place, six distinct times. I am disposed to think, however, that this was occasioned by his not aiming at that object; as there was a white marble hearth before the fender, which was more convenient, and may have suited his purpose better.

The Patent Office at Washington, furnishes an extraordinary example of American enterprise and ingenuity; for the immense number of models it contains, are the accumulated inventions of only five years: the whole of the previous collection having been destroyed by fire. The elegant structure in which they are arranged, is one of design rather than execution, for there is but one side erected out of four, though the works are stopped. The Post Office is a very compact, and very beautiful building. In one of the departments, among a collection of rare and curious articles, are deposited the presents which have been made from time to time to the American Ambassadors at foreign courts by the various potentates to whom they were the accredited agents of the Republic: gifts which by the law they are not permitted to retain. I confess that I looked upon this as a very painful exhibition, and one by no means flattering to the national standard of honesty and honor. That can scarcely be a high state of moral feeling which imagines a gentleman of repute and station, likely to be corrupted, in the discharge of his duty, by the present of a snuff-box, or a richly-mounted sword, or an Eastern shawl; and surely the Nation who reposes confidence in her appointed servants, is likely to be better served, than she who makes them the subject of such very mean and paltry suspicions.

At George Town, in the suburbs, there is a Jesuit College; delightfully situated, and, so far as I had an opportunity of seeing, well managed. Many persons who are not members of the Romish Church, avail themselves, I believe, of these institutions, and of the advantageous opportunities they afford for the education of their children. The heights in this neighborhood, above the Potomac River, are very picturesque; and are free I should conceive, from some of the insalubrities of Washington. The air at that elevation, was quite cool and refreshing, when in the city it was burning hot.

The President's mansion is more like an English club-house, both within and without, than any other kind of establishment with which I can compare it. The ornamental ground about it has been laid out in garden walks; they are pretty, and agreeable to the eye; though they have that uncomfortable air of having been made yesterday, which is far from favorable to the display of such beauties.

My first visit to this house was on the morning after my arrival, when I was carried thither by an official gentleman, who was so kind as to charge himself with my presentation to the President.

We entered a large hall, and having twice or thrice rung a

bell which nobody answered, walked without further ceremony through the rooms on the ground floor, as divers other gentlemen (mostly with their hats on, and their hands in their pocket) were doing very leisurely. Some of these had ladies with them, to whom they were showing the premises; others were lounging on the chairs and sofas; others, in a perfect state of exhaustion from listlessness, were yawning drearily. The greater portion of this assemblage were rather asserting their supremacy than doing anything else, as they had no particular business there, that anybody knew of. A few were closely eyeing the movables, as if to make quite sure that the President (who was far from popular) had not made away with any of the furniture, or sold the fixtures for his private benefit.

After glancing at these loungers; who were scattered over a pretty drawing-room, opening upon a terrace which commanded a beautiful prospect of the river and the adjacent country: and who were sauntering too, about a larger state-room called the Eastern Drawing-room; we went up-stairs into another chamber, where were certain visitors, waiting for audiences. At sight of my conductor, a black in plain clothes and yellow slippers who was gliding noiselessly about, and whispering messages in the ears of the more impatient, made a sign of recognition, and glided off to announce him.

We had previously looked into another chamber fitted all round with a great bare wooden desk or counter, whereon lay files of newspapers, to which sundry gentlemen were referring. But there were no such means of beguiling the time in this apartment, which was as unpromising and tiresome as any waiting-room in one of our public establishments, or any physician's dining-room during his hours of consultation at home.

There were some fifteen or twenty persons in the room. One, a tall, wiry, muscular old man, from the west; sunburnt and swarthy; with a brown-white hat on his knee, and a giant umbrella resting between his legs; who sat bolt upright in his chair, frowning steadily at the carpet, and twitching the hard lines about his mouth, as if he had made up his mind "to fix" the President on what he had to say, and wouldn't bate him a grain. Another, a Kentucky farmer, six-feet-six in height, with his hat on, and his hands under his coat-tails, who leaned against the wall and kicked the floor with his heel, as though he had Time's head under his shoe, and were literally "killing" him. A third, an oval-faced, bilious-looking man, with sleek black hair cropped close, and whiskers and beard shaved down to blue dots, who sucked the head of a thick stick, and from time to time took it out of his mouth, to see how it was getting on. A fourth did nothing but whistle. A fifth did nothing but spit. And indeed all these gentlemen were so very persevering and energetic in this latter particular, and bestowed their favors so abundantly upon the carpet, that I take it for granted the Presidential housemaids have high wages, or, to speak more genteelly, an ample amount of "compensation:" which is the American word for salary, in the case of all public servants.

We had not waited in this room many minutes, before the black messenger returned, and conducted us into another of smaller dimensions, where, at a business-like table covered with papers, sat the President himself. He looked somewhat worn and anxious, and well he might: being at war with everybody—but the expression of his face was mild and pleasant, and his manner was remarkably unaffected, gentlemanly, and agreeable. I thought that in his whole carriage and demeanor, he became his station singularly well.

Being advised that the sensible etiquette of the republican court, admitted of a traveller, like myself, declining, without any impropriety, an invitation to dinner, which did not reach me until I had concluded my arrangements for leaving Washington some days before that to which it referred, I only returned to this house once. It was on the occasion of one of those general assemblies which are held on certain nights, between the hours of nine and twelve o'clock, and are called, rather oddly, Levees.

I went, with my wife, at about ten. There was a pretty dense crowd of carriages and people in the court-yard, and so far as I could make out, there were no very clear regulations for the taking up or setting down of company. There were certainly no policemen to soothe startled horses, either by sawing at their bridles or flourishing truncheons in their eyes; and I am ready to make oath that no inoffensive persons were knocked violently on the head, or poked acutely in their backs or stomachs; or brought to a stand-still by any such gentle means, and then taken into custody for not moving on. But these was no confusion or disorder. Our carriage reached the porch in its turn, without any blustering, swearing, shouting, backing, or other disturbance: and we dismounted with as much ease and comfort as though we had been escorted by the whole Metropolitan Force from A to Z inclusive.

The suite of rooms on the ground-floor, were lighted up; and a military band was playing in the hall. In the smaller drawing-room, the centre of a circle of company, were the President and his daughter-in-law, who acted as the lady of the mansion: and a very interesting, graceful, and accomplished lady too. One gentleman who stood among this group, appeared to take upon himself the functions of a master of the ceremonies. I saw no other officers or attendants, and none were needed.

The great drawing-room, which I have already mentioned, and the other chambers on the ground-floor, were crowded to excess. The company was not, in our sense of the term, select, for it comprehended persons of very many grades, and classes; not was there any great display of costly attire: indeed some of the costumes may have been, for aught I know, grotesque enough. But the decorum and propriety of behavior which prevailed, were unbroken by any rude or disagreeable incident; and every man, even among the miscellaneous crowd in the hall who were admitted without any orders or tickets to look on, appeared to feel that he was a part of the Institution, and was responsible for its preserving a becoming character, and appearing to the best advantage.

That these visitors, too, whatever their station, were not without some refinement of taste and appreciation of intellectual gifts, and gratitude to those men who, by the peaceful exercise of great abilities shed new charms and associations upon the homes of their countrymen, and elevate their character in other lands, was most earnestly testified by their reception of Washington Irving, my dear friend, who had recently been appointed Minister at the court of Spain, and who was among them that night, in his new character, for the first and last time before going abroad. I sincerely believe that in all the madness of American politics, few public men would have beenso earnestly, devotedly, and affectionately caressed, as this most charming writer: and I have seldom respected a public assembly more, than I did this eager throng, when I saw them turning with one mind from noisy orators and officers of state, and flocking with a generous and honest impulse round the man of quiet pursuits: proud in his promotion as reflecting back upon their country: and grateful to him with their whole hearts for the store of graceful fancies he had poured out among them. Long may he dispense such treasures with unsparing hand; and long may they remember him as worthily!

The term we had assigned for the duration of our stay in Washington, was now at an end, and we were to begin to travel; for the railroad distances we had traversed yet, in journeying among these older towns, are on that great continent looked upon as nothing.

I had at first intended going South—to Charleston. But when I came to consider the length of time which this journey would occupy, and the premature heat of the season, which even at Washington had been often very trying; and weighed moreover, in my own mind, the pain of living in the constant centemplation of slavery, against the more than doubtful chances of my ever seeing it, in the time I had to spare, stripped of the disguises in which it would certainly be dressed, and so adding any item to the host of facts already heaped together on the subject; I began to listen to old whisperings which had often been present to me at home in England, when I little thought of ever being here; and to dream again of cities growing up, like palaces in fairy tales, among the wilds and forests of the west.

The advice I received in most quarters when I began to yield to my desire of travelling towards that point of the compass was, according to custom, sufficiently cheerless: my companion being threatened with more perils, dangers, and discomforts, than I can remember or would catalogue if I could; but of which it will be sufficient to remark that blowings-up in steamboats and breakings-down in coaches were among the least. But, having a western route sketched out for me by the best and kindest authority to which I could have resorted, and putting no great faith in these discouragements, I soon determined on my plan of action.

This was to travel south, only to Richmond in Virginia; and then to turn, and shape our course for the Far West; whither I beseech the reader's company, in a new chapter.

## CHAPTER IX.

A NIGHT STEAMER ON THE POTOMAC RIVER. VIRGINIA ROAD AND A BLACK DRIVER. RICHMOND. BALTIMORE. THE HARRISBURG MAIL, AND A GLIMPSE OF THE CITY. A CANAL BOAT.

WE were to proceed in the first instance by steamboat: and as it is usual to sleep on board, in consequence of the starting-hour being four o'clock in the morning, we went down to where she lay, at that very uncomfortable time for such expeditions when slippers are most valuable, and a familiar bed, in the perspective of an hour or two, looks uncommonly pleasant.

It is ten o'clock at night; say half-past ten; moonlight, warm, and dull enough. The steamer (not unlike a child's Noah's ark in form, with the machinery on the top of the roof,) is riding lazily up and down, and bumping clumsily against the wooden pier, as the ripple of the river trifles with its unwieldy carcase. The wharf is some distance from the city. There is nobody down here; and one or two dull lamps upon the steamer's decks are the only signs of life remaining when our coach has driven away. As soon as our footsteps are heard upon the planks, a fat negress, particularly favored by nature in respect of bustle, emerges from some dark stairs, and marshals my wife towards the ladies' cabin, to which retreat she goes, followed by a mighty bale of cloaks and great-coats. I valiantly resolve not to go to bed at all, but to walk up and down the pier till morning.

I begin my promenade—thinking of all kinds of distant things and persons, and of nothing near—and pace up and down for half-an-hour. Then I go on board again; and getting into the light of one of the lamps, look at my watch and think it must have stopped; and wonder what has become of the faithful secretary whom I brought along with me from Boston. He is supping with our late landlord (a Field Marshal, at least, no doubt) in honor of our departure, and may be two hours longer. I walk again, but it gets duller and duller; the moon goes down: next June seems farther off in the dark, and the echoes of my footsteps make me nervous. It has turned cold too; and walking up and down without any companion in such lonely circumstances, is but poor amusement. So I break my staunch resolution, and think it may be, perhaps, as well to go to bed.

I go on board again; open the door of the gentleman's cabin; and walk in. Somehow or other—from its being so quiet, I suppose—I have taken it into my head that there is nobody there. To my horror and amazement it is full of sleepers in every stage, shape, attitude, and variety of slumber; in the berths, on the chairs, on the floors, on the tables, and particularly round the stove, my detested enemy. I take another step forward, and slip upon the shining face of a black steward, who lies rolled in a blanket on the floor. He jumps up, grins half in pain and half in hospitality; whispers my own name in my ear; and groping among the sleepers, leads me to my berth. Standing beside it, I count these slumbering passengers, and get past forty. There is no use in going further, so I begin to undress. As the chairs are all occupied, and there is nothing else to put my clothes on, I deposit them upon the ground: not without soiling my hands, for it is in the same condition as the carpets in the Capitol, and from the same cause. Having but partially undressed, I clamber on my shelf, and hold the curtain open for a few minutes while I look round on all my fellow travellers again. That done, I let it fall on them, and on the world; and go to sleep.

I wake, of course, when we get under weigh, for there is a good deal of noise. The day is then just breaking. Everybody wakes at the same time. Some are self-possessed directly, and some are much perplexed to make out where they are until they have rubbed their eyes, and leaning on one elbow, looked about them. Some yawn, some groan nearly all spit, and a few get up. I am among the risers; for it is easy to feel, without going into the fresh air, that the atmosphere of the cabin is vile in the last degree. I huddle on my clothes, go down into the fore-cabin, get shaved by the barber, and wash myself. The washing and dressing apparatus for the passengers generally, consists of two jack-towels, three small wooden basins, a keg of water and a ladle to serve it out with, six square inches of looking-glass, two ditto ditto of yellow soap, a comb and brush for the head, and nothing for the teeth. Everybody uses the comb and brush, except myself. Everybody stares to see me using my own; and two or three gentlemen are strongly disposed to banter me on my prejudices, but don't. When I have made my toilet, I go upon the hurricane-deck, and set in for two hours of hard walking up and down. The sun is rising brilliantly; we are passing Mount Vernon, where Washington lies buried; the river is wide and rapid; and its banks are beautiful. All the glory and splendor of the day are coming on, and growing brighter every minute.

At eight o'clock, we breakfast in the cabin where I passed the night, but the windows and doors are all thrown open, and now it is fresh enough. There is no hurry or greediness apparent in the despatch of the meal. It is longer than a travelling breakfast with us; more orderly; and more polite.

Soon after nine o'clock we come to Potomac Creek, where we are to land; and then comes the oddest part of the journey.

Seven stage-coaches are preparing to carry us on. Some of them are ready, some of them are not ready. Some of the drivers are blacks, some whites. There are four horses to each coach, and all the horses, harnessed or unharnessed, are there. The passengers are getting out of the steamboat, and into the coaches; the luggage is being transferred in noisy wheelbarrows; the horses are frightened, and impatient to start; the black drivers are chattering to them like so many monkeys; and the white ones whooping like so many drovers: for the main thing to be done in all kinds of hostlering here, is to make as much noise as possible. The coaches are something like the French coaches, but not nearly so good. In lieu of springs, they are hung on bands of the strongest leather. There is very little choice or difference between them; and they may be likened to the car portion of the swings at an English fair, roofed, put upon axle-trees and wheels, and curtained with painted canvas. They are covered with mud from the roof to the wheel-tire, and have never been cleaned since they were first built.

The tickets we have received on board the steamboat are marked No. 1, so we belong to coach No. 1. I throw my coat on the box, and hoist my wife and her maid into the inside. It has only one step and that being about a yard from the ground, is usually approached by a chair: when there is no chair, ladies trust in Providence. The coach holds nine inside, having a seat across from door to door, where we in England put our legs: so that there is only one feat more difficult in the performance than getting in, and that is, getting out again. There is only one outside passenger, and he sits upon the box. As I am that one, I climb up; and while they are strapping the luggage on the roof, and heaping it into a kind of a tray behind, have a good opportunity of looking at the driver.

He is a negro—very black indeed. He is dressed in a coarse pepper-and-salt suit excessively patched and darned (particularly at the knees), grey stockings, enormous unblacked high-low shoes, and very short trousers. He has two odd gloves; one of parti-colored worsted, and one of leather.

He has a very short whip, broken in the middle and bandaged up with string. And yet he wears a low-crowned, broad-brimmed, black hat: faintly shadowing forth a kind of insane imitation of an English coachman! But somebody in authority cries "Go ahead!" as I am making these observations. The mail takes the lead in a four horse wagon, and all the coaches follow in procession: headed by No. 1.

By the way, whenever an Englishman would cry "All right!" an American cries "Go ahead!" which is somewhat expressive of the national character of the two countries.

The first half mile of the road is over bridges made of loose planks laid across two parallel poles which tilt up as the wheels roll over them; and IN the river. The river has a clayey bottom and is full of holes, so that half a horse is constantly disappearing unexpectedly, and can't be found again for some time.

But we get past even this, and come to the road itself, which is a series of alternate swamps and gravel-pits. A tremendous place is close before us, the black driver rolls his eyes, screws his mouth up very round, and looks straight between the two leaders, as if he were saying to himself, "we have done this often before, but *now* I think we shall have a crash." He takes a rein in each hand; jerks and pulls at both; and dances on the splashboard with both feet (keeping his seat of course) like the late lamented Ducrow on two of his fiery coursers. We come to the spot, sink down in the mire nearly to the coach windows, tilt on one side at an angle of forty-five degrees, and stick there. The insides scream dismally; the coach stops: the horses flounder; all the other six coaches stop; and their four-and twenty horses flounder likewise: but merely for company, and in sympathy with ours. Then the following circumstances occur.

BLACK DRIVER (to the horses). "Hi!"

Nothing happens. Insides scream again.

BLACK DRIVER (to the horses). "Ho!"

Horses plunge, and splash the black driver.

GENTLEMAN INSIDE (looking out). "Why, what on arth—"

Gentleman receives a variety of splashes and draws his head in again, without finishing his question or waiting for an answer.

Black Driver (still to the horses). "Jiddy! Jiddy!"

Horses pull violently, drag the coach out of the hole, and draw it up a bank; so steep that the black driver's legs fly up into the air, and he goes back among the luggage on the roof. But he immediately recovers himself, and cries (still to the horses),

"Pill!"

No effect. On the contrary, the coach begins to roll back upon No. 2, which rolls back upon No. 3, which rolls back upon No. 4, and so on, until No. 7 is heard to curse and swear, nearly a quarter of a mile behind.

Black Driver (louder than before). "Pill!"

Horses make another struggle to get up the bank, and again the coach rolls brackward.

Black Driver (louder than before). "Pe-e-e-ill!"

Horses make a desperate struggle.

Black Driver (recovering spirits). "Hi, Jiddy, Jiddy Pill!"

Horses made another effort.

Black Driver (with great vigor). "Ally Loo! Hi. Jiddy, Jiddy. Pill. Ally Loo!"

Horses almost do it.

Black Driver (with his eyes starting out of his head) "Lee, den, Lee, dere. Hi. Jiddy, Jiddy. Pill. Ally Loo Leee-e-e!"

They run up the bank, and go down again on the other side at a fearful pace. It is impossible to stop them, and at the bottom there is a deep hollow, full of water. The coach rolls frightfully. The insides scream. The mud and water fly about us. The black driver dances like a madman. Suddenly we are all right by some extraordinary means, and stop to breathe.

A black friend of the black driver is sitting on a fence. The black driver recognizes him by twirling his head round and round like a harlequin, rolling his eyes, shrugging his shoulders, and grinning from ear to ear. He stops short, turns to me and says :

"We shall get you through sa, like a fiddle, and hope a please you when we get you through sa. Old 'ooman at home sir:" chuckling very much. "Outside gentleman sa, he often remember old 'ooman at home, sa," grinning again.

"Aye, aye, we'll take care of the old woman. Don't be afraid."

The black driver grins again, but there is another hole, and beyond that, another bank, close before us. So he stops short: cries (to the horses again) "Easy, Easy den. Ease. Steady. Hi. Jiddy. Pill. Ally. Loo," but never "Lee!" until we are rendered to the very last extremity, and are in the midst of difficulties, extrication from which appears to be all but impossible.

And so we do the ten miles or thereabouts in two hours and a half; breaking no bones, though bruising a great many; and in short getting through the distance, "like a fiddle."

This singular kind of coaching terminates at Fredericksburgh, whence there is a railway to Richmond. The tract of country through which it takes its course was once productive; but the soil has been exhausted by the system of employing a great amount of slave labor in forcing crops, without strengthening the land: and it is now little better than a sandy desert overgrown with trees. Dreary and uninteresting as its aspect is, I was glad to the heart to find anything on which one of the curses of this horrible institution has fallen; and had greater pleasure in contemplating the withered ground, than the richest and most thriving cultivation in the same place could possibly have afforded me.

In this district, as in all others where slavery sits brooding, (I have frequently heard this admitted, even by those who are its warmest advocates:) there is an air of ruin and decay abroad, which is inseparable from the system. The barns and outhouses are mouldering away; the sheds are patched and half roofless; the log cabins (built in Virginia with external chimneys made of clay or wood), are squalid in the last degree. There is no look of decent comfort anywhere. The miserable stations by the railway side; the great wild woodyards, whence the engine is supplied with fuel; the negro children rolling on the ground before the cabin doors, with dogs and pigs; the biped beasts of burden slinking past: gloom and dejection are upon them all.

In the negro car belonging to the train in which we made this journey, were a mother and her children who had just been purchased; the husband and father being left behind with their old owner. The children cried the whole way, and the mother was misery's picture. The champion of Life, Liberty, and the Pursuit of Happiness, who had bought them, rode in the same train; and, every time we stopped, got down to see that they were safe. The black in Sinbad's Travels with one eye in the middle of his forehead which shone like a burning coal, was nature's aristocrat compared with this white gentleman.

It was between six and seven o'clock in the evening, when we drove to the hotel: in front of which, and on the top of the broad flight of steps leading to the door, two or three citizens were balancing themselves on rocking-chairs, and smoking cigars. We found it a very large and elegant establishment, and were as well entertained as travellers need desire to be. The climate being a thirsty one, there was never, at any hour of the day, a scarcity of loungers in the spacious bar, or a cessation of the mixing of cool liquors: but they were a merrier people here, and had musical instruments playing to them o'nights, which it was a treat to hear again.

The next day, and the next, we rode and walked about the town, which is delightfully situated on eight hills, overhanging James River; a sparkling stream, studded here and there with bright islands, or brawling over broken rocks. Although it was yet but the middle of March, the weather in this southern temperature was extremely warm; the peach-trees and magnolias were in full bloom; and the trees were green. In a low ground among the hills, is a valley known as "Bloody Run," from a terrible conflict with the Indians which once occurred there. It is a good place for such a struggle, and, like every other spot I saw associated with any legend of that wild people now so rapidly fading from the earth, interested me very much.

The city is the seat of the local parliament of Virginia; and in its shady legislative halls, some orators were drowsily holding forth to the hot noon day. By dint of constant repetition, however, these constitutional sights had very little more interest for me than so many parochial vestries; and I was glad to exchange this one for a lounge in a well-arranged public library of some ten thousand volumes, and a visit to a tobacco manufactory, where the workmen were all slaves.

I saw in this place the whole process of picking, rolling, pressing, drying, packing in casks, and branding. All the tobacco thus dealt with, was in course of manufacture for chewing; and one would have supposed there was enough in that one storehouse to have filled even the comprehensive jaws of America. In this form, the weed looks like the oil-cake on which we fatten cattle; and even without reference to its consequences, is sufficiently uninviting.

Many of the workmen appeared to be strong men, and it is hardly necessary to add that they were all laboring quietly, then. After two o'clock in the day, they were allowed to sing, a certain number at a time. The hour striking while I was there, some twenty sang a hymn in parts, and sang it by no means ill; pursuing their work meanwhile. A bell rang as I was about to leave, and they all poured forth into a building on the opposite side of the street to dinner. I said several times that I should like to see them at their meal; but as the gentleman to whom I mentioned this desire appeared to be suddenly taken rather deaf, I did not pursue the request. Of their appearance I shall have something to say, presently.

On the following day, I visited a plantation or farm, of about twelve hundred acres, on the opposite bank of the river, Here again, although I went down with the owner of the estate, to "the quarter," as that part of it in which the slaves live is called, I was not invited to enter into any of their huts. All I saw of them, was, that they were very crazy, wretched cabins, near to which groups of half-naked children basked in the sun, or wallowed on the dusty ground. But I believe that this gentleman is a considerate and excellent master, who inherited his fifty slaves, and is neither a buyer nor a seller of human stock; and I am sure, from my own observation and conviction, that he is a kind-hearted, worthy man.

The planter's house was an airy rustic dwelling, that brought Defoe's description of such places strongly to my recollection. The day was very warm, but the blinds being all closed, and the windows and doors set wide open, a shady coolness rustled through the rooms, which was exquisitely refreshing after the glare and heat without. Before the windows was an open piazza, where, in what they call the hot weather—whatever that may be—they sling hammocks, and drink and doze luxuriously. I do not know how their cool refections may taste within the hammocks, but, having experience, I can report that, out of them, the mounds of ices and the bowls of mint-julep and sherry-cobler they make in these latitudes, are refreshments never to be thought of afterwards, in summer, by those who would preserve contented minds.

There are two bridges across the river: one belongs to the railroad, and the other, which is a very crazy affair, is the private property of some old lady in the neighborhood, who levies tolls upon the town's people. Crossing this bridge, on my way back, I saw a notice painted on the gate, cautioning all persons to drive slowly: under a penalty, if the offender were a white man, of five dollars; if a negro, fifteen stripes.

The same decay and gloom that overhang the way by which it is approached, hover above the town of Richmond. There are pretty villas and cheerful houses in its streets, and Nature smiles upon the country round; but jostling its handsome residences, like slavery itself going hand in hand with many lofty virtues, are deplorable tenements, fences unrepaired, walls crumbling into ruinous heaps. Hinting gloomily at things below the surface, these, and many other tokens of the same description, force themselves upon the notice, and are remembered with depressing influence, when livelier features are forgotten.

To those who are happily unaccustomed to them, the countenances in the streets and laboring-places, too, are shocking. All men who know that there are laws against instructing slaves, of which the pains and penalties greatly exceed in their amount the fines imposed on those who maim and torture them, must be prepared to find their faces very low in the scale of intellectual expression. But the darkness—not of skin, but mind—which meets the stranger's eye at every turn; the brutalizing and blotting out of all fairer characters traced by Nature's hand; immeasurably outdo his worst belief. That travelled creation of the great satirist's brain, who fresh from living among horses, peered from a high casement down upon his own kind with trembling horror, was scarcely more repelled and daunted by the sight, than those who look upon some of these faces for the first time must surely be.

I left the last of them behind me in the person of a wretched drudge, who, after running to and fro all day till midnight, and moping in his stealthy winks of sleep upon the stairs betweenwhiles, was washing the dark passages at four o'clock in the morning; and went upon my way with a grateful heart that I was not doomed to live where slavery was, and had never had my senses blunted to its wrongs and horrors in a slave-rocked cradle.

It had been my intention to proceed by James River and Chesapeake Bay to Baltimore; but one of the steamboats being absent from her station through some accident, and the means of conveyance being consequently rendered uncertain, we returned to Washington by the way we had come (there were two constables on board the steamboat, in pursuit of runaway slaves), and halting there again for one night, went on to Baltimore next afternoon.

The most comfortable of all the hotels of which I had any experience in the United States, and they were not a few, is Barnum's, in that city: where the English traveller will find curtains to his bed, for the first and probably the last time in America (this is a disinterested remark, for I never use them) and where he will be likely to have enough water for washing himself, which is not at all a common case.

This capital of the state of Maryland is a bustling busy

town, with a great deal of traffic of various kinds, and in particular of water commerce. That portion of the town which it most favors is none of the cleanest, it is true; but the upper part is of a very different character, and has many agreeable streets and public buildings. The Washington Monument, which is a handsome pillar with a statue on its summit; the Medical College; and the Battle Monument in memory of an engagement with the British at North Point; are the most conspicuous among them.

There is a very good prison in this city, and the state Penitentiary is also among its institutions. In this latter establishment there were two curious cases.

One, was that of a young man, who had been tried for the murder of his father. The evidence was entirely circumstantial, and was very conflicting and doubtful; nor was it possible to assign any motive which could have tempted him to the commission of so tremendous a crime. He had been tried twice; and on the second occasion the jury felt so much hesitation in convicting him, that they found a verdict of manslaughter, or murder in the second degree; which it could not possibly be, as there had, beyond all doubt, been no quarrel or provocation, and if he were guilty at all, he was unquestionably guilty of murder in its broadest and worst signification.

The remarkable feature in the case was, that if the unfortunate deceased were not really murdered by this own son of his, he must have been murdered by his own brother. The evidence lay in a most remarkable manner, between those two. On all the suspicious points the dead man's brother was the witness; all the explanations for the prisoner, (some of them extremely plausible) went, by construction and inference, to inculpate him as plotting to fix the guilt upon his nephew. It must have been one of them: and the jury had to decide between two sets of suspicions, almost equally unnatural, unaccountable, and strange.

The other case, was that of a man who once went to a certain distiller's and stole a copper measure containing a quantity of liquor. He was pursued and taken with the property in his possession, and was sentenced to two years' imprisonment. On coming out of the jail, at the expiration of that term, he went back to the same distiller's and stole the same copper measure containing the same quantity of liquor. There was not the slightest reason to suppose that the man wished to return to prison: indeed everything, but the commission of the offence, made directly against that assumption. There are only two ways of accounting for this extraordinary proceeding. One is, that after undergoing so much for this copper measure he conceived he had established a sort of claim and right to it. The other that, by dint of long thinking about, it had become a monomania with him, and had acquired a fascination which he found it impossible to resist: swelling from an Earthly Copper Gallon into an Ethereal Golden Vat.

After remaining here a couple of days I bound myself to a rigid adherence to the plan I had laid down so recently, and resolved to set forward on our western journey without any more delay. Accordingly, having reduced the luggage within the smallest possible compass (by sending back to New York, to be afterwards forwarded to us in Canada, so much of it as was not absolutely wanted); and having procured the necessary credentials to banking-houses on the way; and having moreover looked for two evenings at the setting sun, with as well defined an idea of the country before us as if we had been going to travel into the very centre of that planet; we left Baltimore by another railway at half-past eight in the morning, and reached the town of York, some sixty miles off, by the early dinner time of the Hotel which was the starting-place of the four-horse coach, wherein we were to proceed to Harrisburg.

This conveyance, the box of which I was fortunate enough to secure, had come down to meet us at the railroad station, and was as muddy and cumbersome as usual. As more passengers were waiting for us at the inn-door, the coachman observed under his breath, in the usual self-communicative voice, looking the while at his mouldy harness as if it were to that he was addressing himself,

"I expect we shall want *the big* coach."

I could not help wondering within myself what the size of this big coach might be, and how many persons it might be designed to hold; for the vehicle which was too small for our purpose was something larger than two English heavy night coaches, and might have been the twin-brother of a French Diligence. My speculations were speedily set at rest, however, for as soon as we had dined, there came rumbling up the street, shaking its sides like a corpulent giant, a kind of barge on wheels. After much blundering and backing, it stopped at the door: rolling heavily from side to side when its other motion had ceased, as if it had taken cold in its damp stable, and between that, and the having been required in its dropsical old age to move any faster pace than a walk, were distressed by shortness of wind.

"If here ain't the Harrisburg mail at last, and dreadful bright and smart to look at too," cried an elderly gentleman in some excitement, "darn my mother!"

I don't know what the sensation of being darned may be, or whether a man's mother has a keener relish or disrelish of the process than anybody else; but if the endurance of this mysterious ceremony by the old lady in question had depended on the accuracy of her son's vision in respect to the abstract brightness and smartness of the Harrisburg mail, she would certainly have undergone its infliction. However, they booked twelve people inside; and the luggage (including such trifles as a large rocking-chair, and a good-sized dining-table) being at length made fast upon the roof, we started off in great state.

At the door of another hotel, there was another passenger to be taken up.

"Any room, sir?" cries the new passenger to the coachman.

"Well there's room enough," replies the coachman, without getting down, or even looking at him.

"There ain't no room at all, sir," bawls a gentleman inside. Which another gentleman (also inside) confirms, by predicting that the attempt to introduce any more passengers "won't fit nohow."

The new passenger, without any expression of anxiety, looks into the coach, and then looks up at the coachman; "Now, how do you mean to fix it?" says he, after a pause: "for I *must* go."

The coachman employs himself in twisting the lash of his whip into a knot, and takes no more notice of the question: clearly signifying that it is anybody's business but his, and that the passengers would do well to fix it, among themselves. In this state of things, matters seem to be approximating to a fix of another kind, when another inside passenger in a corner, who is nearly suffocated, cries faintly,

"I'll get out."

This is no matter of relief or self-congratulation to the driver, for his immovable philosophy is perfectly undisturbed by anything that happens in the coach. Of all things in the world, the coach would seem to be the very last upon his mind. The exchange is made, however, and then the passenger who has given up his seat makes a third upon the box, seating himself in what he calls the middle: that is, with half his person on my legs, and the other half on the driver's.

"Go a-head cap'en," cries the colonel, who directs.

"Gŏ-lāng!" cries the cap'en to his company, the horses, and away we go.

We took up at a rural bar-room, after we had gone a few miles, an intoxicated gentleman, who climbed upon the roof among the luggage, and subsequently slipping off without hurting himself, was seen in the distant perpective reeling back to the grog-shop where we had found him. We also parted with more of our freight at different times, so that when we came to change horses, I was again alone outside.

The coachmen always change with the horses, and are usually as dirty as the coach. The first was dressed like a very shabby English baker; the second like a Russian peasant: for he wore a loose purple camlet robe with a fur collar, tied round his waist with a parti-colored worsted sash; grey trousers; light blue gloves; and a cap of bear-skin. It had by this time come on to rain very heavily, and there was a cold damp mist besides, which penetrated to the skin. I was very glad to take advantage of a stoppage and get down to stretch my legs, shake the water off my great-coat, and swallow the usual anti-temperance recipe for keeping out the cold.

When I mounted to my seat again, I observed a new parcel lying on the coach roof, which I took to be a rather large fiddle in a brown bag. In the course of a few miles, however, I discovered that it had a glazed cap at one end and a pair of muddy shoes at the other; and further observation demonstrated it to be a small boy in a snuff-colored coat, with his arms quite pinioned to his sides, by deep forcing into his pockets. He was, I presume, a relative or friend of the coachman's, as he lay a-top of the luggage with his face towards the rain; and except when a change of position brought his shoes in contact with my hat, he appeared to be asleep. At last, on some occasion of our stopping, this thing slowly upreared itself to the height of three feet six, and fixing its eyes on me, observed in piping accents, with a complaisant yawn, half quenched in an obliging air of friendly patronage, "Well now, stranger, I guess you find this a'most like an English arternoon, hey?"

The scenery which had been tame enough at first, was, for the last ten or twelve miles, beautiful. Our road wound through the pleasant valley of the Susquehanna; the river, dotted with innumerable green islands, lay upon our right; and on the left, a steep ascent, craggy with broken rock, and dark with pine-trees. The mist, wreathing itself into a hundred fantastic shapes, moved solemnly upon the water: and the gloom of evening gave to all an air of mystery and silence which greatly enhance its natural interest.

We crossed this river by a wooden bridge, roofed and covered in on all sides, and nearly a mile in length. It was profoundly dark; perplexed, with great beams, crossing and re-crossing it at every possible angle; and through the broad chinks and crevices in the floor, the rapid river gleamed, far down below, like a legion of eyes. We had no lamps; and as the horses stumbled and floundered through this place, towards the distant speck of dying light, it seemed interminable. I really could not at first persuade myself as we rumbled heavily on, filling the bridge with hollow noises, and I held down my head to save it from the rafters above, but that I was in a painful dream; for I have often dreamed of toiling through such places, and as often argued, even at the time, "this cannot be reality."

At length, however, we emerged upon the streets of Harrisburg, whose feeble lights, reflected dismally from the wet ground, did not shine out upon a very cheerful city. We were soon established in a snug hotel, which though smaller and far less splendid than many we put up at, is raised above them all in my remembrance, by having for its landlord the most obliging, considerate, and gentlemanly person I ever had to deal with.

As we were not to proceed upon our journey until the afternoon, I walked out, after breakfast the next morning, to look about me; and was duly shown a model prison on the solitary system, just erected, and as yet without an inmate; the trunk of an old tree to which Harris, the first settler here (afterwards buried under it) was tied by hostile Indians, with his funeral pile about him, when he was saved by the timely appearance of a friendly party on the opposite shore of the river; the local legislature (for there was another of those bodies here, again, in full debate); and the other curiosities of the town.

I was very much interested in looking over a number of treaties made from time to time with the poor Indians, signed by the different chiefs at the period of their ratification, and preserved in the office of the Secretary to the Commonwealth. These signatures, traced of course by their own hands, are rough drawings of the creatures or weapons they were called after. Thus the Great Turtle makes a crooked pen-and-ink outline of a great turtle; the Buffalo sketches a buffalo; the War Hatchet sets a rough image of that weapon for his mark. So with the Arrow, the Fish, the Scalp, the Big Canoe, and all of them.

I could not but think—as I looked at the feeble and tremulous production of hands which could draw the longest arrow to the head in a stout elk-horn bow, or split a bead or feather with a rifle-ball—of Crabbe's musings over the Parish Register, and the irregular scratches made with a pen, by men who would plough a lengthy furrow straight from end to end. Nor could I help bestowing many sorrowful thoughts upon the simple warriors whose hands and hearts were set there, in all truth and honesty; and who only learned in course of time from white men how to break their faith, and quibble out of forms and bonds. I wondered, too, how many times the credulous Big Turtle, or trusting Little Hatchet, had put his mark to treaties which were falsely read to him; and had signed away, he knew not what, until it went and cast him loose upon the new possessors of the land, a savage indeed.

Our host announced, before our early dinner, that some members of the legislative body proposed to do us the honor of calling. He had kindly yielded up to us his wife's own little parlor, and when I begged that he would show them in, I saw him look with painful apprehension at its pretty carpet; though, being otherwise occupied at the time, the cause of his uneasiness did not occur to me.

It certainly would have been more pleasant to all parties concerned, and would not, I think, have compromised their independence in any material degree, if some of these gentlemen had not only yielded to the prejudice in favor of spittoons, but had abandoned themselves, for the moment, even to the conventional absurdity of pocket-handkerchiefs.

It still continued to rain heavily, and when we went down to the Canal Boat (for that was the mode of conveyance by which we were to proceed) after dinner, the weather was as unpromising and obstinately wet as one would desire to see. Nor was the sight of this canal boat, in which we were to spend three or four days, by any means a cheerful one; as it involved some uneasy speculations concerning the disposal of the passengers at night, and opened a wide field of inquiry touching the other domestic arrangements of the establishment, which was sufficiently disconcerting.

However, there it was—a barge with a little house in it,

viewed from the outside; and a caravan at a fair, viewed from within: the gentlemen being accommodated, as the spectators usually are, in one of those locomotive museums of penny wonders; and the ladies being partitioned off bv a red curtain, after the manner of the dwarfs and giants in the same establishments, whose private lives are passed in rather close exclusiveness.

We sat here, looking silently at the row of little tables, which extended down both sides of the cabin, and listening to the rain as it dripped and pattered on the boat, and plashed with a dismal merriment in the water, until the arrival of the railway train, for whose final contribution to our stock of passengers, our departure was alone deferred. It brought a great many boxes, which were bumped and tossed upon the roof, almost as painfully as if they had been deposited on one's own head, without the intervention of a porter's knot; and several damp gentlemen, whose clothes, on their drawing round the stove, began to steam again. No doubt it would have been a thought more comfortable if the driving rain, which now poured down more soakingly than ever, had admitted of a window being opened, or if our number had been something less than thirty; but there was scarcely time to think as much, when a train of three horses was attached to the tow-rope, the boy upon the leader smacked his whip, the rudder creaked and groaned complainingly, and we had begun our journey.

---

## CHAPTER X.

SOME FURTHER ACCOUNT OF THE CANAL BOAT, ITS DOMESTIC ECONOMY, AND ITS PASSENGERS. JOURNEY TO PITTSBURG ACROSS THE ALLEGHANY MOUNTAINS. PITTSBURG.

As it continued to rain most perseveringly, we all remained below: the damp gentlemen round the stove, gradually becoming mildewed by the action of the fire; and the dry gentlemen lying at full length upon the seats, or slumbering uneasily with their faces on the tables, or walking up and down the cabin, which it was barely possible for a man of the middle height to do, without making bald places on his head by scraping it against the roof. At about six o'clock, all the small tables were put together to form one long table, and everybody sat down to tea, coffee, bread, butter, salmon, shad, liver, steak, potatoes, pickles, ham, chops, black puddings, and sausages.

"Will you try," said my opposite neighbor, handing me a dish of potatoes, broken up in milk and butter, "will you try some of these fixings?"

There are few words which perform such various duties as this word "fix." It is the Caleb Quotem of the American vocabulary. You call upon a gentleman in a country town, and his help informs you that he is "fixing himself" just now, but will be down directly: by which you are to understand that he is dressing. You inquire, on board a steamboat, of a fellow passenger, whether breakfast will be ready soon, and he tells you he should think so, for when he was last below, they were "fixing the tables:" in other words, laying the cloth. You beg a porter to collect your luggage, and he entreats you not to be uneasy, for he'll "fix it presently;" and if you complain of indisposition, you are advised to have recourse to Doctor so and so, who will "fix you" in no time.

One night, I ordered a bottle of mulled wine at an hotel where I was staying, and waited a long time for it; at length it was put upon the table with an apology from the landlord that he feared it wasn't "fixed properly." And I recollect once, at a stage-coach dinner overhearing a very stern gentleman demand of a waiter who presented him with a plate of underdone roast-beef, "whether he called *that*, fixing God A'mighty's vittles?"

There is no doubt that the meal, at which the invitation was tendered to me which has occasioned this digression, was disposed of somewhat ravenously; and that the gentlemen thrust the broad-bladed knives and the two-pronged forks further down their throats than I ever saw the same weapons go before, except in the hands of a skillful juggler: but no man sat down until the ladies were seated; or omitted any little act of politeness which could contribute to their comfort. Nor did I ever once, on any occasion, anywhere, during my rambles in America, see a woman exposed to the slightest act of rudeness, incivilty, or even inattention.

By the time the meal was over, the rain, which seemed to have worn itself out by coming down so fast, was nearly over too; and it became feasible to go on deck: which was a great relief, notwithstanding its being a very small deck, and being rendered still smaller by the luggage, which was heaped together in the middle under a tarpaulin covering; leaving, on either side, a path so narrow, that it became a science to walk to and fro without tumbling overboard into the canal. It was somewhat embarrassing at first, too, to have to duck nimbly every five minutes whenever the man at the helm cried "Bridge!" and sometimes, when the cry was "Low Bridge," to lie down nearly flat. But custom familiarizes one to anything, and there were so many bridges that it took a very short time to get used to this.

As night came on, and we drew in sight of the first range of hills, which are the outposts of the Alleghany mountains, the scenery, which had been uninteresting hitherto, became more bold and striking. The wet ground reeked and smoked, after the heavy fall of rain; and the croaking of the frogs (whose noise in these parts is almost incredible) sounded as though a million of fairy teams with bells, were travelling through the air, and keeping pace with us. The night was cloudy yet, but moonlight too: and when we crossed the Susquehanna river—over which there is an extraordinary wooden bridge with two galleries, one above the other, so that even there, two boat-teams meeting, may pass without confusion—it was wild and grand.

I have mentioned my having been in some uncertainty and doubt, at first, relative to the sleeping arrangements on board this boat. I remained in the same vague state of mind until ten o'clock or thereabouts, when going below, I found suspended on either side of the cabin, three long tiers of hanging book-shelves, designed apparently for volumes of the small octavo size. Looking with greater attention at these contrivances (wondering to find such literary preparations in such a place), I descried on each shelf a sort of microscopic sheet and blanket; then I began dimly to comprehend that the passengers were the library, and that they were to be arranged, edge-wise, on those shelves, till morning.

I was assisted to this conclusion by seeing some of them gathered round the master of the boat, at one of the tables, drawing lots with all the anxieties and passions of gamesters depicted in their countenances; while others, with small pieces of cardboard in their hands, were groping among the shelves in search of numbers corresponding with those they had drawn. As soon as any gentleman found his number, he took possession of it by immediately undressing himself and crawling into bed. The rapidity with which an agitated gambler subsided into a snoring slumberer, was one of the most singular effects I have ever witnessed. As to the ladies, they were already a-bed, behind the red curtain, which was carefully drawn and pinned up the centre; though as every cough, or sneeze, or whisper, behind this curtain, was perfectly audible before it, we had still a lively consciousness of their society.

The politeness of the person in authority had secured to me a shelf in a nook near this red curtain, in some degree removed from the great body of sleepers: to which place I retired, with many acknowledgments to him for his attention. I found it, on after-measurement, just the width of an ordinary sheet of Bath post letter-paper; and I was at first in some uncertainty as to the best means of getting into it. But the shelf being a bottom one, I finally determined on lying upon the floor, rolling gently in, stopping immediately I touched the mattress, and remaining for the night with that side uppermost, whatever it might be. Luckily, I came upon my back at exactly the right moment. I was much alarmed on looking upward, to see, by the shape of his half yard of sacking (which his weight had bent into an exceedingly tight bag), that there was a very heavy gentleman above me, whom the slender cords seemed quite incapable of holding; and I could not help reflecting upon the grief of my wife and family in the event of his coming down in the night. But as I could not have got up again without a severe bodily struggle, which might have alarmed the ladies; and as I had nowhere to go to, even if I had; I shut my eyes upon the danger, and remained there.

One of two remarkable circumstances is indisputably a fact, with reference to that class of society who travel in these boats. Either they carry their restlessness to such a pitch that they never sleep at all; or they expectorate in dreams, which would be a remarkable mingling of the real and ideal. All night long, and every night, on this canal, there was a perfect storm and tempest of spitting; and once my coat being in the very centre of a hurricane sustained by five gentlemen (which moved vertically, strictly carrying out Reid's Theory of the Law of Storms,) I was fain the next morning to lay it on the deck, and rub it down with fair water before it was in a condition to be worn again.

Between five and six o'clock in the morning we got up, and some of us went on deck, to give them an opportunity of taking the shelves down; while others, the morning being very cold, crowded round the rusty stove, cherishing the newly kindled fire, and filling the grate with those voluntary contributions of which they had been so liberal all night. The washing accommodations were primitive. There was a tin ladle chained to the deck, with which every gentleman who thought it necessary to cleanse himself (many were superior to this weakness), fished the dirty water out of the canal, and poured it into a tin basin, secured in like manner. There was also a jack-towel. And, hanging up before a little looking-glass in the bar, in the immediate vicinity of the bread and cheese and biscuits, were a public comb and hair-brush.

At eight o'clock, the shelves being taken down and put away, and the tables joined together, everybody sat down to the tea, coffee, bread, butter, salmon, shad, liver, steak, potatoes, pickles, ham, chops, black puddings, and sausages, all over again. Some were fond of compounding this variety, and having it all on their plates at once. As each gentleman got through his own personal amount of tea, coffee, bread, butter, salmon, shad, liver, steak, potatoes, pickles, ham, chops, black puddings, and sausages, he rose up and walked off. When everybody had done with everything, the fragments were cleared away: and one of the waiters appearing anew in the character of a barber, shaved such of the company as desired to be shaved; while the remainder looked on, or yawned over their newspapers. Dinner was breakfast again, without the tea and coffee; and supper and breakfast were identical.

There was a man on board this boat, with a light fresh-colored face, and a pepper-and-salt suit of clothes, who was the most inquisitive fellow that can possibly be imagined. He never spoke otherwise than interrogatively. He was an embodied inquiry. Sitting down or standing up, still or moving, walking the deck or taking his meals, there he was, with a great note of interrogation in each eye, two in his cocked ears, two more in his turned-up nose and chin, at least half a dozen more about the corners of his mouth, and the largest one of all in his hair, which was brushed pertly off his forehead in a flaxen clump. Every button in his clothes said, "Eh? What's that? Did you speak? Say that again, will you?" He was always wide awake, like the enchanted bride who drove her husband frantic; always restless; always thirsting for answers; perpetually seeking and never finding. There never was such a curious man.

I wore a fur great-coat at that time, and before we were well clear of the wharf, he questioned me concerning it, and its price, and where I bought it, and when, and what fur it was, and what it weighed, and what it cost. Then he took notice of my watch, and asked what *that* cost, and whether it was a French watch, and where I got it, and how I got, and whether I bought it or had it given me, and how it went, and where the keyhole was, and when I wound it, every night or every morning, and whether I ever forgot to wind it at all, and if I did, what then? Where had I been to last, and where I was going next, and where was I going after that, and had I seen the President, and what did he say, and what did I say, and what did he say when I had said that? Eh? Lor now! do tell!

Finding that nothing would satisfy him, I evaded his questions after the first score or two, and in particular pleaded ignorance respecting the name of the fur whereof the coat was made. I am unable to say whether this was the reason, but that coat fascinated him ever afterwards; he usually kept close behind me as I walked, and moved as I moved, that he might look at it the better; and he frequently dived into narrow places after me at the risk of his life, that he might have the satisfaction of passing his hand up the back, and rubbing it the wrong way.

We had another odd specimen on board, of a different kind. This was a thin-faced, spare-figured man of middle age and stature, dressed in a dusty drabbish-colored suit, such as I never saw before. He was perfectly quiet during the first part of the journey: indeed I don't remember having so much as seen him until he was brought out by circumstances, as great men often are. The conjunction of events which made him famous, happened, briefly, thus.

The canal extends to the foot of the mountain, and there, of course, it stops; the passengers being conveyed across it by land carriage, and taken on afterwards by another canal boat, the counterpart of the first, which awaits them on the other side. There are two canal lines of passage-boats; one is called The Express, and one (a cheaper one) The Pioneer. The Pioneer gets first to the mountain, and waits for the Express people to come up; both sets of passengers being conveyed across at the same time. We were the Express company; but when we had crossed the mountain, and come to the second boat, the proprietors took it into their heads to draft all the Pioneers into it likewise, so that we were five-and-forty at least, and the accession of passengers was not all of that kind which improved the prospect of sleeping at night. Our people grumbled at this, as people do in such cases; but suffered the boat to be towed off with the whole freight aboard nevertheless; and away we went down the canal. At home,

I should have protested lustily, but being a foreigner here, I held my peace. Not so this passenger. He cleft a path among the people on deck (we were nearly all on deck), and without addressing anybody whomsoever, soliloquized as follows:

"This may suit *you*, this may, but it don't suit *me*. This may be all very well with Down Easters, and men of Boston raising, but it won't suit my figure no how; and no two ways about *that;* and so I tell you. Now! I'm from the brown forests of the Mississippi, *I* am, and when the sun shines on me, it does shine—a little. It don't glimmer where *I* live, the sun don't. No. I'm a brown forester, I am. I an't a Johnny Cake. There are no smooth skins where I live. We're rough men there. Rather. If Down Easters and men of Boston raising like this, I'm glad of it, but I'm none of that raising nor of that breed. No. This company wants a little fixing, *it* does. I'm the wrong sort of man for 'em, *I* am. They won't like me, *they* won't. This is piling of it up, a little too moŭntaĭnoŭs, this is." At the end of every one of these short sentences he turned upon his heel and walked the other way; checking himself abruptly when he had finished another short sentence, and turning back again.

It is impossible for me to say what terrific meaning was hidden in the words of this brown forester, but I know that the other passengers looked on in a sort of admiring horror, and that presently the boat was put back to the wharf, and as many of the Pioneers as could be coaxed or bullied into going away, were got rid of.

When we started again, some of the boldest spirits on board made bold to say to the obvious occasion of this improvement in our prospects, "Much obliged to you, sir:" whereunto the brown forester (waving his hand, and still walking up and down as before), replied, "No you an't. You're none o' my raising. You may act for yourselves, *you* may. I have pinted out the way. Down Easters and Johnny Cakes can follow if they please. I an't a Johnny Cake, *I* an't. I am from the brown forests of the Mississippi, *I* am"—and so on, as before.

He was unanimously voted one of the tables for his bed at night—there is a great contest for the tables—in consideration of his public service: and he had the warmest corner by the stove throughout the rest of the journey. But I never could find out that he did anything except sit there; nor did I hear him speak again until, in the midst of the bustle and turmoil of getting the luggage ashore in the dark at Pittsburg, I stumbled over him as he sat smoking a cigar on the cabin steps, and heard him muttering to himself, with a short laugh of defiance, "I an't a Johnny Cake, *I* an't. I'm from the brown forests of the Mississippi, *I* am, damme!" I am inclined to argue from this, that he had never left off saying so; but I could not make affidavit of that part of the story, if required to do so by my Queen and Country.

As we have not reached Pittsburg yet, however, in the order of our narrative, I may go on to remark that breakfast was perhaps the least desirable meal of the day, as an addition to the many savory odors arising from the eatables already mentioned, there were whiffs of gin, whiskey, brandy, and rum, from the little bar hard by, and a decided seasoning of stale tobacco. Many of the gentlemen passengers were far from particular in respect of their linen, which was in some cases as yellow as the little rivulets that had trickled from the corners of their mouths in chewing, and dried there. Nor was the atmosphere quite free from zephyr whisperings of the thirty beds which had just been cleared away, and of which we were further and more pressingly reminded by the occasional appearance on the table-cloth of a kind of Game, not mentioned in the Bill of Fare.

And yet despite these oddities—and even they had, for me at least, a humor of their own—there was much in this mode of travelling which I heartily enjoyed at the time, and look back upon with great pleasure. Even the running up, bare-necked, at five o'clock in the morning, from the tainted cabin to the dirty deck; scooping up the icy water, plunging one's head into it, and drawing it out, all fresh and glowing with the cold; was a good thing. The fast, brisk walk upon the towing-path, between that time and breakfast, when every vein and artery seemed to tingle with health; the exquisite beauty of the opening day, when light came gleaming off from everything; the lazy motion of the boat, when one lay idly on the deck, looking through, rather than at, the deep blue sky; the gliding on at night, so noiselessly, past frowning hills, sullen with dark trees, and sometimes angry in one red burning spot high up, where unseen men lay crouching round a fire; the shining out of the bright stars, undisturbed by noise of wheels or steam, or any other sound than the liquid rippling of the water as the boat went on: all these were pure delights.

Then, there were new settlements and detached log cabins and frame-houses, full of interest for strangers from an old country: cabins with simple ovens, outside, made of clay; and lodgings for the pigs nearly as good as many of the human quarters; broken windows, patched with worn-out hats, old clothes, old boards, fragments of blankets and paper; and home-made dressers standing in the open air without the door, whereon was ranged the household store, not hard to count, of earthen jars and pots. The eye was pained to see the stumps of great trees thickly strewn in every field of wheat, and seldom to lose the eternal swamp and dull morass, with hundreds of rotten trunks and twisted branches steeped in its unwholsome water. It was quite sad and oppressive, to come upon great tracts where settlers had been burning down the trees, and where their wounded bodies lay about, like those of murdered creatures, while here and there some charred and blackened giant reared aloft two withered arms, and seemed to call down curses on his foes. Sometimes, at night, the way wound through some lonely gorge, like a mountain pass in Scotland, shining and coldly glittering in the light of the moon, and so closed in by high steep hills all round, that there seemed to be no egress save through the narrower path by which we had come, until one rugged hill-side seemed to open, and, shutting out the moonlight as we passed into its gloomy throat, wrapped our new course in shade and darkness. We had left Harrisburg on Friday. On Sunday morning we arrived at the foot of the mountain, which is crossed by railroad. There are ten inclined planes; five *a*scending, and five *de*scending; the carriages are dragged up the former, and let slowly down the latter, by means of stationary engines; the comparatively level spaces between being traversed, sometimes by horse, and sometimes by engine power, as the case demands. Occasionally the rails are laid upon the extreme verge of a giddy precipice; and looking from the carriage window, the traveller gazes sheer down, without a stone or scrap of fence between, into the mountain depths below. The journey is very carefully made, however; only two carriages travelling together; and, while proper precautions are taken, is not to be dreaded for its dangers.

It was very pretty travelling thus, at a rapid pace along the heights of the mountain in a keen wind, to look down into a valley full of light and softness: catching glimpses, through the tree-tops, of scattered cabins; children running to the doors; dogs bursting out to bark, whom we could see without hearing; terrified pigs scampering homewards; families sitting out in their rude gardens; cows gazing upward with a stupid indifference; men in their shirt-sleeves looking on at their unfinished houses, planning out to-morrow's work; and we riding onward, high above them, like a whirlwind. It was amusing, too, when we had dined, and rattled down a steep pass, having no other moving power than the weight of the carriages themselves, to see the engine released, long after us, come buzzing down alone, like a great insect, its back of green and gold so shining in the sun, that if it had spread a pair of wings and soared away, no one would have had occasion, as I fancied, for the least surprise. But it stopped short of us in a very business-like manner when we reached the canal; and before we left the wharf, went panting up this hill again, with the passengers who had waited our arrival for the means of traversing the road by which we had come.

On the Monday evening, furnace fires and clanking hammers on the banks of the canal, warned us that we approached the termination of this part of our journey. After going through another dreamy place—a long aqueduct across the Alleghany River, which was stranger than the bridge at

Harrisburg, being a vast low wooden chamber full of water—we emerged upon that ugly confusion of backs of buildings and crazy galleries and stairs, which always abuts on water, whether it be river, sea, canal, or ditch: and were at Pittsburg.

Pittsburg is like Birmingham in England; at least its townspeople say so. Setting aside the streets, the shops, the houses, wagons, factories, public buildings, and population, perhaps it may be. It certainly has a great quantity of smoke hanging about it, and is famous for its iron-works. Besides the prison to which I have already referred, this town contains a pretty arsenal and other institutions. It is very beautifully situated on the Alleghany River, over which there are two bridges; and the villas of the wealthier citizens sprinkled about the high grounds in the neighborhood, are pretty enough. We lodged at a most excellent hotel, and were admirably served. As usual it was full of boarders, was very large, and had a broad colonnade to every story of the house.

We tarried here, three days. Our next point was Cincinnati: and as this was a steamboat journey, and western steamboats usually blow up one or two a week in the season, it was advisable to collect opinions in reference to the comparative safety of the vessels bound that way, then lying in the river. One called The Messenger was the best recommended. She had been advertised to start positively, every day for a fortnight or so, and had not gone yet, nor did her captain seem to have any very fixed intention on the subject. But this is the custom: for if the law were to bind down a free and independent citizen to keep his word with the public, what would become with the liberty of the subject? Besides, it is in the way of trade. And if passengers be decoyed in the way of trade, and people be inconvenienced in the way of trade, what man, who is a sharp tradesman himself, shall say "We must put a stop to this?"

Impressed by the deep solemnity of the public announcement, I (being then ignorant of these usages) was for hurrying on board in a breathless state, immediately; but receiving private and confidential information that the boat would certainly not start until Friday, April the First, we made ourselves very comfortable in the mean while, and went on board at noon that day.

## CHAPTER XI.

### FROM PITTSBURG TO CINCINNATI IN A WESTERN STEAMBOAT. CINCINNATI.

THE Messenger was one among a crowd of high-pressure steamboats, clustered together by the wharf-side, which, looked down upon from the rising ground that forms the landing-place, and backed by the lofty bank on the opposite side of the river, appeared no larger than so many floating models. She had some forty passengers on board, exclusive of the poorer persons on the lower deck; and in half an hour, or less, proceeded on her way.

We had for ourselves, a tiny state-room with two berths in it, opening out of the ladies' cabin. There was, undoubtedly, something satisfactory in this "location," inasmuch as it was in the stern, and we had been a great many times very gravely recommended to keep as far aft as possible, "because the steamboats generally blew up forward." Nor was this an unnecessary caution, as the occurrence and circumstances of more than one such fatality during our stay sufficiently testified. Apart from this source of self-congratulation, it was an unspeakable relief to have any place, no matter how confined, where one could be alone: and as the row of little chambers of which this was one, had each a second glass-door besides that in the ladies' cabin, which opened on a narrow gallery outside the vessel, where the other passengers seldom came, and where one could sit in peace and gaze upon the shifting prospect, we took possession of our new quarters with much pleasure.

If the native packets I have already described be unlike anything we are in the habit of seeing on water, these western vessels are still more foreign to all the ideas we are accustomed to entertain of boats. I hardly know what to liken them to, or how to describe them.

In the first place, they have no mast, cordage, tackle, rigging, or other such boat-like gear; nor have they anything in their shape at all calculated to remind one of a boat's head, stern, sides, or keel. Except that they are in the water, and display a couple of paddle-boxes, they might be intended, for anything that appears to the contrary, to perform some unknown service, high and dry, upon a mountain top. There is no visible deck, even: nothing but a long, black, ugly roof, covered with burnt-out feathery sparks; above which tower two iron chimneys, and a hoarse escape valve, and a glass steerage-house. Then, in order as the eye descends towards the water, are the sides, and doors, and windows of the state-rooms, jumbled as oddly together as though they formed a small street, built by the varying tastes of a dozen men: the whole is supported on beams and pillars resting on a dirty barge, but a few inches above the water's edge: and in the narrow space between this upper structure and this barge's deck, are the furnace fires and machinery, open at the sides to every wind that blows, and every storm of rain it drives along its path.

Passing one of these boats at night, and seeing the great body of fire, exposed as I have just described, that rages and roars beneath the frail pile of painted wood: the machinery, not warded off or guarded in any way, but doing its work in the midst of the crowd of idlers and emigrants and children, who throng the lower deck: under the management, too, of reckless men whose acquaintance with its mysteries may have been of six months' standing: one feels directly that the wonder is, not that there should be so many fatal accidents, but that any journey should be safely made.

Within, there is one long narrow cabin, the whole length of the boat; from which the state-rooms open, on both sides. A small portion of it at the stern is partitioned off for the ladies; and the bar is at the opposite extreme. There is a long table down the centre, and at either end a stove. The washing apparatus is forward, on the deck. It is a little better than on board the canal boat, but not much. In all modes of travelling, the American customs, with reference to the means of personal cleanliness and wholesome ablution, are extremely negligent and filthy; and I strongly incline to the belief that a considerable amount of illness is referable to this cause.

We are to be on board the Messenger three days: arriving at Cincinnati (barring accidents) on Monday morning. There are three meals a day. Breakfast at seven, dinner at half-past twelve, supper about six. At each, there are a great many small dishes and plates upon the table, with very little in them; so that although there is every appearance of a mighty "spread," there is seldom really more than a joint: except for those who fancy slices of beet-root, shreds of dried beef, complicated entanglements of yellow pickle; maize, Indian corn, apple-sauce, and pumpkin.

Some people fancy all these little dainties together (and sweet preserves beside), by way of relish to their roast pig. They are generally those dyspeptic ladies and gentlemen who eat unheard-of quantities of hot corn bread (almost as good for the digestion as a kneaded pin-cushion) for breakfast and for supper. Those who do not observe this custom, and who help themselves several times instead, usually suck their knives and forks meditatively, until they have decided what to take next: then pull them out of their mouths: put them in the dish; help themselves; and fall to work again. At dinner, there is nothing to drink upon the table, but great jugs full of cold water. Nobody says anything, at any meal, to anybody. All the passengers are very dismal, and seem to have tremendous secrets weighing on their minds. There is no conversation, no laughter, no cheerfulness, no sociality, except in spitting; and that is done in silent fellowship round the stove, when the meal is over. Every man sits down, dull and languid; swallows his fare as if breakfasts, dinners, and suppers, were necessities of nature never to be coupled with recreation or enjoyment; and having bolted his food in a gloomy silence bolts himself, in the same state. But for these animal observances, you might suppose the whole male portion of the company to be the melancholy ghosts of departed bookkeepers, who had fallen dead at the desk: such is their weary air of business and calculation. Undertakers on duty would be sprightly beside them; and a collation of funeral-baked meats in comparison with these meals, would be a sparkling festivity.

The people are all alike, too. There is no diversity of character. They travel about on the same errands, say and do the same things in exactly the same manner, and follow in the same dull cheerless round. All down the long table, there is scarcely a man who is in anything different from his neighbor. It is quite a relief to have, sitting opposite, that little girl of fifteen with the loquacious chin: who, to do her justice, acts up to it, and fully identifies nature's handwriting, for of all the small chatterboxes that ever invaded the repose of drowsy ladies' cabin, she is the first and foremost. The beautiful girl, who sits a little beyond her—farther down the table there—married the young man with the dark whiskers, who sits beyond *her*, only last month. They are going to settle in the very Far West, where he has lived four years, but where she has never been. They were both overturned in a stage-coach the other day (a bad omen anywhere else, where overturns are not so common), and his head, which bears the marks of a recent wound, is bound up still. She was hurt too, at the same time, and lay insensible for some days; bright as her eyes are, now.

Further down still, sits a man who is going some miles beyond their place of destination, to "improve" a newly discovered copper mine. He carries the village—that is to be—with him: a few frame cottages, and an apparatus for smelting the copper. He carries its people too. They are partly American and partly Irish, and herd together on the lower deck; where they amused themselves last evening till the night was pretty far advanced, by alternately firing off pistols and singing hymns.

They, and the very few who have been left at table twenty minutes, rise, and go away. We do so too; and passing through our little state-room, resume our seats in the quiet gallery without.

A fine broad river always, but in some parts much wider than in others: and then there is usually a green island, covered with trees, dividing it into two streams. Occasionally, we stop for a few minutes, maybe to take in wood, maybe for passengers, at some small town or village (I ought to say city, every place is a city here); but the banks are for the most part deep solitudes, overgrown with trees, which, hereabouts, are already in leaf and very green. For miles, and miles, and miles, these solitudes are unbroken by any sign of human life or trace of human footsteps; nor is anything seen to move about them but the blue jay, whose color is so bright, and yet so delicate, that it looks like a flying flower. At lengthened intervals a log-cabin, with its little space of cleared land about it, nestles under a rising ground, and sends its thread of blue smoke curling up into the sky. It stands in the corner of the poor field of wheat, which is full of great unsightly stumps, like earthy butchers'-blocks. Sometimes the ground is only just now cleared: the felled trees lying yet upon the soil: and the log-house only this morning begun. As we pass this clearing, the settler leans upon his axe or hammer, and looks wistfully at the people from the world. The children creep out of the temporary hut, which is like a gipsy tent upon the ground, and clap their hands and shout. The dog only glances round at us; and then looks up into his master's face again, as if he were rendered uneasy by any suspension of the common business, and had nothing more to do with pleasures. And still there is the same, eternal foreground. The river had washed away its banks, and stately trees have fallen down into the stream. Some have been there so long, that they are mere dry grizzly skeletons. Some have just toppled over, and having earth yet about their roots, are bathing their green heads in the river, and putting forth new shoots and branches. Some are almost sliding down, as you look at them. And some were drowned so long ago, that their bleached arms start out from the middle of the current, and seem to try to grasp the boat, and drag it under water.

Through such a scene as this, the unwieldy machine takes its hoarse sullen way: venting, at every revolution of the paddles, a loud high-pressure blast; enough, one would think, to waken up the host of Indians who lie buried in a great mound yonder: so old, that mighty oaks and other forest trees have struck their roots into its earth; and so high, that it is a hill, even among the hills that Nature planted round it. The very river, as though it shared one's feelings of compassion for the extinct tribes who lived so pleasantly here, in their blessed ignorance of white existence, hundreds of years ago, steals out of its way to ripple near this mound: and there are few places where the Ohio sparkles more brightly than in the Big Grave Creek.

All this I see as I sit in the little stern-gallery mentioned just now. Evening slowly steals upon the landscape, and changes it before me, when we stop to set some emigrants ashore.

Five men, as many women, and a little girl. All their worldly goods are a bag, a large chest and an old chair: one, old, high-backed, rush-bottomed chair: a solitary settler in itself. They are rowed ashore in the boat, while the vessel stands a little off awaiting its return, the water being shallow. They are landed at the foot of a high bank, on the summit of which are a few log cabins, attainable only by a long winding path. It is growing dusk; but the sun is very red, and shines in the water and on some of the tree-tops, like fire.

The men get out of the boat first; help out the women; take out the bag, the chest, the chair; bid the rowers "good bye;" and shove the boat off for them. At the first plash of the oars in the water, the oldest woman of the party sits down in the old chair, close to the water's edge, without speaking a word. None of the others sit down, though the chest is large enough for many seats. They all stand where they landed, as if stricken into stone; and look after the boat. So they remain, quite still and silent: the old woman and her old chair, in the centre; the bag and chest upon the shore, without anybody heeding them: all eyes fixed upon the boat. It comes alongside, is made fast, the men jump on board, the engine is put in motion, and we go hoarsely on again. There they stand yet, without the motion of a hand. I can see them, through my glass, when, in the distance and increasing darkness, they are mere specks to the eye: lingering there still: the old woman in the old chair, and all the rest about her: not stirring in the least degree. And thus I slowly lose them.

The night is dark, and we proceed within the shadow of the wooded bank, which makes it darker. After gliding past the sombre maze of boughs for a long time, we come upon an open space where the tall trees are burning. The shape of every branch and twig is expressed in a deep red glow, and as the light wind stirs and ruffles it, they seem to vegetate in fire. It is such a sight as we read of in legends of enchanted forests: saving that it is sad to see these noble works wasting away so awfully, alone; and to think how many years must come and go before the magic that created them will rear their like upon this ground again. But the time will come: and when, in their changed ashes, the growth of centuries unborn has struck its roots, the restless men of distant ages will repair to these again unpeopled solitudes; and their fellows, in cities far away, that slumber now, perhaps, beneath the rolling sea, will read, in language strange to any ears in being now but very old to them, of primeval forests where the axe was never heard, and where the jungled ground was never trodden by a human foot.

Midnight and sleep blot out these scenes and thoughts: and when the morning shines again, it gilds the house-tops of a lively city, before whose broad paved wharf the boat is moored: with other boats, and flags, and moving wheels, and hum of men around it; as though there were not a solitary or silent rood of ground within the compass of a thousand miles.

Cincinnati is a beautiful city; cheerful, thriving, and animated. I have not often seen a place that commends itself so favorably and pleasantly to a stranger at the first glance as this does: with its clean houses of red and white, its well-paved roads, and foot-ways of bright tile. Nor does it become less prepossessing on a closer acquaintance. The streets are broad and airy, the shops extremely good, the private residences remarkable for their elegance and neatness. There is something of invention and fancy in the varying styles of these latter erections, which, after the dull company of the steamboat, is perfectly delightful, as conveying an assurance that there are such qualities still in existence. The disposition to ornament these pretty villas and render them attractive, leads to the culture of trees and flowers, and the laying out of well-kept gardens, the sight of which, to those who walk along the streets, is inexpressibly refreshing and agreeable. I was quite charmed with the appearance of the town, and its adjoining suburb of Mount Auburn; from which the city, lying in an amphitheatre of hills, forms a picture of remarkable beauty, and is seen to great advantage.

There happened to be a great Temperance Convention held here on the day after our arrival; and as the order of march brought the procession under the windows of the hotel in which we lodged, when they started in the morning, I had a good opportunity of seeing it. It comprised several thousand men; the members of various "Washington Auxiliary Temperance Societies;" and was marshalled by officers on horseback, who cantered briskly up and down the line, with scarves and ribbons of bright colors fluttering out behind them gaily. There were bands of music too, and banners out of number: and it was a fresh, holiday-looking concourse altogether.

I was particularly pleased to see the Irishmen, who formed a distinct society among themselves, and mustered very strong with their green scarves; carrying their national Harp and their Portrait of Father Mathew, high above the people's heads. They looked as jolly and good-humored as ever; and, working (here) the hardest for their living and doing any kind of sturdy labor that came in their way, were the most independent fellows there, I thought.

The banners were very well painted, and flaunted down the street famously. There was the smiting of the rock, and the gushing forth of the waters; and there was a temperate man with "considerable of a hatchet" (as the standard-bearer would probably have said), aiming a deadly blow at a serpent which was apparently about to spring upon him from the top of a barrel of spirits. But the chief feature of this part of the show was a huge allegorical device, borne among the ship-carpenters, on one side whereof the steamboat Alcohol was represented bursting her boiler and exploding with a great crash, while upon the other, the good ship Temperance sailed away with a fair wind, to the heart's content of the captain, crew, and passengers.

After going round the town, the procession repaired to a certain appointed place, where as the printed programme set forth, it would be received by the children of the different free schools, "singing Temperance Songs." I was prevented from getting there in time to hear these Little Warblers, or to report upon this novel kind of vocal entertainment: novel, at least, to me: but I found, in a large open space, each society gathered round its own banners, and listening in silent attention to its own orator. The speeches, judging from the little I could hear of them, were certainly adapted to the occasion, as having that degree of relationship to cold water which wet blankets may claim: but the main thing was the conduct and appearance of the audience throughout the day; and that was admirable and full of promise.

Cincinnati is honorably famous for its free-schools, of which it had so many that no person's child among its population can, by possibility, want the means of education which are extended, upon an average, to four thousand pupils annually. I was only present in one of these establishments during the hours of instruction. In the boys' department, which was full of little urchins (varying in their ages, I should say, from six years old to ten or twelve), the master offered to institute an extemporary examination of the pupils in Algebra; a proposal, which, as I was by no means confident of my ability to detect mistakes in that science, I declined with some alarm. In the girls' school, reading was proposed; and as I felt tolerably equal to that art, I expressed my willingness to hear a class. Books were distributed accordingly, and some half dozen girls relieved each other in reading paragraphs from English history. But it seemed to be a dry compilation, infinitely above their powers; and when they had blundered through three or four dreary passages concerning the treaty of Amiens, and other thrilling topics of the same nature (obviously without comprehending ten words), I expressed myself quite satisfied. It is very possible that they only mounted to this exalted stave in the Ladder of Learning for the astonishment of a visitor; and that at other times they keep upon its lower rounds; but I should have been much better pleased and satisfied if I had heard them exercised in simpler lessons, which they understood.

As in every other place I visited, the Judges here were gentlemen of high character and attainments. I was in one of the courts for a few minutes, and found it like those to which I have already referred. A nuisance cause was trying; there were not many spectators; and the witnesses, counsel, and jury, formed a sort of family circle, sufficiently jocose and snug.

The society with which I mingled, was intelligent, courteous, and agreeable. The inhabitants of Cincinnati are proud of their city, as one of the most interesting in America: for beautiful and thriving as it is now, and containing as it does, a population of fifty thousand souls, but two-and-fifty years have passed away since the ground on which it stands (bought at that time for a few dollars) was a wild wood, and its citizens were but a handful of dwellers in scattered log huts upon the river's shore.

## CHAPTER XII.

FROM CINCINNATI TO LOUISVILLE IN ANOTHER WESTERN STEAMBOAT; AND FROM LOUISVILLE TO ST. LOUIS IN ANOTHER. ST. LOUIS.

LEAVING Cincinnati at eleven o'clock in the forenoon, we embarked for Louisville in the Pike steamboat, which, carrying the mails, was a packet of a much better class than that in which we had come from Pittsburg. As this passage does not occupy more than twelve or thirteen hours, we arranged to go ashore that night: not coveting the distinction of sleeping in a state-room, when it was possible to sleep anywhere else.

There chanced to be on board this boat, in addition to the usual dreary crowd of passengers, one Pitchlynn, a chief of the Choctaw tribe of Indians, who *sent in his card* to me, and with whom I had the pleasure of a long conversation.

He spoke English perfectly well, though he had not begun te learn the language, he told me, until he was a young man grown. He had read many books; and Scott's poetry appeared to have left a strong impression on his mind: especially the opening of the Lady of the Lake, and the great battle scene in Marmion, in which, no doubt from the congeniality of the subjects to his own pursuits and tastes, he had great interest and delight. He appeared to understand correctly all he had read; and whatever fiction had enlisted his sympathy in its belief, had done so keenly and earnestly, I might almost say fiercely. He was dressed in our ordinary every-day costume, which hung about his fine figure loosely, and with indifferent grace. On my telling him that I regretted not to see him in his own attire, he threw up his right arm, for a moment, as though he were brandishing some heavy weapon, and answered, as he let it fall again, that his race were losing many things besides their dress, and would soon be seen upon the earth no more: but he wore it at home, he added proudly.

He told me that he had been away from his home, west of the Mississippi, seventeen months: and was now returning. He had been chiefly at Washington on some negotiations pending between his Tribe and the Government: which were not settled yet (he said in a melancholy way), and he feared never would be: for what could a few poor Indians do, against such well-skilled men of business as the whites? He had no love for Washington; tired of towns and cities very soon; and longed for the Forest and the Prairie.

I asked him what he thought of Congress? He answered, with a smile, that it wanted dignity, in an Indian's eyes.

He would very much like, he said, to see England before he died; and spoke with much interest about the great things to be seen there. When I told him of that chamber in the British Museum wherein are preserved household memorials of a race that ceased to be, thousands of years ago, he was very attentive, and it was not hard to see that he had a reference in his mind to the gradual fading away of his own people.

This led us to speak of Mr. Catlin's gallery, which he praised highly: observing that his own portrait was among the collection, and that all the likenesses were "elegant." Mr. Cooper, he said, had painted the Red Man well; and so would I, he knew, if I would go home with him and hunt buffaloes, which he was quite anxious I should do. When I told him that supposing I went, I should not be very likely to damage the buffaloes much, he took it as a great joke and laughed heartily.

He was a remarkably handsome man; some years past forty I should judge; with long black hair, an aquiline nose, broad cheek bones, a sun-burnt complexion, and a very bright, keen, dark, and piercing eye. There were but twenty thousand of the Choctaws left, he said, and their number was decreasing every day. A few of his brother chiefs had been obliged to become civilized, and to make themselves acquainted with what the whites knew, for it was their only chance of existence. But they were not many; and the rest were as they always had been. He dwelt on this: and said several times that unless they tried to assimilate themselves to their conquerors, they must be swept away before the strides of civilized society.

When we shook hands at parting, I told him he must come to England, as he longed to see the land so much: that I should hope to see him there, one day: and that I could promise him he would be well received and kindly treated. He was evidently pleased by this assurance, though he rejoined with a good-humored smile and an arch shake of his head, that the English used to be very fond of the Red Men when they wanted their help, but had not cared much for them, since.

He took his leave; as stately and complete a gentleman of Nature's making, as ever I beheld; and moved among the people in the boat, another kind of being. He sent me a lithographed portrait of himself soon afterwards; very like, though scarcely handsome enough; which I have carefully preserved in memory of our brief acquaintance.

There was nothing very interesting in the scenery of this day's journey, which brought us at midnight to Louisville. We slept at the Gault House; a splendid hotel; and were as handsomely lodged as though we had been in Paris, rather than hundreds of miles beyond the Alleghanies.

The city presenting no objects of sufficient interest to detain us on our way, we resolved to proceed next day by another steamboat, the Fulton, and to join it, about noon, at a suburb called Portland, where it would be delayed some time in passing through a canal.

The interval, after breakfast, we devoted to riding through the town, which is regular and cheerful: the streets being laid out at right angles, and planted with young trees. The buildings are smoky and blackened, from the use of bituminous coal, but an Englishman is well used to that appearance, and indisposed to quarrel with it. There did not appear to be much business stirring; and some unfinished buildings and improvements seemed to intimate that the city had been overbuilt in the ardor of "going a-head," and was suffering under the re-action consequent upon such feverish forcing of its powers.

On our way to Portland, we passed a "Magistrate's office," which amused me, as looking far more like a dame school than any police establishment: for this awful Institution was nothing but a little lazy, good-for-nothing front parlor, open to the street; wherein two or three figures (I presume the magistrate and his myrmidons) were basking in the sunshine, the very effigies of languor and repose. It was a perfect picture of Justice retired from business for want of customers; her sword and scales sold off; napping comfortably with her legs upon the table.

Here, as elsewhere in these parts, the road was perfectly

alive with pigs of all ages; lying about in every direction, fast asleep; or grunting along in quest of hidden dainties. I had always a sneaking kindness for these odd animals, and found a constant source of amusement, when all others failed, in watching their proceedings. As we were riding along this morning, I observed a little incident between two youthful pigs, which was so very human as to be inexpressibly comical and grotesque at the time, though I dare say, in telling, it is tame enough.

One young gentleman (a very delicate porker with several straws sticking about his nose, betokening recent investigations in a dunghill), was walking deliberately on, profoundly thinking, when suddenly his brother, who was lying in a miry hole unseen by him, rose up immediately before his startled eyes, ghostly with damp mud. Never was pig's whole mass of blood so turned. He started back at least three feet, gazed for a moment and then shot off as hard as he could go: his excessively little tail vibrating with speed and terror like a distracted pendulum. But before he had gone very far, he began to reason with himself as to the nature of this frightful appearance; and as he reasoned, he relaxed his speed by gradual degrees; until at last he stopped, and faced about. There was his brother, with the mud upon him glazing in the sun, yet staring out of the very same hole, perfectly amazed at his proceedings! He was no sooner assured of this; and he assured himself so carefully that one may almost say he shaded his eyes with his hand to see the better; than he came back at a round trot, pounced upon him, and summarily took off a piece of his tail; as a caution to him to be careful what he was about for the future, and never to play tricks with his family any more.

We found the steamboat in the canal, waiting for the slow process of getting through the lock, and went on board, where we shortly afterwards had a new kind of visitor in the person of a certain Kentucky Giant whose name is Porter, and who is of the moderate height of seven feet eight inches, in his stockings.

There never was a race of people who so completely gave

the lie to history as these giants, or whom all the chroniclers have cruelly libelled. Instead of roaring and ravaging about the world, constantly catering for their cannibal larders, and perpetually going to market in an unlawful manner, they are the meekest people in any man's acquaintance: rather inclining to milk and vegetable diet, and bearing any thing for a quiet life. So decidedly are amiability and mildness their characteristics, that I confess I look upon that youth who distinguished himself by the slaughter of these inoffensive persons, as a false-hearted brigand, who, pretending to philanthropic motives, was secretly influenced only by the wealth stored up within their castles, and the hope of plunder. And I lean the more to this opinion from finding that even the historian of those exploits, with all his partiality for his hero, is fain to admit that the slaughtered monsters in question were of a very innocent and simple turn; extremely guileless and ready of belief; lending a credulous ear to the most improbable tales; suffering themselves to be easily entrapped into pits; and even (as in the case of the Welsh Giant) with an excess of the hospitable politeness of a landlord, ripping themselves open; rather than hint at the possibility of their guests being versed in the vagabond arts of sleight-of-hand and hocus-pocus.

The Kentucky Giant was but another illustration of the truth of this position. He had a weakness in the region of the knees, and a trustfulness in his long face which appealed even to five-feet-nine for encouragement and support. He was only twenty-five years old, he said, and had grown recently, for it had been found necessary to make an addition to the legs of his inexpressibles. At fifteen he was a short boy, and in those days his English father and his Irish mother had rather snubbed him, as being too small of stature to sustain the credit of the family. He added that his health had not been good, though it was better now; but short people are not wanting who whisper that he drinks too hard.

I understand he drives a hackney-coach, though how he does it, unless he stands on the footboard behind, and lies along the roof upon his chest, with his chin in the box, it would be difficult to comprehend. He brought his gun with him, as a curiosity. Christened "The Little Rifle," and displayed outside a shop-window, it would make the fortune of any retail business in Holborn. When he had shown himself and talked a little while, he withdrew with his pocket-instrument, and went bobbing down the cabin, among men of six feet high and upwards, like a lighthouse walking among lamp-posts.

Within a few minutes afterwards, we were out of the canal, and in the Ohio river again.

The arrangements of the boat were like those of the Messenger, and the passengers were of the same order of people. We fed at the same times, on the same kind of viands, in the same dull manner, and with the same observances. The company appeared to be oppressed by the same tremendous concealments, and had as little capacity of enjoyment or light-heartedness. I never in my life did see such listless, heavy dullness as brooded over these meals; the very recollection of it weighs me down, and makes me, for the moment, wretched. Reading and writing on my knee, in our little cabin, I really dreaded the coming of the hour that summoned us to table; and was as glad to escape from it again, as if it had been a penance or a punishment. Healthy cheerfulness and good spirits forming a part of the banquet, I could soak my crusts in the fountain with Le Sage's strolling player, and revel in their glad enjoyment; but sitting down with so many fellow-animals to ward off thirst and hunger as a business; to empty, each creature his Yahoo's trough as quickly as he can, and then slink sullenly away; to have these social sacraments stripped of everything but the mere greedy satisfaction of the natural cravings; goes so against the grain with me, that I seriously believe the recollection of the funeral feasts will be a waking nightmare to me all my life.

There was some relief in this boat, too, which there had not been in the other, for the captain (a blunt good-natured fellow,) had his handsome wife with him, who was disposed to be lively and agreeable, as were a few other lady-passengers who had their seats about us at the same end of the table.

But nothing could have made head against the depressing influence of the general body. There was a magnetism of dullness in them which would have beaten down the most facetious companion that the earth ever knew. A jest would have been a crime, and a smile would have faded into a grinning horror. Such deadly leaden people; such systematic plodding weary insupportable heaviness; such a mass of animated indigestion in respect of all that was genial, jovial, frank, social, or hearty; never, sure, was brought together elsewhere since the world began.

Nor was the scenery, as we approached the junction of the Ohio and Mississippi rivers, at all inspiring in its influence. The trees were stunted in their growth; the banks were low and flat; the settlements and log cabins fewer in number: their inhabitants more wan and wretched than any we had encountered yet. No songs of birds were in the air, no pleasant scents, no moving lights and shadows from swift passing clouds. Hour after hour, the changeless glare of the hot, unwinking sky, shone upon the same monotonous objects. Hour after hour, the river rolled along, as wearily and slowly as the time itself.

At length, upon the morning of the third day, we arrived at a spot so much more desolate than any we had yet beheld, that the folornest places we had passed, were, in comparison with it, full of interest. At the junction of the two rivers, on ground so flat and low and marshy, that at certain seasons of the year it is inundated to the house-tops, lies a breeding-place of fever, ague, and death; vaunted in England as a mine of Golden Hope, and speculated in, on the faith of monstrous representations, to many people's ruin. A dismal swamp, on which the half-built houses rot away; cleared here and there for the space of a few yards; and teeming, then, with rank unwholesome vegetation, in whose baleful shade the wretched wanderers who are tempted hither, droop, and die, and lay their bones; the hateful Mississippi circling and eddying before it, and turning off upon its southern course a slimy monster hideous to behold; a hotbed of disease, an ugly sepulchre, a grave uncheered by any gleam of promise: a place without one single quality, in earth or air or water, to commend it: such is this dismal Cairo.

But what words shall describe the Mississippi, great father of rivers, who (praise be to Heaven) has no young children like him! An enormous ditch, sometimes two or three miles wide, running liquid mud, six miles an hour: its strong and frothy current choked and obstructed everywhere by huge logs and whole forest trees: now twining themselves together in great rafts, from the interstices of which a sedgy lazy foam works up, to float upon the water's top now rolling past like monstrous bodies, their tangled roots showing like matted hair; now glancing singly by like giant leeches; and now writhing round and round in the vortex of some small whirlpool like wounded snakes. The banks low, the trees dwarfish, the marshes swarming with frogs, the wretched cabins few and far apart, their inmates hollow-cheeked and pale, the weather very hot, mosquitoes penetrating into every crack and crevice of the boat, mud and slime on everything: nothing pleasant in its aspect, but the harmless lightning which flickers every night upon the dark horizon.

For two days we toiled up this foul stream, striking constantly against the floating timber, or stopping to avoid those more dangerous obstacles, the snags, or sawyers, which are the hidden trunks of trees that have their roots below the tide. When the nights are very dark, the look-out stationed in the head of the boat, knows by the ripple of the water if any great impediment be near at hand, and rings a bell beside him, which is the signal for the engine to be stopped; but always in the night this bell has work to do, and after every ring, there comes a blow which renders it no easy matter to remain in bed.

The decline of day here was very gorgeous; tinging the firmament deeply with red and gold up to the very keystone of the arch above us. As the sun went down behind the bank, the slightest blades of grass upon it seemed to become as distinctly visible as the arteries in the skeleton of a leaf, and when as it slowly sank, the red and golden bars upon the water grew dimmer, and dimmer yet, as if they were sinking too; and all the glowing colors of departing day paled, inch by inch, before the sombre night; the scene became a thousand times more lonesome and more dreary than before, and all its influences darkened with the sky.

We drank the muddy water of this river while we were upon it. It is considered wholesome by the natives, and is something more opaque than gruel. I have seen water like it at the Filter-shops, but nowhere else.

On the fourth night after leaving Louisville, we reached St. Louis, and here I witnessed the conclusion of an incident, trifling enough in itself but very pleasant to see, which had interested me during the whole journey.

There was a little woman on board, with a little baby; and both little woman and little child were cheerful, good-looking, bright-eyed, and fair to see. The little woman had been passing a long time with her sick mother in New York, and had left her home in St. Louis, in that condition in which ladies who truly love their lords desire to be. The baby was born in her mother's house; and she had not seen her husband (to whom she was now returning), for twelve months: having left him a month or two after their marriage.

Well, to be sure there never was a little woman so full of hope, and tenderness, and love, and anxiety, as this little woman was: and all day long she wondered whether "He" would be at the wharf; and whether "He" had got her letter; and whether, if she sent the baby ashore by somebody else, "He" would know it, meeting it in the street: which, seeing that he had never set eyes upon it in his life, was not very likely in the abstract, but was probable enough, to the young mother. She was such an artless little creature; and was in such a sunny, beaming, hopeful state; and let out all this matter clinging close about her heart, so freely; that all the other lady-passengers entered into the spirit of it as much as she; and the captain (who heard all about it from his wife), was wondrous sly, I promise you: inquiring, every time we met at table, as in forgetfulness, whether she expected anybody to meet her at St. Louis, and whether she should want to go ashore the night we reached it (but he supposed she wouldn't), and cutting many other dry jokes of that nature. There was one little weazen, dried-apple-faced old woman, who took occasion to doubt the constancy of husbands in such circumstances of bereavement; and there was another lady (with a lap dog) old enough to moralize on the lightness of human affections, and yet not so old that she could help nursing the baby, now and then, or laughing with the rest, when the little woman called it by its father's name, and asked it all manner of fantastic questions concerning him in the joy of her heart.

It was something of a blow to the little woman, that when we were within twenty miles of our destination, it became clearly necessary to put this baby to bed. But she got over it with the same good humor; tied a handkerchief round her head; and came out into the little gallery with the rest. Then, such an oracle as she became in reference to the localities! and such facetiousness as was displayed by the married ladies! and such sympathy as was shown by the single ones! and such peals of laughter as the little woman herself (who would just as soon have cried) greeted every jest with!

At last, there were the lights of St. Louis, and here was the wharf, and those were the steps: and the little woman covering her face with her hands, and laughing (or seeming to laugh) more than ever, ran into her own cabin, and shut herself up. I have no doubt that in the charming inconsistency of such excitement, she stopped her ears, lest she should hear "Him" asking for her: but I did not see her do it.

Then, a great crowd of people rushed on board, though the boat was not yet made fast, but was wandering about, among the other boats, to find a landing place: and everybody looked for the husband: and nobody saw him: when, in the midst of us all—Heaven knows how she ever got there—there was the little woman clinging with both arms tight round the neck of a fine, good-looking, sturdy young fellow! and in a moment afterwards, there she was again, actually clapping her little hands for joy, as she dragged him through the small door of her small cabin, to look at the baby as he lay asleep!

We went to a large hotel, called the Planter's House: built

like an English hospital, with long passages and bare walls, and skylights above the room-doors for the free circulation of air. There were a great many boarders in it; and as many lights sparkled and glistened from the windows down into the street below, when we drove up, as if it had been illuminated on some occasion of rejoicing. It is an excellent house, and the proprietors have most bountiful notions of providing the creature comforts. Dining alone with my wife in our own room, one day, I counted fourteen dishes on the table at once.

In the old French portion of the town, the thoroughfares are narrow and crooked, and some of the houses are very quaint and picturesque: being built of wood, with tumble-down galleries before the windows, approachable by stairs or rather ladders from the street. There are queer little barbers' shops and drinking-houses too, in this quarter; and abundance of crazy old tenements with blinking casements, such as may be seen in Flanders. Some of these ancient habitations, with high garret gable-windows perking into the roofs, have a kind of French shrug about them; and being lop-sided with age, appear to hold their heads askew, besides, as if they were grimacing in astonishment at the American Improvements.

It is hardly necessary to say, that these consist of wharves and warehouses, and new buildings in all directions; and of a great many vast plains which are still "progressing." Already, however, some very good houses, broad streets, and marble-fronted shops, have gone so far a-head as to be in a state of completion; and the town bids fair in a few years to improve considerably: though it is not likely ever to vie, in point of elegance or beauty, with Cincinnati.

The Roman Catholic religion, introduced here by the early French settlers, prevails extensively. Among the public institutions are a Jesuit College; a convent for "the Ladies of the Sacred Heart;" and a large chapel attached to the college, which was in course of erection at the time of my visit, and was intended to be consecrated on the second of December, in the next year. The architect of this building, is one of the reverend fathers of the school, and the works proceed under his sole direction. The organ will be sent from Belgium.

In addition to these establishments, there is a Roman Catholic cathedral, dedicated to Saint Francis Xavier; and a hospital, founded by the munificence of a deceased resident, who was a member of that church. It also sends missionaries from hence among the Indian tribes.

The Unitarian church is represented, in this remote place, as in most other parts of America, by a gentleman of great worth and excellence. The poor have good reason to remember and bless it; for it befriends them, and aids the cause of rational education, without any sectarian or selfish views. It is liberal in all its actions; of kind construction; and of wide benevolence.

There are three free-schools already erected, and in full operation in this city. A fourth is building, and will soon be opened.

No man ever admits the unhealthiness of the place he dwells in (unless he is going away from it), and I shall therefore, I have no doubt, be at issue with the inhabitants of St. Louis, in questioning the perfect salubrity of its climate, and in hinting that I think it must rather dispose to fever, in the summer and autumnal seasons. Just adding, that it is very hot, lies among great rivers, and has vast tracts of undrained swampy land around it, I leave the reader to form his own opinion.

As I had a great desire to see a Prairie before turning back from the furthest point of my wandering; and as some gentlemen of the town had, in their hospitable consideration, an equal desire to gratify me; a day was fixed, before my departure, for an expedition to the Looking-Glass Prairie, which is within thirty miles of the town. Deeming it possible that my readers may not object to know what kind of thing such a gipsy party may be at that distance from home, and among what sort of objects it moves, I will describe the jaunt in another chapter.

## CHAPTER XIII.

### A JAUNT TO THE LOOKING-GLASS PRAIRIE AND BACK.

I MAY premise that the word Prairie is variously pronounced *paraaer*, *parearer*, and *paroarer*. The latter mode of pronunciation is perhaps the most in favor.

We were fourteen in all, and all young men: indeed it is a singular though very natural feature in the society of these distant settlements, that it is mainly composed of adventurous persons in the prime of life, and has very few grey heads among it. There were no ladies: the trip being a fatiguing one: and we were to start at five o'clock in the morning punctually.

I was called at four, that I might be certain of keeping nobody waiting; and having got some bread and milk for breakfast, threw up the window and looked down into the street, expecting to see the whole party busily astir, and great preparations going on below. But as everything was very quiet, and the street presented that hopeless aspect with which five o'clock in the morning is familiar elsewhere, I deemed it as well to go to bed again, and went accordingly.

I awoke again at seven o'clock, and by that time the party had assembled, and were gathered round, one light carriage, with a very stout axletree; one something on wheels like an amateur carrier's cart; one double phaeton of great antiquity and unearthly construction; one gig with a great hole in its back and a broken head; and one rider on horseback who was to go on before. I got into the first coach with three companions; the rest bestowed themselves in the other vehicles; two large baskets were made fast to the lightest; two large stone jars in wicker cases, technically known as demi-johns, were consigned to the "least rowdy" of the party for safe keeping; and the procession moved off to the ferry-boat, in which it was to cross the river bodily, men, horses, carriages, and all, as the manner in these parts is.

We got over the river in due course, and mustered again

before a little wooden box on wheels, hove down all aslant in a morass, with "MERCHANT TAILOR" painted in very large letters over the door. Having settled the order of proceeding, and the road to be taken, we started off once more and began to make our way through an ill-favored Black Hollow, called less expressively, the American Bottom.

The previous day had been—not to say hot, for the term is weak and lukewarm in its power of conveying an idea of the temperature. The town had been on fire; in a blaze. But at night it had come on to rain in torrents, and all night long it had rained without cessation. We had a pair of very strong horses, but travelled at the rate of little more than a couple of miles an hour, through one unbroken slough of black mud and water. It had no variety but in depth. Now it was only half over the wheels, now it hid the axletree, and now the coach sank down in it almost to the windows. The air resounded in all directions with the loud chirping of the frogs, who, with the pigs (a coarse, ugly breed, as unwholesome-looking as though they were the spontaneous growth of the country), had the whole scene to themselves. Here and there we passed a log hut; but the wretched cabins were wide apart and thinly scattered, for though the soil is very rich in this place few people can exist in such a deadly atmosphere. On either side of the track, if it deserves the name, was the thick "bush;" and everywhere was stagnant, slimy, rotten, filthy water.

As it is the custom in these parts to give a horse a gallon or so of cold water whenever he is in a foam with heat, we halted for that purpose, at a log inn in the wood, far removed from any other residence. It consisted of one room, bare-roofed and bare-walled of course, with a loft above. The ministering priest was a swarthy young savage, in a shirt of cotton print like bed-furniture, and a pair of ragged trousers. There were a couple of young boys, too, nearly naked, lying idly by the well; and they, and he, and *the* traveller at the inn, turned out to look at us.

The traveller was an old man with a grey grisly beard two inches long, a shaggy moustache of the same hue, and enormous eyebrows; which almost obscured his lazy, semi-drunken glance, as he stood regarding us with folded arms: poising himself alternately upon his toes and heels. On being addressed by one of the party, he drew nearer, and said, rubbing his chin (which scraped under his horny hand like fresh gravel beneath a nailed shoe), that he was from Delaware, and had lately bought a farm "down there" pointing into one of the marshes where the stunted trees were thickest. He was "going," he added to St. Louis, to fetch his family, whom he had left behind; but he seemed in no great hurry to bring on these incumbrances, for when we moved away, he loitered back into the cabin, and was plainly bent on stopping there so long as his money lasted. He was a great politician of course, and explained his opinions at some length to one of our company; but I only remember that he concluded with two sentiments, one of which was, Somebody for ever; and the other, Blast everybody else! which is by no means a bad abstract of the general creed in these matters.

When the horses were swollen out to about twice their natural dimensions (there seems to be an idea here, that this kind of inflation improves their going), we went forward again, through mud and mire, and damp, and festering heat, and brake and bush, attended always by the music of the frogs and pigs, until nearly noon, when we halted at a place called Belleville.

Belleville was a small collection of wooden houses, huddled together in the very heart of the bush and swamp. Many of them had singularly bright doors of red and yellow; for the place had been lately visited by a travelling painter, "who got along," as I was told, "by eating his way." The criminal court was sitting, and was at that moment trying some criminals for horse-stealing: with whom it would most likely go hard: for live stock of all kinds being necessarily very much exposed in the woods, is held by the community in rather higher value than human life; and for this reason, juries generally make a point of finding all men indicted for cattle-stealing, guilty, whether or no.

The horses belonging to the bar, the judge, and witnesses,

were tied to temporary racks set up roughly in the road; by which is to be understood, a forest path, nearly knee-deep in mud and slime.

There was an hotel in this place which like all hotels in America, had its large dining-room for the public table. It was an odd, shambling, low-roofed out-house, half-cowshed and half-kitchen, with a coarse brown canvas table-cloth, and tin sconces stuck against the walls, to hold candles at supper-time.

The horseman had gone forward to have coffee and some eatables prepared, and they were by this time nearly ready. He had ordered "wheat-bread and chicken-fixings," in preference to "corn-bread and common doings." The latter kind of refection includes only pork and bacon. The former comprehends broiled ham, sausages, veal cutlets, steaks, and such other viands of that nature as may be supposed, by a tolerably wide poetical construction, "to fix" a chicken comfortably in the digestive organs of any lady or gentleman.

On one of the door-posts at this inn, was a tin plate, whereon was inscribed in characters of gold "Doctor Crocus;" and on a sheet of paper, pasted up by the side of this plate was a written announcement that Dr. Crocus would that evening deliver a lecture on Phrenology for the benefit of the Belleville public; at a charge for admission, of so much a head.

Straying up-stairs, during the preparation of the chicken-fixings, I happened to pass the Doctor's chamber; and as the door stood wide open, and the room was empty, I made bold to peep in.

It was a bare, unfurnished, comfortless room, with an unframed portrait hanging up at the head of the bed; a likeness, I take it, of the Doctor, for the forehead was fully displayed, and great stress was laid by the artist upon its phrenological developments. The bed itself was covered with an old patchwork counterpane. The room was destitute of carpet or of curtain. There was a damp fire-place without any stove, full of wood ashes; a chair, and a very small table; and on the last named piece of furniture was displayed, in grand array, the doctor's library, consisting of some half-dozen greasy old books.

Now, it certainly looked about the last apartment on the whole earth out of which any man would be likely to get anything to do him good. But the door, as I have said, stood coaxingly open, and plainly said in conjunction with the chair, the portrait, the table, and the books, "Walk in, gentlemen, walk in! Don't be ill, gentlemen, when you may be well in no time. Doctor Crocus is here, gentlemen, the celebrated Doctor Crocus! Doctor Crocus has come all this way to cure you, gentlemen. If you haven't heard of Doctor Crocus, it's your fault, gentlemen, who live a little way out of the world here: not Doctor Crocus's. Walk in, gentlemen, walk in!"

In the passage below, when I went down-stairs again, was Doctor Crocus himself. A crowd had flocked in from the Court House, and a voice from among them called out to the landlord, "Colonel! introduce Doctor Crocus."

"Mr. Dickens," says the colonel, "Doctor Crocus."

Upon which Doctor Crocus, who is a tall, fine-looking Scotchman, but rather fierce and warlike in appearance for a professor of the peaceful art of healing, bursts out of the concourse with his right arm extended, and his chest thrown out as far as it will possibly come, and says:

"Your countryman, sir!"

Whereupon Doctor Crocus and I shake hands; and Doctor Crocus looks as if I didn't by any means realize his expectations, which, in a linen blouse, and a great straw hat with a green ribbon, and no gloves, and my face and nose profusely ornamented with the stings of mosquitoes and the bites of bugs, it is very likely I did not.

"Long in these parts, sir?" says I.

"Three or four months, sir," says the Doctor.

"Do you think of soon returning to the old country, sir?" says I.

Doctor Crocus makes no verbal answer, but gives me an imploring look, which says so plainly "Will you ask me that again, a little louder, if you please?" that I repeat the question.

"Think of soon returning to the old country, sir!" repeats the Doctor.

"To the old country, sir," I rejoin.

Doctor Crocus looks round upon the crowd to observe the effect he produces, rubs his hands, and says, in a very loud voice:

"Not yet awhile, sir, not yet. You won't catch me at that just yet, sir. I am a little too fond of freedom for *that*, sir. Ha, ha! It's not so easy for a man to tear himself from a free country such as this is, sir. Ha, ha! No, no! Ha, ha! None of that till one's obliged to do it, sir. No, no!"

As Doctor Crocus says these latter words, he shakes his head, knowingly, and laughs again. Many of the bystanders shake their heads in concert with the doctor, and laugh too, and look at each other as much as to say, 'A pretty bright and first-rate sort of chap is Crocus!' and unless I am very much mistaken, a good many people went to the lecture that night, who never thought about phrenology, or about Doctor Crocus either, in all their lives before.

From Belleville, we went on, through the same desolate kind of waste, and constantly attended, without the interval of a moment, by the same music; until, at three o'clock in the afternoon, we halted once more at a village called Lebanon to inflate the horses again, and give them some corn besides: of which they stood much in need. Pending this ceremony, I walked into the village, where I met a full-sized dwelling-house coming down-hill at a round trot, drawn by a score or more of oxen.

The public-house was so very clean and good a one, that the managers of the jaunt resolved to return to it and put up there for the night, if possible. This course decided on, and the horses being well refreshed, we again pushed forward, and came upon the Prairie at sunset.

It would be difficult to say why, or how—though it was possibly from having heard and read so much about it—but the effect on me was disappointment. Looking towards the setting sun, there lay, stretched out before my view, a vast expanse of level ground; unbroken, save by one thin line of trees, which scarcely amounted to a scratch upon the great blank; until it met the glowing sky, wherein it seemed to dip: mingling with its rich colors, and mellowing in its distant blue. There it lay, a tranquil sea or lake without water, if such a simile be admissible, with the day going down upon it: a few birds wheeling here and there: and solitude and silence reigning paramount around. But the grass was not yet high: there were bare black patches on the ground; and the few wild flowers that the eye could see, were poor and scanty. Great as the picture was, its very flatness and extent, which left nothing to the imagination, tamed it down and cramped its interest. I felt little of that sense of freedom and exhilaration which a Scottish heath inspires, or even our English downs awaken. It was lonely and wild, but oppressive in its barren monotony. I felt that in traversing the Prairies, I could never abandon myself to the scene, forgetful of all else; as I should do instinctively, were the heather underneath my feet, or an iron-bound coast beyond; but should often glance towards the distant and frequently receding line of the horizon, and wish it gained and passed. It is not a scene to be forgotten, but it is scarcely one, I think (at all events, as I saw it), to remember with much pleasure, or to covet the looking-on again, in after life.

We encamped near a solitary log house, for the sake of its water, and dined upon the plain. The baskets contained roast fowls, buffalo's tongue (an exquisite dainty, by the way), ham, bread, cheese and butter; biscuits, champagne, sherry, lemons and sugar for punch; and abundance of rough ice. The meal was delicious, and the entertainers were the soul of kindness and good humor. I have often recalled that cheerful party to my pleasant recollection since, and shall not easily forget, in junketings nearer home with friends of older date, my boon companions on the Prairie.

Returning to Lebanon that night, we lay at the little inn at which we had halted in the afternoon. In point of cleanliness and comfort it would have suffered by no comparison with any village alehouse, of a homely kind, in England.

Rising at five o'clock next morning, I took a walk about the village: none of the houses were strolling about to-day, but it was early for them yet, perhaps: and then amused myself by lounging in a kind of farm-yard behind the tavern, of which the leading features were, a strange jumble of rough sheds for stables; a rude colonnade, built as a cool place of summer resort; a deep well; a great earthen mound for keeping vegetables in, in winter time; and a pigeon-house, whose little apertures looked, as they do in all pigeon-houses, very much too small for the admission of the plump and swelling-breasted birds who were strutting about it, though they tried to get in never so hard. That interest exhausted, I took a survey of the inn's two parlors, which were decorated with colored prints of Washington, and President Madison, and of a white-faced young lady (much speckled by the flies), who held up her gold neck-chain for the admiration of the spectator, and informed all admiring comers that she was "Just Seventeen:" although I should have thought her older. In the best room there were two oil portraits of the kit-cat size, representing the landlord and his infant son; both looking as bold as lions, and staring out of the canvas with an intensity that would have been cheap at any price. They were painted, I think, by the artist who had touched up the Belleville doors with red and gold; for I seemed to recognize his style immediately.

After breakfast, we started to return by a different way from that which we had taken yesterday, and coming up at ten o'clock with an encampment of German emigrants carrying their goods in carts, who had made a rousing fire which they were just quitting, stopped there to refresh. And very pleasant the fire was; for, hot though it had been yesterday, it was quite cold to-day, and the wind blew keenly. Looming in the distance, as we rode along, was another of the ancient Indian burial-places, called the Monk's Mound; in memory of a body of fanatics of the order of La Trappe, who founded a desolate convent there, many years ago, when there were no settlers within a thousand miles, and were all swept off by the pernicious climate: in which lamentable fatality, few rational people will suppose, perhaps, that society experienced any very severe deprivation.

The track of to-day had the same features as the track of

yesterday. There was the swamp, the bush, the perpetual chorus of frogs, the rank unseemly growth, the unwholesome steaming earth. Here and there, and frequently too, we encountered a solitary broken-down wagon, full of some new settler's goods. It was a pitiful sight to see one of these vehicles deep in the mire; the axle-tree broken; the wheel lying idly by its side; the man gone miles away, to look for assistance; the woman seated among their wandering household gods, with a baby at her breast, a picture of forlorn dejected patience; the team of oxen crouching down mournfully in the mud, and breathing forth such clouds of vapor from their mouths and nostrils, that all the damp mist and fog around seemed to have come direct from them.

In due time we mustered once again before the merchant tailor's, and having done so, crossed over to the city in the ferry-boat: passing, on the way, a spot called Bloody Island, the duelling-ground of St. Louis, and so designated in honor of the last fatal combat fought there, which was with pistols, breast to breast. Both combatants fell dead upon the ground; and possibly some rational people may think of them as of the gloomy madmen on the Monk's Mound, that they were no great loss to the community.

## CHAPTER XIV.

RETURN TO CINCINNATI. A STAGE-COACH RIDE FROM THAT CITY TO COLUMBUS, AND THENCE TO SANDUSKY. SO, BY LAKE ERIE, TO THE FALLS OF NIAGARA.

As I had a desire to travel through the interior of the state of Ohio, and to "strike the lakes," as the phrase is, at a small town called Sandusky, to which that route would conduct us on our way to Niagara, we had to return from St. Louis by the way we had come, and to retrace our former track as far as Cincinnati.

The day on which we were to take leave of St. Louis being

very fine; and the steamboat which was to have started I don't know how early in the morning, postponing, for the third or fourth time, her departure until the afternoon; we rode forward to an old French village on the river, called properly Carondelet, and nicknamed Vide Poche, and arranged that the packet should call for us there.

The place consisted of a few poor cottages, and two or three public-houses; the state of whose larders certainly seemed to justify the second designation of the village, for there was nothing to eat in any of them. At length, however, by going back some half a mile or so, we found a solitary house where ham and coffee were procurable; and there we tarried to await the advent of the boat, which would come in sight from the green before the door, a long way off.

It was a neat, unpretending village tavern, and we took our repast in a quaint little room with a bed in it, decorated with some old oil paintings, which in their time had probably done duty in a Catholic chapel or monastery. The fare was very good, and served with great cleanliness. The house was kept by a characteristic old couple, with whom we had a long talk, and who were perhaps a very good sample of that kind of people in the West.

The landlord was a dry, tough, hard-faced old fellow (not so very old either, for he was but just turned sixty, I should think), who had been out with the militia in the last war with England, and had seen all kinds of service,—except a battle; and he had been very near seeing that, he added: very near. He had all his life been restless and locomotive, with an irresistible desire for change; and was still the son of his old self: for if he had nothing to keep him at home, he said (slightly jerking his hat and his thumb towards the window of the room in which the old lady sat, as we stood talking in front of the house) he would clean up his musket, and be off to Texas to-morrow morning. He was one of the very many descendants of Cain proper to this continent, who seem destined from their birth to serve as pioneers in the great human army: who gladly go on from year to year extending its outposts, and leaving home after home behind them; and die at last, utterly regardless of their graves being left thousands of miles behind, by the wandering generation who succeed.

His wife was a domesticated kind-hearted old soul, who had come with him "from the queen city of the world," which, it seemed, was Philadelphia; but had no love for this Western country, and indeed had little reason to bear it any; having seen her children, one by one, die here of fever, in the full prime and beauty of their youth. Her heart was sore, she said, to think of them; and to talk on this theme, even to strangers, in that blighted place, so far from her old home, eased it somewhat, and became a melancholy pleasure.

The boat appearing towards evening, we bade adieu to the poor old lady and her vagrant spouse, and making for the nearest landing-place, were soon on board The Messenger again, in our old cabin, and steaming down the Mississippi.

If the coming up this river, slowly making head against the stream, be an irksome journey, the shooting down it with the turbid current is almost worse; for then the boat, proceeding at the rate of twelve or fifteen miles an hour, has to force its passage through a labyrinth of floating logs, which, in the dark, it is often impossible to see beforehand or avoid. All that night, the bell was never silent for five minutes at a time; and after every ring the vessel reeled again, sometimes beneath a single blow, sometimes beneath a dozen dealt in quick succession, the lightest of which seemed more than enough to beat in her frail keel, as though it had been pie-crust. Looking down upon the filthy river after dark, it seemed to be alive with monsters, as these black masses rolled upon the surface, or came starting up again, head first, when the boat, in ploughing her way among a shoal of such obstructions, drove a few among them, for the moment, under water. Sometimes, the engine stopped during a long interval, and then before her and behind, and gathering close about her on all sides, were so many of these ill-favored obstacles that she was fairly hemmed in; the centre of a floating island; and was constrained to pause until they parted somewhere, as dark clouds will do before the wind, and opened by degrees a channel out.

In good time next morning, however, we came again in sight of the detestable morass called Cairo; and stopping there to take in wood, lay alongside a barge, whose starting timbers scarcely held together. It was moored to the bank, and on its side was painted "Coffee House;" that being, I supposed, the floating paradise to which the people fly for shelter when they lose their houses for a month or two beneath the hideous waters of the Mississippi. But looking southward from this point, we had the satisfaction of seeing that intolerable river dragging its slimy length and ugly freight abruptly off towards New Orleans; and passing a yellow line which stretched across the current, were again upon the clear Ohio, never, I trust, to see the Mississippi more, saving in troubled dreams and nightmares. Leaving it for the company of its sparkling neighbor, was like the transition from pain to ease, or the awakening from a horrible vision to cheerful realities.

We arrived at Louisville on the fourth night, and gladly availed ourselves of its excellent hotel. Next day we went on in the Ben Franklin, a beautiful mail steamboat, and reached Cincinnati shortly after midnight. Being by this time nearly tired of sleeping upon shelves, we had remained awake to go ashore straightway; and groping a passage across the dark decks of other boats, and among labyrinths of engine-machinery and leaking casks of molasses, we reached the streets, knocked up the porter at the hotel where we had staid before, and were, to our great joy, safely housed soon afterwards.

We rested but one day at Cincinnati, and then resumed our journey to Sandusky. As it comprised two varieties of stage-coach travelling, which, with those I have already glanced at, comprehend the main characteristics of this mode of transit in America, I will take the reader as our fellow-passenger, and pledge myself to perform the distance with all possible despatch.

Our place of destination in the first instance is Columbus. It is distant about a hundred and twenty miles from Cincinnati, but there is a macadamized road (rare blessing!) the whole way, and the rate of travelling upon it is six miles an hour.

We start at eight o'clock in the morning, in a great mail-coach, whose huge cheeks are so very ruddy and plethoric, that it appears to be troubled with a tendency of blood to the head. Dropsical it certainly is, for it will hold a dozen passengers inside. But, wonderful to add, it is very clean and bright, being nearly new; and rattles through the streets of Cincinnati gaily.

Our way lies through a beautiful country, richly cultivated, and luxuriant in its promise of an abundant harvest. Sometimes we pass a field where the strong bristling stalks of Indian corn look like a crop of walking-sticks, and sometimes an enclosure where the green wheat is springing up among a labyrinth of stumps; the primitive worm-fence is universal, and an ugly thing it is; but the farms are neatly kept, and, save for these differences, one might be travelling just now in Kent.

We often stop to water at a roadside inn, which is always dull and silent. The coachman dismounts and fills his bucket, and holds it to the horses' heads. There is scarcely ever any one to help him; there are seldom any loungers standing round: and never any stable-company with jokes to crack. Sometimes, when we have changed our team, there is a difficulty in starting again, arising out of the prevalent mode of breaking a young horse: which is to catch him, harness him against his will, and put him in a stage-coach without further notice: but we get on somehow or other, after a great many kicks and a violent struggle; and jog on as before again.

Occasionally, when we stop to change, some two or three half-drunken loafers will come loitering out with their hands in their pockets, or will be seen kicking their heels in rocking-chairs, or lounging on the window-sill, or sitting on a rail within the colonnade: they have not often anything to say though, either to us or to each other, but sit there idly staring at the coach and horses. The landlord of the inn is usually among them, and seems, of all the party, to be the least connected with the business of the house. Indeed he is with reference to the tavern, what the driver is in relation to the coach and passengers; whatever happens in his sphere of action, he is quite indifferent, and perfectly easy in his mind.

The frequent change of coachmen works no change or variety in the coachman's character. He is always dirty, sullen, and taciturn. If he be capable of smartness of any kind, moral or physical, he has a faculty of concealing it which is truly marvellous. He never speaks to you as you sit beside him on the box, and if you speak to him, he answers (if at all) in monosyllables. He points out nothing on the road, and seldom looks at anything: being, to all appearance, thoroughly weary of it, and of existence generally. As to doing the honors of his coach, his business, as I have said, is with the horses. The coach follows because it is attached to them and goes on wheels; not because you are in it. Sometimes, towards the end of a long stage, he suddenly breaks out into a discordant fragment of an election song, but his face never sings along with him; it is only his voice, and not often that. He always chews and always spits, and never incumbers himself with a pocket-handkerchief. The consequences to the box passenger, especially when the wind blows towards him, are not agreeable.

Whenever the coach stops, and you can hear the voices of the inside passengers; or whenever any bystander addresses them, or any one among them; or they address each other; you will hear one phrase repeated over and over and over again to the most extraordinary extent. It is an ordinary and unpromising phrase enough, being neither more nor less than "Yes, sir;" but it is adapted to every variety of circumstance, and fills up every pause in the conversation. Thus:

The time is one o'clock at noon. The scene, a place where we are to stay to dine on this journey. The coach drives up to the door of an inn. The day is warm, and there are several idlers lingering about the tavern, and waiting for the public dinner. Among them, is a stout gentleman in a brown hat, swinging himself to and fro in a rocking-chair on the pavement.

As the coach stops, a gentleman in a straw hat looks out of the window.

STRAW HAT. (To the stout gentleman in the rocking-chair). I reckon that's Judge Jefferson, ain't it?

BROWN HAT. (Still swinging; speaking very slowly; and without any emotion whatever.) Yes, sir.

STRAW HAT. Warm weather, Judge.

BROWN HAT. Yes, sir.

STRAW HAT. There was a snap of cold, last week.

BROWN HAT. Yes, sir.

STRAW HAT. Yes, sir.

A pause. They look at each other very seriously.

STRAW HAT. I calculate you'll have got through that case of the corporation, judge, by this time, now?

BROWN HAT. Yes, sir.

STRAW HAT. How did the verdict go, sir?

BROWN HAT. For the defendant, sir.

SRAW HAT. (Interrogatively.) Yes, sir.

BROWN HAT. (Affirmatively.) Yes, sir.

BOTH. (Musingly, as each gazes down the street.) Yes, sir.

Another pause. They look at each other again, still more seriously than before.

BROWN HAT. This coach is rather behind its time to-day, I guess.

STRAW HAT. (Doubtingly.) Yes, sir.

BROWN HAT. (Looking at his watch.) Yes, sir; nigh upon two hours.

STRAW HAT. (Raising his eyebrows in very great surprise.) Yes, sir!

BROWN HAT. (Decisively, as he puts up his watch.) Yes, sir.

ALL THE OTHER INSIDE PASSENGERS (among themselves.) Yes, sir.

COACHMAN (in a very surly tone.) No it an't.

STRAW HAT (to the coachman.) Well, I don't know, sir. We were a pretty tall time coming that last fifteen mile. That's a fact.

The coachman making no reply, and plainly declining to enter into any controversy on a subject so far removed from his sympathies and feelings, another passenger says "Yes, sir;" and the gentleman in the straw hat in acknowledgment of his courtesy, says "Yes, sir," to him in return. The straw hat then inquires of the brown hat, whether that coach in which he (the straw hat) then sits, is not a new one? To which the brown hat again makes answer, "Yes, sir."

STRAW HAT. I thought so. Pretty loud smell of varnish, sir?

BROWN HAT. Yes, sir.

ALL THE OTHER INSIDE PASSENGERS. Yes, sir.

BROWN HAT. (To the company in general.) Yes, sir.

The conversational powers of the company having been by this time pretty heavily taxed, the straw hat opens the door and gets out; and all the rest alight also. We dine soon afterwards with the boarders in the house, and have nothing to drink but tea and coffee. As they are both very bad and the water is worse, I ask for brandy; but it is a Temperance Hotel, and spirits are not to be had for love or money. This preposterous forcing of unpleasant drinks down the reluctant throats of travellers is not at all uncommon in America, but I never discovered that the scruples of such wincing landlords induced them to preserve any unusally nice balance between the quality of their fare, and their scale of charges: on the contrary, I rather suspected them of diminishing the one and exalting the other, by way of recompense for the loss of their profit on the sale of spirituous liquors. After all, perhaps, the plainest course for persons of such tender consciences, would be, a total abstinence from tavern-keeping.

Dinner over, we get into another vehicle which is ready at the door (for the coach has been changed in the interval), and resume our journey; which continues through the same kind of country until evening, when we come to the town where we are to stop for tea and supper; and having delivered the mail bags at the Post-office, ride through the usual wide street, lined with the usual stores and houses (the drapers always having hung up at their door, by way of sign, a piece of bright red cloth), to the hotel where this meal is prepared. There being many boarders here, we sit down a large party, and a very melancholy one as usual. But there is a buxom hostess at the head of the table, and opposite, a simple Welsh schoolmaster with his wife and child; who came here, on a speculation of greater promise than performance, to teach the classics: and they are sufficient subjects of interest until the meal is over, and another coach is ready. In it we go on once more, lighted by a bright moon, until midnight; when we stop to change the coach again, and remain for half an hour or so in a miserable room, with a blurred lithograph of Washington over the smoky fire-place, and a mighty jug of cold water on the table: to which refreshment the moody passengers do so apply themselves that they would seem to be, one and all, keen patients of Doctor Sangrado. Among them is a very little boy, who chews tobacco like a very big one; and a droning gentleman, who talks arithmetically and statistically on all subjects, from poetry downwards; and who always speaks in the same key, with exactly the same emphasis, and with very grave deliberation. He came outside just now, and told me how that the uncle of a certain young lady who had been spirited away and married by a certain captain, lived in these parts; and how this uncle was so valiant and ferocious that he shouldn't wonder if he were to follow the said captain to England, "and shoot him down in the street, wherever he found him;" in the feasibility of which strong measure I, being for the moment rather prone to contradiction, from feeling half asleep and very tired, declined to acquiesce, assuring him that if the uncle did resort to it, or gratified any other little whim of the like nature, he would find himself one morning prematurely throttled at the Old Bailey; and that he would do well to make his will before he went, as he would certainly want it before he had been in Britain very long.

On we go, all night, and by-and-by the day begins to break, and presently the first cheerful rays of the warm sun comes slanting on us brightly. It sheds its light upon a miserable waste of sodden grass, and dull trees, and squalid huts, whose aspect is forlorn and grievous in the last degree. A very desert in the wood, whose growth of green is dank and noxious like that upon the top of standing water: where poisonous fungus grows in the rare footprint on the oozy ground, and sprouts like witches' coral from the crevices in the cabin wall and floor; it is a hideous thing to lie upon the very threshold of a city. But it was purchased years ago, and as the owner cannot be discovered, the State has been unable to reclaim it. So there it remains, in the midst of cultivation and improvement, like ground accursed, and made obscene and rank by some great crime.

We reached Columbus shortly before seven o'clock, and stayed there, to refresh, that day and night; having excellent apartments in a very large unfinished hotel called the Neill House, which were richly fitted with the polished wood of the black walnut, and opened on a handsome portico and stone verandah, like rooms in some Italian mansion. The town is clean and pretty, and of course is "going to be" much larger. It is the seat of the State legislature of Ohio, and lays claim, in consequence, to some consideration and importance.

There being no stage-coach next day, upon the road we wished to take, I hired "an extra," at a reasonable charge, to carry us to Tiffin: a small town from whence there is a railroad to Sandusky. This extra was an ordinary four-horse stage-coach, such as I have described, changing horses and drivers, as the stage-coach would, but was exclusively our own for the journey. To ensure our having horses at the proper stations, and being incommoded by no strangers, the proprietors sent an agent on the box, who was to accompany us the whole way through; and thus attended, and bearing with us, besides, a hamper full of savory cold meats, and fruit, and wine; we started off again, in high spirits, at half-past six e'clock next morning, very much delighted to be by ourselves, and disposed to enjoy even the roughest journey.

It was well for us that we were in this humor, for the road we went over that day, was certainly enough to have shaken tempers that were not resolutely at Set Fair, down to some inches below Stormy. At one time we were all flung together in a heap at the bottom of the coach, and at another we were crushing our heads against the roof. Now, one side was down deep in the mire, and we were holding on to the other.

Now, the coach was lying on the tails of the two wheelers; and now it was rearing up in the air, in a frantic state, with all four horses standing on the top of an insurmountable eminence, looking coolly back at it, as though they would say "unharness us. It can't be done." The drivers on these roads who certainly get over the ground in a manner which is quite miraculous, so twist and turn the team about in forcing a passage, corkscrew fashion, through the bogs and swamps, that it was quite a common circumstance on looking out of the window, to see the coachman with the ends of a pair of reins in his hands, apparently driving nothing, or playing at horses, and the leaders staring at one unexpectedly from the back of the coach, as if they had some idea of getting up behind. A great portion of the way was over what is called a corduroy road, which is made by throwing trunks of trees into a marsh, and leaving them to settle there. The very slightest of the jolts with which the ponderous carriage fell from log to log, was enough, it seemed, to have dislocated all the bones in the human body. It would be impossible to experience a similar set of sensations, in any other circumstances, unless perhaps in attempting to go up to the top of St. Paul's in an omnibus. Never, never once, that day, was the coach in any position, attitude, or kind of motion to which we are accustomed in coaches. Never did it make the smallest approach to one's experience of the proceedings of any sort of vehicle that goes on wheels.

Still, it was a fine day, and the temperature was delicious, and though we had left Summer behind us in the west, and were fast leaving Spring, we were moving towards Niagara and home. We alighted in a pleasant wood towards the middle of the day, dined on a fallen tree, and leaving our best fragments with a cottager, and our worst with the pigs (who swarm in this part of the country like grains of sand on the sea-shore, to the great comfort of our commissariat in Canada), we went forward again, gaily.

As night came on, the track grew narrower and narrower, until at last it so lost itself among the trees, that the driver seemed to find his way by instinct. We had the comfort of knowing, at least, that there was no danger of his falling asleep, for every now and then a wheel would strike against an unseen stump with such a jerk, that he was fain to hold on pretty tight and pretty quick, to keep himself upon the box. Nor was there any reason to dread the least danger from furious driving, inasmuch as over that broken ground the horses had enough to do to walk; as to shying, there was no room for that; and a herd of wild elephants could not have run away in such a wood, with such a coach at their heels. So we stumbled along, quite satisfied.

These stumps of trees are a curious feature in American travelling. The varying illusions they present to the unaccustomed eye as it grows dark, are quite astonishing in their number and reality. Now, there is a Grecian urn erected in the centre of a lonely field; now there is a woman weeping at a tomb; now a very common-place old gentleman in a white waistcoat, with a thumb thrust into each arm-hole of his coat; now a student poring on a book; now a crouching negro; now, a horse, a dog, a cannon, an armed man; a hunch-back throwing off his cloak and stepping forth into the light. They were often as entertaining to me as so many glasses in a magic lantern, and never took their shapes at my bidding, but seemed to force themselves upon me, whether I would or no; and strange to say, I sometimes recognized in them counterparts of figures once familiar to me in pictures attached to childish books, forgotten long ago.

It soon became too dark, however, even for this amusement, and the trees were so close together that their dry branches rattled against the coach on either side, and obliged us all to keep our heads within. It lightened too, for three whole hours; each flash being very bright, and blue, and long; and as the vivid streaks came darting in among the crowded branches, and the thunder rolled gloomily above the tree tops, one could scarcely help thinking that there were better neighborhoods at such a time than thick woods afforded.

At length, between ten and eleven o'clock at night, a few feeble lights appeared in the distance, and Upper Sandusky, an Indian village, where we were to stay till morning, lay before us.

They were gone to bed at the log Inn, which was the only house of entertainment in the place, but soon answered to our knocking, and got some tea for us in a sort of kitchen or common room, tapestried with old newspapers, pasted against the wall. The bed-chamber to which my wife and I were shown, was a large, low, ghostly room; with a quantity of withered branches on the hearth, and two doors without any fastening, opposite to each other, both opening on the black night and wild country, and so contrived, that one of them always blew the other open: a novelty in domestic architecture, which I do not remember to have seen before, and which I was somewhat disconcerted to have forced on my attention after getting into bed, as I had a considerable sum in gold for our travelling expenses, in my dressing-case. Some of the luggage, however, piled against the panels, soon settled this difficulty, and my sleep would not have been very much affected that night, I believe, though it had failed to do so.

My Boston friend climbed up to bed, somewhere in the roof, where another guest was already snoring hugely. But being bitten beyond his power of endurance, he turned out again, and fled for shelter to the coach, which was airing itself in front of the house. This was not a very politic step, as it turned out; for the pigs scenting him, and looking upon the coach as a kind of pie with some manner of meat inside, grunted round it so hideously, that he was afraid to come out again, and lay there shivering, till morning. Nor was it possible to warm him, when he did come out, by means of a glass of brandy; for in Indian villages, the legislature, with a very good and wise intention, forbids the sale of spirits by tavern keepers. The precaution, however, is quite inefficacious, for the Indians never fail to procure liquor of a worse kind, at a dearer price, from travelling pedlars.

It is a settlement of the Wyandot Indians who inhabit this place. Among the company at breakfast was a mild old gentleman, who had been for many years employed by the United States Government in conducting negotiations with the Indians, and who had just concluded a treaty with these people by which they bound themselves, in consideration of a certain annual sum, to remove next year to some land provided for them, west of the Mississippi, and a little way beyond St. Louis. He gave me a moving account of their strong attachment to the familiar scenes of their infancy, and in particular to the burial-places of their kindred; and of their great reluctance to leave them. He had witnessed many such removals, and always with pain, though he knew that they departed for their own good. The question whether this tribe should go or stay, had been discussed among them a day or two before, in a hut erected for the purpose, the logs of which still lay upon the ground before the inn. When the speaking was done, the ayes and noes were ranged on opposite sides, and every male adult voted in his turn. The moment the result was known, the minority (a large one) cheerfully yielded to the rest, and withdrew all kind of opposition.

We met some of these poor Indians afterwards, riding on shaggy ponies. They were so like the meaner sort of gipsies that if I could have seen any of them in England, I should have concluded, as a matter of course, that they belonged to that wandering and restless people.

Leaving this town directly after breakfast, we pushed forward again, over a rather worse road than yesterday, if possible, and arrived about noon at Tiffin, where we parted with the extra. At two o'clock we took the railroad; the travelling on which was very slow, its construction being indifferent, and the ground wet and marshy; and arrived at Sandusky in time to dine that evening. We put up at a comfortable little hotel on the brink of Lake Erie, lay there that night, and had no choice but to wait there next day, until a steamboat bound for Buffalo appeared. The town, which was sluggish, and uninteresting enough, was something like the back of an English watering-place, out of the season.

Our host, who was very attentive and anxious to make us comfortable, was a handsome middle-aged man, who had come to this town from New England, in which part of the country he was "raised." When I say that he constantly walked in and out of the room with his hat on; and stopped to converse in the same free-and-easy state; and lay down on our sofa, and pulled his newspaper out of his pocket, and read it at his ease; I merely mention these traits as characteristic of the country: not at all as being matter of complaint, or as having been disagreeable to me. I should undoubtedly be offended by such proceedings at home, because there they are not the custom, and where they are not, they would be impertinences; but in America, the only desire of a good-natured fellow of this kind, is to treat his guests hospitably and well; and I had no more right, and I can truly say no more disposition, to measure his conduct by our English rule and standard, than I had to quarrel with him for not being of the exact stature which would qualify him for admission into the Queen's grenadier guards. As little inclination had I to find fault with a funny old lady who was an upper domestic in this establishment, and who, when she came to wait upon us at any meal, sat herself down comfortably in the most convenient chair, and producing a large pin to pick her teeth with, remained performing that ceremony, and steadfastly regarding us meanwhile with much gravity and composure (now and then pressing us to eat a little more), until it was time to clear away. It was enough for us, that whatever we wished done was done with great civility and readiness, and a desire to oblige, not only here, but everywhere else; and that all our wants were in general, zealously anticipated.

We were taking an early dinner at this house, on the day after our arrival, which was Sunday, when a steamboat came in sight and presently touched at the wharf. As she proved to be on her way to Buffalo, we hurried on board with all speed, and soon left Sandusky far behind us.

She was a large vessel of five hundred tons, and handsomely fitted up, though with high-pressure engines; which always conveyed that kind of feeling to me, which I should be likely to experience, I think, if I had lodgings on the first floor of a powder-mill. She was laden with flour, some casks of which commodity were stored upon the deck. The captain coming up to have a little conversation, and to introduce a friend, seated himself astride of one of these barrels, like a

Bacchus of private life; and pulling a great clasp-knife out of his pocket, began to "whittle" it as he talked, by paring thin slices off the edges. And he whittled with such industry and hearty good will, that but for his being called away very soon, it must have disappeared bodily, and left nothing in its place but grist and shavings.

After calling at one or two flat places, with low dams stretching out into the lake, whereon were stumpy lighthouses, like windmills without sails, the whole looking like a Dutch vignette, we came at midnight to Cleveland, where we lay all night, and until nine o'clock next morning.

I entertained quite a curiosity in reference to this place, from having seen at Sandusky a specimen of its literature in the shape of a newspaper, which was very strong indeed upon the subject of Lord Ashburton's recent arrival at Washington, to adjust the points in dispute between the United States Government and Great Britain: informing its readers that as America had "whipped" England in her infancy, and whipped her again in her youth, so it was clearly necessary that she must whip her once again in her maturity: and pledging its credit to all True Americans, that if Mr. Webster did his duty in the approaching negotiations, and sent the English Lord home again in double quick time, they should, within two years, sing "Yankee Doodle in Hyde Park, and Hail Columbia in the scarlet courts of Westminster!" I found it a pretty town, and had the satisfaction of beholding the outside of the office of the journal from which I have just quoted. I did not enjoy the delight of seeing the wit who indited the paragraphs in question, but I have no doubt he is a prodigious man in his way, and held in high repute by a select circle.

There was a gentleman on board, to whom, as I unintentionally learned through the thin partition which divided our state-room from the cabin in which he and his wife conversed together, I was unwittingly the occasion of very great uneasiness. I don't know why or wherefore, but I appeared to run in his mind perpetually, and to dissatisfy him very much. First of all I heard him say: and the most ludicrous part of the business was, that he said it in my very ear, and could not have communicated more directly with me, if he had leaned upon my shoulder, and whispered me: "Boz is on board still, my dear." After a considerable pause, he added, complainingly, "Boz keeps himself very close:" which was true enough, for I was not very well, and was lying down, with a book. I thought he had done with me after this, but I was deceived; for a long interval having elapsed, during which I imagine him to have been turning restlessly from side to side, and trying to go to sleep; he broke out again, with "I suppose *that* Boz will be writing a book by-and-by, and putting all our names in it!" at which imaginary consequence of being on board a boat with Boz, he groaned, and became silent.

We called at the town of Erie, at eight o'clock that night, and lay there an hour. Between five and six next morning, we arrived at Buffalo, where we breakfasted; and being too near the Great Falls to wait patiently anywhere else, we set off by the train, the same morning at nine o'clock, to Niagara.

It was a miserable day; chilly and raw; a damp mist falling; and the trees in that northern region quite bare and wintry. Whenever the train halted, I listened for the roar; and was constantly straining my eyes in the direction where I knew the Falls must be, from seeing the river rolling on towards them; every moment expecting to behold the spray. Within a few minutes of our stopping, not before, I saw two great white clouds rising up slowly and majestically from the depths of the earth. That was all. At length we alighted: and then for the first time, I heard the mighty rush of water, and felt the ground tremble underneath my feet.

The bank is very steep, and was slippery with rain, and half-melted ice. I hardly know how I got down, but I was soon at the bottom, and climbing, with two English officers who were crossing and had joined me, over some broken rocks, deafened by the noise, half-blinded by the spray, and wet to the skin. We were at the foot of the American Fall. I could see an immense torrent of water tearing headlong down from some great height, but had no idea of shape, or situation, or anything but vague immensity.

When we were seated in the little ferry-boat, and were crossing the swollen river immediately before both cataracts, I began to feel what it was: but I was in a manner stunned, and unable to comprehend the vastness of the scene. It was not until I came on Table Rock, and looked—Great Heaven, on what a fall of bright-green water!—that it came upon me in its full might and majesty.

Then, when I felt how near to my Creator I was standing, the first effect, and the enduring one—instant and lasting—of the tremendous spectacle, was Peace. Peace of Mind, tranquillity, calm recollections of the Dead, great thoughts of Eternal Rest and Happiness: nothing of gloom or terror. Niagara was at once stamped upon my heart, an Image of Beauty; to remain there, changeless and indelible, until its pulses cease to beat, for ever.

Oh, how the strife and trouble of daily life receded from my view, and lessened in the distance, during the ten memorable days we passed on that Enchanted Ground! What voices spoke from out the thundering water; what faces, faded from the earth, looked out upon me from its gleaming depths; what Heavenly promise glistened in those angels' tears, the drops of many hues, that showered around, and twined themselves about the gorgeous arches which the changing rainbows made!

I never stirred in all that time from the Canadian side, whither I had gone at first. I never crossed the river again; for I knew there were people on the other shore, and in such a place it is natural to shun strange company. To wander to and fro all day, and see the cataracts from all points of view; to stand upon the edge of the Great Horse Shoe Fall, marking the hurried water gathering strength as it approached the verge, yet seeming, too, to pause before it shot into the gulf below; to gaze from the river's level up at the torrent as it came streaming down; to climb the neighboring heights and watch it through the trees, and see the wreathing water in the rapids hurrying on to take its fearful plunge; to linger in the shadow of the solemn rocks three miles below; watching the river as, stirred by no visible cause, it heaved and eddied and awoke the echoes, being troubled yet, far down beneath the surface, by its giant leap; to have Niagara before me, lighted by the sun and by the moon, red in the day's decline, and grey as evening slowly fell upon it; to look upon it every day, and wake up in the night and hear its ceaseless voice: this was enough.

I think in every quiet season now, still do those waters roll and leap, and roar and tumble, all day long; still are the rainbows spanning them, a hundred feet below. Still, when the sun is on them, do they shine and glow like molten gold. Still, when the day is gloomy, do they fall like snow, or seem to crumble away like the front of a great chalk cliff, or roll down the rock like dense white smoke. But always does the mighty stream appear to die as it comes down, and always from its unfathomable grave arises that tremendous ghost of spray and mist, which is never laid: which has haunted this place with the same dread solemnity since Darkness brooded on the deep, and that first flood before the Deluge—Light—came rushing on creation at the word of God.

## CHAPTER XV.

IN CANADA; TORONTO; KINGSTON; MONTREAL; QUEBEC; ST. JOHN'S. IN THE UNITED STATES AGAIN; LEBANON; THE SHAKER VILLAGE; AND WEST POINT.

I WISH to abstain from instituting any comparison, or drawing any parallel whatever, between the social features of the United States and those of the British possessions in Canada. For this reason, I shall confine myself to a very brief account of our journeyings in the latter territory.

But before I leave Niagara, I must advert to one disgusting circumstance, which can hardly have escaped the observation of any decent traveller who has visited the Falls.

On Table Rock, there is a cottage belonging to a Guide, where little relics of the place are sold, and where visitors register their names in a book kept for the purpose. On the wall of the room in which a great many of these volumes are preserved, the following request is posted: "Visitors will please not copy nor extract the remarks and poetical effusions from the registers and albums kept here."

But for this intimation, I should have let them lie upon the tables upon which they were strewn with careful negligence, like books in a drawing-room: being quite satisfied with the stupendous silliness of certain stanzas with an anti-climax at at the end of each, which were framed and hung up on the wall. Curious, however, after reading this announcement, to see what kind of morsels were so carefully preserved, I turned a few leaves, and found them scrawled all over with the vilest and the filthiest ribaldry that ever human hogs delighted in.

It is humiliating enough to know that there are among men, brutes so obscene and worthless, that they can delight in laying their miserable profanations upon the very steps of Nature's greatest altar. But that these should be hoarded up for the delight of their fellow swine, and kept in a public place where any eyes may see them, is a disgrace to the English language in which they are written (though I hope few of these entries have been made by Englishmen), and a reproach to the English side, on which they are preserved.

The quarters of our soldiers at Niagara, are finely and airily situated. Some of them are large detached houses on the plain above the Falls, which were originally designed for hotels; and in the evening time, when the women and children were leaning over the balconies watching the men as they played at ball and other games upon the grass before the door, they often presented a little picture of cheerfulness and animation which made it quite a pleasure to pass that way.

At any garrisoned point where the line of demarcation between our country and another is so very narrow as at Niagara, desertion from the ranks can scarcely fail to be of frequent occurrence: and it may be reasonably supposed that when the soldiers entertain the wildest and maddest hopes of the fortune and independence that await them on the other side, the impulse to play traitor, which such a place suggests to dishonest minds, is not weakened. But it very rarely happens that the men who do desert, are happy or contented afterwards; and many instances have been known in which they have confessed their grievous disappointment, and their earnest desire to return to their old service if they could but be assured of pardon, or of lenient treatment. Many of their comrades, notwithstanding, do the like, from time to time; and instances of loss of life in the effort to cross the river with this object, are far from being uncommon. Several men were drowned in the attempt to swim across, not long ago; and one, who had the madness to trust himself upon a table as a raft, was swept down to the whirlpool, where his mangled body eddied round and round some days.

I am inclined to think that the noise of the Falls is very much exaggerated; and this will appear the more probable when the depth of the great basin in which the water is received, is taken into account. At no time during our stay there, was the wind at all high or boisterous, but we never heard them, three miles off, even at the very quiet time of sunset, though we often tried.

Queenston, at which place the steamboats start for Toronto (or I should rather say at which place they call, for their wharf is at Lewiston on the opposite shore), is situated in a delicious valley, through which the Niagara river, in color a very deep green, pursues its course. It is approached by a road that takes its winding way among the heights by which the town is sheltered; and seen from this point is extremely beautiful and picturesque. On the most conspicuous of these heights stood a monument erected by the Provincial legislature in memory of General Brock, who was slain in a battle with the American Forces, after having won the victory. Some vagabond, supposed to be a fellow of the name of Lett, who is now, or who lately was, in prison as a felon, blew up this monument two years ago, and it is now a melancholy ruin, with a long fragment of iron railing hanging dejectedly from its top, and waving to and fro like a wild ivy branch or broken vine stem. It is of much higher importance than it may seem, that this statue should be repaired at the public cost, as it ought to have been long ago. Firstly, because it is beneath the dignity of England to allow a memorial raised in honor of one of her defenders, to remain in this condition, on the very spot where he died. Secondly, because the sight of it in its present state, and the recollection of the unpunished outrage which brought it to this pass, is not very likely to soothe down border feelings among English subjects here, or compose their border quarrels and dislikes.

I was standing on the wharf at this place, watching the passengers embarking in a steamboat which preceded that whose coming we awaited, and participating in the anxiety with which a sergeant's wife was collecting her few goods together—keeping one distracted eye hard upon the porters, who were hurrying them on board, and the other on a hoopless washing tub for which, as being the most utterly worthless of all her movables, she seemed to entertain particular affection—when three or four soldiers with a recruit came up and went on board.

The recruit was a likely young fellow enough, strongly built and well made, but by no means sober: indeed he had all the air of a man who had been more or less drunk for some days. He carried a small bundle over his shoulder, slung at the end of a walking-stick, and had a short pipe in his mouth. He was as dusty and dirty as recruits usually are, and his shoes betokened that he had travelled on foot some distance, but he was in a very jocose state, and shook hands with this soldier, and clapped that one on the back, and talked and laughed continually, like a roaring dog as he was.

The soldiers rather laughed at this blade than with him: seeming to say, as they stood straightening their canes in their hands, and looking coolly at him over their glazed stocks, "Go on, my boy, while you may! you'll know better by-and-by;" when suddenly the novice, who had been backing towards the gangway in his noisy merriment, fell overboard before their eyes, and splashed heavily down into the river between the vessel and the dock.

I never saw such a good thing as the change that came over

these soldiers in an instant. Almost before the man was down, their professional manner, their stiffness and constraint, were gone, and they were filled with the most violent energy. In less time than is required to tell it, they had him out again feet first, with the tails of his coat flapping over his eyes, everything about him hanging the wrong way, and the water streaming off at every thread in his threadbare dress. But the moment they set him upright and found that he was none the worse, they were soldiers again, looking over their glazed stocks more composedly than ever.

The half-sobered recruit glanced round for a moment, as if his first impulse were to express some gratitude for his preservation, but seeing them with this air of total unconcern, and having his wet pipe presented to him with an oath by the soldier who had been by far the most anxious of the party, he stuck it in his mouth, thrust his hands into his moist pockets, and without even shaking the water off his clothes, walked on board whistling; not to say as if nothing had happened, but as if he meant to do it, and it had been a perfect success.

Our steamboat came up directly this had left the wharf, and soon bore us to the mouth of the Niagara; where the stars and stripes of America flutter on one side, and the Union Jack of England on the other: and so narrow is the space between them that the sentinels in either fort can often hear the watchword of the other country given. Thence we emerged on Lake Ontario, an inland sea; and by half-past six o'clock were at Toronto.

The country round this town being very flat, is bare of scenic interest; but the town itself is full of life and motion, bustle, business, and improvement. The streets are well paved, and lighted with gas; the houses are large and good; the shops excellent. Many of them have a display of goods in their shop windows, such as may be seen in thriving county towns in England; and there are some which would do no discredit to the metropolis itself. There is a good stone prison here; and there are, besides, a handsome church, a court-house, public offices, many commodious private residences, and a government observatory for noting and recording the magnetic variations. In the College of Upper Canada, which is one of the public establishments of the city, a sound education in every department of polite learning can be had, at a very moderate expense: the annual charge for the instruction of each pupil, not exceeding nine pounds sterling. It has pretty good endowment in the way of land, and is a valuable and useful institution.

The first stone of a new college had been laid but a few days before, by the Governor General. It will be a handsome, spacious edifice, approached by a long avenue, which is already planted and made available as a public walk. The town is well adapted for wholesome exercise at all seasons, for the footways in the thoroughfares which lie beyond the principal street, are planked like floors, and kept in very good and clean repair.

It is a matter of deep regret that political differences should have run high in this place, and led to most discreditable and disgraceful results. It is not long since guns were discharged from a window in this town at the successful candidates in an election, and the coachman of one of them was actually shot in the body, though not dangerously wounded. But one man was killed on the same occasion; and from the very window whence he received his death, the very flag which shielded his murderer (not only in the commission of his crime, but from its consequence), was displayed again on the occasion of the public ceremony performed by the Governor General, to which I have just adverted. Of all the colors in the rainbow, there is but one which could be so employed: I need not say that flag was orange.

The time of leaving Toronto for Kingston, is noon. By eight o'clock next morning, the traveller is at the end of his journey, which is performed by steamboat upon Lake Ontario, calling at Port Hope and Coburg, the latter a cheerful thriving little town. Vast quantities of flour form the chief item in the freight of these vessels. We had no fewer than one thousand and eighty barrels on board, between Coburg and Kingston.

The latter place, which is now the seat of government in

Canada, is a very poor town, rendered still poorer in the appearance of its market-place by the ravages of a recent fire. Indeed, it may be said of Kingston, that one half of it appears to be burnt down, and the other half not to be built up. The Government House is neither elegant nor commodious, yet it is almost the only house of any importance in the neighborhood.

There is an admirable jail here, well and wisely governed, and excellently regulated, in every respect. The men were employed as shoemakers, ropemakers, blacksmiths, tailors, carpenters, and stonecutters; and in building a new prison, which was pretty far advanced towards completion. The female prisoners were occupied in needlework. Among them was a beautiful girl of twenty, who had been there nearly three years. She acted as bearer of secret despatches for the self-styled Patriots on Navy Island, during the Canadian Insurrection: sometimes dressing as a girl, and carrying them in her stays; sometimes attiring herself as a boy, and secreting them in the lining of her hat. In the latter character she always rode as a boy would, which was nothing to her, for she could govern any horse that any man could ride, and could drive four-in-hand with the best whip in those parts. Setting forth on one of her patriotic missions, she appropriated to herself the first horse she could lay hands on; and this offence had brought her where I saw her. She had quite a lovely face, though, as the reader may suppose from this sketch of her history, there was a lurking devil in her bright eye, which looked out pretty sharply from between her prison bars.

There is a bomb-proof fort here of great strength, which occupies a bold position, and is capable, doubtless, of doing good service; though the town is much too close upon the frontier to be long held, I should imagine, for its present purpose in troubled times. There is also a small navy-yard, where a couple of Government steamboats were building, and getting on vigorously.

We left Kingston for Montreal on the tenth of May, at half-past nine in the morning, and proceeded in a steamboat down the St. Lawrence river. The beauty of this noble stream at almost any point, but especially in the commencement of this journey when it winds its way among the thousand Islands, can hardly be imagined. The number and constant successions of these islands, all green and richly wooded; their fluctuating sizes, some so large that for half an hour together one among them will appear as the opposite bank of the river, and some so small that they are mere dimples on its broad bosom; their infinite variety of shapes; and the numberless combinations of beautiful forms which the trees growing on them, present: all form a picture fraught with uncommon interest and pleasure.

In the afternoon we shot down some rapids where the river boiled and bubbled strangely, and where the force and headlong violence of the current were tremendous. At seven o'clock we reached Dickenson's Landing, whence travellers proceed for two or three hours by stage-coach: the navigation of the river being rendered so dangerous and difficult in the interval, by rapids, that steamboats do not make the passage. The number and length of those *portages*, over which the roads are bad, and the travelling slow, render the way between the towns of Montreal and Kingston somewhat tedious.

Our course lay over a wide, uninclosed tract of country at a little distance from the river side, whence the bright warning lights on the dangerous parts of the St. Lawrence shone vividly. The night was dark and raw, and the way dreary enough. It was nearly ten o'clock when we reached the wharf where the next steamboat lay; and went on board, and to bed.

She lay there all night, and started as soon as it was day. The morning was ushered in by a violent thunderstorm, and was very wet, but gradually improved and brightened up. Going on deck after breakfast, I was amazed to see floating down with the stream, a most gigantic raft, with some thirty or forty wooden houses upon it, and at least as many flag masts, so that it looked like a nautical street. I saw many of these rafts afterwards, but never one so large. All the timber, or "lumber," as it is called in America, which is brought down the St. Lawrence, is floated down in this manner. When the raft reaches its place of destination, it is broken up; the materials are sold; and the boatmen return for more.

At eight we landed again, and travelled by a stage-coach for four hours through a pleasant and well-cultivated country, perfectly French in every respect: in the appearance of the cottages; the air, language, and dress of the peasantry, the sign-boards on the shops and taverns; and the Virgin's shrines and crosses by the wayside. Nearly every common laborer and boy, though he had no shoes to his feet, wore round his waist a sash of some bright color: generally red: and the women, who were working in the fields and gardens, and doing all kinds of husbandry, wore, one and all, great flat straw hats with most capacious brims. There were Catholic Priests and Sisters of Charity in the village streets; and images of the Saviour at the corners of cross-roads, and in other public places.

At noon we went on board another steamboat, and reached the village of Lachine, nine miles from Montreal, by three o'clock. There, we left the river, and went on by land.

Montreal is pleasantly situated on the margin of the St. Lawrence, and is backed by some bold heights, about which there are charming rides and drives. The streets are generally narrow and irregular, as in most French towns of any age; but in the more modern parts of the city, they are wide and airy. They display a great variety of very good shops; and both in the town and suburbs there are many excellent private dwellings. The granite quays are remarkable for their beauty, solidity, and extent.

There is a very large Catholic cathedral here, recently erected; with two tall spires, of which one is yet unfinished.[1] In the open space in front of this edifice, stands a solitary, grim-looking, square brick tower, which has a quaint and remarkable appearance, and which the wiseacres of the place have consequently determined to pull down immediately. The Government House is very superior to that at Kingston, and the town is full of life and bustle. In one of the suburbs is a plank road—not footpath—five or six miles long, and a famous road it is too. All the rides in the vicinity were made doubly interesting by the bursting out of spring, which is here so rapid, that it is but a day's leap from barren winter, to the blooming youth of summer.

The steamboats to Quebec perform the journey in the night; that is to say, they leave Montreal at six in the evening and arrive in Quebec at six next morning. We made this excursion during our stay in Montreal (which exceeded a fortnight), and were charmed by its interest and beauty.

The impression made upon the visitor by this Gibraltar of America: its giddy heights; its citadel suspended, as it were, in the air; its picturesque steep streets and frowning gateways; and the splendid views which burst upon the eye at every turn: is at once unique and lasting.

It is a place not to be forgotten or mixed up in the mind with other places, or altered for a moment in the crowd of scenes a traveller can recall. Apart from the realities of this most picturesque city, there are associations clustering about it which would make a desert rich in interest. The dangerous precipice along whose rocky front Wolfe and his brave companions climbed to glory; the Plains of Abraham, where he received his mortal wound; the fortress so chivalrously defended by Montcalm; and his soldier's grave, dug for him while yet alive, by the bursting of a shell; are not the least among them, or among the gallant incidents of history. That is a noble Monument too, and worthy of two great nations, which perpetuates the memory of both brave generals, and on which their names are jointly written.

The city is rich in public institutions and in Catholic churches and charities, but it is mainly in the prospect from the site of the Old Government House, and from the Citadel, that its surpassing beauty lies. The exquisite expanse of country, rich in field and forest, mountain-height and water, which lies stretched out before the view, with miles of Canadian villages, glancing in long white streaks, like veins along the landscape; the motley crowd of gables, roofs, and chimney tops in the old hilly town immediately at hand; the beautiful St. Lawrence sparkling and flashing in the sunlight: and the tiny ships below the rock from which you gaze, whose distant rigging looks like spiders' webs against the light, while casks and barrels on their decks dwindle into toys, and busy mariners become so many puppets: all this, framed by a sunken window in the fortress and looked at from the shadowed room within, forms one of the brightest and most enchanting pictures that the eye can rest upon.

In the spring of the year, vast numbers of emigrants who have newly arrived from England or from Ireland, pass between Quebec and Montreal on their way to the back woods and new settlements of Canada. If it be an entertaining lounge (as I very often found it) to take a morning stroll upon the quay at Montreal, and see them grouped in hundreds on the public wharves about their chests and boxes, it is matter of deep interest to be their fellow-passenger on one of these steamboats, and, mingling with the concourse, see and hear them unobserved.

The vessel in which we returned from Quebec to Montreal was crowded with them, and at night they spread their beds between decks (those who had beds at least,) and slept so close and thick about our cabin door, that the passage to and fro was quite blocked up. They were nearly all English; from Gloucestershire the greater part; and had had a long winter-passage out; but it was wonderful to see how clean the children had been kept, and how untiring in their love and self-denial all the poor parents were.

Cant as we may, and as we shall to the end of all things, it is very much harder for the poor to be virtuous than it is for the rich; and the good that is in them, shines the brighter for it. In many a noble mansion lives a man, the best of husbands and of fathers, whose private worth in both capacities is justly lauded to the skies. But bring him here, upon this crowded deck. Strip from his fair young wife her silken dress and jewels, unbind her braided hair, stamp early wrinkles on her brow, pinch her pale cheek with care and much privation, array her faded form in coarsely patched attire, let there be nothing but his love to set her forth or deck her out, and you shall put it to the proof indeed. So change his station in the world, that he shall see in those young things who climb about his knee: not records of his wealth and name: but little wrestlers with him for his daily bread; so many poachers on his scanty meal; so many units to divide his every sum of comfort, and farther to reduce its small amount. In lieu of the endearments of childhood in its sweetest aspect, heap upon him all its pains and wants, its sicknesses and ills, its fretfulness, caprice and querulous endurance; let its prattle be, not of engaging infant fancies, but of cold, and thirst, and hunger; and if his fatherly affection outlive all this, and he be patient, watchful, tender; careful of his children's lives, and mindful always of their joys and sorrows; then send him back to Parliament, and Pulpit, and to Quarter Sessions, and when he hears fine talk of the depravity of those who live from hand to mouth, and labor hard to do it, let him speak up, as one who knows, and tell those holders forth, that they, by parallel with such a class, should be High Angels in their daily lives, and lay but humble siege to Heaven at last.

Which of us shall say what he would be, if such realities, with small relief or change all through his days, were his! Looking round upon these people; far from home, houseless, indigent, wandering, weary with travel and hard living: and seeing how patiently they nursed and tended their young children; how they consulted ever their wants first, then half supplied their own; what gentle ministers of hope and faith the women were; how the men profited by their example; and how very, very seldom even a moment's petulance or harsh complaint broke out among them: I felt a stronger love and honor of my kind come glowing on my heart, and wished to God there had been many Atheists in the better part of human nature there, to read this simple lesson in the book of Life.

We left Montreal for New York again, on the thirtieth of May; crossing to La Prairie, on the opposite shore of the St.

Lawrence, in a steamboat; we then took the railroad to St. John's which is on the brink of Lake Champlain. Our last greeting in Canada was from the English officers in the pleasant barracks at that place (a class of gentlemen who had made every hour of our visit memorable by their hospitality and friendship); and with "Rule Britannia" sounding in our ears, soon left it far behind.

But Canada has held, and always will retain, a foremost place in my remembrance. Few Englishmen are prepared to find it what it is. Advancing quietly; old differences settling down, and being fast forgotten; public feeling and private enterprise alike in a sound and wholesome state; nothing of flush or fever in its system, but health and vigor throbbing in its steady pulse: it is full of hope and promise. To me—who had been accustomed to think of it as something left behind in the strides of advancing society, as something neglected and forgotten, slumbering and wasting in its sleep—the demand for labor and the rates of wages; the busy quays of Montreal; the vessels taking in their cargoes, and discharging them; the amount of shipping in the different ports; the commerce, roads, and public works, all made *to last;* the respectability and character of the public journals; and the amount of rational comfort and happiness which honest industry may earn: were very great surprises. The steamboats on the lakes, in their conveniences, cleanliness, and safety; in the gentlemanly character and bearing of their captains; and in the politeness and perfect comfort of their social regulations; are unsurpassed even by the famous Scotch vessels, deservedly so much esteemed at home. The inns are usually bad; because the custom of boarding at hotels is not so general here as in the States, and the British officers, who form a large portion of the society of every town, live chiefly at the regimental messes: but in every other respect, the traveller in Canada will find as good provision for his comfort as in any place I know.

There is one American boat—the vessel which carried us on Lake Champlain, from St. John's to Whitehall—which I praise very highly, but no more than it deserves, when I say that it is superior even to that in which we went from Queenston to Toronto, or to that in which we travelled from the latter place to Kingston, or I have no doubt I may add, to any other in the world. This steamboat, which is called the Burlington, is a perfectly exquisite achievement of neatness, elegance, and order. The decks are drawing-rooms; the cabins are boudoirs, choicely furnished and adorned with prints, pictures, and musical instruments; every nook and corner in the vessel is a perfect curiosity of graceful comfort and beautiful contrivance. Captain Sherman her commander, to whose ingenuity and excellent taste these results are solely attributable, has bravely and worthily distinguished himself on more than one trying occasion: not least among them, in having the moral courage to carry British troops, at a time (during the Canadian rebellion) when no other conveyance was open to them. He and his vessel are held in universal respect, both by his own countrymen and ours; and no man ever enjoyed the popular esteem, who, in his sphere of action, won and wore it better than this gentleman.

By means of this floating palace we were soon in the United States again, and called that evening at Burlington; a pretty town, where we lay an hour or so. We reached Whitehall, where we were to disembark, at six next morning; and might have done so earlier, but that these steamboats lie by for some hours in the night, in consequence of the lake becoming very narrow at that part of the journey, and difficult of navigation in the dark. Its width is so contracted at one point, indeed, that they are obliged to warp round by means of a rope.

After breakfasting at Whitehall, we took the stage-coach for Albany: a large and busy town, where we arrived between five and six o'clock that afternoon; after a very hot day's journey, for we were now in the height of summer again. At seven we started for New York on board a great North River steamboat, which was so crowded with passengers that the upper deck was like the box lobby of a theatre between the pieces, and the lower one like Tottenham Court Road on a Saturday night. But we slept soundly notwithstanding, and soon after five o'clock next morning, reached New York.

Tarrying here, only that day and night to recruit after our late fatigues, we started off once more upon our last journey in America. We had yet five days to spare before embarking for England, and I had a great desire to see "the Shaker Village," which is peopled by a religious sect from whom it takes its name.

To this end, we went up the North River again, as far as the town of Hudson, and there hired an extra to carry us to Lebanon thirty miles distant: and of course another and a different Lebanon, from that village where I slept on the night of the Prairie trip.

The country through which the road meandered, was rich and beautiful; the weather very fine; and for many miles the Kaatskill mountains, where Rip Van Winkle and the ghastly Dutchmen played at ninepins one memorable gusty afternoon, towered in the blue distance, like stately clouds. At one point, as we ascended a steep hill, athwart whose base a railroad, yet constructing, took its course, we came upon an Irish colony. With means at hand of building decent cabins, it was wonderful to see how clumsy, rough, and wretched, its hovels were. The best were poor protection from the weather; the worst let in the wind and rain through wide breaches in the roofs of sodden grass, and in the walls of mud; some had neither door nor window; some had nearly fallen down, and were imperfectly propped up by stakes and poles; all were ruinous and filthy. Hideously ugly old women and very buxom young ones, pigs, dogs, men, children, babies, pots, kettles, dunghills, vile refuse, rank straw, and standing water, all wallowing together in an inseparable heap, composed the furniture of every dark and dirty hut.

Between nine and ten o'clock at night, we arrived at Lebanon: which is renowned for its warm baths, and for a great hotel, well adapted, I have no doubt, to the gregarious taste of those seekers after health or pleasure who repair here, but inexpressibly comfortless to me. We were shown into an immense apartment, lighted by two dim candles, called the

16

drawing-room: from which there was a descent by a flight of steps, to another vast desert called the dining-room: our bed chambers were among certain long rows of little white-washed cells, which opened from either side of a dreary passage; and were so like rooms in a prison that I half expected to be locked up when I went to bed, and listened involuntarily for the turning of the key on the outside. There need be baths somewhere in the neighborhood, for the other washing arrangements were on as limited a scale as I ever saw, even in America: indeed, these bedrooms were so very bare of even such common luxuries as chairs, that I should say they were not provided with enough of anything, but that I bethink myself of our having been most bountifully bitten all night.

The house is very pleasantly situated, however, and we had a good breakfast. That done, we went to visit our place of destination, which was some two miles off, and the way to which was soon indicated by a finger-post, whereon was painted, "To the Shaker Village."

As we rode along, we passed a party of Shakers, who were at work upon the road; who wore the broadest of all broad-brimmed hats; and were in all visible respects such very wooden men, that I felt about as much sympathy for them, and as much interest in them, as if they had been so many figure-heads of ships. Presently we came to the beginning of the village, and alighting at the door of a house where the Shaker manufactures are sold, and which is the head-quarters of the elders, requested permission to see the Shaker worship.

Pending the conveyance of this request to some person in authority, we walked into a grim room, where several grim hats were hanging on grim pegs, and the time was grimly told by a grim clock, which uttered every tick with a kind of struggle, as if it broke the grim silence reluctantly, and under protest. Ranged against the wall were six or eight stiff high-backed chairs, and they partook so strongly of the general grimness, that one would much rather have sat on the floor than incurred the smallest obligation to any of them.

Presently, there stalked into this apartment, a grim old Shaker, with eyes as hard, and dull, and cold, as the great round metal buttons on his coat and waistcoat; a sort of calm goblin. Being informed of our desire, he produced a newspaper wherein the body of elders, whereof he was a member, had advertised but a few days before, that in consequence of certain unseemly interruptions which their worship had received from strangers, their chapel was closed to the public for the space of one year.

As nothing was to be urged in opposition to this reasonable arrangement, we requested leave to make some trifling purchases of Shaker goods; which was grimly conceded. We accordingly repaired to a store in the same house and on the opposite side of the passage, where the stock was presided over by something alive in a russet case, which the elder said was a woman; and which I suppose *was* a woman, though I should not have suspected it.

On the opposite side of the road was their place of worship; a cool clean edifice of wood, with large windows and green blinds: like a spacious summer-house. As there was no getting into this place, and nothing was to be done but walk up and down, and look at it and the other buildings in the village (which were chiefly of wood, painted a dark red like English barns, and composed of many stories like English factories), I have nothing to communicate to the reader beyond the scanty results I gleaned the while our purchases were making.

These people are called Shakers from their peculiar form of adoration, which consists of a dance, performed by the men and women of all ages, who arrange themselves for that purpose in opposite parties: the men first divesting themselves of their hats and coats, which they gravely hang against the wall before they begin; and tying a ribbon round their shirt-sleeves, as though they were going to be bled. They accompany themselves with a droning humming noise, and dance until they are quite exhausted, alternately advancing and retiring in a preposterous sort of trot. The effect is said to be unspeakably absurd: and if I may judge from a print of this ceremony which I have in my possession; and which I am informed by those who have visited the chapel, is perfectly accurate; it must be infinitely grotesque.

They are governed by a woman, and her rule is understood to be absolute, though she has the assistance of a council of elders. She lives, it is said, in strict seclusion, in certain rooms above the chapel, and is never shown to profane eyes. If she at all resemble the lady who presided over the store, it is a great charity to keep her as close as possible, and I cannot too strongly express my perfect concurrence in this benevolent proceeding.

All the possessions and revenues of the settlement are thrown into a common stock, which is managed by the elders. As they have made converts among people who were well to do in the world, and are frugal and thrifty, it is understood that this fund prospers: the more especially as they have made large purchases of land. Nor is this at Lebanon the only Shaker settlement: there are, I think, at least, three others.

They are good farmers, and all their produce is eagerly purchased and highly esteemed. "Shaker seeds," "Shaker herbs," and "Shaker distilled waters," are commonly announced for sale in the shops of towns and cities. They are good breeders of cattle, and are kind and merciful to the brute creation. Consequently, Shaker beasts seldom fail to find a ready market.

They eat and drink together, after the Spartan model, at a great public table. There is no union of the sexes: and every Shaker, male and female, is devoted to a life of celibacy. Rumor has been busy upon this theme, but here again I must refer to the lady of the store, and say, that if many of the sister Shakers resemble her, I treat all such slander as bearing on its face the strongest marks of wild improbability. But that they take as proselytes, persons so young that they cannot know their own minds, and cannot possess much strength of resolution in this or any other respect, I can assert from my own observation of the extreme juvenility of certain youthful Shakers whom I saw at work among the party on the road.

They are said to be good drivers of bargains, but to be honest and just in their transactions, and even in horse-dealing to resist those thievish tendencies which would seem, for some undiscovered reason, to be almost inseparable from that branch of traffic. In all matters they hold their own course quietly, live in their gloomy silent commonwealth, and show little desire to interfere with other people.

This is well enough, but nevertheless I cannot, I confess, incline towards the Shakers; view them with much favor, or extend towards them any very lenient construction. I so abhor, and from my soul detest that bad spirit, no matter by what class or sect it may be entertained, which would strip life of its healthful graces, rob youth of its innocent pleasures, pluck from maturity and age their pleasant ornaments, and make existence but a narrow path towards the grave: that odious spirit which, if it could have had full scope and sway upon the earth, must have blasted and made barren the imaginations of the greatest men, and left them, in their power of raising up enduring images before their fellow-creatures yet unborn, no better than the beasts: that, in these very broad-brimmed hats and very sombre coats—in stiff-necked solemn-visaged piety, in short, no matter what its garb, whether it have cropped hair as in a Shaker village, or long nails as in a Hindoo temple—I recognize the worst among the enemies of Heaven and Earth, who turn the water at the marriage feasts of this poor world, not into wine but gall. And if there must be people vowed to crush the harmless fancies and the love of innocent delights and gaieties, which are a part of human nature; as much a part of it as any other love or hope that is our common portion: let them, for me, stand openly revealed among the ribald and licentious; the very idiots know that *they* are not on the Immortal road, and will despise them, and avoid them readily.

Leaving the Shaker village with a hearty dislike of the old Shakers, and a hearty pity for the young ones: tempered by the strong probability of their running away as they grow older and wiser, which they not uncommonly do: we returned to Lebanon, and so to Hudson, by the way we had come upon the previous day. There, we took steamboat down the North River towards New York, but stopped, some four hours' journey short of it, at West Point, where we remained that night, and all next day, and next night too.

In this beautiful place: the fairest among the fair and lovely Highlands of the North River: shut in by deep green heights and ruined forts, and looking down upon the distant town of Newburgh, along a glittering path of sunlit water, with here and there a skiff, whose white sail often bends on some new tack as sudden flaws of wind come down upon her from the gullies in the hills: hemmed in besides, all round with memories of Washington, and events of the revolutionary war: is the Military School of America.

It could not stand on more appropriate ground, and any ground more beautiful can hardly be. The course of education is severe, but well devised, and manly. Through June, July, and August, the young men encamp upon the spacious plain whereon the college stands; and all the year their military exercises are performed there, daily. The term of study at this institution, which the State requires from all cadets, is four years; but, whether it be from the rigid nature of the discipline, or the national impatience of restraint, or both causes combined, not more than half the number who begin their studies here, ever remain to finish them.

The number of cadets being about equal to that of the members of Congress, one is sent here from every Congressional district: its member influencing the selection. Commissions in the service are distributed on the same principle. The dwellings of the various Professors are beautifully situated; and there is a most excellent hotel for strangers, though it has the two drawbacks of being a total abstinence house (wines and spirits being forbidden to the students), and of serving the public meals at rather uncomfortable hours: to wit, breakfast at seven, dinner at one, and supper at sunset.

The beauty and freshness of this calm retreat, in the very dawn and greenness of summer—it was then the beginning of June—were exquisite indeed. Leaving it upon the sixth, and returning to New York, to embark for England on the succeeding day, I was glad to think that among the last memorable beauties which had glided past us, and softened in the bright perspective, were those whose pictures, traced by no common hand, are fresh in most men's minds; not easily to grow old, or fade beneath the dust of Time: The Kaatskill Mountains, Sleepy Hollow, and the Tappaan Zee.

---

## CHAPTER XVI.

### THE PASSAGE HOME.

I NEVER had so much interest before, and very likely I shall never have so much interest again, in the state of the wind, as on the long-looked-for morning of Tuesday the Seventh of June. Some nautical authority had told me a day or two previous, "anything with west in it, will do;" so when I darted out of bed at daylight, and throwing up the window was saluted by a lively breeze from the north-west which had sprung up in the night, it came upon me so freshly, rustling with so many happy associations, that I conceived upon the spot a special regard for all airs blowing from that quarter of the compass, which I shall cherish, I dare say, until my own wind has breathed its last frail puff, and withdrawn itself for ever from the mortal calendar.

The pilot had not been slow to take advantage of this favorable weather, and the ship which yesterday had been in such a crowded dock that she might have retired from trade for good and all, for any chance she seemed to have of going to sea, was now full sixteen miles away. A gallant sight she was, when we, fast gaining on her in a steamboat, saw her in the distance riding at anchor: her tall masts pointing up in graceful lines against the sky, and every rope and spar expressed in delicate and thread-like outline: gallant, too, when we, being all on board, the anchor came up to the sturdy chorus "Cheerily men, oh cheerily!" and she followed proudly in the towing steamboat's wake: but bravest and most gallant of all, when the tow-rope being cast adrift, the canvas fluttered from her masts, and spreading her white wings she soared away upon her free and solitary course.

In the after-cabin we were only fifteen passengers in all, and the grater part were from Canada, where some of us had known each other. The night was rough and squally, so were the next two days, but they flew by quickly, and we were were soon as cheerful and as snug a party, with an honest, manly-hearted captain at our head, as ever came to the resolution of being mutually agreeable on land or water.

We breakfasted at eight, lunched at twelve, dined at three, and took our tea at half-past seven. We had abundance of amusement, and dinner was not the least among them: firstly for its own sake; secondly, because of its extraordinary length: its duration, inclusive of all the long pauses between the courses, being seldom less than two hours and a half; which was the subject of never-failing entertainment. By way of beguiling the tediousness of these banquets, a select association was formed at the lower end of the table, below the mast, to whose distinguished president modesty forbids me to make any further allusion, which, being a very hilarious and jovial institution, was (prejudice apart) in high favor with the rest of the community, and particularly with a black steward, who lived for three weeks in a broad grin at the marvellous humor of these incorporated worthies.

Then, we had chess for those who played it, whist, cribbage, books, backgammon, and shovelboard. In all weathers, fair or foul, calm or windy, we were every one on deck, walking up and down in pairs, lying in the boats, leaning over the side, or chatting in a lazy group together. We had no lack of music, for one played the accordion, another the violin, and another (who usually began at six o'clock A.M.) the key-bugle: the combined effect of which instruments, when they all played different tunes in different parts of the ship, at the same time, and within hearing of each other, as they sometimes did (everybody being intensely satisfied with his own performance), was sublimely hideous.

When all these means of entertainment failed, a sail would heave in sight; looming, perhaps, the very spirit of a ship, in the misty distance, or passing us so close that through our glasses we could see the people on her decks, and easily make out her name, and whither she was bound. For hours together we could watch the dolphins and porpoises as they rolled and leaped and dived around the vessel; or those small creatures ever on the wing, the Mother Carey's chickens, which had borne us company from New York bay, and for a whole fortnight fluttered about the vessel's stern. For some days we had a dead calm, or very light winds, during which the crew amused themselves with fishing, and hooked an unlucky dolphin, who expired, in all his rainbow colors, on the deck: an event of such importance in our barren calendar, that afterwards we dated from the dolphin, and made the day on which he died, an era.

Besides all this, when we were five or six days out, there began to be much talk of icebergs, of which wandering islands an unusual number had been seen by the vessels that had come into New York a day or two before we left that port, and of whose dangerous neighborhood we were warned by the sudden coldness of the weather, and the sinking of the mercury in the barometer. While these tokens lasted, a double lookout was kept, and many dismal tales were whispered, after dark, of ships that had struck upon the ice and gone down in the night; but the wind obliging us to hold a southward course, we saw none of them, and the weather soon grew bright and warm again.

The observation every day at noon, and the subsequent working of the vessel's course, was, as may be supposed, a feature in our lives of paramount importance; nor were there wanting (as there never are) sagacious doubters of the captain's calculations, who, so soon as his back was turned, would, in the absence of compasses, measure the chart with bits of string, and ends of pocket-handkerchiefs, and points of snuffers, and clearly prove him to be wrong by an odd thousand miles or so. It was very edifying to see these unbelievers shake their heads and frown, and hear them hold forth strongly upon navigation: not that they knew anything about it, but that they always mistrusted the captain in calm weather, or when the wind was adverse. Indeed, the mercury itself is not so variable as this class of passengers, whom you will see, when the ship is going nobly through the water, quite pale with admiration, swearing that the captain beats all captains ever known, and even hinting at subscription for a piece of plate; and who, next morning, when the breeze has lulled, and all the sails hang useless in the idle air, shake their despondent heads again, and say, with screwed-up lips, they hope that the captain is a sailor—but they shrewdly doubt him.

It even became an occupation in the calm, to wonder when the wind *would* spring up in the favorable quarter, where, it was clearly shown by all the rules and precedents, it ought to have sprung up long ago. The first mate, who whistled for it zealously, was much respected for his perseverance, and was regarded even by the unbelievers as a first-rate sailor. Many gloomy looks would be cast upward through the cabin skylights at the flapping sails while dinner was in progress; and some, growing bold in ruefulness, predicted that we should land about the middle of July. There are always on board ship, a Sanguine One, and a Despondent One. The latter character carried it hollow at this period of the voyage, and triumphed over the Sanguine One at every meal, by inquiring where he supposed the Great Western (which left New York a week after us) was *now*: and where he supposed the "Cunard" steam-packet was *now*: and what he thought of sailing vessels as compared with steam-ships *now*: and so beset his life with pestilent attacks of that kind, that he too was obliged to affect despondency, for very peace and quietude.

These were additions to the list of entertaining incidents, but there was still another source of interest. We carried in the steerage, nearly a hundred passengers: a little world of poverty: and as we came to know individuals among them by sight, from looking down upon the deck where they took the air in the day-time, and cooked their food, and very often ate it too, we became curious to know their histories, and with what expectations they had gone out to America, and on what errands they were going home, and what their circumstances were. The information we got on these heads from the carpenter, who had charge of these people, was often of the strangest kind. Some of them had been in America but three days, some but three months, and some had gone out in the last voyage of that very ship in which they were now returning home. Others had sold their clothes to raise the passage-money, and had hardly rags to cover them; others had no food, and lived upon the charity of the rest: and one man, it was discovered nearly at the end of the voyage, not before—for he kept his secret close, and did not court compassion—had had no sustenance whatever but the bones and scraps of fat he took from the plates used in the after-cabin dinner, when they were put out to be washed.

The whole system of shipping and conveying these unfortunate persons, is one that stands in need of thorough revision. If any class deserve to be protected and assisted by the Government, it is that class who are banished from their native land in search of the bare means of subsistence. All that could be done for these poor people by the great compassion and humanity of the captain and officers was done, but they require much more. The law is bound at least upon the English side, to see that too many of them are not put on board one ship: and that their accommodations are decent: not demoralizing and profligate. It is bound, too, in common humanity, to declare that no man shall be taken on board without his stock of provisions being previously inspected by some proper officer, and pronounced moderately sufficient for his support upon the voyage. It is bound to provide, or to require that there be provided, a medical attendant; whereas in these ships there are none, though sickness of adults, and deaths of children, on the passage, are matters of the very commonest occurrence. Above all it is the duty of any Government, be it monarchy or republic, to interpose and put an end to that system by which a firm of traders in emigrants purchase of the owners the whole 'tween-decks of a ship, and send on board as many wretched people as they can lay hold of, on any terms they can get, without the smallest reference to the conveniences of the steerage, the number of berths, the slightest separation of the sexes, or anything but their own immediate profit. Nor is even this the worst of the vicious system: for, certain crimping agents of these houses, who have a per-centage on all the passengers they inveigle, are constantly travelling about those districts where poverty and discontent are rife, and tempting the credulous into more misery, by holding out monstrous inducements to emigration which can never be realized.

The history of every family we had on board was pretty much the same. After hoarding up, and borrowing, and begging, and selling everything to pay the passage, they had gone out to New York, expecting to find its streets paved with gold; and had found them paved with very hard and very real stones. Enterprise was dull; laborers were not wanted; jobs of work were to be got, but the payment was not. They were coming back, even poorer than they went. One of them was carrying an open letter from a young English artisan, who had been in New York a fortnight, to a friend near Manchester, whom he strongly urged to follow him. One of the officers brought it to me as a curiosity. "This is the country, Jem," said the writer. "I like America. There is no despotism here; that's the great thing. Employment of all sorts is going a-begging, and wages are capital. You have only to choose a trade, Jem, and be it. I haven't made choice of one yet, but I shall soon. *At present I have'nt quite made up my mind whether to be a carpenter—or a tailor.*"

There was yet another kind of passenger, and but one more, who, in the calm and the light winds, was a constant theme of conversation and observation among us. This was an English sailor, a smart, thorough-built, English man-of-war's-man from his hat to his shoes, who was serving in the American navy, and having got leave of absence was on his way home to see his friends. When he presented himself to take and pay for his passage, it had been suggested to him that being an able seaman he might as well work it and save the money, but this piece of advice he very indignantly rejected: saying, "He'd be damned but for once he'd go aboard-ship, as a gentleman." Accordingly they took his money, but he no sooner came aboard, than he stowed his kit in the forecastle, arranged to mess with the crew, and the very first time the hands were turned up, went aloft like a cat, before anybody. And all through the passage there he was, first at the braces, outermost on the yards, perpetually lending a hand everywhere, but always with a sober dignity in his manner, and a sober grin on his face, which plainly said, "I do it as a gentleman. For my own pleasure mind you!"

At length and at last, the promised wind came up in right good earnest, and away we went before it, with every stitch of canvas set, slashing through the water nobly. There was a grandeur in the motion of the splendid ship, as overshadowed by her mass of sails, she rode at a furious pace upon the waves, which filled one with an indescribable sense of pride and exultation. As she plunged into a foaming valley, how I loved to see the green waves, bordered deep with white, come rushing on astern, to buoy her upward at their pleasure, and curl about her as she stooped again, but always own her for their haughty mistress still! On, on we flew, with changing lights upon the water, being now in the blessed region of fleecy skies; a bright sun lighting us by day, and a bright moon by night; the vane pointing directly homeward, alike the truthful index to the favoring wind and to our cheerful hearts; until at sunrise, one fair Monday morning—the twenty-seventh of June, I shall not easily forget the day,—there lay before us, old Cape Clear, God bless it, showing, in the mist of early morning, like a cloud: the brightest and most welcome cloud, to us, that ever hid the face of Heaven's fallen sister—Home.

Dim speck as it was in the wide prospect, it made the sunrise a more cheerful sight, and gave to it that sort of human interest which it seems to want at sea. There, as elsewhere, the return of day is inseparable from some sense of renewed hope and gladness; but the light shining on the dreary waste of water, and showing it in all its vast extent of loneliness, presents a solemn spectacle, which even night, veiling it in darkness and uncertainty, does not surpass. The rising of the moon is more in keeping with the solitary ocean; and has an air of melancholy grandeur, which in its soft and gentle influence, seems to comfort while it saddens. I recollect when I was a very young child having a fancy that the reflection of the moon in water was a path to Heaven, trodden by the spirits of good people on their way to God; and this old feeling often came over me again, when I watched it on a tranquil night at sea.

The wind was very light on this same Monday morning, but it was still in the right quarter, and so, by slow degrees, we left Cape Clear behind, and sailed along within sight of the coast of Ireland. And how merry we all were, and how loyal to the George Washington, and how full of mutual congratulations, and how venturesome in predicting the exact hour at which we should arrive at Liverpool, may be easily imagined and readily understood. Also, how heartily we drank the captain's health that day at dinner; and how restless we became about packing up; and how two or three of the most sanguine spirits rejected the idea of going to bed at all that night as something it was not worth while to do, so near the shore, but went nevertheless, and slept soundly; and how to be so near our journey's end, was like a pleasant dream, from which one feared to wake.

The friendly breeze freshened again next day, and on we went once more before it gallantly: descrying now and then an English ship going homeward under shortened sail, while we with every inch of canvas crowded on, dashed gaily past, and left her far behind. Towards evening, the weather turned hazy, with a drizzling rain; and soon became so thick, that we sailed, as it were, in a cloud. Still we swept onward like a phantom ship, and many an eager eye glanced up to where the Look-out on the mast kept watch for Holyhead.

At length his long-expected cry was heard, and at the same moment there shone out from the haze and mist ahead, a gleaming light, which presently was gone, and soon returned, and soon was gone again. Whenever it came back, the eyes of all on board, brightened and sparkled like itself; and there we all stood, watching this revolving light upon the rock at Holyhead, and praising it for its brightness and its friendly warning, and lauding it, in short, above all other signal lights that ever were displayed, until it once more glimmered faintly in the distance, far behind us.

Then, it was time to fire a gun, for a pilot; and almost before its smoke had cleared away, a little boat with a light at her mast-head came bearing down upon us, through the darkness, swiftly. And presently, our sails being backed, she ran alongside; and the hoarse pilot, wrapped and muffled in pea-coats and shawls to the very bridge of his weather-ploughed-up nose, stood bodily among us on the deck. And I think if that pilot had wanted to borrow fifty pounds for an indefinite period on no security, we should have engaged to lend it him, among us, before his boat had dropped astern, or (which is the same thing) before every scrap of news in the paper he brought with him had become the common property of all on board.

We turned in pretty late that night, and turned out pretty early next morning. By six o'clock we clustered on the deck, prepared to go ashore; and looked upon the spires and roofs, and smoke of Liverpool. By eight we all sat down in one of its Hotels, to eat and drink together for the last time. And by nine we had shaken hands all round, and broken up our social company forever.

The country by the railroad, seemed, as we rattled through it, like a luxuriant garden. The beauty of the fields (so small they looked!), the hedge-rows, and the trees; the pretty cottages, the beds of flowers, the old churchyards, the antique houses, and every well-known object; the exquisite delights of that one journey, crowding in the short compass of a summer's day, the joy of many years, and winding up with Home and all that makes it dear; no tongue can tell, or pen of mine can describe.

## CHAPTER XVII.

### SLAVERY.

The upholders of slavery in America—of the atrocities of which system, I shall not write one word for which I have not ample proof and warrant—may be divided into three great classes.

The first are those more moderate and rational owners of human cattle, who have come into the possession of them as so many coins in their trading capital, but who admit the frightful nature of the Institution in the abstract, and perceive the dangers to society with which it is fraught: dangers which, however distant they may be, or howsoever tardy in their coming on, are as certain to fall upon its guilty head, as is the Day of Judgment.

The second consists of all those owners, breeders, users, buyers and sellers of slaves, who will, until the bloody chapter has a bloody end, own, breed, use, buy, and sell them at all hazards; who doggedly deny the horrors of the system, in the teeth of such a mass of evidence as never was brought to bear on any other subject, and to which the experience of every day contributes its immense amount; who would, at this or any other moment, gladly involve America in a war, civil or foreign, provided that it had for its sole end and object the assertion of their right to perpetuate slavery, and to whip and work and torture slaves, unquestioned by any human authority, and unassailed by any human power; who, when they speak of Freedom, mean the Freedom to oppress their kind, and to be savage, merciless, and cruel; and of whom every man on his own ground, in republican America, is a more exacting, and a sterner, and a less responsible despot than the Caliph Haroun Alraschid in his angry robe of scarlet.

The third, and not the least numerous or influential, is composed of all that delicate gentility which cannot bear a superior, and cannot brook an equal; of that class whose Republicanism means, "I will not tolerate a man above me:

and of those below, none must approach too near;" whose pride, in a land where voluntary servitude is shunned as a disgrace, must be ministered to by slaves; and whose inalienable rights can only have their growth in negro wrongs.

It has been sometimes urged that, in the unavailing efforts which have been made to advance the cause of Human Freedom in the republic of America (strange cause for history to treat of!), sufficient regard has not been had to the existence of the first class of persons; and it has been contended that they are hardly used, in being confounded with the second. This is, no doubt, the case; noble instances of pecuniary and personal sacrifice have already had their growth among them; and it is much to be regretted that the gulf between them and the advocates of emancipation should have been widened and deepened by any means: the rather, as there are, beyond dispute, among these slave-owners, many kind masters who are tender in the exercise of their unnatural power. Still it is to be feared that this injustice is inseparable from the state of things with which humanity and truth are called upon to deal. Slavery is not a whit the more endurable because some hearts are to be found which can partially resist its hardening influences; nor can the indignant tide of honest wrath stand still, because in its onward course it overwhelms a few who are comparatively innocent, among a host of guilty.

The ground most commonly taken by these better men among the advocates of slavery is this: "It is a bad system; and for myself I would willingly get rid of it, if I could; most willingly. But it is not so bad as you in England take it to be. You are deceived by the representations of the emancipationists. The greater part of my slaves are much attached to me. You will say that I do not allow them to be severely treated; but I will put it to you whether you believe that it can be a general practice to treat them inhumanly, when it would impair their value, and would be obviously against the interests of their masters."

Is it the interest of any man to steal, to game, to waste his health and mental faculties by drunkenness, to lie, forswear himself, indulge hatred, seek desperate revenge, or do murder?

No. All these are roads to ruin. And why, then, do men tread them? Because such inclinations are among the vicious qualities of mankind. Blot out, ye friends of slavery, from the catalogue of human passions, brutal lust, cruelty, and the abuse of irresponsible power (of all earthly temptations the most difficult to be resisted), and when ye have done so, and not before, we will inquire whether it be the interest of a master to lash and maim the slaves, over whose lives and limbs he has an absolute control!

But again: this class, together with that last one I have named, the miserable aristocracy spawned of a false republic, lift up their voices and exclaim, "Public opinion is all sufficient to prevent such cruelty as you denounce." Public opinion! Why, public opinion in the slave States is slavery, is it not? Public opinion in the slave States has delivered the slaves over to the gentle mercies of their masters. Public opinion has made the laws, and denied the slaves legislative protection. Public opinion has knotted the lash, heated the branding-iron, loaded the rifle, and shielded the murderer. Public opinion threatens the abolitionist with death, if he venture to the South; and drags him with a rope about the middle, in broad unblushing noon, through the first city in the East. Public opinion has, within a few years, burned a slave alive at a slow fire in the city of St. Louis; and public opinion has to this day maintained upon the bench that estimable Judge who charged the Jury, impanelled there to try his murderers, that their most horrid deed was an act of public opinion, and being so must not be punished by the laws the public sentiment had made. Public opinion hailed this doctrine with a howl of wild applause, and set the prisoners free, to walk the city, men of mark, and influence, and station as they had been before.

Public opinion! what class of men have an immense preponderance over the rest of the community, in their power of representing public opinion in the legislature? the slave owners. They send from their twelve States one hundred members, while the fourteen free States, with a free population nearly double, return but a hundred and forty-two. Before whom do the presidential candidates bow down the most humbly, on whom do they fawn the most fondly, and for whose taste do they cater the most assiduously in their servile protestations? The slave owners always.

Public opinion! hear the public opinion of the free South, as expressed by its own members in the House of Representatives at Washington. "I have a great respect for the chair," quoth North Carolina, "I have a great respect for the chair as an officer of the house, and a great respect for him personally; nothing but that respect prevents me from rushing to the table and tearing that petition which has just been presented for the abolition of slavery in the district of Columbia, to pieces." — "I warn the abolitionists," says South Carolina, "ignorant, infuriated barbarians as they are, that if chance shall throw any of them into our hands, he may expect a felon's death."—"Let an abolitionist come within the borders of South Carolina," cries a third; mild Carolina's colleague; "and if we can catch him, we will try him, and notwithstanding the interference of all the governments on earth, including the Federal government, we will HANG him."

Public opinion has made this law.—It has declared that in Washington, in that city which takes its name from the father of American liberty, any justice of the peace may bind with fetters any negro passing down the street, and thrust him into jail: no offence on the black man's part is necessary. The justice says, "I choose to think this man a runaway:" and locks him up. Public opinion impowers the man of law when this is done, to advertise the negro in the newspapers, warning his owner to come and claim him, or he will be sold to pay the jail fees. But supposing he is a free black, and has no owner, it may naturally be presumed that he is set at liberty. No: HE IS SOLD TO RECOMPENSE HIS JAILER. This has been done again, and again, and again. He has no means of proving his freedom; has no adviser, messenger, or assistance of any sort or kind; no investigation into his case is made, or inquiry instituted. He, a free man, who may have served for years, and bought his liberty, is thrown into jail on no process, for no crime, and on no pretence of crime: and is sold to pay the jail fees. This seems incredible, even of America, but it is the law.

Public opinion is deferred to, in such cases as the following; which is headed in the newspapers:—

"*Interesting Law-Case.*

"An interesting case is now on trial in the Supreme Court, arising out of the following facts. A gentleman residing in Maryland had allowed an aged pair of his slaves, substantial though not legal freedom for several years. While thus living, a daughter was born to them, who grew up in the same liberty, until she married a free negro, and went with him to reside in Pennsylvania. They had several children, and lived unmolested until the original owner died, when his heir attempted to regain them; but the magistrate before whom they were brought, decided that he had no jurisdiction in the case. *The owner seized the woman and her children in the night, and carried them to Maryland.*"

"Cash for negroes," "cash for negroes," "cash for negroes," is the heading of advertisements in great capitals down the long columns of the crowded journals. Woodcuts of a runaway negro with manacled hands, crouching beneath a bluff pursuer in top boots, who having caught him, grasps him by the throat, agreeably diversify the pleasant text. The leading article protests against "that abominable and hellish doctrine of abolition, which is repugnant alike to every law of God and nature." The delicate mamma, who smiles her acquiescence in this sprightly writing as she reads the paper in her cool piazza, quiets her youngest child who clings about her skirts, by promising the boy "a whip to beat the little niggers with."—But the negroes, little and big, are protected by public opinion.

Let us try this public opinion by another test, which is important in three points of view: first, as showing how desperately timid of the public opinion slave owners are, in their delicate descriptions of fugitive slaves in widely circulated newspapers; secondly, as showing how perfectly contented the slaves are, and how very seldom they run away; thirdly, as exhibiting their entire freedom from scar, or blemish, or any mark of cruel infliction, as their pictures are drawn, not by lying abolitionists, but by their own truthful masters.

The following are a few specimens of the advertisements in the public papers. It is only four years since the oldest among them appeared; and others of the same nature continue to be published every day, in shoals.

"Ran away, Negress Caroline. Had on a collar with one prong turned down."

"Ran away, a black woman, Betsy. Had an iron bar on her right leg."

"Ran away, the negro Manuel. Much marked with irons."

"Ran away, the negress Fanny. Had on an iron band about her neck."

"Ran away, a negro boy about twelve years old. Had round his neck a chain dog-collar with 'De Lampert' engraved on it."

"Ran away, the negro Hown. Has a ring of iron on his left foot. Also, Grise, *his wife*, having a ring and chain on the left leg."

"Ran away, a negro boy named James. Said boy was ironed when he left me."

"Committed to jail, a man who calls his name John. He has a clog of iron on his right foot which will weigh four or five pounds."

"Detained at the police jail, the negro wench, Myra. Has several marks of LASHING, and has irons on her feet."

"Ran away, a negro woman and two children. A few days before she went off, I burnt her with a hot iron, on the left side of her face. I tried to make the letter M."

"Ran away, a negro man named Henry; his left eye out, some scars from a dirk on and under his left arm, and much scarred with the whip."

"One hundred dollars reward, for a negro fellow, Pompey, 40 years old. He is branded on the left jaw."

"Committed to jail, a negro man. Has no toes on the left foot."

"Ran away, a negro woman named Rachel. Has lost all her toes except the large one."

"Ran away, Sam. He was shot a short time since through the hand, and has several shots in his left arm and side."

"Ran away, my negro man Dennis. Said negro has been shot in the left arm between the shoulders and elbow, which has paralyzed the left hand."

"Ran away, my negro man named Simon. He has been shot badly, in his back and right arm."

"Ran away, a negro named Arthur. Has a considerable scar across his breast and each arm, made by a knife; loves to talk much of the goodness of God."

"Twenty-five dollars reward for my man Isaac. He has a scar on his forehead, caused by a blow; and one on his back, made by a shot from a pistol."

"Ran away, a negro girl called Mary. Has a small scar over her eye, a good many teeth missing, the letter A is branded on her cheek and forehead."

"Ran away, negro Ben. Has a scar on his right hand; his thumb and forefinger being injured by being shot last fall. A part of the bone came out. He has also one or two large scars on his back and hips."

"Detained at the jail, a mulatto, named Tom. Has a scar on the right cheek, and appears to have been burned with powder on the face."

"Ran away, a negro man named Ned. Three of his fingers are drawn into the palm of his hand by a cut. Has a scar on the back of his neck, nearly half round, done by a knife."

"Was committed to jail, a negro man. Says his name is Josiah. His back very much scarred by the whip; and branded on the thigh and hips in three or four places, thus (J. M.) The rim of his right ear has been bit or cut off."

"Fifty dollars reward, for my fellow Edward. He has a scar on the corner of his month, two cuts on and under his arm, and the letter E on his arm."

"Ran away, negro boy Ellie. Has a scar on one of his arms from the bite of a dog."

"Ran away, from the plantation of James Surgette, the following negroes: Randal, has one ear cropped; Bob, has lost one eye; Kentucky Tom, has one jaw broken."

"Ran away, Anthony. One of his ears cut off, and his left hand cut with an axe."

"Fifty dollars reward for the negro Jim Blake. Has a piece cut out of each ear, and the middle finger of the left hand cut off to the second joint."

"Ran away, a negro woman named Maria. Has a scar on one side of her cheek, by a cut. Some scars on her back."

"Ran away, the Mulatto wench Mary. Has a cut on the left arm, a scar on the left shoulder, and two upper teeth missing."

I should say, perhaps, in explanation of this latter piece of description, that among the other blessings which public opinion secures to the negroes, is the common practice of violently punching out their teeth. To make them wear iron collars by day and night, and to worry them with dogs, are practices almost too ordinary to deserve mention.

"Ran away, my man Fountain. Has holes in his ears, a scar on the right side of his forehead, has been shot in the hind part of his legs, and is marked on the back with the whip."

"Two hundred and fifty dollars reward for my negro man Jim. He is much marked with shot in his right thigh. The shot entered on the outside, halfway between the hip and knee joints."

"Brought to jail, John. Left ear cropped."

"Taken up, a negro man. Is very much scarred about the face and body, and has the left ear bit off."

"Ran away, a black girl, named Mary. Has a scar on her cheek, and the end of one of her toes cut off."

"Ran away, my mulatto woman, Judy. She has had her right arm broke."

"Ran away, my negro man, Levi. His left hand has been burnt, and I think the end of his forefinger is off."

"Ran away, a negro man, NAMED WASHINGTON. Has lost a part of his middle finger, and the end of his little finger."

"Twenty-five dollars reward for my man John. The tip of his nose is bit off."

"Twenty-five dollars reward for the negro slave Sally. Walks *as though* crippled in the back."

"Ran away, Joe Dennis. Has a small notch in one of his ears."

"Ran away, negro boy, Jack. Has a small crop out of his left ear."

"Ran away, a negro man, named Ivory. Has a small piece cut out of the top of each ear."

While upon the subject of ears, I may observe that a distinguished abolitionist in New York once received a negro's ear, which had been cut off close to the head, in a general post letter. It was forwarded by the free and independent gentleman who had caused it to be amputated, with a polite request that he would place the specimen in his "collection."

I could enlarge this catalogue with broken arms, and broken legs, and gashed flesh, and missing teeth, and lacerated backs, and bites of dogs, and brands of red-hot irons innumerable: but as my readers will be sufficiently sickened and repelled already, I will turn to another branch of the subject.

These advertisements, of which a similar collection might be made for every year, and month, and week, and day; and which are coolly read in families as things of course, and as a part of the current news and small-talk; will serve to show how very much the slaves profit by public opinion, and how tender it is in their behalf. But it may be worth while to inquire how the slave owners, and the class of society to which great numbers of them belong, defer to public opinion in their conduct, not to their slaves but to each other; how they are accustomed to restrain their passions; what their bearing is among themselves; whether they are fierce or gentle; whether their social customs be brutal, sanguinary, and violent, or bear the impress of civilization and refinement.

That we may have no partial evidence from abolitionists in this inquiry, either, I will once more turn to their own newspapers, and I will confine myself, this time, to a selection from paragraphs which appeared from day to day, during my visit to America, and which refer to occurrences happening while I was there. The italics in these extracts, as in the foregoing, are my own.

These cases did not ALL occur, it will be seen, in territory actually belonging to legalized Slave States, though most and those the very worst among them did, as their counterparts constantly do; but the position of the scenes of action in reference to places immediately at hand, where slavery is the law; and the strong resemblance between that class of outrages and the rest; lead to the just presumption that the character of the parties concerned was formed in slave districts, and brutalized by slave customs.

"*Horrible Tragedy.*

"By a slip from *The Southport Telegraph*, Wisconsin, we learn that the Hon. Charles C. P. Arndt, Member of the Council for Brown county, was shot dead *on the floor of the Council chamber*, by James R. Vinyard, Member from Grant county. *The affair* grew out of a nomination for Sheriff of Grant county. Mr. E. S. Baker was nominated and supported by Mr. Arndt. This nomination was opposed by Vinyard, who wanted the appointment to vest in his own brother. In the course of debate, the deceased made some statements which Vinyard pronounced false, and made use of violent and insulting language, dealing largely in personalities, to which Mr. A. made no reply. After the adjournment, Mr. A. stepped up to Vinyard, and requested him to retract, which he refused to do, repeating the offensive words. Mr. Arndt then made a blow at Vinyard, who stepped back a pace, drew a pistol, and shot him dead.

"The issue appears to have been provoked on the part of Vinyard, who was determined at all hazards to defeat the appointment of Baker, and who, himself defeated, turned his ire and revenge upon the unfortunate Arndt."

"*The Wisconsin Tragedy.*

"Public indignation runs high in the territory of Wisconsin, in relation to the murder of C. C. P. Arndt, in the Legislative Hall of the Territory. Meetings have been held in different counties of Wisconsin, denouncing *the practice of secretly bearing arms in the Legislative chambers of the country.* We have seen the account of the expulsion of James R. Vinyard, the perpetrator of the bloody deed, and are amazed to hear, that, after this expulsion by those who saw Vinyard kill Mr. Arndt in the presence of his aged father, who was on a visit to see his son, little dreaming that he was to witness his murder, *Judge Dunn has discharged Vinyard on bail.* The Miners' Free Press speaks *in terms of merited rebuke* at the outrage upon the feelings of the people of Wisconsin. Vinyard was within arm's length of Mr. Arndt, when he took such deadly aim at him, that he never spoke. Vinyard might at pleasure, being so near, have only wounded him, but he chose to kill him."

"*Murder.*

"By a letter in a St. Louis paper of the 14th, we notice a terrible outrage at Burlington, Iowa. A Mr. Bridgman having had a difficulty with a citizen of the place, Mr. Ross; a brother-in-law of the latter provided himself with one of Colt's revolving pistols, met Mr. B. in the street, *and discharged the contents of five of the barrels at him: each shot taking effect.* Mr. B., though horribly wounded, and dying, returned the fire, and killed Ross on the spot.

*Terrible death of Robert Potter.*

"From the 'Caddo Gazette,' of the 12th inst., we learn the frightful death of Colonel Robert Potter. . . . . He was beset in his house by an enemy, named Rose. He sprang from his couch, seized his gun, and, in his night clothes, rushed from the house. For about two hundred yards his speed seemed to defy his pursuers; but, getting entangled in a thicket, he was captured. Rose told him *that he intended to act a generous part*, and give him a chance for his life. He then told Potter he might run, and he should not be interrupted till he reached a certain distance. Potter started at the word of command, and before a gun was fired he had reached the lake. His first impulse was to jump in the water and dive for it, which he did. Rose was close behind him and formed his men on the bank ready to shoot him as he rose. In a few seconds he came up to breathe; and scarce had his head reached the surface of the water when it was completely riddled with the shot of their guns, and he sunk, to rise no more!"

"*Murder in Arkansas.*

"We understand *that a severe rencontre came off* a few days since in the Seneca Nation, between Mr. Loose, the sub-agent of the mixed band of the Senecas, Quapaw, and Shawnees, and Mr. James Gillespie, of the mercantile firm of Thomas G. Allison and Co., of Maysville, Benton, County Ark, in which the latter was slain with a bowie-knife. Some difficulty had for some time existed between the parties. It is said that Major Gillespie brought on the attack with a cane. A severe conflict ensued, during which two pistols were fired by Gillespie and one by Loose. Loose then stabbed Gillespie with one of those never failing weapons, a bowie-knife. The death of Major G. is much regretted, as he was a liberal-minded and energetic man. Since the above was in type, we have learned that Major Allison has stated to some of our citizens in town that Mr. Loose gave the first blow. We forbear to give any particulars, as *the matter will be the subject of judicial investigation.*"

"*Foul Deed.*

"The steamer Thames, just from Missouri river, brought us a handbill, offering a reward of 500 dollars for the person who assassinated Lilburn W. Baggs, late Governor of this State, at Independence, on the night of the 6th inst. Governor Baggs, it is stated in a written memorandum, was not dead but mortally wounded.

"Since the above was written, we received a note from the clerk of the Thames, giving the following particulars. Gov Baggs was shot by some villain on Friday, 6th inst., in the evening, while sitting in a room in his own house in Independence. His son, a boy, hearing a report, ran into the room, and found the Governor sitting in his chair, with his jaw fallen down, and his head leaning back; on discovering the injury done his father, he gave the alarm. Foot tracks were found in the garden below the window, and a pistol picked up supposed to have been overloaded, and thrown from the hand of the scoundrel who fired it. Three buck shots of a heavy load, took effect; one going through his mouth, one into the brain, and another probably in or near the brain; all going into the back part of the neck and head. The Governor was still alive on the morning of the 7th; but no hopes for his recovery by his friends, and but slight hopes from his physicians.

"A man was suspected, and the Sheriff most probably has possession of him by this time.

"The pistol was one of a pair stolen some days previous from a baker in Independence, and the legal authorities have the description of the other."

"*Rencontre.*

"An unfortunate *affair* took place on Friday evening in Chartres Street, in which one of our most respectable citizens received a dangerous wound, from a poignard in the abdomen. From the Bee (New Orleans) of yesterday, we learn the following particulars. It appears that an article was published in the French side of the paper on Monday last, containing some strictures on the Artillery Battalion for firing their guns on Sunday morning, in answer to those from the Ontario and Woodbury, and thereby much alarm was caused to the families of those persons who were out all night preserving the peace of the city. Major C. Gally, Commander of the battalion resenting this, called at the office and demanded the author's name; that of M. P. Arpin was given to him, who was absent at the time. Some angry words then passed with one of the proprietors, and a challenge followed; the friends of both parties tried to arrange the affair, but failed to do so. On Friday evening, about seven o'clock, Major Gally met Mr. P. Arpin in Chartres Street, and accosted him. 'Are you Mr. Arpin?'

"'Yes, Sir.'

"'Then I have to tell you that you are a——'" (applying an appropriate epithet.)

"'I shall remind you of your words, sir.'

"'But I have said I would break my cane on your shoulders.'

"'I know it, but I have not received the blow.'

"'At these words, Major Gally, having a cane in his hands, struck Mr. Arpin across the face, and the latter drew a poignard from his pocket and stabbed Major Gally in the abdomen.

"Fears are entertained that the wound will be mortal. *We understand that Mr. Arpin has given security for his appearance at the Criminal Court to answer the charge.*"

"*Affray in Mississippi.*

"On the 27th ult., in an affray near Carthage, Leake county Mississippi, between James Cottingham and John Wilburn, the latter was shot by the former, and so horribly wounded, that there was no hope of his recovery. On the 2nd instant, there was an affray at Carthage between A. C. Sharkey and George Goff, in which the latter was shot, and thought mortally wounded. Sharkey delivered himself up to the authorities, *but changed his mind and escaped!*"

"*Personal Encounter.*

"An encounter took place in Sparta, a few days since, between the barkeeper of an hotel, and a man named Bury. It appears that Bury had become somewhat noisy, *and that the barkeeper, determined to preserve order, had threatened to shoot Bury,* whereupon Bury drew a pistol and shot the barkeeper down. He was not dead at last accounts, but slight hopes were entertained of his recovery."

"*Duel.*

"The clerk of the steamboat *Tribune* informs us that another duel was fought on Tuesday last, Mr. Robbins, a bank officer in Vicksburg, and Mr. Fall, the editor of the Vicksburg Sentinel. According to the arrangement, the parties had six pistols each, which, after the word 'Fire!' *they were to discharge as fast as they pleased.* Fall fired two pistols without effect. Mr. Robbins' first shot took effect in Fall's thigh, who fell, and was unable to continue the combat."

"*Affray in Clark County.*

"An *unfortunate affray* occurred in Clark county (Mo.) near Waterloo, on Tuesday the 19th ult., which originated in settling the partnership concerns of Messrs. M'Kane and M'Allister, who had been engaged in the business of distilling, and resulted in the death of the latter, who was shot down by Mr. M'Kane, because of his attempting to take possession of seven barrels of whiskey, the property of M'Kane, which had been knocked off to M'Allister at a sheriff's sale at one dollar per barrel. M'Kane immediately fled *and at the latest dates had not been taken.*

" *This unfortunate affray* caused considerable excitement in the neighborhood, as both the parties were men with large families depending upon them and stood well in the community."

I will quote but one more paragraph, which, by reason of its monstrous absurdity, may be a relief to these atrocious deeds.

"*Affair of Honor.*

"We have just heard the particulars of a meeting which took place on Six Mile Island, on Tuesday, between two young bloods of our city: Samuel Thurston, *aged fifteen*, and William Hine, *aged thirteen years.* They were attended by young gentlemen of the same age. The weapons used on this occasion, were a couple of Dickson's best rifles; the distance, thirty yards. They took one fire, without any damage being sustained by either party, except the ball of Thurston's gun passing through the crown of Hine's hat. *Through the intercession of the Board of Honor*, the challenge was withdrawn, and the difference amicably adjusted."

If the reader will picture to himself the kind of Board of Honor which amicably adjusted the difference between these two little boys, who in any other part of the world would have been amicably adjusted on two porters' backs and soundly flogged with birchen rods, he will be possessed, no doubt, with as strong a sense of its ludicrous character, as that which sets me laughing whenever its image rises up before me.

Now I appeal to every human mind, imbued with the commonest of common sense, and the commonest of common humanity; to all dispassionate, reasoning creatures, of any shade of opinion; and ask, with these revolting evidences of the state of society which exists in and about the slave districts of America before them, can they have a doubt of the real condition of the slave, or can they for a moment make a compromise between the institution or any of its flagrant fearful features, and their own just consciences? Will they say of any tale of cruelty and horror, however aggravated in degree, that it is improbable, when they can turn to the public prints, and, running, read such signs as these, laid before them by the men who rule the slaves: in their own acts, and under their own hands?'

Do we not know that the worst deformity and ugliness of slavery are at once the cause and the effect of the reckless licence taken by these free-born outlaws? Do we not know that the man who has been born and bred among its wrongs; who has seen in his childhood husbands obliged at the word of command to flog their wives; women, indecently compelled to hold up their own garments that men might lay the heavier stripes upon their legs, driven and harried by brutal overseers in their time of travail, and becoming mothers on the field of toil, under the very lash itself; who has read in youth, and seen his virgin sisters read, descriptions of runaway men and women, and their disfigured persons, which could not be published elsewhere, of so much stock upon a farm, or at a show of beasts :—do we not know that that man, whenever his wrath is kindled up, will be a brutal savage? Do we not know that as he is a coward in his domestic life, stalking among his shrinking men and women slaves armed with his heavy whip, so he will be a coward out of doors, and carrying cowards' weapons hidden in his breast will shoot men down and stab them when he quarrels? And if our reason did not teach us this and much beyond; if we were such idiots as to close our eyes to that fine mode of training which rears up such men; should we not know that they who among their equals stab and pistol in the legislative halls, and in the counting-house, and on the market-place, and in all the elsewhere peaceful pursuits of life, must be to their dependants, even though they were free servants, so many merciless and unrelenting tyrants?

What! shall we declaim against the ignorant peasantry of Ireland, and mince the matter when these American taskmasters are in question? Shall we cry shame on the brutality of those who ham-string cattle; and share the lights of Freedom upon earth who notch the ears of men and women, cut pleasant posies in the shrinking flesh, learn to write with pens of red-hot iron on the human face, rack their poetic fancies for liveries of mutilation which their slaves shall wear for life and carry to the grave, break living limbs as did the soldiery who mocked and slew the Saviour of the world, and set defenceless creatures up for targets? Shall we whimper over legends of the tortures practised on each other by the Pagan Indians, and smile upon the cruelties of Christian men? Shall we, so long as these things last, exult above the scattered remnants of that stately race, and triumph in the white enjoyment of their broad possessions? Rather, for me, restore the forest and the Indian village; in lieu of stars and stripes, let some poor feather flutter in the breeze; replace the streets and squares by wigwams; and though the death-song of a hundred haughty warriors fill the air, it will be music to the shriek of one unhappy slave.

On one theme, which is commonly before our eyes, and in respect of which our national character is changing fast, let the plain Truth be spoken, and let us not, like dastards, beat about the bush by hinting at the Spaniard and the fierce Italian. When knives are drawn by Englishmen in conflict let it be said and known: "We owe this change to Republican Slavery. These are the weapons of Freedom. With sharp points and edges such as these, Liberty in America hews and hacks her slaves; or, failing that pursuit, her sons devote them to a better use, and turn them on each other."

---

## CHAPTER XVIII.

### CONCLUDING REMARKS.

THERE are many passages in this book, where I have been at some pains to resist the temptation of troubling my readers with my own deductions and conclusions: preferring that they should judge for themselves, from such premises as I have laid before them. My only object in the outset, was, to carry them with me faithfully wheresoever I went: and that task I have discharged.

But I may be pardoned, if on such a theme as the general character of the American people, and the general character of their social system, as presented to a stranger's eyes, I desire to express my own opinions in a few words, before I bring these volumes to a close.

They are, by nature, frank, brave, cordial, hospitable, and affectionate. Cultivation and refinement seem but to enhance their warmth of heart and ardent enthusiasm; and it is the possession of these latter qualities in a most remarkable degree, which renders an educated American one of the most endearing and most generous of friends. I never was so won upon, as by this class; never yielded up my full confidence and esteem so readily and pleasurably, as to them; never can make again, in half-a-year, so many friends for whom I seem to entertain the regard of half a life.

These qualities are natural, I implicitly believe, to the whole people. That they are, however, sadly sapped and blighted in their growth among the mass; and that there are influences at work which endanger them still more, and give but little present promise of their healthy restoration; is a truth that ought to be told.

It is an essential part of every national character to pique itself mightily upon its faults, and to deduce tokens of its virtue or its wisdom from their very exaggeration. One great blemish in the popular mind of America, and the prolific parent of an innumerable brood of evils, is Universal Distrust. Yet the American citizen plumes himself upon this spirit, even when he is sufficiently dispassionate to perceive the ruin it works; and will often adduce it, in spite of his own reason, as an instance of the great sagacity and acuteness of the people, and their superior shrewdness and independence.

"You carry," says the stranger, "this jealousy and distrust into every transaction of public life. By repelling worthy men from your legislative assemblies, it has bred up a class of candidates for the suffrage, who, in their every act, disgrace your Institutions and your people's choice. It has rendered you so fickle, and so given to change, that your inconstancy has passed into a proverb; for you no sooner set up an idol firmly, than you are sure to pull it down and dash it into fragments: and this, because directly you reward a benefactor, or a public servant, you distrust him, merely because he *is* rewarded; and immediately apply yourselves to find out, either that you have been too bountiful in your acknowledgments, or he remiss in his deserts. Any man who attains a high place among you, from the President downwards, may date his downfall from that monent; for any printed lie that any notorious villain pens, although it militate directly against the character and conduct of a life, appeals at once to your distrust, and is believed. You will strain at a gnat in the way of trustfulness and confidence, however fairly won and well deserved; but you will swallow a whole caravan of camels, if they be laden with unworthy doubts and mean suspicions. Is this well, think you, or likely to elevate the character of the governors or the governed, among you?"

The answer is invariably the same: "There's freedom of opinion here, you know. Every man thinks for himself, and we are not to be easily overreached. That's how our people come to be suspicious."

Another prominent feature in the love of "smart" dealing: which gilds over many a swindle and gross breach of trust; many a defalcation, public and private; and enables many a knave to hold his head up with the best, who well deserves a halter: though it has not been without its retributive operation, for this smartness has done more in a few years to impair the public credit, and to cripple the public resources, than dull honesty, however rash, could have effected in a century. The merits of a broken speculation, or a bankruptcy or of a successful scoundrel, are not gauged by its or his observance of the golden rule, "Do as you would be done by," but are considered with reference to their smartness. I recollect, on both occasions of our passing that ill-fated Cairo on the Mississippi, remarking on the bad effects such gross deceits must have when they exploded, in generating a want of confidence abroad, and discouraging foreign investment: but I was given to understand that this was a very smart scheme by which a deal of money had been made: and that its smartest feature was that they forgot these things abroad, in a very short time, and speculated again, as freely as ever. The following dialogue I have held a hundred times: "Is it not a very disgraceful circumstance that such a man as So and So should be acquiring a large property by the most infamous and odious means, and notwithstanding all the crimes of which he has been guilty, should be tolerated and abetted by your Citizens? He is a public nuisance, is he not?" "Yes, sir." "A convicted liar?" "Yes, sir." "He has been kicked, and cuffed, and caned?" "Yes, sir." "And he is utterly dishonorable, debased, and profligate?" "Yes, sir." "In the name of wonder, then, what is his merit?" "Well, sir, he is a smart man."

In like manner, all kinds of deficient and impolitic usages are referred to the national love of trade; though, oddly enough, it would be a weighty charge against a foreigner that he regarded the Americans as a trading people. The love of trade is assigned as a reason for that comfortless custom, so very prevalent in country towns, of married persons living in hotels, having no fireside of their own, and seldom meeting from early morning until late at night, but at the hasty public meals. The love of trade is a reason why the literature of America is to remain for ever unprotected: "For we are a trading people, and don't care for poetry:" though we *do*, by the way, profess to be very proud of our poets: while healthful amusements, cheerful means of recreation, and wholesome fancies, must fade before the stern utilitarian joys of trade.

These three characteristics are strongly presented at every turn, full in the stranger's view. But, the foul growth of America has a more tangled root than this; and it strikes its fibres, deep in its licentious Press.

Schools may be erected, East, West, North, and South; pupils be taught, and masters reared, by scores upon scores of thousands; colleges may thrive, churches may be crammed, temperance may be diffused, and advancing knowledge in all other forms walk through the land with giant strides: but while the newspaper press of America is in, or near, its present abject state, high moral improvement in that country is hopeless. Year by year, it must and will go back; year by year, the tone of public feeling must sink lower down; year by year, the Congress and the Senate must become of less account before all decent men; and year by year, the memory of the Great Fathers of the Revolution must be outraged more and more, in the bad life of their degenerate child.

Among the herd of journals which are published in the States, there are some, the reader scarcely need be told, of character and credit. From personal intercourse with accomplished gentlemen connected with publications of this class, I have derived both pleasure and profit. But the name of these is Few, and of the others Legion; and the influence of the good is powerless to counteract the mortal poison of the bad.

Among the gentry of America; among the well-informed and moderate: in the learned professions; at the bar and on the bench: there is, as there can be, but one opinion, in reference to the vicious character of these infamous journals. It is sometimes contended—I will not say strangely, for it is natural to seek excuses for such a disgrace—that their influence is not so great as a visitor would suppose. I must be pardoned for saying that there is no warrant for this plea, and that every fact and circumstance tends directly to the opposite conclusion.

When any man, of any grade of desert in intellect or character, can climb to any public distinction, no matter what, in America, without first grovelling down upon earth, and bending the knee before this monster of depravity; when any private excellence is safe from its attacks; when any social confidence is left unbroken by it, or any tie of social decency and honor is held in the least regard; when any man in that Free Country has freedom of opinion, and presumes to think for himself, and speak for himself, without humble reference to a censorship which, for its rampant ignorance and base dishonesty, he utterly loathes and despises in his heart; when those who most acutely feel its infamy and the reproach it casts upon the nation, and who most denounce it to each other, dare to set their heels upon, and crush it openly, in the sight of all men: then, I will believe that its influence is lessening, and men are returning to their manly senses. But while that Press has its evil eye in every house, and its black hand in every appointment in the state, from a president to a postman; while, with ribald slander for its only stock in trade, it is the standard literature of an enormous class, who must find their reading in a newspaper, or they will not read at all; so long must its odium be upon the country's head, and so long must the evil it works be plainly visible in the Republic.

To those who are accustomed to the leading English journals, or to the respectable journals of the Continent of Europe; to those who are accustomed to anything else in print and paper; it would be impossible, without an amount of extract for which I have neither space nor inclination, to convey an adequate idea of this frightful engine in America. But if any man desire confirmation of my statement on this head, let him repair to any place in this city of London, where scattered numbers of these publications are to be found; and there, let him form his own opinion.*

It would be well, there can be no doubt, for the American people as a whole, if they loved the Real less, and the Ideal somewhat more. It would be well, if there were greater encouragement to lightness of heart and gaiety, and a wider cultivation of what is beautiful, without being eminently and directly useful. But here, I think the general remonstrance, "we are a new country," which is so often advanced as an excuse for defects which are quite unjustifiable, as being of right only the slow growth of an old one, may be very reasonably urged: and I yet hope to hear of there being some other national amusement in the United States, besides newspaper politics.

They certainly are not a humorous people, and their temperament always impressed me as being of a dull and gloomy character. In shrewdness of remark, and a certain cast-iron quaintness, the Yankees, or people of New England, unquestionably take the lead; as they do in most other evidences of intelligence. But in travelling about out of the large cities—as I have remarked in former parts of these volumes—I was quite oppressed by the prevailing seriousness and melancholy air of business: which was so general and unvarying, that at every new town I came to I seemed to meet the very same people whom I had left behind me, at the last. Such defects as are perceptible in the national manners, seem, to me, to be referable, in a great degree, to this cause: which has generated a dull, sullen persistence in coarse usages, and rejected the graces of life as undeserving of attention. There is no doubt that Washington, who was always most scrupulous

*NOTE TO THE ORIGINAL EDITION.—Or let him refer to an able, and perfectly truthful article, in *The Foreign Quarterly Review*, published in the present month of October; to which my attention has been attracted, since these sheets have been passing through the press. He will find some specimens there, by no means remarkable to any man who has been in America, but sufficiently striking to one who has not.

and exact on points of ceremony, perceived the tendency towards this mistake, even in his time, and did his utmost to correct it.

I cannot hold with other writers on these subjects that the prevalence of various forms of dissent in America, is in any way attributable to the non-existence there of an established church: indeed I think the temper of the people, if it admitted of such an Institution being founded amongst them, would lead them to desert it, as a matter of course, merely because it *was* established. But, supposing it to exist, I doubt its probable efficacy in summoning the wandering sheep to one great fold, simply because of the immense amount of dissent which prevails at home; and because I do not find in America any one form of religion with which we in Europe, or even in England, are unacquainted. Dissenters resort thither in great numbers, as other people do, simply because it is a land of resort; and great settlements of them are founded, because ground can be purchased, and towns and villages reared, where there were none of the human creation before. But even the Shakers emigrated from England; our country is not unknown to Mr. Joseph Smith, the apostle of Mormonism, or to his benighted disciples; I have beheld religious scenes myself in some of our populous towns which can hardly be surpassed by an American camp-meeting; and I am not aware that any instance of superstitious imposture on the one hand, and superstitious credulity on the other, has had its origin in the United States, which we cannot more than parallel by the precedents of Mrs. Southcote, Mary Tofts the rabbit-breeder, or even Mr. Thom of Canterbury: which latter case arose sometime after the dark ages had passed away.

The Republican Institutions of America undoubtedly lead the people to assert their self-respect and their equality; but a traveller is bound to bear those Institutions in his mind, and not hastily to resent the near approach of a class of strangers, who at home, would keep aloof. This characteristic, when it was tinctured with no foolish pride, and stopped short of no honest service, never offended me; and I very seldom, if ever experienced its rude or unbecoming display. Once or twice it was comically developed, as in the following case; but this was an amusing incident, and not the rule or near it.

I wanted a pair of boots at a certain town, for I had none to travel in, but these with the memorable cork soles, which were much too hot for the fiery decks of a steamboat. I therefore sent a message to an artist in boots, importing, with my compliments, that I should be happy to see him, if he would do me the polite favor to call. He very kindly returned for answer, that he would "look round" at six o'clock that evening.

I was lying on the sofa, with a book and a wine-glass, at about that time, when the door opened, and a gentleman in a stiff cravat, within a year or two on either side of thirty, entered, in his hat and gloves; walked up to the looking-glass; arranged his hair; took off his gloves; slowly produced a measure from the uttermost depths of his coat pocket; and requested me, in a languid tone, to "unfix" my straps. I complied, but looked with some curiosity at his hat, which was still upon his head. It might have been that, or it might have been the heat—but he took it off. Then, he sat himself down on a chair opposite to me; rested an arm on each knee; and, leaning forward very much, took from the ground, by a great effort, the specimen of metropolitan workmanship which I had just pulled off: whistling, pleasantly, as he did so. He turned it over and over; surveyed it with a contempt no language can express; and inquired if I wished him to fix me a boot like *that?* I courteously replied, that provided the boots were large enough, I would leave the rest to him; that, if convenient and practicable, I should not object to their bearing some resemblance to the model then before him; but that I would be entirely guided by, and would beg to leave the whole subject to, his judgment and discretion. "You an't partickler, about this scoop in the heel I suppose then?" says he: "We don't foller that, here." I repeated my last observation. He looked at himself in the glass again: went closer to it to dash a grain or two of dust out of the corner of his eye; and settled his cravat. All this time, my leg and foot were in the air. "Nearly ready, sir?" I inquired. "Well, pretty nigh," he said; "keep steady." I kept as steady as I could, both in foot and face; and havimg by this time got the dust out, and found his pencil-case, he measured me, and made the necessary notes. When he had finished, he fell into his old attitude, and taking up the boot again, mused for some time. "And this," he said, at last, "is an English boot, is it! This is a London boot, eh?" "That, sir," I replied, "is a London boot." He mused over it again after the manner of Hamlet with Yorick's skull; nodded his head, as who should say, "I pity the Institutions that led to the production of this boot!"; rose; put up his pencil, notes, and paper—glancing at himself in the glass all the time—put on his hat; drew on his gloves very slowly; and finally walked out. When he had been gone about a minute, the door reopened, and his hat and his head reappeared. He looked round the room, and at the boot again, which was still lying on the floor; appeared thoughtful for a minute; and then said "Well, good arternoon." "Good afternoon, sir," said I: and that was the end of the interview.

There is but one other head on which I wish to offer a remark; and that has reference to the public health. In so vast a country, where there are thousands of millions of acres of land yet unsettled and uncleared, and on every rood of which, vegetable decomposition is annually taking place; where there are so many great rivers, and such opposite varieties of climate; there cannot fail to be a great amount of sickness at certain seasons. But I may venture to say, after conversing with many members of the medical profession in America, that I am not singular in the opinion that much of the disease which does prevail, might be avoided, if a few common precautions were observed. Greater means of personal cleanliness, are indispensable to this end; the custom of hastily swallowing large quantities of animal food, three times a-day, and rushing back to sedentary pursuits after each meal, must be changed; the gentler sex must go more wisely clad, and take more healthful exercise; and in the latter clause, the males must be included also. Above all, in public institutions, and throughout the whole of every town and city, the system of ventilation, and drainage, and removal of impurities requires to be thoroughly revised. There is no local Legislature in America which may not study Mr. Chadwick's excellent Report upon the Sanitary Condition of our Laboring Classes, with immense advantage.

I HAVE now arrived at the close of this book. I have little reason to believe, from certain warnings I have had since I returned to England, that it will be tenderly or favorably received by the American people; and as I have written the Truth in relation to the mass of those who form their judgments and express their opinions, it will be seen that I have no desire to court, by any adventitious means, the popular applause.

It is enough for me to know, that what I have set down in these pages cannot cost me a single friend on the other side of the Atlantic, who is, in anything, deserving of the name. For the rest, I put my trust, implicitly, in the spirit in which they have been conceived and penned; and I can bide my time.

I have made no reference to my reception, nor have I suffered it to influence me in what I have written; for, in either case, I should have offered but a sorry acknowledgement, compared with that I bear within my breast, towards those partial readers of my former books across the Water, who met me with an open hand, and not with one that closed upon an iron muzzle.

# THE UNCOMMERCIAL TRAVELER.

# THE UNCOMMERCIAL TRAVELER.

ALLOW me to introduce myself—first, negatively.

No landlord is my friend and brother, no chambermaid loves me, no waiter worships me, no boots admires and envies me. No round of beef or tongue or ham is expressly cooked for me, no pigeon-pie is especially made for me, no hotel-advertisement is personally addressed to me, no hotel-room tapestried with great coats and railway-wrappers is set apart for me, no house of public entertainment in the United Kingdom greatly cares for my opinion of its brandy or its sherry. When I go upon my journeys, I am not usually rated at a low figure in the bill; when I come home from my journeys, I never get any commission. I know nothing about prices, and should have no idea, if I were put to it, how to wheedle a man into ordering something he doesn't want. As a town traveler, I am never to be seen driving a vehicle externally like a young and volatile pianoforte van, and internally like an oven in which a number of flat boxes are baking in layers. As a country traveler, I am rarely to be found in a gig, and am never to be encountered by a pleasure train, waiting on the platform of a branch station, quite a Druid in the midst of a light Stonehenge of samples.

And yet—proceeding now, to introduce myself positively—I am both a town traveler and a country traveler, and am always on the road. Figuratively speaking, I travel for the great house of Human Interest Brothers, and have rather a large connection in the fancy goods way. Literally speaking, I am always wandering here and there from my rooms in Covent-garden, London—now about the city streets: now, about the country by-roads—seeing many little things and some great things, which, because they interest me, I think may interest others.

These are my brief credentials as the Uncommercial Traveler. Business is business, and I start.

---

NEVER had I seen a year going out, or going on, under quieter circumstances. Eighteen hundred and fifty-nine had but another day to live, and truly its end was Peace on that sea-shore that morning.

So settled and orderly was every thing seaward, in the bright light of the sun and under the transparent shadows of the clouds, that it was hard to imagine the bay otherwise, for years past or to come, than it was that very day. The tug-steamer lying a little off the shore, the Lighter lying still nearer to the shore, the boat alongside the Lighter, the regularly turning windlass aboard the Lighter, the methodical figures at work, all slowly and regularly heaving up and down with the breathing of the sea, all seemed as much a part of the nature of the place as the tide itself. The tide was on the flow, and had been for some two hours and a half; there was a slight obstruction in the sea, within a few yards of my feet; as if the stump of a tree, with earth enough about it to keep it from lying horizontally on the water, had slipped a little from the land—and as I stood upon the beach and observed it dimpling the light swell that was coming in, I cast a stone over it.

So orderly, so quiet, so regular—the rising and falling of the tug-steamer, the Lighter, and the boat—the turning of the windlass—the coming in of the tide—that I myself seemed, to my own thinking, any thing but new to the spot. Yet, I had never seen it in my life, a minute before, and had traversed two hundred miles to get at it. That very morning I had come bowling down, and struggling up, hill-country roads; looking back at snowy summits; meeting courteous peasants, well to do, driving fat pigs, and cattle to market; noting the neat and thrifty dwellings, with their unusual quantity of clean white linen, drying on the bushes; having windy weather, suggested by every cotter's little rick, with its thatch, straw-ridged and extra straw-ridged into overlapping compartments, like the back of a rhinoceros. Had I not given a lift of fourteen miles to the Coast-Guardsman (kit and all), who was coming to his spell of duty, there, and had we not just now parted company? So it was; but the journey seemed to glide down into the placid sea, with other chafe and trouble, and for the moment nothing was so calmly and monotonously real under the sunlight as the gentle rising and falling of the water with its freight, the regular turning of the windlass aboard the Lighter, and the slight obstruction so very near my feet.

O reader, haply turning this page by the fireside at home and hearing the night wind rumble in the chimney, that slight obstruction was the uppermost fragment of the wreck of the Royal Charter, Australian trader and passenger ship, homeward bound that struck here on the terrible morning of the twenty-sixth of last October, broke into three parts, went down with her treasure of at least five hundred human lives, and has never stirred since!

From which point, or from which, she drove ashore, stern foremost; on which side, or on which, she passed the little Island in the bay, for ages henceforth to be aground certain yards outside her; these are rendered bootless questions by the darkness of that night and the darkness of death. Here she went down.

Even as I stood on the beach, with the words "Here she went down!" in my ears, a diver in his grotesque dress, dipped heavily over the side of the boat alongside the Lighter, and dropped to the bottom. On the shore by the water's edge, was a rough tent, made of fragments of wreck, where other divers and workmen sheltered themselves, aud where they had kept Christmas-day with rum and roast beef, to the destruction of their frail chimney. Cast up among the stones and boulders of the beach, were great spars of the lost vessel, and masses of iron twisted by the fury of the sea into the strangest forms. The timber was already bleached and the iron rusted, and even these objects did no violence to the prevailing air the whole scene wore, of having been exactly the same for years and years.

Yet, only two short months had gone, since a man, living on the nearest hill-top overlooking the sea, being blown out of bed at about daybreak by the wind that had begun to strip his roof off, and getting upon a ladder with his nearest neighbor to construct some temporary device for keeping his house over his head, saw, from the ladder's elevation as he looked down by chance toward the shore, some dark troubled object close in with the land. And he and the other, descending to the beach, and finding the sea mercilessly beating over a great broken ship, had clambered up the stony ways like staircases without stairs, on which the wild village hangs in little clusters, as fruit hangs on boughs, and had given the alarm. And so, over the hill-slopes, and past the waterfall, and down the gullies where the land drains off into the ocean, the scattered quarrymen and fishermen inhabiting that part of Wales had come running to the dismal sight—their clergyman among them. And as they stood in the leaden morning, stricken with pity leaning hard against the wind, their breath and vision often failing as the sleet and spray rushed at them from the ever forming and dissolving mountains of sea, and as the wool which was a part of the vessel's cargo blew in with the salt foam and remained upon the land when the foam melted, they saw the ship's life-boat put off from one of the heaps of wreck; and first, there were three men in her, and in a moment she capsized, and there were but two; and again, she was struck by a vast mass of water, and there was but one; and again, she was thrown bottom upward, and that one, with his arm stuck through the broken planks and waving as if for the help that could never reach him, went down into the deep.

It was the clergyman himself from whom I heard this, while I stood on the shore, looking in his kind wholesome face as it turned to the spot where the boat had been. The divers were down then, and busy. They were "lifting" to-day, the gold found yesterday—some five-and-twenty thousand pounds. Of three hundred and fifty thousand pounds worth of gold, three hundred thousand pounds worth, in round numbers, was at that time recovered. The great bulk of the remainder was surely and steadily coming up. Some loss of sovereigns there would be, of course; indeed, at first, sovereigns had drifted in with the sand, and been scattered far and wide over the beach, like sea-shells; but most other golden treasure would be found. As it was brought up, it went aboard the Tug steamer, where good account was taken of it. So tremendous had the force of the sea been when it broke the ship, that it had beaten one great ingot of gold, deep into a strong and heavy piece of her solid iron-work: in which, also, several loose sovereigns that the ingot had swept in before it, had been found, as firmly imbedded as though the iron had been liquid when they were forced there. It had been remarked of such bodies come ashore, too, as had been seen by scientific men, that they had been stunned to death, and not suffocated. Observation, both of the internal change that had been wrought in them, and of their external expression, showed death to have been thus merciful and easy. The report was brought, while I was holding such discourse on the beach, that no more bodies had come ashore since last night. It began to be very doubtful whether many more would be thrown up until the northeast winds of the early spring set in. Moreover, a great number of the passengers, and particularly the second-class women-passengers, were known to have been in the middle of the ship when she parted, and thus the collapsing wreck would have fallen upon them after yawning open, and would keep them down. A diver made known, even then, that he had come upon the body of a man, and had sought to release it from a great superincumbent weight; but that, finding he could not do so without mutilating the remains, he had left it where it was.

It was the kind and wholesome face I have made mention of as being then beside me, that I had purposed to myself to see, when I left home for Wales. I had heard of that clergyman, as having buried many scores of the shipwrecked people; of his having opened his house and heart to their agonized friends; of his having used a most sweet and patient diligence for weeks and weeks, in the performance of the forlornest offices that Man can render to his kind; of his having most tenderly and thoroughly devoted himself to the dead, and to those who were sorrowing for the dead. I had said to myself, "In the Christmas season of the year, I should like to see that man!" And he had swung the gate of his little garden in coming out to meet me, not half an hour ago.

So cheerful of spirit, and guiltless of affectation—as true practical Christianity ever is!—I read more of the New Testament in the fresh frank face going up the village beside me, in five minutes, than I have read in anathematizing discourses (albeit put to press with enormous flourishing of trumpets), in all my life. I heard more of the Sacred Book in the cordial voice that had nothing to say about its owner, than in all the would-be celestial pairs of bellows that have ever blown conceit at me.

We climbed toward the little church, at a cheery pace, among the loose stones, the deep mud, the wet coarse grass, the outlying water, and other obstructions from which frost and snow had lately thawed. It was a mistake (my friend was glad to tell me, on the way) to suppose that the peasantry had shown any superstitious avoidance of the drowned; on the whole, they had done very well, and had assisted readily. Ten shillings had been paid for the bringing of each body up to the church, but the way was steep, and a horse and a cart (in which it was wrapped in a sheet) were necessary, and three or four men, and, all things considered, it was not a great price. The people were none the richer for the wreck, for it was the season of the herring-shoal—and who could cast nets for fish, and find dead men and women in the draught?

He had the church keys in his hand, and opened the churchyard gate, and opened the church door; and we went in.

It is a little church of great antiquity; there is reason to believe that some church has occupied the spot, these thousand years or more. The pulpit was gone, and other things usually belonging to the church were gone, owing to its living congregation having deserted it for the neighboring school-room, and yielded it up to the dead. The very Commandments had been shouldered out of their places in the bringing in of the dead; the black wooden tables on which they were painted, were askew, and on the stone pavement below them, and on the stone pavement all over the church, were the marks and stains where the drowned had been laid down. The eye, with little or no aid from the imagination, could yet see how the bodies had been turned, and where the head had been and where the feet. Some faded traces of the wreck of the Australian ship may be discernible on the stone pavement of this little church, hundreds of years hence, when the digging for gold in Australia shall have long and long ceased out of the land.

Forty-four shipwrecked men and women lay here at one time,

awaiting burial. Here, with weeping and wailing in every room of his house, my companion worked alone for hours, solemnly surrounded by eyes that could not see him, and by lips that could not speak to him, patiently examining the tattered clothing, cutting off buttons, hair, marks from linen, any thing that might lead to subsequent identification, studying faces, looking for a scar, a bent finger, a crooked toe, comparing letters sent to him with the ruin about him. "My dearest brother had bright gray eyes and a pleasant smile," one sister wrote. O poor sister! well for you to be far from here, and keep that as your last remembrance of him!

The ladies of the clergyman's family, his wife and two sisters-in-law, came in among the bodies often. It grew to be the business of their lives to do so. Any new arrival of a bereaved woman would stimulate their pity to compare the description brought, with the dread realities. Sometimes, they would go back, able to say, "I have found him," or, "I think she lies there." Perhaps the mourner, unable to bear the sight of all that lay in the church, would be led in blindfold. Conducted to the spot with many compassionate words, and encouraged to look, she would say, with a piercing cry "This is my boy!" and drop insensible on the insensible figure.

He soon observed that in some cases of women, the identification of person, though complete, was quite at variance with the marks upon the linen; this led him to notice that even the marks upon the linen were sometimes inconsistent with one another; and thus he came to understand that they had dressed in great haste and agitation, and that their clothes had become mixed together. The identification of men by their dress, was rendered extremely difficult, in consequence of a large proportion of them being dressed alike—in clothes of one kind, that is to say, supplied by slopsellers and outfitters, and not made by single garments, but by hundreds. Many of the men were bringing over parrots, and had receipts upon them for the price of the birds, others had bills of exchange in their pockets, or in belts. Some of these documents, carefully unwrinkled and dried, were little less fresh in appearance that day, than the present page will be under ordinary circum stances, after having been opened three or four times.

In that lonely place, it had not been easy to obtain even such common commodities in towns, as ordinary disinfectants. Pitch had been burned in the church, as the readiest thing at hand, and the frying-pan in which it had bubbled over a brazier of coals was still there, with its ashes. Hard by the Communion-Table, were some boots that had been taken off the drowned and preserved—a gold-digger's boot, cut down the leg for its removal—a trodden down man's ankle-boot with a buff cloth top—and others—soaked and sandy, weedy and salt.

From the church, we passed out into the churchyard. Here, there lay, at that time, one hundred and forty-five bodies, that had come ashore from the wreck. He had buried them, when not identified, in graves containing four each. He had numbered each body in a register describing it, and had placed a corresponding number on each coffin, and over each grave. Identified bodies he had buried singly, in private graves, in another part of the churchyard. Several bodies had been exhumed from the graves of four, as relatives had come from a distance and seen his register; and, when recognized, these had been reburied in private graves, so that the mourners might erect separate headstones over the remains. In all such cases he had performed the funeral service a second time, and the ladies of his house had attended. There had been no offense in the poor ashes when they were brought again to the light of day; the beneficent Earth had already absorbed it. The drowned were buried in their clothes. To supply the great sudden demand for coffins, he had got all the neighboring people handy at tools, to work the livelong day, and Sunday likewise. The coffins were neatly formed;—I had seen two, waiting for occupants, under the lee of the ruined walls of a stone hut on the beach, within call of the tent where the Christmas Feast was held. Similarly, one of the graves for four was lying open and ready, here, in the churchyard. So much of the scanty space was already devoted to the wrecked people, that the villagers had begun to express uneasy doubts whether they themselves could lie in their own ground, with their forefathers and descendants, by-and-by. The churchyard being but a step from the clergyman's dwelling-house, we crossed to the latter;

the white surplice was hanging up near the door, ready to be put on at any time, for a funeral service.

The cheerful earnestness of this good Christian minister was as consolatory, as the circumstances out of which it shone were sad. I never have seen any thing more delightfully genuine than the calm dismissal by himself and his household of all they had undergone, as a simple duty that was quietly done and ended. In speaking of it, they spoke of it with great compassion for the bereaved; but laid no stress upon their own hard share in those weary weeks, except as it had attached many people to them as friends, and elicited many touching expressions of gratitude. This clergyman's brother himself the clergyman of two adjoining parishes, who had buried thirty-four of the bodies in his own churchyard, and who had done to them all that his brother had done as to the larger number—must be understood as included in the family. He was there, with his neatly-arranged papers, and made no more account of his trouble than any body else did. Down to yesterday's post outward, my clergyman alone had written one thousand and seventy-five letters to relatives and friends of the lost people. In the absence of all self-assertion, it was only through my now and then delicately putting a question as the occasion arose, that I became informed of these things. It was only when I had remarked again and again, in the church, on the awful nature of the scene of death he had been required so closely to familiarize himself with for the soothing of the living, that he had casually said, without the least abatement of his cheerfulness, "Indeed, it had rendered him unable for a time to eat or drink more than a little coffee now and then, and a piece of bread."

In this noble modesty, in this beautiful simplicity, in this serene avoidance of the least attempt to "improve" an occasion which might be supposed to have sunk of its own weight into my heart, I seemed to have happily come, in a few steps, from the churchyard with its open grave, which was the type of Death, to the Christian dwelling side by side with it, which was the type of Resurrection. I never shall think of the former, without the latter. The two will always rest side by side in my memory. If I had lost any one dear to me in this unfortunate ship, if I made a voyage from Australia to look at the grave in the churchyard, I should go away, thankful to GOD that that house was so close to it, and that its shadow by day and its domestic lights by night fell upon the earth in which its master had so tenderly laid my dear one's head.

The references that naturally arose out of our conversation, to the descriptions sent down of shipwrecked persons, and to the gratitude of relations and friends, made me very anxious to see some of those letters. I was presently seated before a shipwreck of papers, all bordered with black, and from them I made the following few extracts.

A mother writes:

REVEREND SIR. Amongst the many who perished on your shore was numbered my beloved son. I was only just recovering from a severe illness, and this fearful affliction has caused a relapse, so that I am unable at present to go to identify the remains of the loved and lost. My darling son would have been sixteen on Christmas-day next. He was a most amiable and obedient child, early taught the way of salvation. We fondly hoped that as a British seaman he might be an ornament to his profession, but, "it is well;" I feel assured my dear boy is now with the redeemed. Oh, he did not wish to go this last voyage! On the fifteenth of October, I received a letter from him from Melbourne, date August twelfth; he wrote in high spirits, and in conclusion he says: "Pray for a fair breeze, dear mamma, and I'll not forget to whistle for it; and, God permitting, I shall see you and all my little pets again. Good-by, dear mother—good-by, dearest parents. Good-by, dear brother." Oh, it was indeed an eternal farewell. I do not apologize for thus writing you, for oh, my heart is very sorrowful.

A husband writes:

MY DEAR KIND SIR. Will you kindly inform me whether there are any initials upon the ring and guard you have in possession, found, as the Standard says, last Tuesday? Believe, me my dear sir, when I say that I cannot express my deep gratitude in words sufficiently for your kindness to me on that fearful and appalling day. Will you tell me what I can do for you, and will you write me a consoling letter to prevent my mind from going astray?

A widow writes:

Left in such a state as I am, my friends and I thought it best that my dear husband should be buried where he lies, and, much as I should have liked to have had it otherwise, I must submit. I feel, from all I have heard of you, that you will see it done decently and in order. Little does it signify to us, when the soul has departed, where this poor body lies, but we who are left behind would do all we can to show how we loved them. This is denied me, but it is God's hand that afflicts us, and I try to submit. Some day I may be able to visit the spot, and see where he lies, and erect a simple stone to his memory. Oh! it will be long, long before I forget that dreadful night. Is there such a thing in the vicinity, or any shop in Bangor, to which I could send for a small picture of Moelfra or Llanallgo Church, a spot now sacred to me?

Another widow writes:

I have received your letter this morning, and do thank you most kindly for the interest you have taken about my dear husband, as well for the sentiments yours contains, evincing the spirit of a Christian who can sympathize for those who, like myself, are broken down with grief.

May God bless and sustain you, and all in connection with you, in this great trial. Time may roll on and bear all its sons away, but your name as a disinterested person will stand in history, and as successive years pass, many a widow will think of your noble conduct, and the tears of gratitude flow down many a cheek, the tribute of a thankful heart, when other things are forgotten forever.

A father writes:

I am at a loss to find words to sufficiently express my gratitude to you for your kindness to my son Richard upon the melancholy occasion of his visit to his dear brother's body, and also for your ready attention in pronouncing our beautiful burial service over my poor unfortunate son's remains. God grant that your prayers over him may reach the Mercy Seat, and that his soul may be received (through Christ's intercession) into heaven!

His dear mother begs me to convey to you her heartfelt thanks.

Those who were received at the clergyman's house, write thus, after leaving it:

DEAR AND NEVER-TO-BE-FORGOTTEN FRIENDS. I arrived here yesterday morning without accident, and am about to proceed to my home by railway.

I am overpowered when I think of you and your hospitable home. No words could speak language suited to my heart. I refrain. God reward you with the same measure you have meted with!

I enumerate no names, but embrace you all.

MY BELOVED FRIENDS. This is the first day that I have been able to leave my bedroom since I returned, which will explain the reason of my not writing sooner.

If I could only have had my last melancholy hope realized in recovering the body of my beloved and lamented son, I should have returned home somewhat comforted, and I think I could then have been comparatively resigned.

I fear now there is but little prospect, and I mourn as one without hope.

The only consolation to my distressed mind is in my having been so feelingly allowed by you to leave the matter in your hands, by whom I well know that every thing will be done that can be, according to arrangements made before I left the scene of the awful catastrophe, both as to the identification of my dear son, and also his interment.

I feel most anxious to hear whether any thing fresh has transpired since I left you; will you add another to the many deep obligations I am under to you by writing to me? And, should the body of my dear and unfortunate son be identified, let me hear from you immediately, and I will come again.

Words cannot express the gratitude I feel I owe to you all for your benevolent aid, your kindness, and your sympathy.

MY DEARLY BELOVED FRIENDS. I arrived in safety at my house yesterday, and a night's rest has restored and tranquilized me. I must again repeat, that language has no words by which I can express my sense of obligation to you. You are enshrined in my heart of hearts.

I have seen him! and can now realize my misfortune more than I have hitherto been able to do. Oh, the bitterness of the cup I drink! But I bow submissive. God *must* have done right. I do not want to feel less, but to acquiesce more simply.

There were some Jewish passengers on board the Royal Charter, and the gratitude of the Jewish people is feelingly expressed in the following letter, bearing date from "the Office of the Chief Rabbi:"

Reverend Sir. I cannot refrain from expressing to you my heartfelt thanks on behalf of those of my flock whose relatives have unfortunately been among those who perished at the late wreck of the Royal Charter. You have, indeed, like Boaz, "not left off your kindness to the living and the dead."

You have not alone acted kindly towards the living by receiving them hospitably at your house, and energetically assisting them in their mournful duty, but also towards the dead, by exerting yourself to have our co-religionists buried in our ground, and according to our rites. May our heavenly Father reward you for your acts of humanity and true philanthropy!

The "Old Hebrew congregation of Liverpool" thus express themselves through their secretary:

Reverend Sir. The wardens of this congregation have learned with great pleasure that, in addition to those indefatigable exertions, at the scene of the late disaster to the Royal Charter, which have received universal recognition, you have very benevolently employed your valuable efforts to assist such members of our faith as have sought the bodies of lost friends to give them burial in our consecrated grounds, with the observances and rites prescribed by the ordinances of our religion.

The wardens desire me to take the earliest available opportunity to offer to you, on behalf of our community, the expression of their warm acknowledgments and grateful thanks, and their sincere wishes for your continued welfare and prosperity.

A Jewish gentleman writes:

Reverend and dear Sir. I take the opportunity of thanking you right earnestly for the promptness you displayed in answering my note with full particulars concerning my much-lamented brother, and I also herein beg to express my sincere regard for the willingness you displayed and for the facility you afforded for getting the remains of my poor brother exhumed. It has been to us a most sorrowful and painful event, but when we meet with such friends as yourself, it in a measure, somehow or other, abates that mental anguish, and makes the suffering so much easier to be borne. Considering the circumstances connected with my poor brother's fate, it does, indeed, appear a hard one. He had been away in all seven years; he returned four years ago to see his family. He was then engaged to a very amiable young lady. He had been very successful abroad, and was now returning to fulfill his sacred vow; he brought all his property with him in gold, uninsured. We heard from him when the ship stopped at Queenstown, when he was in the highest of hope, and in a few short hours afterwards all was washed away.

Mournful in the deepest degree, but too sacred for quotation here, were the numerous references to those miniatures of women worn round the necks of rough men (and found there after death), those locks of hair, those scraps of letters, those many, many slight memorials of hidden tenderness. One man cast up by the sea bore about him, printed on a perforated lace card, the following singular (and unavailing) charm:

A BLESSING.

May the blessing of God await thee. May the sun of glory shine around thy bed; and may the gates of plenty, honor, and happiness be ever open to thee. May no sorrow distress thy days; may no grief disturb thy nights. May the pillow of peace kiss thy cheek, and the pleasures of imagination attend thy dreams; and when length of years makes thee tired of earthly joys, and the curtain of death gently closes around thy last sleep of human existence, may the Angel of God attend thy bed, and take care that the expiring lamp of life shall not receive one rude blast to hasten on its extinction.

A sailor had these devices on his right arm. "Our Saviour on the Cross, the forehead of the crucifix and the vesture stained red; on the lower part of the arm, a man and woman; on one side of the Cross, the appearance of a half moon, with a face; on the other side, the sun; on the top of the Cross, the letters I.H.S.; on the left arm, a man and woman dancing, with an effort to delineate the female's dress; under which, initials." Another seaman "had, on the lower part of the right arm, the device of a sailor and a female; the man holding the Union Jack with a streamer, the folds of which waved over her head, and the end of it was held in her hand. On the upper part of the arm, a device of Our Lord on the Cross, with stars surrounding the head of the Cross, and one large star on the side in Indian ink. On the left arm, a flag, a true lover's knot, a face, and initials." This tattooing was found still plain, below the discolored outer surface of a mutilated arm, when such surface was carefully scraped away with a knife. It is not improbable that the perpetuation of this marking custom among seamen, may be referred back to their desire to be identified, if drowned and flung ashore.

It was some time before I could sever myself from the many interesting papers on the table, and then I broke bread and drank wine with the kind family before I left them. As I had brought the Coast-guard down, so I took the Postman back, with his leathern wallet, walking-stick, bugle, and terrier dog. Many a heart-broken letter he had brought to the Rectory House within two months; many a benignantly painstaking answer had he carried back.

As I rode along, I thought of the many people, inhabitants of this mother country, who would make pilgrimages to the little churchyard in the years to come; I thought of the many people in Australia, who would have an interest in such a shipwreck, and would find their way here when they visit the Old World; I thought of the writers of all the wreck of letters I had left upon the table; and I resolved to place this little record where it stands. Convocations, Conferences, Diocesan Epistles, and the like, will do a great deal for Religion, I dare say, and Heaven send they may! but I doubt if they will ever do their Master's service half so well, in all the time they last, as the Heavens have seen it done in this bleak spot upon the rugged coast of Wales.

Had I lost the friend of my life, in the wreck of the Royal Charter; had I lost my betrothed, the more than friend of my life; had I lost my maiden daughter, had I lost my hopeful boy, had I lost my little child; I would kiss the hands that worked so busily and gently in the church, and say, "None better could have touched the form, though it had lain at home." I could be sure of it, I could be thankful for it; I could be content to leave the grave near the house the good family pass in and out of every day, undisturbed, in the little churchyard where so many are so strangely brought together.

Without the name of the clergyman to whom—I hope, not without carrying comfort to some heart at some time—I have referred, my reference would be as nothing. He is the Reverend Stephen Roose Hughes, of Llanallgo, near Moelfra, Anglesey. His brother is the Reverend Hugh Robert Hughes, of Penrhos Alligwy.

---

My day's no-business beckoning me to the east end of London, I had turned my face to that point of the metropolitan compass on leaving Covent Garden, and had got past the India House, thinking, in my idle manner of Tippoo-Sahib and Charles Lamb, and had got past my little wooden midshipman, after affectionately patting him on one leg of his knee-shorts for old acquaintance' sake, and had got past Aldgate Pump, and had got past the Saracen's Head (with an ignominious rash of posting bills disfiguring his swarthy countenance), and had strolled up the empty yard of his ancient neighbor the Black or Blue Boar, or Bull, who departed this life I don't know when, and whose coaches are all gone I don't know where, and I had come out again into the age of railways, and I had got past Whitechapel Church, and was—rather inappropriately for an Uncommercial Traveler—in the Commercial Road. Pleasantly wallowing in the abundant mud of that thoroughfare, and greatly enjoying the huge piles of building belonging to the sugar refiners, the little masts and vanes in small back gardens in back streets, the neighboring canals and docks, the India vans lumbering along their stone tramway, and the pawnbroker's shops where hard-up Mates had pawned so many sextants and quadrants, that I should have bought a few cheap if I had the least notion how to use them, I at last began to file off to the right, toward Wapping.

Not that I intended to take boat at Wapping Old Stairs, or that I was going to look at that locality, because I believe (for I don't) in the constancy of the young woman who told her sea-going lover, to such a beautiful old tune, that she had ever continued the same, since she gave him the 'baccer-box marked with his name; I am afraid he usually got the worst of those transactions, and was frightfully taken in. No, I was going to Wapping, because an Eastern police magistrate had said, through the morning papers, that there was no classification at the Wapping workhouse for women, and that it was a disgrace and a shame and divers other hard names, and because I wished to see how the fact really stood. For, that Eastern police magistrates are not always the wisest men of the East, may be inferred from their course of procedure respecting the fancy-dressing and pantomime-posturing at St. George's in that quarter: which is usually, to discuss the matter at issue, in a state of mind betokening the weakest perplexity, with all parties concerned and unconcerned, and, for a final expedient, to consult the complainant as to what he thinks ought to be done with the defendant, and take the defendant's opinion as to what he would recommend to be done with himself.

Long before I reached Wapping I gave myself up as having lost my way, and, abandoning myself to the narrow streets in a Turkish frame of mind, relied on predestination to bring me somehow or other to the place I wanted if I were ever to get there. When I had ceased for an hour or so to take any trouble about the matter, I found myself on a swing-bridge, looking down at some dark locks in some dirty water.

Over against me, stood a creature remotely in the likeness of a young man, with a puffed sallow face, and a figure all dirty and shiny and slimy, who may have been the youngest son of his filthy old father, Thames, or the drowned man about whom there was a placard on the granite post like a large thimble, that stood between us.

I asked this apparition what it called the place? Unto which, it replied, with a ghastly grin and with a sound like gurgling water in its throat:

"Mister Baker's trap."

As it is a point of great sensitiveness with me on such occasions to be equal to the intellectual pressure of the conversation, I deeply considered the meaning of this speech, while I eyed the apparition—then engaged in hugging and sucking a horizontal iron bar at the top of the locks. Inspiration suggested to me that Mr. Baker was the acting Coroner of that neighborhood.

"A common place for suicide," said I, looking down at the locks.

"Sue?" returned the ghost, with a stare. "Yes! And Poll. Likeways Emily. And Nancy. And Jane;" he sucked the iron between each name; "and all the bileing. Ketches off their bonnets or shorls, takes a run, and headers down here, they does. Always a headerin' down here, they is. Like one o'clock."

"And at about that hour of the morning, I suppose?"

"Ah!" said the apparition. "*They* an't partickler. Two 'ull do for *them*. Three. All times 'o night. O'ny mind you!" Here the apparition rested its profile on the bar, and gurgled in a sarcastic manner. "There must be somebody comin'. They don't go a headerin' down here, wen there an't no Bobby nor gen'ral Cove, fur to hear the splash."

According to my interpretation of these words, I was myself a General Cove, or member of the miscellaneous public. In which modest character, I remarked:

"They are often taken out, are they, and restored?"

"I dunno about restored," said the apparition, who, for some occult reason, very much objected to that word; "they're carried into the werkiss and put into a 'ot bath, and brought round. But I dunno about restored," said the apparition; "blow *that!*"—and vanished.

As it had shown a desire to become offensive, I was not sorry to find myself alone, especially as the "werkiss" it had indicated with a twist of its matted head, was close at hand. So I left Mr. Baker's terrible trap (baited with a scum that was like the soapy rinsing of sooty chimneys), and made bold to ring at the workhouse gate, where I was wholly unexpected and quite unknown.

A very bright and nimble little matron, with a bunch of keys in her hand, responded to my request to see the House. I began to doubt whether the police magistrate was quite right in his facts, when I noticed her quick active little figure and her intelligent eyes.

The Traveler (the matron intimated) should see the worst first. He was welcome to see every thing. Such as it was, there it all was.

This was the only preparation for our entering "the Foul wards." They were in an old building, squeezed away in a corner of a paved yard, quite detached from the more modern and spacious main body of the workhouse. They were in a building most monstrously behind the time—a mere series of garrets or lofts, with every inconvenient and objectionable circumstance in their construction, and only accessible by steep and narrow staircases, infamously ill adapted for the passage up-stairs of the sick or down-stairs of the dead.

A-bed in these miserable rooms, here on bedsteads, there (for a change, as I understood it) on the floor, were women in every stage of distress and disease. None but those who have attentively observed such scenes, can conceive the extraordinary variety of expression still latent under the general monotony and uniformity of color, attitude, and condition. The form a little coiled up and turned away, as though it had turned its back on this world forever; the uninterested face at once lead-colored and yellow, looking passively upward from the pillow; the haggard mouth a little dropped, the hand outside the coverlet, so dull and indifferent, so light and yet so heavy; these were on every pallet; but, when I stopped beside a bed, and said ever so slight a word to the figure lying there, the ghost of the old character came into the face, and made the Foul ward as various as the fair world. No one appeared to care to live, but no one complained; all who could speak, said that as much was done for them as could be done there, that the attendance was kind and patient, that their suffering was very heavy, but they had nothing to ask for. The wretched rooms were as clean and sweet as it is possible for such rooms to be; they would become a pest-house in a single week, if they were ill-kept.

I accompanied the brisk matron up another barbarous staircase, into a better kind of loft devoted to the idiotic and imbecile. There was at least Light in it, whereas the windows in the former wards had been like sides of schoolboys birdcages. There was a strong grating over the fire here, and, holding a kind of state on either side of the hearth, separated by the breadth of this grating, were two old ladies in a condition of feeble dignity, which was surely the very last and lowest reduction of self-complacency, to be found in this wonderful humanity of ours. They were evidently jealous of each other, and passed their whole time (as some people do, whose fires are not grated) in mentally disparaging each other, and contemptuously watching their neighbors. One of these parodies on provincial gentlewomen was extremely talkative, and expressed a strong desire to attend the service on Sundays, from which she represented herself to have derived the greatest interest and consolation when allowed that privilege. She gossiped so well, and looked altogether so cheery and harmless, that I began to think this a case for the Eastern magistrate, until I found that on the last occasion of her attending chapel, she had secreted a small stick, and had caused some confusion in the responses by suddenly producing it and belaboring the congregation.

So, these two old ladies, separated by the breadth of the grating—otherwise they would fly at one another's caps—sat all day long, suspecting one another, and contemplating a world of fits. For every body else in the room had fits, except the wardswoman: an elderly, able-bodied pauperess, with a large upper lip, and an air of repressing and saving her strength, as she stood with her hands folded before her, and her eyes slowly rolling, biding her time for catching or holding somebody. This civil personage (in whom I regretted to identify a reduced member of my honorable friend Mrs. Gamp's family) said, "They has 'em continiwal, sir. They drops without no more notice than if they was coach-horses dropped from the moon, sir. And when one drops, another drops, and sometimes there'll be as many as four or five on 'em at once, dear me, a rollin' and a tearin', bless you!—this young woman, now, has 'em dreadful bad."

She turned up this young woman's face with her hand as she said it. This young woman was seated on the floor, pondering, in the foreground of the afflicted. There was nothing repellant, either in her face or head. Many, apparently worse, varieties of epilepsy and hysteria were about her, but she was said to be the worst there. When I had spoken to her a little, she still sat with her face turned up, pondering, and a gleam of the mid-day sun shone in upon her.

Whether this young woman, and the rest of these so sorely troubled, as they sit or lie pondering in their confused dull way, ever get mental glimpses among the motes in the sunlight, of healthy people and healthy things? Whether this young woman, brooding like this in the summer season, ever thinks that somewhere there are trees and flowers, even mountains and the great sea? Whether, not to go so far, this young woman ever has any dim revelation of that young woman—that young woman who is not here and never will come here, who is courted, and caressed, and loved, and has a husband, and bears children, and lives in a home, and who never knows what it is to have this lashing and tearing coming upon her? And whether this young woman, God help her, gives herself up then, and drops like a coach-horse from the moon?

I hardly knew whether the voices of infant children, penetrating into so hopeless a place, made a sound that was pleasant or painful to me. It was something to be reminded that the weary world was not all weary, and was ever renewing itself; but, this young woman was a child not long ago, and a child not long hence might be such as she. Howbeit, the active step and eye of the vigilant matron conducted me past the two provincial gentlewomen (whose dignity was ruffled by the children) and into the adjacent nursery.

There were many babies here, and more than one handsome young mother. There were ugly young mothers also, and sullen young mothers, and callous young mothers. But, the babies had not appropriated to themselves any bad expression as yet, and might have been, for any thing that appeared to the contrary in their soft faces, Princes Imperial, and Princesses Royal. I had the pleasure of giving a poetical commission to the baker's man to make a cake with all dispatch and toss it into the oven for one red-headed young pauper and myself, and felt much the better for it. Without that refreshment, I doubt if I should have been in a condition for "the Refractories," toward whom my quick little matron—for whose adaptation to her office I had by this time conceived a genuine respect—drew me next, and marshaled me the way that I was going.

The Refractories were picking oakum, in a small room giving on a yard. They sat in line on a form, with their backs to a window; before them, a table, and their work. The oldest Refractory was, say twenty; youngest Refractory, say sixteen. I have never yet ascertained, in the course of my uncommercial travels, why a Refractory habit should affect the tonsils and uvula; but, I have always observed that Refractories of both sexes and every grade, between a Ragged School and the Old Bailey, have one voice, in which the tonsils and uvula gain a diseased ascendency.

"Five pound indeed! I hain't a going fur to pick five pound," said the Chief of the Refractories, keeping time to herself with her head and chin. "More than enough to pick what we picks now, in sitch a place as this, and on wot we gets here!"

(This was in acknowledgment of a delicate intimation that the amount of work was likely to be increased. It certainly was not heavy then, for one Refractory had already done her day's task—it was barely two o'clock—and was sitting behind it, with a head exactly matching it.)

"A pretty Ouse this is, matron, ain't it?" said Refractory Two, "where a pleeseman's called in, if a gal says a word!"

"And wen you're sent to prison for nothink or less!" said the Chief, tugging at her oakum, as if it were the matron's hair. "But any place is better than this; that's one thing, and be thankful!"

A laugh of Refractories led by Oakum Head with folded arms—who originated nothing, but who was in command of the skirmishers outside the conversation.

"If any place is better than this," said my brisk guide, in the calmest manner, "it is a pity you left a good place when you had one."

"Ho, no, I didn't, matron," returned the Chief with another

pull at her oakum, and a very expressive look at the enemy's forehead. "Don't say that, matron, 'cos it's lies."

Oakum Head brought up the skirmishers again, skirmished, and retired.

"And *I* warn't a going," exclaimed Refractory Two, "though I was in one place for as long as four year—*I* warn't a going fur to stop in a place that warn't fit for me—there! And where the fam'ly warn't 'spectable characters—there! And where I fort'nately or hunfort'nately found that the people warn't what they pretended to make theirselves out to be—there! And where it wasn't their faults, by chalks, if I warn't made bad and ruinated—Hah!"

During this speech, Oakum Head had again made a diversion with the skirmishers, and had again withdrawn.

The Uncommercial Traveler ventured to remark that he supposed Chief Refractory and Number One, to be the two young women who had been taken before the magistrate?

"Yes!" said the Chief, "we har! and the wonder is, that a a pleeseman an't 'ad in now, and we took off agen. You can't open your lips here, without a pleeseman."

Number Two laughed (very uvularly), and the skirmishers followed suit.

"I'm sure I'd be thankful," protested the Chief, looking sideways at the Uncommercial, "if I could be got into a place, or got abroad. I'm sick and tired of this precious Ouse, I am, with reason."

So would be, and so was, Number Two. So would be, and so was, Oakum Head. So would be, and so were, Skirmishers.

The Uncommercial took the liberty of hinting that he hardly thought it probable that any lady or gentleman in want of a likely young domestic of retiring manners, would be tempted into the engagement of either of the two leading Refractories, on her own presentation of herself as per sample.

"It ain't no good being nothink else here," said the Chief.

The Uncommercial thought it might be worth trying.

"Oh no it ain't," said the Chief.

"Not a bit of good," said Number Two.

"And I'm sure I'd be very thankful to be got into a place, or got abroad," said the Chief

"And so should I," said Number Two. "Truly thankful, I should."

Oakum Head then rose, and announced as an entirely new idea, the mention of which profound novelty might be naturally expected to startle her unprepared hearers, that she would be very thankful to be got into a place, or got abroad. And, as if she had then said, "Chorus, ladies!" all the Skirmishers struck up to the same purpose. We left them, thereupon, and began a long, long walk among the women who were simply old and infirm; but whenever, in the course of this same walk, I looked out of any high window that commanded the yard, I saw Oakum Head and all the other Refractories looking out at their low window for me, and never failing to catch me, the moment I showed my head.

In ten minutes I had ceased to believe in such fables of a golden time as youth, the prime of life, or a hale old age. In ten minutes all the lights of womankind seemed to have been blown out, and nothing in that way to be left this vault to brag of, but the flickering and expiring snuffs.

And what was very curious, was, that these dim old women had one company notion which was the fashion of the place. Every old woman who became aware of a visitor and was not in bed, hobbled over a form into her accustomed seat, and became one of a line of dim old women confronting another line of dim old women across a narrow table. There was no obligation whatever upon them to range themselves in this way; it was their manner of "receiving." As a rule, they made no attempt to talk to one another, or to look at the visitor, or to look at any thing, but sat silently working their mouths, like a sort of poor old Cows. In some of these wards, it was good to see a few green plants; in others, an isolated Refractory acting as nurse, who did well enough in that capacity, when separated from her compeers; every one of these wards, day room, night room, or both combined, was scrupulously clean and fresh. I have seen as many such places as most travelers in my line, and I never saw one such, better kept.

Among the bedridden there was great patience, great reliance on the books under the pillow, great faith in God. All cared for sympathy, but none much cared to be encouraged with hope of recovery; on the whole, I should say, it was considered rather a distinction to have a complication of disorders, and to be in a worse way than the rest. From some of the windows the river could be seen with all its life and movement; the day was bright, but I came upon no one who was looking out.

In one large ward, sitting by the fire in arm-chairs of distinction, like the President and Vice of the good company, were two old women, upward of ninety years of age. The younger of the two, just turned ninety, was deaf, but not very, and could easily be made to hear. In her early time she had nursed a child, who was now another old woman, more infirm than herself, inhabiting the very same chamber. She perfectly understood this when the matron told it, and, with sundry nods and motions of her forefinger, pointed out the woman in question. The elder of this pair, ninety-three, seated before an illustrated newspaper (but not reading it), was a bright-eyed old soul, really not deaf, wonderfully preserved, and amazingly conversational. She had not long lost her husband, and had been in that place little more than a year. At Boston, in the State of Massachusetts, this poor creature would have been individually addressed, would have been tended in her own room, and would have had her life gently assimilated to a comfortable life out of doors. Would that be much to do in England for a woman who has kept herself out of a workhouse more than ninety rough long years? When Britain first, at Heaven's command, arose, with a great deal of allegorical confusion, from out the azure main, did her guardian angels positively forbid it in the Charter which has been so much be-sung?

The object of my journey was accomplished when the nimble matron had no more to show me. As I shook hands with her at the gate, I told her that I thought Justice had not used her very well, and that the wise men of the East were not infallible.

Now, I reasoned with myself, as I made my journey home again, concerning those Foul wards. They ought not to exist; no person of common decency and humanity can see them and doubt it. But what is this Union to do? The necessary alteration would cost several thousands of pounds; it has already to support three work-houses; its inhabitants work hard for their bare lives, and are already rated for the relief of the Poor to the utmost extent of reasonable endurance. One poor parish in this very Union is rated to the amount of FIVE AND SIXPENCE in the pound, at the very same time when the rich parish of Saint George's, Hanover-square, is rated at about SEVENPENCE in the pound, Paddington at about FOURPENCE, Saint James's, Westminster, at about TENPENCE! It is only through the equalization of Poor Rates that what is left undone in this wise, can be done. Much more is left undone, or is ill-done, than I have space to suggest in these notes of a single uncommercial journey; but, the wise men of the East, before they can reasonably hold forth about it, must look to the North and South and West; let them also, any morning before taking the seat of Solomon, look into the shops and dwellings all around the Temple, and first ask themselves "how much more can these poor people—many of whom keep themselves with difficulty enough out of the workhouse—bear?"

I had yet other matter for reflection, as I journeyed home, inasmuch as, before I altogether departed from the neighborhood of Mr. Baker's trap, I had knocked at the gate of the workhouse of St. George's-in-the-East, and had found it to be an establishment highly creditable to those parts, and thoroughly well administered by a most intelligent master. I remarked in it, an instance of the collateral harm that obstinate vanity and folly can do. "This was the Hall where those old paupers, male and female, whom I had just seen, met for the Church service, was it?"—"Yes."—"Did they sing the Psalms to any instrument?"—"They would like to, very much; they would have an extraordinary interest in doing so." "And could none be got?"—"Well, a piano could even have been got for nothing, but these unfortunate dissensions——" Ah! better, far better, my Christian friend in the beautiful garment, to have let the singing boys alone, and left the multitude to sing for themselves! You should know better than I, but I think I have read that they did so, once upon a time, and that "when they had sung an hymn," Some one (not in a beautiful garment) went up into the Mount of Olives.

It made my heart ache to think of this miserable trifling, in the streets of a city where every stone seemed to call to me, as I walked along, "Turn this way, man, and see what waits to be done!" So I decoyed myself into another train of thought to ease my heart. But, I don't know that I did it, for I was so full of paupers, that it was, after all, only a change to a single pauper, who took possession of my remembrance instead of a thousand.

"I beg your pardon, sir," he had said, in a confidential manner, on another occasion, taking me aside; "but I have seen better days."

"I am very sorry to hear it."

"Sir, I have a complaint to make against the master."

"I have no power here, I assure you. And if I had——"

"But allow me, sir, to mention it, as between yourself and a man who has seen better days, sir. The master and myself are both masons, sir, and I make him the sign continually; but, because I am in this unfortunate position, sir, he won't give me the countersign!"

---

As I shut the door of my lodging behind me, and came out into the streets at six on a drizzling Saturday evening in the last past month of January, all that neighborhood of Covent Garden, looked very desolate. It is so essentially a neighborhood which has seen better days, that bad weather affects it sooner than another place which has not come down in the world. In its present reduced condition, it bears a thaw almost worse than any place I know. It gets so dreadfully low-spirited when damp breaks forth. Those wonderful houses about Drury-lane Theatre, which in the palmy days of theatres were prosperous and long-settled places of business, and which now change hands every week, but never change their character of being divided and subdivided on the ground floor into mouldy dens of shops where an orange and half a dozen nuts, or a pomatum pot, one cake of fancy soap, and a cigar-box, are offered for sale and never sold, were most ruefully contemplated that evening, by the statue of Shakespeare, with the rain-drops coursing one another down its innocent nose. Those inscrutable pigeon-hole offices, with nothing in them (not so much as an ink-stand) but a model of a theatre before the curtain, where, in the Italian Opera season, tickets at reduced prices are kept on sale by nomadic gentlemen in smeary hats too tall for them, whom one occasionally seems to have seen on race-courses, not wholly unconnected with strips of cloth of various colors and a rolling ball—those Bedouin establishments, deserted by the tribe, and tenantless except when sheltering in one corner an irregular row of ginger-beer-bottles which would have made one shudder on such a night, but for its being plain that they had nothing in them, shrunk from the shrill cries of the newsboys down at their Exchange in the kennel of Catherine-street, like guilty things upon a fearful summons. At the pipe-shop in Great Russell-street, the Death's-head pipes were like a theatrical memento mori, admonishing beholders of the decline of the play-house as an Institution. I walked up Bow-street, disposed to be angry with the shops there, that were letting out theatrical secrets by exhibiting to work-a-day humanity, the stuff of which diadems and robes of kings are made. I noticed that some shops which had once been in the dramatic line, and had straggled out of it, were not getting on prosperously—like some actors I have known, who took to business and failed to make it answer. In a word, those streets looked so dull, and, considered as theatrical streets, so broken and bankrupt, that the FOUND DEAD on the black-board at the police station might have announced the decease of the Drama, and the pools of water outside the fire-engine maker's at the corner of Long-acre might have been occasioned by his having brought out the whole of his stock to play upon its last smouldering ashes.

And yet, on such a night in so degenerate a time, the object of my journey was theatrical. And yet, within half an hour I was in an immense theatre, capable of holding nearly five thousand people.

What Theatre? Her Majesty's? Far better. Royal Italian Opera? Far better. Infinitely superior to the latter for hearing in; infinitely superior to both, for seeing in. To every part of this Theatre spacious fireproof ways of ingress and egress. For every part of it, convenient places of refreshment and retiring rooms. Every thing to eat and drink carefully supervised as to quality, and sold at an appointed price; respectable female attendants ready for the commonest women in the audience; a general air of consideration, decorum, and supervision, most commendable; an unquestionably humanizing influence in all the social arrangements of the place.

Surely a dear Theatre, then? Because there were in London (not very long ago) Theatres with entrance-prices up to half a guinea a head, whose arrangements were not half so civilized. Surely, therefore, a dear Theatre? Not very dear. A gallery at threepence, another gallery at fourpence, a pit at sixpence, boxes and pit-stalls at a shilling, and six private boxes at half-a-crown.

My uncommercial curiosity induced me to go into every nook of this great place, and among every class of the audience assembled in it—amounting that evening, as I calculated, to about two thousand and odd hundreds. Magnificently lighted by a firmament of sparkling chandeliers, the building was ventilated to perfection. My sense of smell, without being particularly delicate, has been so offended in some of the commoner places of public resort, that I have often been obliged to leave them when I have made an uncommercial journey expressly to look on. The air of this Theatre was fresh, cool, and wholesome. To help toward this end, very sensible precautions had been used ingeniously combining the experience of hospitals and railway stations. Asphalt pavements substituted for wooden floors, honest bare walls of glazed brick and tile—even at the back of the boxes—for plaster and paper, no benches stuffed, and no carpeting or baize used: a cool material with a light glazed surface, being the covering of the seats.

These various contrivances are as well considered in the place in question as if it were a Fever Hospital; the result is, that it is sweet and healthful. It has been constructed from the ground to the roof, with a careful reference to sight and sound in every corner; the result is, that its form is beautiful, and that the appearance of the audience, as seen from the proscenium—with every face in it commanding the stage, and the whole so admirably raked and turned to that centre, that a hand can scarcely move in the great assemblage without the movement being seen from thence—is highly remarkable in its union of vastness with compactness. The stage itself, and all its appurtenances of machinery, cellarage, height, and breadth.

are on a scale more like the Scala at Milan, or the San Carlo at Naples, or the Grand Opera at Paris, than any notion a stranger would be likely to form of the Britannia Theatre at Hoxton, a mile North of Saint Luke's Hospital in the Old street-road, London. The Forty Thieves might be played here, and every thief ride his real horse, and the disguised captain bring in his oil jars on a train of real camels, and nobody be put out of the way. This really extraordinary place is the achievement of one man's enterprise, and was erected on the ruins of an inconvenient old building, in less than five months, at a round cost of five-and-twenty thousand pounds. To dismiss this part of my subject, and still to render to the proprietor the credit that is strictly his due, I must add that his sense of the responsibility upon him to make the best of his audience, and to do his best for them, is a highly agreeable sign of these times.

As the spectators at this theatre, for a reason I will presently show, were the object of my journey, I entered on the play of the night as one of the two thousand and odd hundreds, by looking about me at my neighbors. We were a motley assemblage of people, and we had a good many boys and young men among us; we had also many girls and young women. To represent, however, that we did not include a very great number, and a very fair proportion, of family groups, would be to make a gross misstatement. Such groups were to be seen in all parts of the house; in the boxes and stalls particularly, they were composed of persons of very decent appearance, who had many children with them. Among our dresses there were most kinds of shabby and greasy wear, and much fustian and corduroy that was neither sound nor fragrant. The caps of our young men were mostly of a limp character, and we who wore them, slouched, high-shouldered, into our places with our hands in our pockets, and occasionally twisted our cravats about our necks like eels, and occasionally tied them down our breasts like links of sausages, and occasionally had a screw in our hair over each cheek-bone with a slight thief-flavor in it. Beside prowlers and idlers, we were mechanics, dock-laborers, coster-mongers, petty tradesmen, small clerks, milliners, staymakers, shoe-binders, slop workers, poor workers in a hundred highways and by-ways. Many of us—on the whole, the majority—were not at all clean, and not at all choice in our lives or conversation. But we had all come together in a place where our convenience was well consulted, and where we were well looked after, to enjoy an evening's entertainment in common. We were not going to lose any part of what we had paid for, through any body's caprice, and as a community we had a character to lose. So we were closely attentive, and kept excellent order, and let the man or boy who did otherwise instantly get out from this place, or we would put him out with the greatest expedition.

We began at half-past six with a pantomime—with a pantomime so long, that before it was over I felt as if I had been traveling for six weeks—going to India, say, by the Overland Mail. The Spirit of Liberty was the principal personage in the Introduction, and the Four quarters of the World came out of the globe, glittering, and discoursed with the Spirit, who sang charmingly. We were delighted to understand that there was no Liberty anywhere but among ourselves, and we highly applauded the agreeable fact. In an allegorical way, which did as well as any other way, we and the Spirit of Liberty got into a kingdom of Needles and Pins, and found them at war with a potentate who called in to his aid their old arch-enemy Rust and who would have got the better of them if the Spirit of Liberty had not in the nick of time transformed the leaders into Clown, Pantaloon, Harlequin, Columbine, Harlequina, and a whole family of Sprites, consisting of a remarkably stout father and three spineless sons. We all knew what was coming, when the Spirit of Liberty addressed the King with the big face, and His Majesty backed to the side-scenes and began untying himself behind, with his big face all on one side. Our excitement at that crisis was great, and our delight unbounded. After this era in our existence, we went through all the incidents of a pantomime; it was not by any means a savage pantomime in the way of burning or boiling people, or throwing them out of window, or cutting them up; was often very droll, was always liberally got up, and cleverly presented. I noticed that the people who kept the shops, and who represented the passengers in the thoroughfares and so forth, had no conventionality in them, but were unusually like the real thing—from which I infer that you may take that audience in (if you wish to) concerning Knights and Ladies, Fairies, Angels, or such like, but that they are not to be done as to any thing in the streets. I noticed, also, that when two young men, dressed in exact imitation of the eel-and-sausage-cravated portion of the audience, were chased by policemen, and finding themselves in danger of being caught, dropped so suddenly as to oblige the policemen to tumble over them, there was great rejoicing among the caps—as though it were a delicate reference to something they had heard of before.

The Pantomime was succeeded by a Melo-Drama. Throughout the evening, I was pleased to observe Virtue quite as triumphant as she usually is out of doors, and indeed I thought rather more so. We all agreed (for the time) that honesty was the best policy, and we were as hard as iron upon Vice, and we wouldn't hear of Villany getting on in the world —no, not upon any consideration whatever.

Between the pieces, we almost all of us went out and refreshed. Many of us went the length of drinking beer at the bar of the neighboring public-house, some of us drank spirits, crowds of us had sandwiches and ginger-beer at the refreshment-bars established for us in the Theatre. The sandwich —as substantial as was consistent with portability, and as cheap as possible—we hailed as one of our greatest institutions. It forced its way among us at all stages of the entertainment, and we were always delighted to see it; its adaptability to the varying moods of our nature was surprising; we could never weep so comfortably as when our tears fell on our sandwich; we could never laugh so heartily as when we choked with sandwich; Virtue never looked so beautiful or Vice so deformed as when we paused, sandwich in hand, to consider what would come of that resolution of Wickedness in boots, to sever Innocence in flowered chintz from Honest Industry in striped stockings. When the curtain fell for the night, we still fell back upon sandwich, to help us through the rain and mire, and home to bed.

This, as I have mentioned, was Saturday night. Being Saturday night, I had accomplished but the half of my uncommercial journey; for, its object was to compare the play on Saturday evening, with the preaching in the same Theatre on Sunday evening.

Therefore, at the same hour of half-past six on the similarly damp and muddy Sunday evening, I returned to this Theatre. I drove up to the entrance (fearful of being late, or I should have come on foot), and found myself in a large crowd of people who, I am happy to state, were put into excellent spirits by my arrival. Having nothing to look at but the mud and the closed doors, they looked at me, and highly enjoyed the comic spectacle. My modesty inducing me to draw off, some hundreds of yards, into a dark corner, they at once forgot me, and applied themselves to their former occupation of looking at the mud and looking in at the closed doors: which being of grated iron-work, allowed the lighted passage within to be seen. They were chiefly people of respectable appearance, odd and impulsive as most crowds are, and making a joke of being there as most crowds do.

In the dark corner I might have sat a long while, but that a very obliging passer-by informed me that the Theatre was already full, and that the people whom I saw in the street were all shut out for want of room. After that, I lost no time in worming myself into the building, and creeping to a place in a Proscenium box that had been kept for me.

There must have been full four thousand people present. Carefully estimating the pit alone, I could bring it out as holding little less than fourteen hundred. Every part of the house was well filled, and I had not found it easy to make my way along the back of the boxes to where I sat. The chandeliers in the ceiling were lighted; there was no light on the stage; the orchestra was empty. The green curtain was down, and packed pretty closely on chairs on the small space of stage before it were some thirty gentlemen, and two or three ladies. In the centre of these, in a desk or pulpit covered with red baize, was the presiding minister. The kind of rostrum he occupied, will be very well understood, if I liken it to a boarded-up fire-place turned towards the audience, with a gentleman in a black surtout standing in the stove and leaning forward over the mantle-piece.

A portion of Scripture was being read when I went in. It was followed by a discourse, to which the congregation listened with most exemplary attention and uninterrupted silence and decorum. My own attention comprehended both the auditory and the speaker, and shall turn to both in this recalling of the scene, exactly as it did at the time.

"A very difficult thing," I thought, when the discourse began, 'to speak appropriately to so large an audience, and to speak with tact. Without it, better not to speak at all. Infinitely better to read the New Testament well, and to let *that* speak. In this congregation there is indubitably one pulse; but I doubt if any power short of genius can touch it as one, and make it answer as one."

I could not possibly say to myself as the discourse proceeded, that the minister was a good speaker. I could not possibly say to myself that he expressed an understanding of the general mind and character of his audience. There was a supposititious working-man introduced into the homily to make supposititious objections to our Christian religion and be reasoned down, who was not only a very disagreeable person, but remarkably unlike life—very much more unlike it than any thing I had seen in the pantomime. The native independence of character this artisan was supposed to possess, was represented by a suggestion of a dialect that I certainly never heard in my uncommercial travels, and with a coarse swing of voice and manner any thing but agreeable to his feelings I should conceive, considered in the light of a portrait, and as far away from the fact as a Chinese Tartar. There was a model pauper introduced in like manner, who appeared to me to be the most intolerably arrogant pauper ever relieved, and to show himself in absolute want and dire necessity of a course of Stone Yard. For, how did this pauper testify to his having received the gospel of humility? A gentleman met him in the workhouse, and said (which I myself really thought good-natured of him), "Ah, John? I am sorry to see you here. I am sorry to see you so poor." "Poor, sir!" replied that man, drawing himself up, "I am the son of a Prince! *My* father is the King of Kings. *My* father is the Lord of Lords. *My* father is the ruler of all the Princes of the Earth!" &c. And this was what all the preacher's fellow-sinners might come to, if they would embrace this blessed book—which I must say it did some violence to my own feelings of reverence, to see held out at arm's length at frequent intervals and soundingly slapped, like a slow lot at a sale. Now, could I help asking myself the question, whether the mechanic before me who must detect the preacher as being wrong about the visible manner of himself and the like of himself, and about such a noisy lip-server as that pauper, might not, most unhappily for the usefulness of the occasion, doubt that preacher's being right about things not visible to human senses?

Again. Is it necessary or advisable to address such an audience continually, as "fellow-sinners"? Is it not enough to be fellow-creatures, born yesterday, suffering and striving to-day, dying to-morrow? By our common humanity, my brothers and sisters, by our common capacities for pain and pleasure, by our common laughter and our common tears, by our common aspiration to reach something better than ourselves, by our common tendency to believe in something good, and to invest whatever we love or whatever we lose with some qualities that are superior to our own failings and weaknesses as we know them in our own poor hearts—by these. Hear me! —Surely, it is enough to be fellow-creatures. Surely, it includes the other designation and some touching meanings over and above.

Again. There was a personage introduced into the discourse (not an absolute novelty, to the best of my remembrance of my reading), who had been personally known to the preacher, and had been quite a Crichton in all the ways of philosophy, but had been an infidel. Many a time had the preacher talked with him on that subject, and many a time had he failed to convince that intelligent man. But he fell ill and died, and before he died he recorded his conversion—in words which the preacher had taken down, my fellow-sinners, and would read to you from this piece of paper. I must confess that to me, as one of an uninstructed audience, they did not appear particularly edifying. I thought their tone extremely selfish, and I thought they had a spiritual vanity in them which was of the before-mentioned refractory pauper's family.

All slangs and twangs are objectionable everywhere, but the slang and twang of the conventicle—as bad in its way as that of the House of Commons, and nothing worse can be said of it—should be studiously avoided under such circumstances as I describe. The avoidance was not complete on this occasion. Nor was it quite agreeable to see the preacher addressing his pet "points" to his backers on the stage, as if appealing to those disciples to shore him up, and testify to the multitude that each of those points was a clincher.

But, in respect of the large Christianity of his general tone; of his renunciation of all priestly authority; of his earnest and reiterated assurance to the people that the commonest among them could work out their own salvation if they would, by simply, lovingly, and dutifully following Our Saviour, and that they needed the mediation of no erring man; in these particulars, this gentleman deserved all praise. Nothing could be better than the spirit, or the plain emphatic words of his discourse in these respects. And it was a most significant and encouraging circumstance, that whenever he struck that chord, or whenever he described any thing which Christ himself had done, the array of faces before him was very much more earnest, and very much more expressive of emotion, than at any other time.

And now, I am brought to the fact, that the lowest part of the audience of the previous night, *was not there*. There is no doubt about it. There was no such thing in that building, that Sunday evening. I have been told since, that the lowest part of the audience of the Victoria Theatre has been attracted to its Sunday services. I have been very glad to hear it, but on this occasion of which I write, the lowest part of the usual audience of the Britannia Theatre, decidedly and unquestionably stayed away. When I first took my seat and looked at the house, my surprise at the change in its occupants was as great as my disappointment. To the most respectable class of the previous evening, was added a great number of respectable strangers attracted by curiosity, and drafts from the regular congregations of various chapels. It was impossible to fail in identifying the character of these last, and they were very numerous. I came out in a strong, slow tide of them setting from the boxes. Indeed, while the discourse was in progress, the respectable character of the auditory was so manifest in their appearance, that when the minister addressed a supposititious " outcast," one really felt a little impatient of it, as a figure of speech not justified by any thing the eye could discover.

The time appointed for the conclusion of the proceedings was eight o'clock. The address having lasted until full that time, and it being the custom to conclude with a hymn, the preacher intimated in a few sensible words that the clock had struck the hour, and that those who desired to go before the hymn was sung, could go now, without giving offense. No one stirred. The hymn was then sung, in good time and tune and unison, and its effect was very striking. A comprehensive benevolent prayer dismissed the throng, and in seven or eight minutes there was nothing left in the Theatre but a light cloud of dust.

That these Sunday meetings in Theatres are good things, I do not doubt. Nor do I doubt that they will work lower and lower down in the social scale, if those who preside over them will be very careful on two heads: firstly, not to disparage the places in which they speak, or the intelligence of their hearers; secondly, not to set themselves in antagonism to the natural inborn desire of the mass of mankind to recreate themselves and to be amused.

There is a third head, taking precedence of all others, to which my remarks on the discourse I heard, have tended. In the New Testament there is the most beautiful and affecting history conceivable by man, and there are the terse models for all prayer and for all preaching. As to the models, imitate them, Sunday preachers—else why are they there, consider? As to the history, tell it. Some people cannot read, some people will not read, many people (this especially holds among the young and ignorant) find it hard to pursue the verse-form in which the book is presented to them, and imagine that those breaks imply gaps, and want of continuity. Help them over that first stumbling-block, by setting forth the history in narrative, with no fear of exhausting it. You will never preach so well, you will never move them so profoundly, you will never send them away with half so much to think of. Which is the better interest: Christ's choice of twelve poor men to help in those merciful wonders among the poor and rejected; or the pious bullying of a whole Union-full of paupers? What is your changed philosopher to wretched me, peeping in at the door out of the mud of the streets and of my life, when you have the widow's son to tell me about, the ruler's daughter, the other figure at the door when the brother of the two sisters was dead, and one of the two ran to the mourner, crying, "The Master is come, and calleth for thee"? Let the preacher who will thoroughly forget himself and remember no individuality but one, and no eloquence but one, stand up before four thousand men and women at the Britannia Theatre any Sunday night, recounting that narrative to them as fellow-creatures, and he shall see a sight!

---

Is the sweet little cherub who sits smiling aloft and keeps watch on the life of Poor Jack, commissioned to take charge of Mercantile Jack, as well as Jack of the national navy? If not, who is? What is the cherub about, and what are we all about, when Poor Mercantile Jack is having his brains slowly knocked out by pennyweights, aboard the brig Beelzebub, or the barque Bowie-knife—when he looks his last at that infernal craft, with the first officer's iron boot-heel in his remaining eye, or with his dying body towed overboard in the ship's wake, while the cruel wounds in it do "the multitudinous seas incarnadine"?

Is it unreasonable to entertain a belief that if, aboard the brig Beelzebub or the barque Bowie-knife, the first officer did half the damage to cotton that he does to men, there would presently arise from both sides of the Atlantic so vociferous an invocation of the sweet little cherub who sits calculating aloft, keeping watch on the markets that pay, that such vigilant cherub would, with a winged sword, have that gallant officers' organ of destructiveness out of his head in the space of a flash of lightning?

If it be unreasonable, then am I the most unreasonable of men, for I believe it with all my soul.

This was my thought as I walked the dock-quays at Liverpool, keeping watch on poor Mercantile Jack. Alas for me! I have long outgrown the state of sweet little cherub; but there I was, and there Mercantile Jack was, and very busy he was, and very cold he was: the snow yet lying in the frozen furrows of the land, and the northeast winds snipping off the tops of the little waves in the Mersey, and rolling them into hailstones to pelt him with. Mercantile Jack was hard at it, in the hard weather, as he mostly is in all weathers, poor Jack. He was girded to ships' masts and funnels of steamers, like a forester to a great oak, scraping and painting; he was lying out on yards, furling sails that tried to beat him off; he was dimly discernible up in a world of giant cobwebs, reefing and splicing; he was faintly audible down in holds, stowing and unshipping cargo; he was winding round and round at capstans melodious, monotonous, and drunk; he was of a diabolical aspect, with coaling for the Antipodes; he was washing decks barefoot, with the breast of his red shirt open to the blast, though it was sharper than the knife in his leathern girdle; he was looking over bulwarks, all eyes and hair; he was standing by at the shoot of the Cunard steamer, off to-morrow, as the stocks in trade of several butchers, poulterers, and fishmongers, poured down into the ice-house; he was coming aboard of other vessels, with his kit in a tarpaulin bag, attended by plunderers to the very last moment of his shore-going existence. As though his senses, when released from the uproar of the elements, were under obligation to be confused by other turmoil, there was a rattling of wheels, a clattering of hoofs, a clashing of iron, a jolting of cotton and hides and casks and timber, an incessant deafening disturbance, on the quays, that was the very madness of sound. And as, in the midst of it, he stood swaying about, with his hair blown all manner of wild ways, rather crazedly taking leave of his plunderers, all the rigging in the docks was shrill in the wind, and every little steamer coming and going across the Mersey was sharp in its blowing off, and every buoy in the river bobbed spitefully up and down, as if there were a general taunting chorus of "Come along, Mercantile Jack! Ill-lodged, ill-fed, ill-used, hocussed, entrapped, anticipated, cleaned out. Come along, Poor Mercantile Jack, and be tempest-tossed till you are drowned!"

The uncommercial transaction which had brought me and Jack together, was this:—I had entered the Liverpool police-force, that I might have a look at the various unlawful traps which are every night set for Jack. As my term of service in that distinguished corps was short, and my personal bias in the capacity of one of its members has ceased, no suspicion will attach to my evidence that it is an admirable force. Besides that it is composed, without favor, of the best men that can be picked, it is directed by an unusual intelligence. Its organization against Fires, I take to be much better than the metropolitan system, and in all respects it tempers its remarkable vigilance with a still more remarkable discretion.

Jack had knocked off work in the docks some hours, and I had taken, for purposes of identification, a photograph likeness of a thief in the portrait room at our head police-office (on the whole, he seemed rather complimented by the proceeding), and I had been on police parade, and the small hand of the clock was moving on to ten, when I took up my lantern to follow Mr. Superintendent to the traps that were set for Jack. In Mr. Superintendent I saw, as any body might, a tall, well-looking, well set-up man, of a soldierly bearing, with a cavalry air, a good chest, and a resolute but not by any means ungentle face. He carried in his hand a plain black walking-stick of hard wood; and whenever and wherever, at any after-time of the night, he struck it on the pavement with a ringing sound, it instantly produced a whistle out of the darkness, and a policeman. To this remarkable stick, I refer an air of mystery and magic which pervaded the whole of my perquisition among the traps that were set for Jack.

We began by diving into the obscurest streets and lanes of the port. Suddenly pausing in a flow of cheerful discourse, before a dead wall, apparently some ten miles long, Mr. Superintendent struck upon the ground, and the wall opened and shot out, with military salute of hand to temple, two policemen —not in the least surprised themselves, not in the least surprising Mr. Superintendent.

"All right, Sharpeye?"

"All right, sir."

"All right, Trampfoot?"

"All right, sir."

"Is Quickear there?"

"Here am I, sir."

"Come with us."

"Yes sir."

So, Sharpeye went before, and Mr. Superintendent and I went next, and Trampfoot and Quickear marched as rear-guard. Sharpeye, I soon had occasion to remark, had a skillful and quite professional way of opening doors—touched latches delicately, as if they were keys of musical instruments—opened every door he touched, as if he were perfectly confident that there was stolen property behind it—instantly insinuated himself to prevent its being shut.

Sharpeye opened several doors of traps that were set for Jack, but Jack did not happen to be in any of them. They were all such miserable places that really, Jack, if I were you I would give them a wider berth. In every trap, somebody was sitting over a fire, waiting for Jack. Now, it was a crouching old woman, like the picture of the Norwood Gipsy in the old sixpenny dream-books; now, it was a crimp of the male sex in a checked shirt and without a coat, reading a newspaper; now, it was a man crimp and a woman crimp, who always introduced themselves as united in holy matrimony; now, it was Jack's delight, his (un)lovely Nan; but they were all waiting for Jack, and were all frightfully disappointed to see us.

"Who have you got up-stairs here?" says Sharpeye, generally. (In the Move-on tone.)

"Nobody, surr; sure not a blessed sowl!" (Irish feminine reply.)

"What do you mean by nobody? Didn't I hear a woman's step go upstairs when my hand was on the latch?"

"Ah! sure thin you're rhight, surr, I forgot her! 'Tis on'y Betsy White, surr. Ah! you know Betsy, surr. Come down, Betsy, darlin', and say the gintlemin."

Generally, Betsy looks over the banisters (the steep staircase is in the room) with a forcible expression in her protesting face, of an intention to compensate herself for the present trial by grinding Jack finer than usual when he does come.

Generally, Sharpeye turns to Mr. Superintendent, and says, as if the subjects of his remarks were wax-work:

"One of the worst, sir, this house is. This woman has been indicted three times. This man's a regular bad one likewise. His real name is Pegg. Gives himself out as Waterhouse."

"Never had sitch a name as Pegg near me back, thin, since I was in this house, bee the good Lard!" says the woman.

Generally, the man says nothing at all, but becomes exceedingly roundshouldered, and pretends to read his paper with rapt attention. Generally, Sharpeye directs our observation with a look, to the prints and pictures that are invariably numerous on the walls. Always, Trampfoot and Quickear are taking notice on the door-step. In default of Sharpeye being acquainted with the exact individuality of any gentleman encountered, one of these two is sure to proclaim from the outer air, like a gruff spectre that Jackson is not Jackson, but knows himself to be Fogle; and that Canlon is Walker's brother, against whom there was not sufficient evidence; or that the man who says he never was at sea since he was a boy, came ashore from a voyage last Thursday, or sails to-morrow morning. "And that is a bad class of man, you see," says Mr. Superintendent, when we got out into the dark again, "and very difficult to deal with, who, when he has made this place too hot to hold him, enters himself for a voyage as steward or cook, and is out of knowledge for months, and then turns up again worse than ever."

When we had gone into many such houses, and had come out (always leaving every body relapsing into waiting for Jack,) we started off to a singing-house where Jack was expected to muster strong.

The vocalization was taking place in a long low room upstairs; at one end, an orchestra of two performers, and a small platform; across the room, a series of open pews for Jack, with an aisle down the middle; at the other end, a larger pew than the rest entitled SNUG, and reserved for mates and similar good company. About the room, some amazing coffee-colored pictures varnished an inch deep, and some stuffed creatures in cases; dotted among the audience, in Snug and out of Snug, the "Professionals;" among them, of course, the celebrated comic favorite Mr. Banjo Bones, looking very hideous with his blackened face and limp sugar-loaf hat; beside him, sipping rum-and-water, Mrs. Banjo Bones, in her natural colors—a little heightened.

It was a Friday night, and Friday night was considered not a good night for Jack. At any rate, Jack did not show in very great force even here, though the house was one to which he much resorts, and where a good deal of money is taken. There was British Jack, a little maudlin and sleepy, lolling over his emptied glass, as if he were trying to read his fortune at the bottom; there was Loafing Jack at the Stars and Stripes, rather an unpromising customer, with his long nose, lank cheek, high cheek-bones, and nothing soft about him but his cabbage-leaf hat; there was Spanish Jack, with curls of black hair, rings in his ears, and a knife not far from his hand, if you got into trouble with him; there were Maltese Jack, and Jack of Sweden, and Jack the Finn, looming through the smoke of their pipes, and turning faces that looked as if they were carved out of dark wood, toward the young lady dancing the hornpipe, who found the platform so exceedingly small for it that I had a nervous expectation of seeing her, in the backward steps, disappear through the window. Still, if all hands had been got together, they would not have more than half filled the room. Observe, however, said Mr. Licensed Victualer, the host, that it was Friday night, and, besides, it was getting on for twelve, and Jack had gone aboard. A sharp and watchful man, Mr. Licensed Victualer the host, with tight lips and a complete edition of Cocker's arithmetic in each eye. Attended to his business himself, he said. Always on the spot. When he heard of talent, trusted nobody's account of it, but went off by rail to see it. If true talent, engaged it. Pounds a week for talent—four pound—five pound. Banjo Bones was undoubted talent. Hear this instrument that was going to play—it was real talent! In truth it was very good; a kind of piano-accordeon, played by a young girl of a delicate prettiness of face, figure, and dress, that made the audience look coarser. She sang to the instrument, too; first, a song about village bells, and how they chimed; then a song about how I went to sea; winding up with an imitation of the bagpipes, which Mercantile Jack seemed to understand much the best. A good girl, said Mr. Licensed Victualer. Kept herself select. Sat in Snug, not listening to the blandishments of mates. Lived with mother. Father dead. Once, a merchant well to do, but over-speculated himself. On delicate inquiry as to salary paid for item of talent under consideration, Mr. Victualer's pounds dropped suddenly to shillings—still it was a very comfortable thing for a young person like that, you know; she only went on, six times a night, and was only required to be there from six at night to twelve. What was more congclusive was, Mr. Victualer's assurance that he "never allowed any language, and never suffered any disturbance." Sharpeye confirmed the statement, and the order that prevailed was the best proof of it that could have been cited. So, I came to the conclusion that Poor Mercantile Jack might do (as I am afraid he does) much worse than trust himself to Mr. Victualer, and pass his evenings here.

But we had not yet looked, Mr. Superintendent—said Trampfoot, receiving us in the street again with military salute—for dark Jack. True, Trampfoot. Ring the wonderful stick, rub the wonderful lantern, and cause the spirits of the stick and lantern to convey us to the Darkies.

There was no disappointment in the matter of Dark Jack; *he* was producible. The Genii set us down in the little first floor of a little public-house, and there in a stiflingly close atmosphere, were Dark Jack and Dark Jack's Delight, his *white* unlovely Nan, sitting against the wall all round the room. More than that: Dark Jack's Delight was the least unlovely Nan, both morally and physically, that I saw that night.

As a fiddle and tambourine band were sitting among the company, Quickear suggested why not strike up? "Ah la'ads!" said a negro sitting by the door, "gib the jebblem a darnse. Tak' yah pardlers, jebblem, for 'um QUAD-rill."

This was the landlord, in a Greek cap, and a dress half Greek and half English. As master of the ceremonies, he called all the figures, and occasionally addressed himself parenthetically—after this manner. When he was very loud, I use capitals.

"Now den! Hoy! ONE. Right and left. (Put a steam

on, gib 'um powder.) LA-dies' chail. BAL-loon say. Lemonade! Two. AD-warnse and go back (gib 'ell a breakdown, shake it out o' yerselbs, keep a movil). SWING-corners, BAL-loon say, and Lemonade! (Hoy!) THREE. GENT come for'ard with a lady and go back, hoppersite come for'ard with a lady and go back, ALL four come for'ard and do what yer can. (Aeiohoy!) BAL-loon say, and leetle lemonade (Dat hair nigger by um fire-place 'hind a' time, shake it out o' yerselbs, gib 'ell a breakdown). Now den! Hoy! FOUR! Lemonade. BAL-loon say, and swing. FOUR ladies meet in 'um middle, FOUR gents goes round 'um ladies, FOUR gents passes out under 'um ladies' arms, SWING—and Lemonade till 'a moosic can't play no more! (Hdy, Hoy!)"

The male dancers were all blacks, and one was an unusually powerful man of six feet three or four. The sound of their flat feet on the floor was as unlike the sound of white feet as their faces were unlike white faces. They toed and heeled, shuffled, double-shuffled, double-double-shuffled, covered the buckle, and beat the time out, rarely, dancing with a great show of teeth, and with a childish, good-humoured enjoyment that was very prepossessing. They generally kept together, these poor fellows, said Mr. Superintendent, because they were at a disadvantage singly, and liable to slights in the neighboring streets. But if I were Light Jack, I should be very slow to interfere oppressively with Dark Jack, for, whenever I have had to do with him I have found him a simple and gentle fellow. Bearing this in mind, I asked his friendly permission to leave him restoration of beer, in wishing him good night, and thus it fell out that the last words I heard him say as I blundered down the worn stairs, were, "Jebblem's elth! Ladies drinks fust!"

The night was now well on into the morning, but, for miles and hours we explored a strange world, where nobody ever goes to bed, but every body is eternally sitting up waiting for Jack. This exploration was among a labyrinth of dismal courts and blind alleys, called Entries, kept in wonderful order by the police, and in much better order than by the corporation: the want of gaslight in the most dangerous and infamous of these places being quite unworthy of so spirited a town. I need describe but two or three of the houses in which Jack was waited for, as specimens of the rest. Many we attained by noisome passages so profoundly dark that we felt our way with our hands. Not one of the whole number we visited, was without its show of prints and ornamental crockery; the quantity of the latter set forth on little shelves and in little cases, in otherwise wretched rooms, indicating that Mercantile Jack must have an extraordinary fondness for crockery, to necessitate so much of that bait in his traps.

Among such garniture, in one front parlor in the dead of the night, four women were sitting by a fire. One of them had a male child in her arms. On a stool among them was a swarthy youth with a guitar, who had evidently stopped playing when our footsteps were heard.

"Well! how do *you* do?" says Mr. Superintendent, looking about him.

"Pretty well, sir, and hope you gentlemen are going to treat us ladies, now you have come to see us."

"Order there!" says Sharpeye.

"None of that!" says Quickear.

Trampfoot, outside is heard to confide to himself, "Megisson's lot this is. And a bad 'un!"

"Well!" says Mr. Superintendent, laying his hand on the shoulder of the swarthy youth, and who's this?"

"Antonio, sir."

"And what does *he* do here?"

"Come to give us a bit of music. No harm in that, I suppose?"

"A young foreign sailor?"

"Yes. He's a Spaniard. You're a Spaniard, ain't you, Antonio?"

"Me Spanish."

"And he don't know a word you say, not he, not if you was to talk to him till doomsday." (Triumphantly, as if it redounded to the credit of the house.)

"Will he play something?"

"Oh, yes, if you like. Play something, Antonio. *You* ain't ashamed to play something; are you?"

The cracked guitar raises the feeblest ghost of a tune, and three of the women keep time to it with their heads, and the fourth with the child. If Antonio has brought any money in with him, I am afraid he will never take it out, and it even strikes me that his jacket and guitar may be in a bad way. But, the look of the young man and the tinkling of the instrument so change the place in a moment to a leaf out of Don Quixote, that I wonder where his mule is stabled, until he leaves off.

I am bound to acknowledge (as it tends rather to my uncommercial confusion), that I occasioned a difficulty in this establishment, by having taken the child in my arms. For, on my offering to restore it to a ferocious joker not unstimulated by rum, who claimed to be its mother, that unnatural parent put her hands behind her, and declined to accept it; backing into the fire-place, and very shrilly declaring, regardless of remonstrance from her friends, that she knowed it to be Law, that whoever took a child from its mother of his own will, was bound to stick to it. The uncommercial sense of being in a rather ridiculous position with the poor little child beginning to be frightened, was relieved by my worthy friend and fellow-constable, Trampfoot; who, laying hands on the article as if it were a Bottle, passed it on to the nearest woman, and bade her "take hold of that." As we came out, the Bottle was passed to the ferocious joker, and they all sat down as before, including Antonio and the guitar. It was clear that there was no such thing as a nightcap to this baby's head, and that even he never went to bed, but was always kept up—and would grow up, kept up—waiting for Jack.

Later still in the night, we came (by the court "where the man was murdered," and by the other court across the street, into which his body was dragged) to another parlor in another Entry, where several people were sitting round a fire in just the same way. It was a dirty and offensive place, with some ragged clothes drying in it; but there was a high shelf over the entrance-door (to be out of the reach of marauding hands, possibly), with two large white loaves on it, and a great piece of Cheshire cheese.

"Well!" says Mr. Superintendent, with a comprehensive look all round. "How do *you* do?"

"Not much to boast of, sir." From the courtesying woman of the house. "This is my good man, sir."

"You are not registered as a common Lodging House?"

"No, sir."

Sharpeye (in the Move-on tune) puts in the pertinent inquiry, "Then why ain't you?"

"Ain't got no one here, Mr. Sharpeye," rejoins the woman and my good man together, "but our own family."

"How many are you in family?"

The woman takes time to count, under pretense of coughing, and adds, as one scant of breath, "Seven, sir."

But she has missed one, so Sharpeye, who knows all about it, says:

"Here's a young man here makes eight, who ain't of your family?"

"No, Mr. Sharpeye, he's a weekly lodger."

"What does he do for a living?"

The young man here, takes the reply upon himself, and shortly answers, "Ain't got nothing to do."

The young man here, is modestly brooding behind a damp apron pendent from a clothes-line. As I glance at him I become—but I don't know why—vaguely reminded of Woolwich, Chatham, Portsmouth, and Dover. When we get out, my respected fellow-constable Sharpeye addressing Mr. Superintendent, says:

"You noticed that young man, sir, in at Darby's?"

"Yes. What is he?"

"Deserter, sir."

Mr. Sharpeye further intimates that when we have done with his services, he will step back and take that young man. Which in course of time he does: feeling at perfect ease about finding him, and knowing for a moral certainty that nobody in that region will be gone to bed.

Later still in the night, we came to another parlor up a step or two from the street, which was very cleanly, neatly, even tastefully, kept, and in which, set forth on a draped chest of drawers masking the staircase, was such a profusion of ornamental crockery, that it would have furnished forth a handsome sale-booth at a fair. It backed up a stout old lady—

HOGARTH drew her exact likeness more than once—and a boy who was carefully writing a copy in a copy-book.

"Well, ma'am, how do *you* do?"

Sweetly, she can assure the dear gentlemen, sweetly. Charm ingly, charmingly. And overjoyed to see us.

"Why, this is a strange time for this boy to be writing his copy. In the middle of the night!"

"So it is, dear gentlemen, Heaven bless your welcome faces and send ye prosperous, but he has been to the Play with a young friend for his diversion, and he combinates his improvement with entertainment by doing his school-writhing afterwards, God be good to ye!"

The copy admonished human nature to subjugate the fire of every fierce desire. One might have thought it recommended stirring the fire, the old lady so approved it. There she sat, rosily beaming at the copy-book and the boy, and invoking showers of blessings on our heads, when we left her in the middle of the night, waiting for Jack.

Later still in the night, we came to a nauseous room with an earth floor, into which the refuse scum of an alley trickled. The stench of this habitation was abominable; the seeming poverty of it, diseased and dire. Yet, here again, was visitor or lodger—a man sitting before the fire, like the rest of them elsewhere, and apparently not distasteful to the mistress's niece, who was also before the fire. The mistress herself had the misfortune of being in jail.

Three weird old women of transcendent ghastliness, were at needlework at a table in this room. Says Trampfoot to First Witch, "What are you making?" Says she, "Money-bags."

"*What* are you making?" retorts Trampfoot, a little off his balance.

"Bags to hold your money," says the witch, shaking her head, and setting her teeth; "you as has got it."

She holds up a common cash-bag, and on the table is a heap of such bags. Witch Two laughs at us. Witch Three scowls at us. Witch sisterhood all, stitch, stitch. First Witch has a red circle round each eye. I fancy it like the beginning of the development of a perverted diabolical halo and that when it spreads all round her head, she will die in the odor of devilry.

Trampfoot wishes to be informed what First Witch has got behind the table, down by the side of her, there? Witches Two and Three croak angrily, "Show him the child!"

She drags out a skinny little arm from a brown dust-heap on the ground. Adjured not to disturb the child, she lets it drop again. Thus we find at last that there is one child in the world of Entries who goes to bed—if this be bed.

Mr. Superintendent asks how long are they going to work at those bags?

How long? First Witch repeats. Going to have supper presently. See the cups and saucers, and the plates.

Mr. Superintendent opines, it is rather late for supper, surely.

"Late? Ay! But we has to 'arn our supper afore we eats it!" Both the other witches repeat this after First Witch, and take the Uncommercial measurement with their eyes, as for a charmed winding-sheet. Some grim discourse ensues, referring to the mistress of the cave, who will be released from jail to-morrow. Witches pronounce Trampfoot "right there," when he deems it a trying distance for the old lady to walk; she shall be fetched by niece in a spring-cart.

As I took a parting look at First Witch in turning away, the red marks round her eyes seemed to have already grown larger, and she hungrily and thirstily looked out beyond me into the dark doorway, to see if Jack were there. For, Jack came even here, and the mistress had got into jail through deluding Jack.

When I at last ended this night of travel and got to bed, I failed to keep my mind on comfortable thoughts of Seaman's Homes (not overdone with strictness), and improved dock-regulations giving Jack greater benefit of fire and candle aboard ship, through my mind's wandering among the vermin I had seen. Afterward the same vermin ran all over my sleep. Evermore, when on a breezy day I see Poor Mercantile Jack running into port with a fair wind under all sail, I shall think of the unsleeping host of devourers who never go to bed, and are always in their set traps waiting for him.

In the late high winds I was blown to a great many places —and indeed, wind or no wind, I generally have extensive transactions on hand in the article of Air—but I have not been blown to any English place lately, and I very seldom have been blown to any English place in my life, where I could get any thing good to eat and drink in five minutes, or where if I sought it, I was received with a welcome.

This is a curious thing to consider. But before (stimulated by my own experiences and the representations of many fellow-travelers of every uncommercial and commercial degree) I consider it further, I must utter a passing word of wonder concerning high winds.

I wonder why metropolitan gales always blow so hard at Walworth. I cannot imagine what Walworth has done, to bring such windy punishment upon itself, as I never fail to find recorded in the newspapers when the wind has blown at all hard. Brixton seems to have something on its conscience; Peckham suffers more than a virtuous Peckham might be supposed to deserve; the howling neighborhood of Deptford figures largely in the accounts of the ingenious gentlemen who are out in every wind that blows, and to whom it is an ill high wind that blows no good; but, there can hardly be any Walworth left by this time. It must surely be blown away. I have read of more chimney-stacks and house-copings coming down with terrific smashes at Walworth, and of more sacred edifices being nearly (not quite) blown out to sea from the same accursed locality, than I have read of practiced thieves with the appearance and manners of gentlemen—a popular phenomenon which never existed on earth out of fiction and a police report. Again: I wonder why people are always blown into the Surrey Canal, and into no other piece of water? Why do people get up early and go out in groups, to be blown into the Surrey Canal? Do they say to one another, "Welcome Death, so that we get into the newspapers"? Even that would be an insufficient explanation, because even then they might sometimes put themselves in the way of being blown into the Regent's Canal, instead of always saddling Surrey for the field. Some nameless policemen, too, is constantly, on the slightest provocation, getting himself blown into this same

Surrey Canal. Will SIR RICHARD MAYNE see to it, and re strain that weak-minded and feeble-bodied constable?

To resume the consideration of the curious question of Refreshment. I am a Briton, and, as such, I am aware that I never will be a slave—and yet I have a latent suspicion that there must be some slavery of wrong custom in this matter.

I travel by railroad. I start from home at seven or eight in the morning, after breakfasting hurriedly. What with skimming over the open landscape, what with mining in the damp bowels of the earth, what with banging, booming, and shrieking the scores of miles away, I am hungry when I arrive at the "Refreshment" station where I am expected. Please to observe, expected. I have said, I am hungry; perhaps I might say, with greater point and force, that I am to some extent exhausted, and that I need—in the expressive French sense of the word–to be restored. What is provided for my restoration? The apartment that is to restore me, is a wind trap, cunningly set to inveigle all the draughts in that country-side, and to communicate a special intensity and velocity to them as they rotate in two hurricanes: one, about my wretched head: one, about my wretched legs. The training of the young ladies behind the counter who are to restore me, has been from their infancy directed to the assumption of a defiant dramatic show that I am *not* expected. It is in vain for me to represent to them by my humble and conciliatory manners, that I wish to be liberal. It is in vain for me to represent to myself, for the encouragement of my sinking soul, that the young ladies have a pecuniary interest in my arrival. Neither my reason nor my feelings can make head against the cold glazed glare of eye with which I am assured that I am not expected, and not wanted. The solitary man among the bottles would sometimes take pity on me, if he dared, but he is powerless against the rights and mights of Woman. (Of the page I make no account, for he is a boy, and therefore the natural enemy of Creation.) Chilling fast, in the deadly tornadoes to which my upper and lower extremities are exposed, and subdued by the moral disadvantage at which I stand, I turn my disconsolate eyes on the refreshments that are to restore me. I find that I must either scald my throat by insanely ladling into it, against time and for no wager, brown hot water stiffened with flour; or, I must make myself flaky and sick with Banbury cake; or, I must stuff into my delicate organization, a currant pincushion which I know will swell into immeasurable dimensions when it has got there; or, I must extort from an iron-bound quarry, with a fork, as if I were farming an inhospitable soil, some glutinous lumps of gristle and grease, called pork-pie. While thus forlornly occupied, I find that the depressing banquet on the table is, in every phase of its profoundly unsa-atisfactory character, so like the banquet at the meanest and shabbiest of evening parties, that I begin to think I must have "brought down" to supper, the old lady unknown, blue with cold, who is setting her teeth on edge with a cool orange, at my elbow—that the pastrycook who has compounded for the company on the lowest terms per head, is a fraudulent bankrupt, redeeming his contract with the stale stock from his window—that, for some unexplained reason, the family giving the party have become my mortal foes, and have given it on purpose to affront me. Or, I fancy that I am "breaking up" again, at the evening conversazione at school, charged two-and-sixpence in the half-year's bill; or breaking down again at that celebrated evening party given at Mrs. Bogles's boarding-house when I was a boarder there, on which occasion Mrs. Bogles was taken in execution by a branch of the legal profession who got in as the harp, and was removed (with the keys and subscribed capital) to a place of durance, half an hour prior to the commencement of the festivities.

Take another case.

Mr. Grazinglands, of the Midland Counties, came to London by railroad one morning last week, accompanied by the amiable and fascinating Mrs. Grazinglands. Mr. G. is a gentleman of a comfortable property, and had a little business to transact at the Bank of England, which required the concurrence and signature of Mrs. G. Their business disposed of, Mr. and Mrs. Granzinglands viewed the Royal Exchange, and the exterior of St. Paul's Cathedral. The spirits of Mrs Grazinglands then gradually beginning to flag, Mr. Grazinglands (who is the tenderest of husbands) remarked with sympathy, "Arabella, my dear, I fear you are faint." Mrs

Grazinglands replied, "Alexander, I am rather faint; but don't mind me, I shall be better presently." Touched by the feminine meekness of this answer, Mr. Grazinglands looked in at a pastry-cook's window, hesitating as to the expediency of lunching at that establishment. He beheld nothing to eat, but butter in various forms, slightly charged with jam, and languidly frizzling over tepid water. Two ancient turtle-shells, on which was inscribed the legend, "SOUPS," decorated a glass partition within, inclosing a stuffy alcove, from which a ghastly mockery of a marriage-breakfast spread on a rickety table, warned the terrified traveler. An oblong box of stale and broken pastry at reduced prices, mounted on a stool, ornamented the doorway; and two high chairs that looked as if they were performing on stilts, embellished the counter. Over the whole, a young lady presided, whose gloomy haughtiness as she surveyed the street, announced a deep-seated grievance against society, and an implacable determination to be avenged. From a beetle-haunted kitchen below this institution, fumes arose, suggestive of a class of soup which Mr. Grazinglands knew, from painful experience, enfeebles the mind, distends the stomach, forces itself into the complexion, and tries to ooze out at the eyes. As he decided against entering, and turned away, Mrs. Grazinglands, becoming perceptibly weaker, repeated, "I am rather faint, Alexander, but don't mind me." Urged to new efforts by these words of resignation, Mr. Grazinglands looked in at a cold and floury baker's shop, where utilitarian buns unrelieved by a currant consorted with hard biscuits, a stone filter of cold water, a hard pale clock, and a hard little old woman with flaxen hair, of an undeveloped farinaceous aspect, as if she had been fed upon seeds. He might have entered even here, but for the timely remembrance coming upon him that Jairing's was but round the corner.

Now, Jairing's being an hotel for families and gentlemen, in high repute among the midland counties, Mr. Grazinglands plucked up a great spirit when he told Mrs. Grazinglands she should have a chop there. That lady, likewise, felt that she was going to see Life. Arriving on that gay and festive scene, they found the second waiter, in a flabby undress, cleaning the windows of the empty coffee-room, and the first waiter, denuded of his white tie, making up his cruets behind the Post-office Directory. The latter (who took them in hand) was greatly put out by their patronage, and showed his mind to be troubled by a sense of the pressing necessity of instantly smuggling Mrs. Grazinglands into the obscurest corner of the building. This slighted lady (who is the pride of her division of the county) was immediately conveyed, by several dark passages, and up and down several steps, into a penitential apartment at the back of the house, where five invalided old plate-warmers leaned up against one another under a discarded old melancholy sideboard, and where the wintry leaves of all the dining-tables in the house lay thick. Also, a sofa, of incomprehensible form regarded from any sofane point of view, murmured "Bed;" while an air of mingled fluffiness and heel-taps, added, "Second Waiter's." Secreted in this dismal hold, objects of a mysterious distrust and suspicion, Mr. Grazinglands and his charming partner waited twenty minutes for the smoke (for it never came to a fire), twenty-five minutes for the sherry, half an hour for the table-cloth, forty minutes for the knives and forks, three-quarters of an hour for the chops, and an hour for the potatoes. On settling the little bill—which was not much more than the day's pay of a Lieutenant in the navy—Mr. Grazinglands took heart to remonstrate against the general quality and cost of his reception. To whom the waiter replied, substantially, that Jairing's made it a merit to have accepted him on any terms; "for," added the waiter (unmistakably coughing at Mrs. Grazinglands, the pride of her division of the county), "when individuals is not staying in the 'Ouse, their favors is not as a rule looked upon as making it worth Mr. Jairing's while; nor is it, indeed, a style of business Mr. Jairing wishes." Finally, Mr. and Mrs. Grazinglands passed out of Jairing's hotel for Families and Gentlemen, in a state of the greatest depression, scorned by the bar; and did not recover their self-respect for several days.

Or take another case. Take your own case.

You are going off by railway, from any Terminus. You have twenty minutes for dinner before you go. You want your dinner, and, like Doctor Johnson, sir, you like to dine. You present to your mind, a picture of the refreshment-table at that terminus. The conventional shabby evening party supper—accepted as the model for all termini and all refreshment stations, because it is the last repast known to this state of existence of which any human creature would partake, but in the direst extremity—sickens your contemplation, and your words are these: "I cannot dine on stale sponge-cakes that turn to sand in the mouth. I cannot dine on shining brown patties, composed of unknown animals within, and offering to my view the device of an indigestible star-fish in leaden pie-crust without. I cannot dine on a sandwich that has long been pining under an exhausted receiver. I cannot dine on barley-sugar. I cannot dine on Toffee." You repair to the nearest hotel, and arrive, agitated, in the coffee-room.

It is a most astonishing fact that the waiter is very cold to you. Account for it how you may, smooth it over how you will, you cannot deny that he is cold to you. He is not glad to see you, he does not want you, he would much rather you hadn't come. He opposes to your flushed condition, an immovable composure. As if this were not enough, another waiter, born, as it would seem, expressly to look at you in this passage of your life, stands at a little distance, with his napkin under his arm and his hands folded, looking at you with all his might. You impress on your waiter that you have ten minutes for dinner, and he proposes that you shall begin with a bit of fish which will be ready in twenty. That proposal declined, he suggests—as a neat originality—"a weal or mutton cutlet." You close with either cutlet, any cutlet, any thing. He goes, leisurely, behind a door, and calls down some unseen shaft. A ventriloquial dialogue ensues, tending finally to the effect that weal only, is available on the spur of the moment. You anxiously call out "Veal then!" Your waiter, having settled that point, returns to array your table-cloth, with a table napkin folded cocked-hat-wise, (slowly, for something out of window engages his eye), a white wine-glass, a green wine-glass, a blue finger-glass, a tumbler, and a powerful field battery of fourteen castors with nothing in them: or at all events—which is enough for your purpose—with nothing in them that will come out. All this time, the other waiter looks at you—with an air of mental comparison and curiosity, now, as if it had occurred to him that you are rather like his brother. Half your time gone, and nothing come but the jug of ale and the bread, you implore your waiter to "see after that cutlet, waiter; pray do." He cannot go at once, for he is carrying in seventeen pounds of American cheese for you to finish with, and a small Landed Estate of celery and water-cress. The other waiter changes his leg, and takes a new view of you—doubtfully, now, as if he had rejected the resemblance to his brother, and had begun to think you more like his aunt or his grandmother. Again you beseech your waiter with pathetic indignation, to "see after that cutlet!" He steps out to see after it, and by-and-by, when you are going away without it, comes back with it. Even then, he will not take the sham silver-cover off, without a pause for a flourish, and a look at the musty cutlet as if he were surprised to see it—which cannot possibly be the case, he must have seen it so often before. A sort of fur has been produced upon its surface by the cook's art, and, in a sham silver vessel staggering on two feet instead of three, is a cutaneous kind of sauce, of brown pimples and pickled cucumber. You order the bill, but your waiter cannot bring your bill yet, because he is bringing, instead, three flinty-hearted potatoes and two grim head of broccoli, like the occasional ornaments on area railings, badly boiled. You know that you will never come to this pass, any more than to the cheese and celery, and you imperatively demand your bill; but it takes time to get, even when gone for, because your waiter has to communicate with a lady who lives behind a sash-window in a corner, and who appears to have to refer to several Ledgers before she can make it out—as if you had been staying there a year. You become distracted to get away, and the other waiter, once more changing his leg, still looks at you—but suspiciously, now, as if you had begun to remind him of the party who took the great-coats last winter. Your bill at last brought and paid, at the rate of sixpence a mouthful, your waiter reproachfully reminds you that "attendance is not charged for a single meal," and you have to search in all your pockets for sixpence more. He has a worse opinion of you than ever, when you have given it to him, and lets you out into the street with the air of one saying to himself, as you cannot doubt he is. "I hope we shall never see *you* here again!"

Or, take any other of the numerous traveling instances in which, with more time at your disposal, you are, have been, or may be, equally ill-served. Take the old-established Bull's Head with its old-established knife-boxes on its old-established sideboards, its old-established flue under its old-established four-post bedsteads in its old-established airless rooms, its old-established frouziness up-stairs and down-stairs, its old-established cookery, and its old-established principles of plunder. Count up your injuries, in its side-dishes of ailing sweet breads in white poultices, of apothecaries' powders in rice for curry, of pale stewed bits of calf ineffectually relying for an adventitious interest on forcemeat balls. You have had experience of the old-established Bull's Head's stringy fowls, with lower extremities like wooden legs, sticking up out of the dish; of its cannibalic boiled mutton, gushing horribly among its capers, when carved; of its little dishes of pastry—roofs of spermaceti ointment, erected over half an apple or four gooseberries. Well for you if you have yet forgotten the old-established Bull's Head's fruity port: whose reputation was gained solely by the old-established price the Bull's Head put upon it, and by the old-established air with which the Bull's Head set the glasses and D'Oyleys on, and held that Liquid Gout to the three-and-sixpenny wax-candle, as if its old-established color hadn't come from the dyer's.

Or lastly, take, to finish with, two cases that we all know, every day.

We all know the new hotel near the station, where it is always gusty, going up the lane which is always muddy, where we are sure to arrive at night, and where we make the gas start awfully when we open the front door. We all know the flooring of the passages and staircases that is too new, and the walls that are too new, and the house that is haunted by the ghost of mortar. We all know the doors that have cracked, and the cracked shutters through which we get a glimpse of the disconsolate moon. We all know the new people who have come to keep the new hotel, and who wish they had never come, and who (inevitable result) wish *we* had never come. We all know how much too scant and smooth and bright the new furniture is, and how it has never settled down, and cannot fit itself into right places, and will get into wrong places. We all know how the gas, being lighted, shows maps of damp upon the walls. We all know how the ghost of mortar passes into our sandwich, stirs our negus, goes up to bed with us, ascends the pale bedroom chimney, and prevents the smoke from following. We all know how a leg of our chair comes off at breakfast in the morning, and how the dejected waiter attributes the accident to a general greenness pervading the establishment, and informs us, in reply to a local inquiry, that he is thankful to say he is an entire stranger in that part of the country, and is going back to his own connection on Saturday.

We all know, on the other hand, the great station hotel belonging to the company of proprietors, which has suddenly sprung up in the back outskirts of any place we like to name, and where we look out of our palatial windows, at little back yards and gardens, old summer-houses, fowl-houses, pigeon-traps, and pig-sties. We all know this hotel in which we can get any thing we want, after its kind, for money; but where nobody is glad to see us, or sorry to see us, or minds (our bill paid) whether we come or go, or how, or when, or why, or cares about us. We all know this hotel, where we have no individuality, but put ourselves into the general post, as it were, and are sorted and disposed of according to our division. We all know that we can get on very well indeed at such a place, but still not perfecly well; and this may be, because the place is largely wholesale, and there is a lingering personal retail interest within us that asks to be satisfied.

To sum up. My uncommercial traveling has not yet brought me to the conclusion that we are close to perfection in these matters. And just as I do not believe that the end of the world will ever be near at hand, so long as any of the very tiresome and arrogant people who constantly predict that catastrophe are left in it, so, I shall have small faith in the Hotel Millennium, while any of the uncomfortable superstitions I have glanced at, remain in existence.

---

I GOT into the traveling chariot—it was of German make, roomy, heavy, and unvarnished—I got into the traveling chariot, pulled up the steps after me, shut myself in with a smart bang of the door, and gave the word "Go on!"

Immediately, all that W. and S. W. division of London began to slide away at a pace so lively that I was over the river and past the Old Kent road, and out on Blackheath, and even ascending Shooter's Hill, before I had had time to look about me in the carriage, like a collected traveler.

I had two ample Imperials on the roof, other fitted storage for luggage in front, and other up behind; I had a net for books overhead, great pockets to all the windows, a leathern pouch or two hung up for odds and ends, and a reading-lamp fixed in the back of the chariot, in case I should be benighted. I was amply provided in all respects, and had no idea where I was going (which was delightful), except that I was going abroad.

So smooth was the old high road, and so fresh were the horses, and so fast went I, that it was midway between Gravesend and Rochester, and the widening river was bearing the ships, white-sailed or black-smoked, out to sea, when I noticed by the wayside a very queer small boy.

"Halloa!" said I, to the very queer small boy, "where do you live?"

"At Chatham," says he.

"What do you do there?" says I.

"I go to school," says he.

I took him up in a moment, and we went on. Presently the very queer small boy said, "This is Gadshill we are coming to, where Falstaff went out to rob those travelers, and ran away."

"You know something about Falstaff, eh?" said I.

"All about him," said the very queer small boy. "I am old (I am nine), and I read all sorts of books. But *do* let us stop at the top of the hill, and look at the house there, if you please!"

"You admire that house?" said I.

"Bless you, sir," said the very queer small boy, "when I was not more than half as old as nine, it used to be a treat for me to be brought to look at it. And now, I am nine, I come by myself to look at it. And ever since I can recollect, my father seeing me so fond of it, has often said to me, 'If you were to be very persevering and were to work hard, you might some day come to live in it.' Though that's impossible!" said the very queer small boy, drawing a low breath, and now staring at the house out of window with all his might.

I was rather amazed to be told this by the very queer small boy; for that house happens to be my house, and I have reason to believe that what he said was true.

Well! I made no halt there, and I soon dropped the very queer small boy and went on. Over the road where the old Romans used to march, over the road where the old Canterbury pilgrims used to go, over the road where the traveling trains of the old imperious priests and princes used to jingle on horseback between the continent and this Island through the mud and water, over the road where Shakespeare hummed to himself, "Blow, blow, thou winter wind," as he sat in the saddle at the gate of the inn yard noticing the carriers; all among the cherry orchards, apple orchards, corn-fields, and hop-gardens; so went I, by Canterbury to Dover. There, the sea was tumbling in, with deep sounds, after dark, and the revolving French light on Cape Grinez was seen regularly bursting out and becoming obscured, as if the head of a gigantic light-keeper in an anxious state of mind were interposed every half minute, to look how it was burning.

Early in the morning I was on the deck of the steam-packet, and we were aiming at the bar in the usual intolerable manner, and the bar was aiming at us in the usual intolerable manner, and the bar got by far the best of it, and we got by far the worst—all in the usual intolerable manner.

But, when I was clear of the Custom House on the other side, and when I began to make the dust fly on the thirsty French roads, and when the twigsome trees by the wayside (which, I suppose, never will grow leafy, for they never did) guarded here and there a dusty soldier, or field laborer, baking on a heap of broken stones, sound asleep in a fiction of shade, I began to recover my traveling spirits. Coming upon the breaker of the broken stones, in a hard, hot, shining hat, on which the sun played at a distance as on a burning-glass, I felt that now, indeed, I was in the dear old France of my affections. I should have known it, without the well-remembered bottle of rough ordinary wine, the cold roast fowl, the loaf, and the pinch of salt, on which I lunched with unspeakable satisfaction, from one of the stuffed pockets of the chariot.

I must have fallen asleep after lunch, for when a bright face looked in at the window, I started, and said:

"Good God, Louis, I dreamed you were dead!"

My cheerful servant laughed, and answered:

"Me? Not at all, sir."

"How glad I am to wake! What are we doing, Louis?"

"We go to take relay of horses. Will you walk up the hill?"

"Certainly."

Welcome the old French hill, with the old French lunatic (not in the most distant degree related to Sterne's Maria) living in a thatched dog-kennel half way up, and flying out with his crutch, and his big head and extended nightcap, to be beforehand with the old men and women exhibiting crippled children, and with the children exhibiting old men and women, ugly and blind, who always seemed by resurrectionary process to be recalled out of the elements for the sudden peopling of the solitude!

"It is well," said I, scattering among them what small coin I had; "here comes Louis, and I am quite roused from my nap."

We journeyed on again, and I welcomed every new assurance that France stood where I had left it. There were the posting-houses, with their archways, dirty stable-yards, and clean post-masters' wives, bright women of business, looking on at the putting-to of the horses; there were the postillions counting what money they got, into their hats, and never making enough of it; there were the standard population of gray horses of Flanders descent, invariably biting one another when they got a chance; there were the fleecy sheepskins, looped on over their uniforms by the postillions, like bibbed aprons, when it blew and rained; there were their jack-boots, and their cracking whips; there were the cathedrals that I got out to see, as under some cruel bondage, in no wise desiring to see them;

there were the little towns that appeared to have no reason for being towns, since most of their houses were to let and nobody could be induced to look at them, except the people who couldn't let them and had nothing else to do but look at them all day. I lay a night upon the road and enjoyed delectable cookery of potatoes, and some other sensible things, adoption of which at home would inevitably be shown to be fraught with ruin, somehow or other, to that rickety national blessing, the British farmer; and at last I was rattled, like a single pill in a box, over leagues of stones, until—madly cracking, plunging, and flourishing two gray tails about—I made my triumphal entry into Paris.

At Paris I took an upper apartment for a few days in one of the hotels of the Rue de Rivoli: my front windows looking into the garden of the Tuileries (where the principal difference between the nursemaids and the flowers seemed to be that the former were locomotive, and the latter not): my back windows looking at all the other back windows in the hotel, and deep down into a paved yard, where my German chariot had retired under a tight-fitting arch-way, to all appearance, for life, and where bells rang all day without anybody's minding them but certain chamberlains with feather brooms and green baize caps, who here and there leaned out of some high window placidly looking down, and where neat waiters with trays on their left shoulders passed and repassed from morning to night.

Whenever I am at Paris, I am dragged by invisible force into the Morgue. I never want to go there, but am always pulled there. One Christmas Day, when I would rather have been anywhere else, I was attracted in, to see an old gray man lying all alone on his cold bed, with a tap of water turned on over his gray hair, and running drip, drip, drip, down his wretched face until it got to the corner of his month, where it took a turn and made him look sly. One New Year's Morning (by the same token, the sun was shining outside, and there was a mountebank balancing a feather on his nose, within a yard of the gate), I was pulled in again, to look at a flaxen-haired boy of eighteen with a heart hanging on his breast—"From his mother," was engraven on it—who had come into the net across the river, with a bullet-wound in his fair forehead and his hands cut with a knife, but whence or how was a blank mystery. This time I was forced into the same dread place, to see a large dark man whose disfigurement by water was, in a frightful manner, comic, and whose expression was that of a prize-fighter who had closed his eyelids under a heavy blow, but was going immediately to open them, shake his head, and "come up smiling." Oh what this large dark man cost me in that bright city!

It was very hot weather, and he was none the better for that, and I was much the worse. Indeed, a very neat and pleasant little woman with the key of her lodging on her fore-finger, who had been showing him to her little girl while she and the child ate sweetmeats, observed monsieur looking poorly as we came out together, and asked monsieur, with her wondering little eyebrows prettily raised, if there were any thing the matter? Faintly replying in the negative, monsieur crossed the road to a wine-shop, got some brandy, and resolved to freshen himself with a dip in the great floating bath on the river.

The bath was crowded in the usual airy manner, by a male population in striped drawers of various gay colors, who walked up and down arm in arm, drank coffee, smoked cigars, sat at little tables, conversed politely with the damsels who dispensed the towels, and every now and then pitched themselves into the river head foremost, and came out again to repeat this social routine.

I made haste to participate in the water part of the entertainments, and was in the full enjoyment of a delightful bath, when all in a moment I was seized by an unreasonable idea that the large dark body was floating straight at me.

I was out of the river and dressing instantly. In the shock I had taken some water into my mouth, and it turned me sick, for I fancied that the contamination of the creature was in it. I had got back to my cool darkened room in the hotel, and was lying on a sofa there, before I began to reason with myself.

Of course, I knew perfectly well that the large dark creature was stone dead, and that I should no more come upon him out of the place where I had seen him dead, than I should come upon the cathedral of Notre-Dame in an entirely new situation.

What troubled me was the picture of the creature; and that had so curiously and strongly painted itself upon my brain, that I could not get rid of it until it was worn out.

I noticed the peculiarities of this possession, while it was a real discomfort to me. That very day, at dinner, some morsel on my plate looked like a piece of him, and I was glad to get up and go out. Later in the evening, I was walking along the Rue St. Honoré, when I saw a bill at a public room there, announcing small-sword exercise, broad-sword exercise, wrestling, and other such feats. I went in, and, some of the sword play being very skillful, remained. A specimen of our own national sport, the British Boaxe, was announced to be given at the close of the evening. In an evil hour, I determined to wait for this Boaxe, as became a Briton. It was a clumsy specimen (executed by two English grooms out of place), but, one of the combatants, receiving a straight right-hander with the glove between his eyes, did exactly what the large dark creature in the Morgue had seemed going to do—and finished me for that night.

There was a rather sickly smell (not at all an unusual fragrance in Paris) in the little anteroom of my apartment at the hotel. The large dark creature in the Morgue was by no direct experience associated with my sense of smell, because, when I came to the knowledge of him, he lay behind a wall of thick plate-glass, as good as a wall of steel or marble for that matter. Yet the whiff of the room never failed to reproduce him. What was more curious was the capriciousness with which his portrait seemed to light itself up in my mind, elsewhere; I might be walking in the Palais Royal, lazily enjoying the shop windows, and might be regaling myself with one of the ready-made clothes shops that are set out there. My eyes, wandering over impossible-waisted dressing-gowns and luminous waistcoats, would fall upon the master, or the shopman, or even the very dummy at the door, and would suggest to me, "Something like him!"—and instantly I was sickened again.

This would happen at the theatre, in the same manner. Often, it would happen in the street, when I certainly was not looking for the likeness, and when probably there was no likeness there. It was not because the creature was dead that I was so haunted, because I know that I might have been (and I know it because I have been) equally attended by the image of a living aversion. This lasted about a week. The picture did not fade by degrees, in the sense that it became a whit less forcible and distinct, but in the sense that it obtruded itself less and less frequently. The experience may be worth considering by some who have the care of children. It would be difficult to overstate the intensity and accuracy of an intelligent child's observation. At that impressible time of life, it must sometimes produce a fixed impression. If the fixed impression be of an object terrible to the child, it will be (for want of reasoning upon) inseparable from great fear. Force the child at such a time, be Spartan with it, send it into the dark against its will, leave it in a lonely bedroom against its will, and you had better murder it.

On a bright morning I rattled away from Paris, in the German chariot, and left the large dark creature behind me for good. I ought to confess, though, that I had been drawn back back to the Morgue, after he was put under ground, to look at his clothes, and that I found them frightfully like him—particularly his boots. However, I rattled away for Switzerland, looking forward and not backward, and so we parted company.

Welcome again, the long long spell of France, with the queer country inns, full of vases of flowers, and clocks, in the dull little towns, and with the little population not at all dull on the little Boulevard in the evening, under the little trees! Welcome Monsieur the Curé walking alone in the early morning a short way out of the town, reading that eternal Breviary of yours, which surely might be almost read, without book, by this time? Welcome Monsieur the Curé, later in the day, jolting through the highway dust (as if you had already ascended to the cloudy region), in a very big-headed cabriolet, with the dried mud of a dozen winters on it. Welcome again Monsieur the Curé, as we exchange salutations: you, straightening your back to look at the German chariot, while picking in your little village garden a vegetable or two for the day's soup; I, looking out of the German chariot window in that delicious traveler's-trance which knows no cares, no yesterdays, no to-morrows, nothing but the passing objects and the passing scents and sounds! And so I came in due course of delight, to Strasbourg, where I passed a wet Sunday evening at a window, while an idle trifle of a vaudeville was played for me at the opposite house.

How such a large house came to have only three people living in it, was its own affair. There were at least a score of windows in its high roof alone; how many in its grotesque front, I soon gave up counting. The owner was a shopkeeper, by name Straudenheim; by trade—I couldn't make out what by trade, for he had forborne to write that up, and his shop was shut.

At first, as I looked at Straudenheim's through the steadily falling rain, I set him up in business in the goose-liver line. But, inspection of Straudenheim, who became visible at a window on the second floor, convinced me that there was something more precious than liver in the case. He wore a black velvet skull-cap, and looked usurious and rich. A large-lipped, pear-nosed old man, with white hair, and keen eyes, though near-sighted. He was writing at a desk, was Straudenheim, and ever and again left off writing, put his pen in his mouth, and went through actions with his right hand, like a man steadying piles of cash. Five-franc pieces, Straudenheim, or golden Napoleons? A jeweler, Straudenheim, a dealer in money, a diamond merchant, or what?

Below Straudenheim, at a window on the first floor, sat his housekeeper—far from young, but of a comely presence, suggestive of a well-matured foot and ankle. She was cheerily dressed, had a fan in her hand, and wore large gold earrings and a large gold cross. She would have been out holiday-making (as I settled it) but for the pestilent rain. Strasbourg had given up holiday-making for that once, as a bad job, because the rain was jerking in gushes out of the old roof-spouts, and running in a brook down the middle of the street. The housekeeper, her arms folded on her bosom and her fan tapping her chin, was bright and smiling at her open window, but otherwise Straudenheim's house front was very dreary. The housekeeper's was the only open window in it; Straudenheim kept himself close, though it was a sultry evening when air is pleasant, and though the rain had brought into the town that vague refreshing smell of grass which rain does bring in the summer-time.

The dim appearance of a man at Straudenheim's shoulder inspired me with a misgiving that somebody had come to murder that flourishing merchant for the wealth with which I had handsomely endowed him: the rather, as it was an excited man, lean and long of figure, and evidently stealthy of foot. But, he conferred with Straudenheim instead of doing him a mortal injury, and then they both softly opened the other window of that room—which was immediately over the housekeeper's—and tried to see her by looking down. And my opinion of Straudenheim was much lowered when I saw that eminent citizen spit out of window, clearly with the hope of spitting on the housekeeper.

The unconscious housekeeper fanned herself, tossed her head, and laughed. Though unconscious of Straudenheim, she was conscious of somebody else—of me?—there was nobody else.

After leaning so far out of window, that I confidently expected to see their heels tilt up, Straudenheim and the lean man drew their heads in and shut the window. Presently, the house door secretly opened, and they slowly and spitefully crept forth into the pouring rain. They were coming over to me (I thought) to demand satisfaction for my looking at the housekeeper, when they plunged into a recess in the architecture under my window, and dragged out the puniest of little soldiers begirt with the most innocent of little swords. The tall glazed head-dress of this warrior, Straudenheim instantly knocked off, and out of it fell two sugar-sticks, and three or four large lumps of sugar.

The warrior made no effort to recover his property or to pick up his shako, but looked with an expression of attention at Straudenheim when he kicked him five times, and also at the lean man when *he* kicked him five times, and again at Straudenheim when he tore the breast of his (the warrior's) little coat open, and shook all his ten fingers in his face, as if they were ten thousand. When these outrages had been committed, Straudenheim and his man went into the house again and barred the door. A wonderful circumstance was, that the housekeeper, who saw it all (and who could have taken six such warriors to her buxom bosom at once), only fanned herself, and laughed as she had laughed before, and seemed to have no opinion about it, one way or other.

But, the chief effect of the drama was the remarkable vengeance taken by the little warrior. Left alone in the rain, he picked up his shako; put it on, all wet and dirty as it was; retired into a court, of which Straudenheim's house formed the corner; wheeled about; and bringing his two forefingers close to the top of his nose, rubbed them over one another, crosswise, in derision, defiance, and contempt of Straudenheim. Although Straudenheim could not possibly be supposed to be conscious of this strange proceeding, it so inflated and comforted the little warrior's soul, that twice he went away, and twice came back into the court to repeat it, as though it must goad his enemy to madness. Not only that, but he afterward came back with two other small warriors, and they all three did it together. Not only that—as I live to tell the tale!—but just as it was falling quite dark, the three came back, bringing with them a huge, bearded Sapper, whom they moved, by recital of the original wrong, to go through the same performance, with the same complete absence of all possible knowledge of it on the part of Straudenheim. And then they all went away, arm in arm, singing.

I went away, too, in the German chariot, at sunrise, and rattled on, day after day, like one in a sweet dream; with so many clear little bells on the harness of the horses, that the nursery rhyme about Banbury Cross and the venerable lady who rode in state there, was always in my ears. And now I came into the land of wooden houses, innocent cakes, thin butter soup, and spotless little inn bedrooms with a family likeness to Dairies. And now the Swiss marksmen were for ever rifle-shooting at marks across gorges, so exceedingly near my ear, that I felt like a new Gesler in a Canton of Tells, and went in highly-deserved danger of my tyrannical life. The prizes at these shootings, were watches, smart handkerchiefs, hats, spoons, and (above all) tea-trays; and at these contests I came upon a more than usually accomplished and amiable countryman of my own, who had shot himself deaf in whole years of competition, and had won so many tea-trays, that he went about the country with his carriage full of them, like a glorified Cheap Jack.

In the mountain country into which I had now traveled, a yoke of oxen were sometimes hooked on before the post-horses, and I went lumbering up, up, up, through mist and rain, with the roar of falling water for change of music. Of a sudden, mist and rain would clear away, and I would come down into picturesque little towns with gleaming spires and odd towers; and would stroll afoot into market-places in steep winding streets, where a hundred women in bodices, sold eggs and honey, butter and fruit, and suckled their children as they sat by their clean baskets, and had such enormous goitres (or glandular swellings in the throat) that it became a science to know where the nurse ended and the child began. About this time, I deserted my German chariot for the back of a mule (in color and consistency so very like a dusty old hair trunk I once had at school, that I half expected to see my initials in brass-headed nails on his backbone), and went up a thousand rugged ways, and looked down at a thousand woods of fir and pine, and would on the whole have preferred my mule's keeping a little nearer to the inside, and not usually traveling with a hoof or two over the precipice, though much consoled by explanation that this was to be attributed to his great sagacity, by reason of his carrying broad loads of wood at other times, and not being clear but that I myself belonged to that station of life, and required as much room as they. He brought me safely, in his own wise way, among the passes of the Alps, and here I enjoyed a dozen climates a day; being now (like Don Quixote on the back of the wooden horse) in the region of wind, now in the region of fire, and now in the region of unmelting ice and snow. Here, I passed over trembling domes of ice, beneath which the cataract was roaring; and here was received under arches of icicles, of unspeakable beauty; and here the sweet air was so bracing and so light, that at halting-times I rolled in the snow when I saw my mule do it, thinking that he must know best. At this part of the journey we would come, at mid-day, into half an hour's thaw: when the rough mountain inn would be found on an island of deep mud in a sea of snow, while the baiting strings of mules, and the carts full of casks and bales, which had been in an Arctic condition a mile off, would steam again. By such ways and means, I would come to the cluster of châlets where I had to turn out of the track to see the waterfall; and then, uttering a howl like a young giant, on espying a traveler—in other words, something to eat—coming up the steep, the idiot lying on the wood-pile who sunned himself and nursed his goitre, would rouse the woman-guide within the hut, who would stream out hastily, throwing her child over one of her shoulders and her goitre over the other, as she came along. I slept at religious houses, and bleak refuges of many kinds, on this journey, and by the stove at night heard stories of travelers who had perished within call, in wreaths and drifts of snow. One night the stove within, and the cold outside, awakened childish associations long forgotten, and I dreamed I was in Russia—the identical serf out of a picture-book I had, before I could read it for myself—and that I was going to be knouted by a noble personage in a fur cap, boots, and earrings, who, I think, must have come out of some melo-drama.

Commend me to the beautiful waters among these mountains! Though I was not of their mind: they, being inveterately bent on getting down into the level country, and I ardently desiring to linger where I was. What desperate leaps they took, what dark abysses they plunged into, what rocks they wore away, what echoes they invoked! In one part where I went, they were pressed into the service of carrying wood down, to be burned next winter, as costly fuel, in Italy. But, their fierce savage nature was not to be easily constrained, and they fought with every limb of the wood; whirling it round and round, stripping its bark away, dashing it against pointed corners, driving it out of the course, and roaring and flying at the peasants who steered it back again from the bank with long stout poles. Alas! concurrent streams of time and water carried *me* down fast, and I came, on an exquisitely clear day, to the Lausanne shore of the Lake of Geneva, where I stood looking at the bright blue water, the flushed white mountains opposite, and the boats at my feet with their furled Mediterranean sails, showing like enormous magnifications of this goose-quill pen that is now in my hand.

The sky became overcast without any notice; a wind very like the March east wind of England, blew across me; and a voice said, "How do you like it? Will it do?"

I had merely shut myself, for half a minute, in a German traveling chariot that stood for sale in the Carriage Department of the London Pantechnicon. I had a commission to buy it, for a friend who was going abroad; and the look and manner of the chariot, as I tried the cushion and the springs, brought all these hints of traveling remembrance before me.

"It will do very well," said I, rather sorrowfully, as I got out at the other door, and shut the carriage up.

---

I TRAVEL constantly, up and down a certain line of railway that has a terminus in London. It is the railway for a large military depot, and for other large barracks. To the best of my serious belief, I have never been on that railway by daylight, without seeing some handcuffed deserters in the train.

It is in the nature of things that such an institution as our English army should have many bad and troublesome characters in it. But, this is a reason for, and not against, its being made as acceptable as possible to well-disposed men of decent behavior. Such men are assuredly not tempted into the ranks, by the beastly inversion of natural laws, and the compulsion to live in worse than swinish foulness. Accordingly, when any such Circumlocutional embellishments of the soldiers condition have of late been brought to notice, we civilians, seated in outer darkness cheerfully meditating on an Income Tax, have considered the matter as being our business, and have shown a tendency to declare that we would rather not have it misregulated, if such declaration may, without violence to the Church Catechism, be hinted to those who are put in authority over us.

Any animated description of a modern battle, any private soldier's letter published in the newspapers, any page of the records of the Victoria Cross, will show that in the ranks of the army, there exists under all disadvantages as fine a sense of duty as is to be found in any station on earth. Who doubts that if we all did our duty as faithfully as the soldier does his, this world would be a better place? There may be greater difficulties in our way than in the soldier's. Not disputed. But, let us at least do our duty toward *him*.

I had got back again to that rich port where so many snares are set for Mercantile Jack, and I was walking up a hill there, on a wild March morning. My conversation with my official friend Pangloss, by whom I was accidently accompanied, took this direction as we took the up-hill direction, because the object of my uncommercial journey was to see some discharged soldiers who had recently come home from India. There were men of HAVELOCK'S among them; there were men who had been in many of the great battles of the great Indian campaign, among them; and I was curious to note what our discharged soldiers looked like, when they were done with.

I was not the less interested (as I mentioned to my official friend Pangloss) because these men had claimed to be discharged, when their right to be discharged was not admitted. They had behaved with unblemished fidelity and bravery; but a change of circumstances had arisen, which, as they considered, put an end to their compact and entitled them to enter on a new one. Their demand had been blunderingly resisted by the authorities in India; but, it is to be presumed that the men were not far wrong, inasmuch as the bungle had ended in their being sent home discharged, in pursuance of orders from home. (There was an immense waste of money, of course.)

Under these circumstances—thought I, as I walked up the hill, on which I accidentally encountered my official friend—under these circumstances of the men having successfully opposed themselves to the Pagoda Department of that great Circumlocution Office, on which the sun never sets and the light of reason never rises, the Pagoda Department will have been particularly careful of the national honor. It will have shown these men, in the scrupulous good faith, not to say the generosity, of its dealing with them, that great national authorities can have no small retaliations and revenges. It will have made every provision for their health on the passage home, and will have landed them, restored from their campaigning fatigue by a sea-voyage, pure air, sound food, and good medicines. And I pleased myself with dwelling beforehand, on the great accounts of their personal treatment which these men would carry into their various towns and villages, and on the increasing popularity of the service that would insensibly follow. I almost began to hope that the hitherto-never-failing deserters on my railroad, would by-and-by become a phenomenon.

In this agreeable frame of mind I entered the workhouse of Liverpool—For, the cultivation of Laurels in a sandy soil, had brought the soldiers in question to *that* abode of Glory.

Before going into their wards to visit them, I inquired how they had made their triumphant entry there? They had been brought through the rain in carts, it seemed, from the landing-place to the gate, and had then been carried up stairs on the backs of paupers. Their groans and pains during the performance of this glorious pageant, had been so distressing, as to bring tears into the eyes of spectators but too well accustomed to scenes of suffering. They were so dreadfully cold, that those who could get near the fires were hard to be restrained from thrusting their feet in among the blazing coals. They were so horribly reduced, that they were awful to look upon. Racked with dysentery and blackened with scurvy, one hundred and forty wretched men had been revived with brandy and laid in bed.

My official friend Pangloss is lineally descended from a learned doctor of that name, who was once tutor to Candide, an ingenuous young gentleman of some celebrity. In his personal character, he is as humane and worthy a gentleman as any I know; in his official capacity, he unfortunately preaches the doctrines of his renowned ancestor, by demonstrating on all occasions that we live in the best of all possible official worlds.

"In the name of Humanity," said I, "how did the men fall into this deplorable state? Was the ship well found in stores?"

"I am not here to asseverate that I know the fact, of my own knowledge," answered Pangloss, "but I have grounds for asserting that the stores were the best of all possible stores."

A medical officer laid before us, a handful of rotten biscuit, and a handful of split peas. The biscuit was a honey-combed heap of maggots, and the excrement of maggots. The peas were even harder than this filth. A similar handful had been experimentally boiled, six hours, and had shown no signs of softening. These were the stores on which the soldiers had been fed.

"The beef——" I began, when Pangloss cut me short.

"Was the best of all possible beef," said he.

But, behold, there was laid before us certain evidence given at the Coroner's Inquest, holden on some of the men (who had obstinately died of their treatment), and from that evidence it appeared that the beef was the worst of all possible beef!

"Then I lay my hand upon my heart, and take my stand," said Pangloss, "by the pork, which was the best of all possible pork."

"But look at this food before our eyes, if one may so misuse the word," said I. "Would any Inspector who did his duty, pass such abomination?"

"It ought not to have been passed," Pangloss admitted.

"Then the authorities out there——" I began, when Pangloss cut me short again.

"There would certainly seem to have been something wrong somewhere," said he; "but I am prepared to prove that the authorities out there, are the best of all possible authorities."

I never heard of an impeached public authority in my life, who was not the best public authority in existence.

"We are told of these unfortunate men being laid low by scurvy," said I. "Since lime-juice has been regularly stored and served out in our navy, surely that disease, which used to devastate it, has almost disappeared. Was there lime-juice aboard this transport?"

My official friend was beginning, "The best of all possible——" when an inconvenient medical forefinger pointed out another passage in the evidence, from which it appeared that the lime-juice had been bad too. Not to mention that the vinegar had been bad too, the vegetables bad too, the cooking accommodation insufficient (if there had been any thing worth mentioning to cook), the water supply exceedingly inadequate, and the beer sour.

"Then, the men," said Pangloss, a little irritated, "were the worst of all possible men."

"In what respect?" I asked.

"Oh! Habitual drunkards," said Pangloss.

But, again the same incorrigible medical forefinger pointed out another passage in the evidence, showing that the dead men had been examined after death, and that they, at least, could not possibly have been habitual drunkards, because the organs within them which must have shown traces of that habit, were perfectly sound.

"And besides," said the three doctors present, one and all, "habitual drunkards brought as low as these men have been, could not recover under care and food, as the great majority of these men are recovering. They would not have strength of constitution to do it."

"Reckless and improvident dogs, then," said Pangloss. "Always are—nine times out of ten."

I turned to the master of the workhouse, and asked him whether the men had any money?

"Money?" said he. "I have in my iron safe, nearly four hundred pounds of theirs; the agents have nearly a hundred pounds more; and many of them have left money in Indian banks besides."

"Hah!" said I to myself, as we went up-stairs, "this is not the best of all possible stories, I doubt!"

We went into a large ward, containing some twenty or five-and-twenty beds. We went into several such wards, one after another. I find it very difficult to indicate what a shocking sight I saw in them, without frightening the reader from the perusal of these lines, and defeating my object of making it known.

Oh the sunken eyes that turned to me as I walked between the rows of beds, or—worse still—that glazedly looked at the white ceiling, and saw nothing and cared for nothing! Here, lay the skeleton of a man, so lightly covered with a thin unwholesome skin, that not a bone in the anatomy was clothed, and I could clasp the arm above the elbow, in my finger and thumb. Here, lay a man with the black scurvy eating his legs away, his gums gone, and his teeth all gaunt and bare. This bed was empty, because gangrene had set in, and the patient had died but yesterday. That bed was a hopeless one, because its occupant was sinking fast, and could only be roused to turn the poor pinched mask of face upon the pillow, with a feeble moan. The awful thinness of the fallen cheeks, the awful brightness of the deep-set eyes, the lips of lead, the hands of ivory, the recumbent human images lying in the shadow of death with a kind of solemn twilight on them, like the sixty who had died aboard the ship and were lying at the bottom of the sea. O Pangloss, GOD forgive you!

In one bed, lay a man whose life had been saved (as it was hoped) by deep incisions in the feet and legs. While I was speaking to him, a nurse came up to change the poultices which this operation had rendered necessary, and I had an instinctive feeling that it was not well to turn away, merely to spare myself. He was sorely wasted and keenly susceptible, but the efforts he made to subdue any expression of impatience or suffering, were quite heroic. It was easy to see, in the shrinking of the figure, and the drawing of the bedclothes over the head, how acute the endurance was, and it made me shrink too, as if *I* were in pain; but, when the new bandages were on, and the poor feet were composed again, he made an apology for himself (though he had not uttered a word), and said plaintively, "I am so tender and weak, you see, sir!" Neither from him nor from any one sufferer of the whole ghastly number, did I hear a complaint. Of thankfulness for present solicitude and care, I heard much; of complaint, not a word.

I think I could have recognized in the dismalest skeleton there, the ghost of a soldier. Something of the old air was still latent in the palest shadow of life that I talked to. One emaciated creature, in the strictest literality worn to the bone, lay stretched on his back, looking so like death that I asked one of the doctors if he were not dying, or dead? A few kind words from the doctor, in his ear, and he opened his eyes, and smiled—looked, in a moment, as if he would have made a salute, if he could. "We shall pull him through, please God," said the Doctor. "Plase God, surr, and thank ye," said the patient. "You are much better to-day; are you not?" said the Doctor. "Plase God, surr; 'tis the slape I want, surr; 'tis my breathin' makes the nights so long." "He is a careful fellow this, you must know," said the Doctor, cheerfully; "it was raining hard when they put him in the open cart to bring him here, and he had the presence of mind to ask to have a sovereign taken out of his pocket that he had there, and a cab engaged. Probably it saved his life." The patient rattled out the skeleton of a laugh, and said, proud of the story, "'Deed, surr, an open cairt was a comical means o' bringin' a dyin' man here, and a clever way to kill him." You might have sworn to him for a soldier when he said it.

One thing had perplexed me very much in going from bed to bed. A very significant and cruel thing. I could find no young man, but one. He had attracted my notice, by having got up and dressed himself in his soldier's jacket and trowsers, with the intention of sitting by the fire; but he had found himself too weak, and had crept back to his bed and laid himself down on the outside of it. I could have pronounced him, alone, to be a young man aged by famine and sickness. As we were standing by the Irish soldier's bed, I mentioned my perplexity to the Doctor. He took a board with an inscription on it from the head of the Irishman's bed, and asked me what age I supposed that man to be? I had observed him with attention while talking to him, and answered, confidently, "Fifty." The doctor, with a pitying glance at the patient, who had dropped into a stupor again, put the board back, and said, "Twenty-Four."

All the arrangements of the wards were excellent. They could not have been more humane, sympathizing, gentle, attentive, or wholesome. The owners of the ship, too, had done all they could, liberally. There were bright fires in every room, and the convalescent men were sitting round them, reading various papers and periodicals. I took the liberty of inviting my official friend Pangloss to look at those convalescent men, and to tell me whether their faces and bearing were or were not, generally, the faces and bearing of steady, respectable soldiers? The master of the workhouse, overhearing me, said that he had had a pretty large experience of troops, and that better conducted men than these, he had never had to do with. They were always (he added) as we saw them. And of us visitors (I add) they knew nothing whatever, except that we were there.

It was audacious in me, but I took another liberty with Pangloss. Prefacing it with the observation that of course, I knew beforehand that there was not the faintest desire, any where, to hush up any part of this dreadful business, and that the Inquest was the fairest of all possible Inquests, I besought four things of Pangloss. Firstly, to observe that the Inquest *was not held in that place*, but at some distance off. Secondly, to look round upon those helpless spectres in their beds. Thirdly, to remember that the witnesses produced from among them before that Inquest, could not have been selected because they were the men who had the most to tell it, but because they happened to be in a state admitting of their safe removal. Fourthly, to say whether the Coroner and Jury could have come there, to those pillows, and taken a little evidence? My official friend declined to commit himself to a reply.

There was a sergeant, reading, in one of the fireside groups; as he was a man of a very intelligent countenance, and as I have a great respect for non-commissioned officers as a class, I sat down on the nearest bed, to have some talk with him. (It was the bed of one of the grisliest of the poor skeletons, and he died soon afterward.)

"I was glad to see, in the evidence of an officer at the Inquest, sergeant, that he never saw men behave better on board ship than these men."

"They did behave very well, sir."

"I was glad to see, too, that every man had a hammock."

The sergeant gravely shook his head. "There must be some mistake, sir. The men of my own mess had no hammocks. There were not hammocks enough on board, and the men of the two next messes laid hold of hammocks for themselves as soon as they got on board, and squeezed my men out, as I may say."

"Had the squeezed-out men none then?"

"None, sir. As men died, their hammocks were used by other men, who wanted hammocks; but many men had none at all."

"Then you don't agree with the evidence on that point?"

"Certainly not sir. A man can't, when he knows to the contrary."

"Did any of the men sell their bedding for drink?"

"There is some mistake on that point too, sir. Men were under the impression—I knew it for a fact at the time—that it was not allowed to take blankets or bedding on board, and so men who had things of that sort came to sell them purposely."

"Did any of the men sell their clothes for drink?"

"They did, sir." (I believe there never was a more truthful witness than the sergeant. He had no inclination to make out a case.)

"Many?"

"Some, sir" (considering the question). "Soldier-like. There had been long marching in the rainy season, by bad roads—no roads at all, in short—and when they got to Calcutta, men turned to and drank, before taking a last look at it. Soldier-like."

"Do you see any men in this ward, for example, who sold clothes for drink at that time?"

The sergeant's wan eye, happily just beginning to rekindle with health, traveled round the place and came back to me. "Certainly, sir."

"The marching to Calcutta in the rainy season must have been severe?"

"It was very severe, sir."

"Yet, what with the rest and the sea air, I should have thought that the men (even the men who got drunk) would have soon begun to recover on board ship?"

"So they might; but the bad food told upon them, and when we got into a cold latitude it began to tell more, and the men dropped."

"The sick had a general disinclination for food, I am told, Sergeant?"

"Have you seen the food, sir?"

"Some of it."

"Have you seen the state of their mouths, sir?"

If the sergeant, who was a man of a few orderly words, had spoken the amount of a volume of this publication, he could not have settled that question better. I believe that the sick could as soon have eaten the ship, as the ship's provisions.

I took the additional liberty with my friend Pangloss, when I had left the sergeant with good wishes, of asking Pangloss whether he had ever heard of biscuit getting drunk and bartering its nutritious qualities for putrefaction and vermin : of peas becoming hardened in liquor; of hammocks drinking themselves off the face of the earth ; of lime-juice, vegetables, vinegar, cooking accommodation, water supply, and beer, all taking to drinking together and going to ruin? If not (I asked him,) what did he say in defense of the officers condemned by the Coroner's Jury, who, by signing the General Inspection report relative to the ship Great Tasmania chartered for these troops, had deliberately asserted all that bad and poisonous dunghill refuse, to be good and wholesome food? My official friend replied that it was a remarkable fact, that whereas some officers were only positively good, and other officers only comparatively better, those particular officers were superlatively the very best of all possible officers.

My hand and my heart fail me, in writing my record of this journey. The spectacle of the soldiers in the hospital beds of that Liverpool workhouse, was so shocking and so shameful, that as an Englishman I burn and blush to remember it. It would have been simply unbearable at the time, but for the consideration and pity with which they were soothed in their sufferings.

No punishment that our inefficient laws provide, is worthy of the name when set against the guilt of this transaction. But, if the memory of it die out unavenged, and if it do not result in the inexorable dismissal and disgrace of those who are responsible for it, their escape will be infamous to the Government (no matter of what party) that so neglects its duty and infamous to the nation that tamely suffers such intolerable wrong to be done in its name.

---

If the confession that I have often traveled from this Covent Garden lodging of mine on Sundays, should give offense to those who never travel on Sundays, they will be satisfied (I hope) by my adding that the journeys in question were made to churches.

Not that I have any curiosity to hear powerful preachers. Time was, when Iwas dragged by the hair of my head, as one may say, to hear too many. On summer evenings, when every flower, and tree, and bird, might have better addressed my soft young heart, I have in my day been caught in the palm of a female hand by the crown, have been violently scrubbed from the neck to the roots of the hair as a purification for the Temple, and have then been carried off highly charged with saponaceous electricity, to be steamed like a potato in the unventilated breath of the powerful Boanerges Boiler and his congregation, until what small mind I had was quite steamed out of me. In which pitiable plight I have been hauled out of the place of meeting, at the conclusion of the exercises, and catechised respecting Boanerges Boiler, his fifthly, his sixthly, and his seventhly, until I have regarded that reverend person in the light of a most dismal and oppressive Charade. Time was, when I was carried off to platform assemblages at which no human child, whether of wrath or grace, could possibly keep its eyes open, and when I felt the fatal sleep stealing, stealing over me, and when I gradually heard the orator in possession, spinning and humming like a great top, until he rolled, collapsed, and tumbled over, and I discovered to my burning shame and fear, that as to that last stage, it was not he, but I. I have sat under Boanerges when he has specifically addressed himself to us—us, the infants—and at this present writing I hear his lumbering jocularity (which never amused us, though we basely pretended that it did), and I behold his big round face, and I look up the inside of his outstretched coat-sleeve as if it were a telescope with the stopper on, and I hate him with an unwholesome hatred for two hours. Through such means did it come to pass that I knew the powerful preacher from beginning to end, all over and all through, while I was very young, and that I left him behind at an early period of life. Peace be with him! More peace than he brought to me!

Now, I have heard many preachers since that time—not powerful; merely Christian, unaffected, and reverential—and I have had many such preachers on my roll of friends. But, it was not to hear these, any more than the powerful class, that I made my Sunday journeys. They were journeys of curiosity to the numerous churches in the City of London. It came into my head one day, here had I been cultivating a familiarity with all the churches of Rome, and I knew nothing of the insides of the old churches of London? This befell on a Sunday morning. I began my expeditions that very same day, and they lasted me a year.

I never wanted to know the names of the churches to which I went, and to this hour I am profoundly ignorant in that particular of at least nine-tenths of them. Indeed, saving that I know the church of old GOWER'S tomb (he lies in effigy with his head upon his books) to be the church of Saint Saviour's, Southwark, and the church of MILTON'S tomb to be the church of Cripplegate, and the church on Cornhill with the great golden keys to be the church of Saint Peter, I doubt if I could pass a competitive examination in any of the names. No question did I ever ask of living creature concerning these churches, and no answer to any antiquarian question on the subjects that I ever put to books, shall harass the reader's soul. A full half of my pleasure in them, arose out of their mystery; mysterious I found them; mysterious they shall remain for me.

Where shall I begin my round of hidden and forgotten old churches in the City of London?

It is twenty minutes short of eleven on a Sunday morning, when I stroll down one of the many narrow hilly streets in the City that tend due south to the Thames. It is my first experiment, and I have come to the region of Whittington in an omnibus, and we have put down a fierce-eyed spare old woman, whose slate-colored gown smells of herbs, and who walked up Aldersgate-street to some chapel where she comforts herself with brimstone doctrine, I warrant. We have also put down a stouter and sweeter old lady, with a pretty large prayer-book in an unfolded pocket-handkerchief, who got out at the corner of a court near Stationers' Hall, and who I think must go to church there, because she is the widow of some deceased Old Company's Beadle. The rest of our freight were mere chance pleasure-seekers and rural walkers, and went on to the

Blackwall railway. So many bells are ringing, when I stand undecided at a street corner, that every sheep in the ecclesiastical fold might be a bell wether. The discordance is fearful. My state of indecision is referable to, and about equally divisible among, four great churches, which are all within sight and sound, all within the space of a few square yards. As I stand at the street corner, I don't see as many as four people at once going to church, though I see as many as four churches with their steeples clamoring for people. I choose my church, and go up the flight of steps to the great entrance in the tower. A mouldy tower within, and like a neglected washhouse. A rope comes through the beamed roof, and a man in a corner pulls it and clashes the bell; a whity-brown man, whose clothes were once black; a man with flue on him, and cobweb. He stares at me, wondering how I come there, and I stare at him, wondering how he comes there. Through a screen of wood and glass, I peep into the dim church. About twenty people are discernible, waiting to begin. Christening would seem to have faded out of this church long ago, for the font has the dust of desuetude thick upon it, and its wooden cover (shaped like an old fashioned tureen cover) looks as if it wouldn't come off upon requirement. I perceive the altar to be rickety, and the Commandments damp. Entering after this survey, I jostle the clergyman, who is entering too from a dark lane behind a pew of state with curtains, where nobody sits. The pew is ornamented with four blue wands, once carried by four somebodys, I suppose, before somebody else, but which there is nobody now to hold or receive honor from. I open the door of a family pew, and shut myself in; if I could occupy twenty family pews at once, I might have them. The clerk, a brisk young man, (how does *he* come here?) glances at me knowingly, as who should say, "You have done it now; you must stop." Organ plays. Organ-loft is in a small gallery across the church; gallery congregation, two girls I wonder within myself what will happen when we are required to sing.

There is a pale heap of books in the corner of my pew, and while the organ, which is hoarse and sleepy, plays in such fashion that I can hear more of the rusty working of the stops than of any music, I look at the books, which are mostly bound in faded baize and stuff. They belonged, in 1754, to the Dowgate family; and who were they? Jane Comport must have married Young Dowgate, and come into the family that way; Young Dowgate was courting Jane Comport when he gave her her prayer-book, and recorded the presentation in the fly-leaf; if Jane were fond of Young Dowgate, why did she die and leave the book here? Perhaps at the rickety altar, and before the damp Commandments, she, Comport, had taken him, Dowgate, in a flush of youthful hope and joy, and perhaps it had not turned out in the long run as great a success as was expected?

The opening of the service recalls my wandering thoughts. I then find, to my astonishment, that I have been, and still am, taking a strong kind of invisible snuff, up my nose, into my eyes, and down my throat. I wink, sneeze, and cough. The clerk sneezes; the clergyman winks; the unseen organist sneezes and coughs, (and probably winks); all our little party wink, sneeze, and cough. The snuff seems to be made of the decay of matting, wood, cloth, stone, iron, earth, and something else. Is the something else, the decay of dead citizens in the vaults below? As sure as Death it is! Not only in the cold damp February day, do we cough and sneeze dead citizens all through the service, but dead citizens have got into the very bellows of the organ, and half choked the same. We stamp our feet to warm them, and dead citizens arise in heavy clouds. Dead citizens stick upon the walls, and lie pulverized on the sounding-board over the clergyman's head, and, when a gust of air comes, tumble down upon him.

In this first experience I was so nauseated by too much snuff, made of the Dowgate family, the Comport branch, and other families and branches, that I gave but little heed to our dull manner of ambling through the service; to the brisk clerk's manner of encouraging us to try a note or two at psalm time; to the gallery-congregation's manner of enjoying a shrill duet, without a notion of time or tune; to the whity-brown man's manner of shutting the minister into the pulpit, and being very particular with the lock of the door, as if he were a dangerous animal. But, I tried again next Sunday, and soon accustomed myself to the dead citizens when I found that I could not possibly get on without them among the City churches.

Another Sunday. After being again rung for by conflicting bells, like a leg of mutton or a laced hat a hundred years ago, I make selection of a church oddly put away in a corner among a number of lanes—a smaller church than the last, and an ugly: of about the date of Queen Anne. As a congregation we are fourteen strong: not counting an exhausted charity school in a gallery, which has dwindled away to four boys and two girls. In the porch, is a benefaction of loaves of bread, which there would seem to be nobody left in the exhausted congregation to claim, and which I saw an exhausted beadle, long faded out of uniform, eating with his eyes for self and family when I passed in. There is also an exhausted clerk in a brown wig, and two or three exhausted doors and windows have been bricked up, and the service books are musty, and the pulpit cushions are threadbare, and the whole of the church furniture is in a very advanced stage of exhaustion. We are three old women (habitual), two young lovers (accidental), two tradesmen, one with a wife and one alone, an aunt and nephew, again two girls (these two girls dressed out for church with evey thing about them limp that should be stiff, and *vice versa*, are an invariable experience), and three sniggering boys. The clergyman is, perhaps, the chaplain of a civic company; he has the moist and vinous look, and eke the bulbous boots, of one acquainted with 'Twenty port, and comet vintages.

We are so quiet in our dullness that the three sniggering boys, who have got away into a corner by the altar-railing, give us a start, like crackers, whenever they laugh. And this reminds me of my own village church where, during sermon-time on bright Sundays when the birds are very musical indeed, farmers' boys patter out over the stone pavement, and the clerk steps out from his desk after them, and is distinctly heard in the summer repose to pursue and punch them in the churchyard, and is seen to return with a meditative countenance, making believe that nothing of the sort has happened. The aunt and nephew in this City church are much disturbed by the sniggering boys. The nephew is himself a boy, and the sniggerers tempt him to secular thoughts of marbles and string, by secretly offering such commodities to his distant contemplation. This young Saint Anthony for a while resists, but presently becomes a backslider, and in dumb show defies the sniggerers to "heave" a marble or two in his direction. Herein he is detected by the aunt (a rigorous reduced gentlewoman who has the charge of offices), and I perceive that worthy relative to poke him in the side, with the corrugated hooked handle of an ancient umbrella. The nephew revenges himself for this, by holding his breath and terrifying his kinswoman with the dread belief that he has made up his mind to burst. Regardless of whispers and shakes, he swells and becomes discolored, and yet again swells and becomes discolored, until the aunt can bear it no longer, but leads him out, with no visible neck, and with his eyes going before him like a prawn's. This causes the sniggerers to regard flight as an eligible move, and I know which of them will go out first, because of the over-devout attention that he suddenly concentrates on the clergyman. In a little while, this hypocrite, with an elaborate demonstration of hushing his footsteps, and with a face generally expressive of having until now forgotten a religious appointment elsewhere, is gone. Number two gets out in the same way, but rather quicker. Number three getting safely to the door, there turns reckless, and banging it open, flies forth with a Whoop! that vibrates to the top of the tower above us.

The clergyman, who is of a prandial presence and a muffled voice, may be scant of hearing as well as of breath, but he only glances up, as having an idea that somebody has said Amen in a wrong place, and continues his steady jog-trot, like a farmer's wife going to market. He does all he has to do, in the same easy way, and gives us a concise sermon, still like the jog-trot of the farmer's wife on a level road. Its drowsy cadence soon lulls the three old women asleep, and the unmarried tradesman sits looking out at window, and the married tradesman sits looking at his wife's bonnet, and the lovers sit looking at one another, so superlatively happy, that I mind when I, turned of eighteen, went with my Angelica to a City church on account of a shower (by this special coincidence that it was in Huggin-lane), and when I said to my Angelica,

"Let the blessed event, Angelica, occur at no altar but this!" and when my Angelica consented that it should occur at no other—which it certainly never did, for it never occurred anywhere. And O, Angelica, what has become of you, this present Sunday morning when I can't attend to the sermon: and, more difficult question than that, what has become of Me as I was when I sat by your side!

But we receive the signal to make that unanimous dive which surely is a little conventional—like the strange rustlings and settlings and clearings of throats and noses, which are never dispensed with, at certain points of the Church service, and are never held to be necessary under any other circumstances. In a minute more it is all over, and the organ expresses itself to be as glad of it as it can be of any thing in its rheumatic state, and in another minute we are all of us out of the church, and Whity-brown has locked it up. Another minute or little more, and, in the neighboring churchyard—not the yard of that church, but of another—a churchyard like a great shabby old mignonette-box, with two trees in it and one tomb—I meet Whity-brown, in his private capacity, fetching a pint of beer for his dinner from the public-house in the corner, where the keys of the rotting fire-ladders are kept and were never asked for, and where there is a ragged, white-seamed, out-at-elbowed bagatelle-board on the first floor.

In one of these city churches, and only in one, I found an individual who might have been claimed as expressly a City personage. I remember the church, by the feature that the clergyman couldn't get to his own desk without going through the clerk's, or couldn't get to the pulpit without going through the reading-desk—I forget which, and it's no matter—and by the presence of this personage among the exceedingly sparse congregation. I doubt if we were a dozen, and we had no exhausted charity school to help us out. The personage was dressed in black of square cut, and was stricken in years, and wore a black velvet cap and cloth shoes. He was of a staid, wealthy, and dissatisfied aspect. In his hand, he conducted to church a mysterious child: a child of the feminine gender. The child had a beaver hat, with a stiff drab plume that surely never belonged to any bird of the air. The child was further attired in a nankeen frock and spencer, brown boxing-gloves and a vail. It had a blemish, in the nature of currant jelly, on its chin; and was a thirsty child. Insomuch that the personage carried in his pocket a green bottle, from which, when the first psalm was given out, the child was openly refreshed. At all other times throughout the service it was motionless, and stood on the seat of the large pew, closely fitted into the corner, like a rain-water pipe.

The personage never opened his book, and never looked at the clergyman. *He* never sat down either, but stood with his arms leaning on the top of the pew, and his forehead sometimes shaded with his right hand, always looking at the church door. It was a long church for a church of its size, and he was at the upper end, but he always looked at the door. That he was an old bookkeeper, or an old trader who had kept his own books, and that he might be seen at the Bank of England about Dividend times, no doubt. That he had lived in the city all his life and was disdainful of other localities, no doubt. Why he looked at the door, I never absolutely proved, but it is my belief that he lived in expectation of the time when the citizens would come back to live in the city, and its ancient glories would be renewed. He appeared to expect that this would occur on a Sunday, and that the wanderers would first appear in the deserted churches, penitent and humbled. Hence, he looked at the door which they never darkened. Whose child the child was, whether the child of a disinherited daughter, or some parish orphan whom the personage had adopted, there was nothing to lead up to. It never played, or skipped, or smiled. Once, the idea occurred to me that it was an automaton, and that the personage had made it; but following the strange couple out one Sunday, I heard the personage say to it, "Thirteen thousand pounds;" to which it added, in a weak human voice, "Seventeen and fourpence." Four Sundays I followed them out, and this is all I ever heard or saw them say. One Sunday, I followed them home. They lived behind a pump, and the personage opened their abode with an exceeding large key. The one solitary inscription on their house related to a fire-plug. The house was partly undermined by a deserted and closed gateway; its windows were blind with dirt; and it stood with its face disconsolately turned to a wall. Five great churches and two small ones rang their Sunday bells between this house and the church the couple frequented, so they must have had some special reason for going a quarter of a mile to it. The last time I saw them, was on this wise. I had been to explore another church at a distance, and happened to pass the church they frequented, at about two of the afternoon when that edifice was closed. But a little side-door, which I had never observed before, stood open, and disclosed certain cellarous steps. Methought, "They are airing the vaults to-day," when the personage and the child silently arrived at the steps, and silently descended. Of course, I came to the conclusion that the personage had at last despaired of the looked-for return of the penitent citizens, and that he and the child went down to get themselves buried.

In the course of my pilgrimages I came upon one obscure church which had broken out in the melodramatic style, and was got up with various tawdry decorations, much after the manner of the extinct London Maypoles. These attractions had induced several young priests or deacons in black bibs for waistcoats, and several young ladies interested in that holy order (the proportion being, as I estimated, seventeen young ladies to a deacon,) to come into the City as a new and odd excitement. It was wonderful to see how these young people played out their little play in the heart of the city, all among themselves, without the deserted city's knowing any thing about it. It was as if you should take an empty counting-house on a Sunday, and act one of the old Mysteries there. They had impressed a small school (from what neighborhood I don't know) to assist in the performances, and it was pleasant to notice frantic garlands of inscription on the walls, especially addressing those poor innocents in characters impossible for them to decipher. There was a remarkably agreeable smell of pomatum in this congregation.

But, in other cases, rot and mildew and dead citizens formed the uppermost scent, while, infused into it in a dreamy way not at all displeasing, was the staple character of the neighborhood. In the churches about Mark-lane, for example, there was a dry whiff of wheat; and I accidentally struck an airy sample of barley out of an aged hassock in one of them. From Rood-lane to Tower street, and thereabouts, there was often a subtle flavor of wine: sometimes, of tea. One church near Mincing lane smelt like a druggist's drawer. Behind the Monument, the service had a flavor of damaged oranges, which, a little further down toward the river, tempered into herrings, and gradually toned into a cosmopolitan blast of fish. In one church, the exact counterpart of the church in the Rake's Progress where the hero is being married to the horrible old lady, there was no speciality of atmosphere, until the organ shook a perfume of hides all over us from some adjacent warehouse.

Be the scent what it would, however, there was no speciality in the people. There were never enough of them to represent any calling or neighborhood. They had all gone elsewhere over-night, and a few stragglers in the many churches languished there inexpressively.

Among the uncommercial travels in which I have engaged, this year of Sunday travel occupies its own place, apart from all the rest. Whether I think of the church where the sails of the oyster-boats in the river almost flapped against the windows, or of the church where the railroad made the bells hum as the train rushed by above the roof, I recall a curious experience. On summer Sundays, in the gentle rain or the bright sunshine—either, deepening the idleness of the idle city—I have sat, in that singular silence which belongs to resting-places usually astir, in scores of buildings at the heart of the world's metropolis, unknown to far greater numbers of people speaking the English tongue, than the ancient edifices of the Eternal City, or the Pyramids of Egypt. The dark vestries and registries into which I have peeped, and the little hemmed-in churchyards that have echoed to my feet, have left impressions on my memory as distinct and quaint as any it has in that way received. In all those dusty registers that the worms are eating there is not a line but made some hearts leap, or some tears flow, in their day. Still and dry now, still and dry! and the old tree at the window with no room for its branches, has seen them all out. So with the tomb of the old Master of the old Company, on which it drips. His son restored it and died, his daughter restored it and died, and then he had been remembered long enough, any the tree took possession of him, and his name cracked out.

There are few more striking indications of the changes of manners and customs that two or three hundred years have brought about, than these deserted Churches. Many of them are handsome and costly structures, several of them were designed by WREN, many of them arose from the ashes of the great fire, others of them outlived the plague and the fire too, to die a slow death in these latter days. No one can be sure of the coming time; but it is not too much to say of it that it has no sign in its outsetting tides, of the reflux to these churches of their congregations and uses. They remain, like the tombs of the old citizens who lie beneath them and around them, Monuments of another age. They are worth a Sunday-exploration now and then, for they yet echo, not unharmoniously, to the time when the city of London really was London; when the 'Prentices and Trained Bands were of mark in the state; when even the Lord Mayor himself was a Reality—not a Fiction conventionally be-puffed on one day in the year by illustrious friends, who no less conventionally laugh at him on the remaining three hundred and sixty-four days.

---

So much of my traveling is done on foot, that if I cherished betting propensities, I should probably be found registered in sporting newspapers, under some such title as the Elastic Novice, challenging all eleven-stone mankind to competition in walking. My last special feat was turning out of bed at two, after a hard day, pedestrian and otherwise, and walking thirty miles into the country to breakfast. The road was so lonely in the night, that I fell asleep to the monotonous sound of my own feet, doing their regular four miles an hour. Mile after mile I walked, without the slightest sense of exertion, dozing heavily and dreaming constantly. It was only when I made a stumble like a drunken man, or struck out into the road to avoid a horseman close upon me on the path—who had no existence—that I came to myself and looked about. The day broke mistily (it was autumn time), and I could not disembarrass myself of the idea that I had to climb those heights and banks of cloud, and that there was an Alpine Convent somewhere behind the sun, where I was going to breakfast. This sleepy notion was so much stronger than such substantial objects as villages and haystacks, that, after the sun was up and bright, and when I was sufficiently awake to have a sense of pleasure in the prospect, I still occasionally caught myself looking about for wooden arms to point the right track up the mountain, and wondering there was no snow yet. It is a curiosity of broken sleep, that I made immense quantities of verses on that pedestrian occasion,—of course I never make any when I am in my right senses,—and that I spoke a certain language once pretty familiar to me, but which I had nearly forgotten from disuse, with fluency. Of both these phenomena I have such frequent experience in the state between sleeping and waking, that I sometimes argue with myself that I know I cannot be awake, for, if I were, I should not be half so ready. The readiness is not imaginary, because I can often recall long strings of the verses, and many turns of the fluent speech, after I am broad awake.

My walking is of two kinds; one straight on end to a definite goal at a round pace; one, objectless, loitering, and purely vagabond. In the latter state, no gipsy on earth is a greater vagabond than myself; it is so natural to me and strong with me, that I think I must be the descendant, at no great distance, of some irreclaimable tramp.

One of the pleasantest things I have lately met with, in a vagabond course of shy metropolitan neighborhoods and small shops, is the fancy of a humble artist as exemplified in two portraits representing Mr. Thomas Sayers, of Great Britain, and Mr. John Heenan, of the United States of America. These illustrious men are highly colored, in fighting trim, and fighting attitude. To suggest the pastoral and meditative nature of their peaceful calling, Mr. Heenan is represented on emerald sward, with primroses and other modest flowers springing up at the heels of his half-boots; while Mr. Sayers is impelled to the administration of his favorite blow, the Auctioneer, by the silent eloquence of a village church. The humble homes of England, with their domestic virtues and honeysuckle porches, urge both heroes to go in and win; and the lark and other singing-birds are observable in the upper air, ecstatically caroling their thanks to Heaven for a fight. On the whole, the associations entwined with the pugilistic art by this artist are much in the manner of Izaak Walton.

But, it is with the lower animals of back streets and by-ways that my present purpose rests. For human notes, we may return to such neighborhoods when leisure and inclination serve.

Nothing in shy neighborhoods perplexes my mind more than the bad company birds keep. Foreign birds often get into good society, but British birds are inseparable from low associates There is a whole street of them in Saint Giles's; and I always find them in poor and immoral neighborhoods, convenient to the public-house and the pawnbroker's. They seem to lead the people into drinking, and even the man who makes their cages usually gets into a chronic state of black eye. Why is this? Also, they will do things for people in short-skirted velveteen coats with bone buttons, or in sleeved waistcoats and fur caps, which they cannot be persuaded by the respectable orders of society to undertake. In a dirty court in Spitalfields, once, I found a goldfinch drawing his own water, and drawing as much of it as if he were in a consuming fever. That goldfinch lived at a bird-shop, and offered in writing, to barter himself against old clothes, empty bottles, or even kitchen stuff. Surely a low thing and a depraved taste in any finch! I bought that goldfinch for money. He was sent home, and hung upon a nail over against my table. He lived outside a counterfeit dwelling-house, supposed (as I argued) to be a dyer's; otherwise it would have been impossible to account for his perch sticking out of the garret window. From the time of his appearance in my room, either he left off being thirsty—which was not in the bond—or he could not make up his mind to hear his little bucket drop back into his well when he let it go; a shock which in the best of times had made him tremble. He drew no water but by stealth and under the cloak of night. After an interval of futile and at length hopeless expectation, the merchant who had educated him was appealed to. The merchant was a bow-legged character, with a flat and cushiony nose, like the last new strawberry. He wore a fur cap, and shorts, and was of the velveteen race, velveteeny. He sent word that he would "look round." He looked round, appeared in the doorway of the room, and slightly cocked up his evil eye at the goldfinch. Instantly, a raging thirst beset that bird; when it was appeased, he still drew several unnecessary buckets of water; and finally, leaped about his perch and sharpened his bill, as if he had been to the nearest wine-vaults and got drunk.

Donkeys again. I know shy neighborhoods where the Donkey goes in at the street door, and appears to live up-stairs, for I have examined the back yard from over the palings, and have been unable to make him out. Gentility, Nobility, Royalty, would appeal to that donkey in vain to do what he does for a costermonger. Feed him with oats at the highest price, put an infant prince and princess in a pair of panniers on his back, adjust his delicate trappings to a nicety, take him to the softest slopes at Windsor, and try what pace you can get out of him. Then, starve him, harness him any how to a truck with a flat tray on it, and see him bowl from Whitechapel to Bayswater. There appears to be no particular private understanding between birds and donkeys, in a state of nature; but in the shy neighborhood state you shall see them always in the same hands, and always developing their very best energies for the very worst company. I have known a donkey—by sight; we were not on speaking terms—who lived over on the Surrey side of London-bridge, among the fastnesses of Jacob's Island and Dockhead. It was the habit of that animal, when his services were not in immediate requisition, to go out alone, idling. I have met him a mile from his place of residence, loitering about the streets; and the expression of his countenance at such times was most degraded. He was attached to the establishment of an elderly lady who sold periwinkles, and he used to stand on Saturday nights with a cartful of those delicacies outside a gin-shop, pricking up his ears when a customer came to the cart, and too evidently deriving satisfaction from the knowledge that they got bad measure. His mistress was sometimes overtaken by inebriety. The last time I ever saw him (about five years ago) he was in circumstances of difficulty, caused by this failing. Having been left alone with the cart of periwinkles, and forgotten, he went off idling. He prowled among his usual low haunts for some time, gratifying his depraved taste, until, not taking the cart into his calculations, he endeavored to turn up a narrow alley, and became greatly involved. He was taken into custody by the police, and, the Green Yard of the district being near at hand, was backed into that place of durance. At that crisis, I encountered him; the stubborn sense he evinced of being—not to compromise the expression—a blackguard, I never saw exceeded in the human subject. A flaring candle in a paper shade, stuck in among his periwinkles, showed him, with his ragged harness broken and his cart extensively shattered, twitching his mouth and shaking his hanging head, a picture of disgrace and obduracy. I have seen boys being taken to station-houses, who were as like him as his own brother.

The dogs of shy neighborhoods, I observe to avoid play, and to be conscious of poverty. They avoid work too, if they can, of course; that is in the nature of all animals. I have the pleasure to know a dog in a back street in the neighborhood of Walworth, who has greatly distinguished himself in the minor drama, and who takes his portrait with him when he makes an engagement, for the illustration of the play-bill. His portrait (which is not at all like him) represents him in the act of dragging to the earth a recreant Indian, who is supposed to have tomahawked, or essayed to tomahawk a British officer. The design is pure poetry, for there is no such Indian in the piece, and no such incident. He is a dog of the Newfoundland breed, for whose honesty I would be bail to any amount; but whose intellectual qualities in association with dramatic fiction, I cannot rate high. Indeed, he is too honest for the profession he has entered. Being at a town in Yorkshire last summer, and seeing him posted in the bill of the night, I attended the performance. His first scene was eminently successful; but, as it occupied a second in its representation (and five lines in the bill), it scarcely afforded ground for a cool and deliberate judgment of his powers. He had merely to bark, run on, and jump through an inn window after a comic fugitive. The next scene of importance to the fable was a little marred in its interest by his over-anxiety: orasmuch as while his master (a belated soldier in a den of robbers on a tempestuous night) was feelingly lamenting the absence of his faithful dog, and laying great stress on the fact that he was thirty leagues away, the faithful dog was barking furiously in the prompter's box, and clearly choking himself against his collar. But it was in his greatest scene of all, that his honesty got the better of him. He had to enter a dense and trackless forest, on the trail of the murderer, and there to fly at the murderer when he found him resting at the foot of a tree, with his victim bound ready for slaughter. It was a hot night, and he came into the forest from an altogether unexpected direction, in the sweetest temper, at a very deliberate trot, not in the least excited; trotted to the footlights with his tongue out; and there sat down, panting, and amiably surveying the audience, with his tail beating on the boards, like a Dutch clock. Meanwhile the murderer, impatient to receive his doom, was audibly calling to him "Co-o-OME here!" while the victim, struggling with his bonds, assailed him with the most injurious expressions. It happened through these means, that when he was in course of time persuaded to trot up and rend the murderer limb from limb, he made it (for dramatic purposes) a little too obvious that he worked out that awful retribution by licking butter off his blood-stained hands.

In a shy street behind Long-acre, two honest dogs live, who perform in Punch's shows. I may venture to say that I am on terms of intimacy with both, and that I never saw either guilty of the falsehood of failing to look down at the man inside the show, during the whole performance. The difficulty other dogs have in satisfying their minds about these dogs, appears to be never overcome by time. The same dogs must encounter them over and over again, as they trudge along in their off-minutes behind the legs of the show and beside the drum; but all dogs seem to suspect their frills and jackets, and to sniff at them as if they thought those articles of personal adornment an eruption—a something in the nature of mange, perhaps. From this Covent Garden window of mine, I noticed a country dog, only the other day, who had come up to Covent Garden Market under a cart, and had broken his cord, an end of which he still trailed along with him. He loitered about the corners of the four streets commanded by my window; and bad London dogs came up, and told him lies that he didn't believe; and worse London dogs came up, and made proposals to him to go and steal in the market, which his principles rejected; and the ways of the town confused him, and he crept aside and lay down in a doorway. He had scarcely got a wink of sleep, when up comes Punch with Toby. He was darting to Toby for consolation and advice, when he saw the frill, and stopped in the middle of the street, appalled. The show was pitched, Toby retired behind the drapery, the audience formed, the drum and pipes struck up. My country dog remained immovable, intently staring at these strange appearances, until Toby opened the drama by appearing on his ledge, and to him entered Punch, who put a tobacco-pipe into Toby's mouth. At this spectacle, the country dog threw up his head, gave one terrible howl, and fled due west.

We talk of men keeping dogs, but we might often talk more expressively of dogs keeping men. I know a bulldog in a shy corner of Hammersmith who keeps a man. He keeps him up a yard, and makes him go to public houses and lay wagers on him, and obliges him to lean against posts and look at him, and forces him to neglect work for him, and keeps him under rigid coercion. I once knew a fancy terrier that kept a gentleman—a gentleman who had been brought up at Oxford, too. The dog kept the gentleman entirely for his glorification, and the gentleman never talked about any thing but the terrier. This, however, was not in a shy neighborhood, and is a digression consequently.

There are a great many dogs in shy neighborhoods, who keep boys. I have my eye on a mongrel in Somers-town who keeps three boys. He feigns that he can bring down sparrows, and unburrow rats (he can do neither), and he takes the boys out on sporting pretenses into all sorts of suburban fields. He has likewise made them believe that he possesses some mysterious knowledge of the art of fishing, and they consider themselves to be incompletely equipped for the Hampstead ponds, with a pickle-jar and a wide-mouthed bottle, unless he is with them and barking tremendously. There is a dog residing in the Borough of Southwark, who keeps a blind man. He may be seen, most days, in Oxford-street, hauling the blind man away on expeditions wholly uncontemplated by, and unintelligible to, the man: wholly of the dog's conception and execution. Contrariwise, when the man has projects, the dog will sit down in a crowded thoroughfare and meditate. I saw him yesterday, wearing the money-tray like an easy collar instead of offering it to the public, taking the man against his will, on the invitation of a disreputable cur, apparently to visit a dog at Harrow—he was so intent on that direction. The north wall of Burlington House Gardens, between the Arcade and the Albany, offers a shy spot for appointments among blind men at about two or three o'clock in the afternoon. They sit (very uncomfortable) on a sloping board there, and compare notes. Their dogs may always be observed at the same time, openly disparaging the men they keep, to one another, and settling where they shall respectively take their men when they begin to move again. At a small butcher's, in a shy neighborhood (there is no reason for suppressing the name; it is by Notting-hill, and gives upon the district called the Potteries), I know a shaggy black and white dog who keeps a drover. He is a dog of an easy disposition, and too frequently allows this drover to get drunk. On these occasions, it is the dog's custom to sit outside the public-house, keeping his eye on a few sheep, and thinking. I have seen him with six sheep, plainly casting-up in his mind how many he began with when he left the market, and at what places he has left the rest. I have seen him perplexed by not being able to account to himself for certain particular sheep. A light has gradually broken on him, he has remembered at what butcher's he left them, and in a burst of grave satisfaction has caught a fly off his nose, and shown himself much relieved. If I could at any time have doubted the fact that it was he who kept the drover, and not the drover who kept him, it would have been abundantly proved by his way of taking undivided charge of the six sheep, when the drover came out besmeared with red ochre and beer, and gave him wrong directions, which he calmly disregarded. He has taken the sheep entirely into his own hands, has merely remarked with respectful firmness, "That instruction would place them under an omnibus; you had better confine your attention to yourself—you will want it all;" and has driven his charge away, with an intelligence of ears and tail, and a knowledge of business, that has left his lout of a man very, very far behind.

As the dogs of shy neighborhoods usually betray a slinking consciousness of being in poor circumstances—for the most part manifested in an aspect of anxiety, an awkwardness in their play, and a misgiving that somebody is going to harness them to something, to pick up a living—so the cats of shy neighborhoods exhibit a strong tendency to relapse into barbarism. Not only are they made selfishly ferocious by ruminating on the surplus population around them, and on the densely crowded state of all the avenues to cat's meat; not only is there a moral and politico-economical haggardness in them, traceable to these reflections; but they evince a physical deterioration. Their linen is not clean, and is wretchedly got up; their black turns rusty, like old mourning; they wear very indifferent fur; and take to the shabbiest cotton velvet, instead of silk velvet. I am on terms of recognition with several small streets of cats, about the Obelisk in Saint George's Fields, and also in the vicinity of Clerkenwell-green, and also in the back settlements of Drury-lane. In appearance, they are very like the women among whom they live. They seem to turn out of their unwholesome beds into the street, without any preparation. They leave their young families to stagger about the gutters, unassisted, while they frouzily quarrel and swear and scratch and spit, at street corners. In particular, I remark that when they are about to increase their families (an event of frequent recurrence) the resemblance is strongly expressed in a certain dusty dowdiness, down-at-heel self-neglect, and general giving up of things. I cannot honestly report that I have ever seen a feline matron of this class washing her face when in an interesting condition.

Not to prolong these notes of uncommercial travel among the lower animals of shy neighborhoods, by dwelling at length upon the exasperated moodiness of the tom-cats, and their resemblance in many respects to a man and a brother, I will come to a close with a word on the fowls of the same localities.

That any thing born of an egg and invested with wings, should have got to the pass that it hops contentedly down a ladder into a cellar, and calls *that* going home, is a circumstance so amazing as to leave one nothing more in this connection to wonder at. Otherwise I might wonder at the completeness with which these fowls have become separated from all the birds of the air—have taken to groveling in bricks and mortar and mud—have forgotten all about live trees, and make roosting-places of shop-boards, barrows, oyster-tubs, bulk-heads, and door-scrapers. I wonder at nothing concerning them, and take them as they are. I accept as products of Nature and things of course, a reduced Bantam family of my acquaintance in the Hackney-road, who are incessantly at the pawnbroker's I cannot say that they enjoy themselves, for they are of a melancholy temperament; but what enjoyment they are capable of, they derive from crowding together in the pawnbroker's side-entry. Here, they are always to be found in a feeble flutter, as if they were newly come down in the world, and were afraid of being identified. I know a low fellow, originally of a good family from Dorking, who takes his whole establishment of wives, in single file, in at the door of the Jug Department of a disorderly tavern near the Haymarket, manœuvres them among the company's legs, emerges with them at the Bottle Entrance, and so passes his life: seldom, in the season, going to bed before two in the morning. Over Waterloo-bridge, there is a shabby old speckled couple (they belong to the wooden French-bedstead, washing-stand, and towel-horse-making trade), who are always trying to get in at the door of a chapel. Whether the old lady, under a delusion reminding one of Mrs. Southcott, has an idea of intrusting an egg to that particular denomination, or merely understands that she has no business in the building, and is consequently frantic to enter it, I cannot determine; but she is constantly endeavoring to undermine the principal door: while her partner, who is infirm upon his legs, walks up and down, encouraging her and defying the Universe. But the family I have been best acquainted with, since the removal from this trying sphere of a Chinese circle at Brentford, reside in the densest part of Bethnal-green. Their abstraction from the objects among which they live, or rather their conviction that those objects have all come into existence in express subservience to fowls, has so enchanted me, that I have made them the subject of many journeys at divers hours. After careful observation of the two lords and the ten ladies of whom this family consists, I have come to the conclusion that their opinions are represented by the leading lord and leading lady; the latter, as I judge, an aged personage, afflicted with a paucity of feather and visibility of quill, that gives her the appearance of a bundle of office pens. When a railway goods-van that would crush an elephant comes round the corner, tearing over these fowls, they emerge unharmed from under the horses perfectly satisfied that the whole rush was a passing property in the air, which may have left something to eat behind it. They look upon old shoes, wrecks of kettles and saucepans, and fragments of bonnets, as a kind of meteoric discharge, for fowls to peck at. Peg-tops and hoops they account, I think, as a sort of hail; shuttlecocks, as rain, or dew. Gaslight comes quite as natural to them as any other light; and I have more than a suspicion that, in the minds of the two lords, the early public-house at the corner has superseded the sun. I have established it as a certain fact, that they always begin to crow when the public-house shutters begin to be taken down, and that they salute the potboy, the instant he appears to perform that duty, as if he were Phœbus in person.

---

The chance use of the word "Tramp" in my last paper, brought that numerous fraternity so vividly before my mind's eye, that I had no sooner laid down my pen than a compulsion was upon me to take it up again, and make notes of the Tramps whom I perceived on all the summer roads in all directions.

Whenever a tramp sits down to rest by the wayside, he sits with his legs in a dry ditch; and whenever he goes to sleep (which is very often indeed), he goes to sleep on his back. Yonder, by the high road, glaring white in the bright sunshine, lies, on the dusty bit of turf under the bramble-bush that fences the coppice from the highway, the tramp of the order savage, fast asleep. He lies on the broad of his back, with his face turned up to the sky and one of his ragged arms loosely thrown across his face. His bundle (what can be the contents of that mysterious bundle, to make it worth his while to carry it about?) is thrown down beside him, and the waking woman with him sits with her legs in the ditch, and her back to the road. She wears her bonnet rakishly perched on the front of her head, to shade her face from the sun in walking, and she ties her skirts round her in conventionally tight tramp-fashion with a sort of apron. You can seldom catch signt of her, resting thus, without seeing her in a despondently defiant manner doing something to her hair or her bonnet, and glancing at you between her fingers. She does not often go to sleep herself in the daytime, but will sit for any length of time beside the man. And his slumberous propensities would not seem to be referable to the fatigue of carrying the bundle, for she carries it much oftener and further than he. When they are afoot, you will mostly find him slouching on ahead, in a gruff temper, while she lags heavily behind with the burden. He is given to personally correcting her, too—which phase of his character develops itself oftenest, on benches outside alehouse doors—and she appears to become strongly attached to him for these reasons: it may usually be noticed that when the poor creature has a bruised face, she is the most affectionate. He has no occupation whatever, this order of tramp, and has no object whatever in going anywhere. He will sometimes call himself a brickmaker, or a sawyer, but only when he takes an imaginative flight. He generally represents himself, in a vague way, as looking out for a job of work; but he never did work, he never does, and he never never will. It is a favorite fiction with him, however (as if he were the most industrious character on earth), that *you* never work; and as he goes past your garden and sees you looking at your flowers, you will overhear him growl, with a strong sense of contrast, "*You* are a lucky hidle devil, *you* are!"

The slinking tramp is of the same hopeless order, and has the same injured conviction on him that you were born to whatever you possess, and never did any thing to get it; but he is of a less audacious disposition. He will stop before your gate, and say to his female companion with an air of constitutional humility and propitiation—to edify any one who may be within hearing behind a blind or a bush—"This is a sweet spot, ain't it? A lovelly spot! And I wonder if they'd give two poor foot sore travelers like me and you, a drop of fresh water out of such a pretty gen-teel crib? We'd take it wery koind on 'em, wouldn't us? Wery koind, upon my word, us would!" He has a quick sense of a dog in the vicinity, and will extend his modestly-injured propitiation to the dog chained up in your yard: remarking, as he slinks at the yard gate, "Ah! You are a foine breed o' dog, too, and *you* ain't kep for nothink! I'd take it wery koind o' your master if he'd elp a traveler and his woife as envies no gentlefolk their good fortun, wi' a bit o' your broken wittles. He'd never know the want of it, nor more would you. Don't bark like that, at poor persons as never done you no arm; the poor is down-trodden and broke enough without that; O DON'T!" He generally heaves a prodigious sigh in moving away, and always looks up the lane and down the lane, and up the road and down the road, before going on.

Both of these orders of tramp are of a very robust habit; let the hard-working laborer at whose cottage door they prowl and beg, have the ague never so badly, these tramps are sure to be in good health.

That is another kind of tramp, whom you encounter this bright summer day—say, on a road with the sea-breeze making its dust lively, and sails of ships in the blue distance beyond the slope of Down. As you walk enjoyingly on, you descry in the perspective at the bottom of a steep hill up which your way lies, a figure that appears to be sitting airily on a gate, whistling in a cheerful and disengaged manner. As you approach nearer to it, you observe the figure to slide down from the gate, to desist from whistling, to uncock its hat, to become tender of foot, to depress its head and elevate its shoulders, and to present all the characteristics of profound despondency. Arriving at the bottom of the hill and coming close to the figure, you observe it to be the figure of a shabby young man. He is moving painfully forward, in the direction in which you are going, and his mind is so preoccupied with his misfortunes that he is not aware of your approach until you are close upon him at the hill-foot. When he is aware of you, you discover him to be a remarkably well-behaved young man, and a remarkably well-spoken young man. You know him to be well-behaved, by his respectful manner of touching his hat; you know him to be well-spoken, by his smooth manner of expressing himself. He says in a flowing confidential voice, and without punctuation, "I ask your pardon sir but if you would excuse the liberty of being so addressed upon the public Iway by one who is almost reduced to rags though it as not always been so and by no fault of his own but through ill elth in his family and many unmerited sufferings it would be a great obligation sir to know the time." You give the well-spoken young man, the time. The well-spoken young man, keeping well up with you, resumes: "I am aware sir that it is a liberty to intrude a further question on a gentleman walking for his entertainment but might I make so bold as ask the favor of the way to Dover sir and about the distance?" You inform the well-spoken young man that the way to Dover is straight on, and the distance some eighteen miles. The well-spoken young man becomes greatly agitated. "In the condition to which I am reduced," says he, "I could not ope to reach Dover before dark even if my shoes were in a state to take me there or my feet were in a state to old out over the flinty road and were not on the bare ground of which any gentleman has the means to satisfy himself by looking Sir may I take the liberty of speaking to you?" As the well-spoken young man keeps so well up with you that you can't prevent his taking the liberty of speaking to you, he goes on, with fluency: "Sir it is not begging that is my intention for I was brought up by the best of mothers and begging is not my trade I should not know sir how to follow it as a trade if such were my shameful wishes for the best of mothers long taught otherwise and in the best of omes though now reduced to take the present liberty on the Iway Sir my business was the law-stationering and I was favorably known to the Solicitor-General the Attorney-General the majority of the Judges and the ole of the legal profession but through ill elth in my family and the treachery of a friend for whom I became security and he no other than my own wife's brother the brother of my own wife I was cast forth with my tender partner and three young children not to beg for

I will sooner die of deprivation but to make my way to the seaport town of Dover where I have a relative i in respect not only that will assist me but that would trust me with untold gold Sir in appier times and hare this calamity fell upon me I made for my amusement when I little thought that I should ever need it excepting for my air this"—here the well-spoken young man puts his hand into his breast—"this comb! Sir I implore you in the name of charity to purchase a tortoise-shell comb which is a genuine article at any price that your humanity may put upon it and may the blessings of a ouseless family awaiting with beating arts the return of a husband and a father from Dover upon the cold stone seats of London Bridge ever attend you Sir may I take the liberty of speaking to you I implore you to buy this comb!" By this time, being a reasonably good walker, you will have been too much for the well-spoken young man, who will stop short and express his disgust and his want of breath, in a long expectoration, as you leave him behind.

Toward the end of the same walk, on the same bright summer-day, at the corner of the next little town or village, you may find another kind of tramp, embodied in the persons of a most exemplary couple whose only improvidence appears to have been, that they spent the last of their little All on soap. They are a man and woman, spotless to behold—John Anderson, with the frost on his short smock-frock instead of his "pow," attended by Mrs. Anderson. John is over ostentatious of the frost upon his raiment, and wears a curious and, you would say, an almost unnecessary demonstration of girdle of white linen wound about his waist—a girdle, snowy as Mrs. Anderson's apron. This cleanliness was the expiring effort of the respectable couple, and nothing then remained to Mr. Anderson but to get chalked upon his spade in snow-white copy-book characters, HUNGRY! and to sit down here. Yes; one thing more remained to Mr. Anderson—his character; Monarchs could not deprive him of his hard-earned character. Accordingly, as you come up with this spectacle of virtue in distress, Mrs. Anderson rises, and with a decent courtesy presents for your consideration a certificate from a Doctor of Divinity, the reverend the Vicar of Upper Dodgington, who informs his

Christian friends and all whom it may concern that the bearers, John Anderson and lawful wife, are persons to whom you cannot be too liberal. This benevolent pastor omitted no work of his hands to fit the good couple out, for with half an eye you can recognize his autograph on the spade.

Another class of tramp is a man, the most valuable part of whose stock-in-trade is a highly perplexed demeanor. He is got up like a countryman, and you will often come upon the poor fellow, while he is endeavoring to decipher the inscription on a milestone—quite a fruitless endeavor, for he cannot read. He asks your pardon, he truly does (he is very slow of speech, this tramp, and he looks in a bewildered way all round the prospect while he talks to you), but all of us shold do as we wold be done by, and he'll take it kind if you'll put a power man in the right road for to jine his eldest son as has broke his leg bad in the masoning, and is in this heere Orspit'l as is wrote down by Squire Pouncerby's own hand as wold not tell a lie fur no man. He then produces from under his dark frock (being always very slow and perplexed) a neat but worn old leathern purse, from which he takes a scrap of paper. On this scrap of paper is written by Squire Pouncerby, of The Grove, "Please to direct the Bearer, a poor but very worthy man, to the Sussex County Hospital, near Brighton"—a matter of some difficulty at the moment, seeing that the request comes suddenly upon you in the depths of Hertfordshire. The more you endeavor to indicate where Brighton is—when you have with the greatest difficulty remembered—the less the devoted father can be made to comprehend, and the more obtusely he stares at the prospect; whereby, being reduced to extremity, you recommend the faithful parent to begin by going to Saint Albans, and present him with half-a-crown. It does him good, no doubt, but scarcely helps him forward, since you find him lying drunk that same evening in the wheelwright's saw pit under the shed where the felled trees are, opposite the sign of the Three Jolly Hedgers.

But the most vicious, by far, of all the idle tramps, is the tramp who pretends to have been a gentleman. "Educated," he writes from the village beer-shop in pale ink of a ferruginous complexion; "educated at Trin. Coll. Cam.—nursed in the lap of afluence—once in my small way the pattron of the Muses," &c., &c., &c.—surely a sympathetic mind will not withhold a trifle, to help him on to the market-town where he thinks of giving a Lecture to the *fruges consumere nati*, on things in general? This shameful creature lolling about hedge tap-rooms in his ragged clothes, now so far from being black that they look as if they never can have been black, is more selfish and insolent than even the savage tramp. He would sponge on the poorest boy for a farthing, and spurn him when he had got it; he would interpose—if he could get any thing by it—between the baby and the mother's breast. So much lower than the company he keeps, for his maudlin assumption of being higher, this pitiless rascal blights the summer road as he maunders on between the luxuriant hedges: where, to my thinking, even the wild convolvulus and rose and sweet-brier, are the worse for his going by, and need time to recover from the taint of him in the air.

The young fellows who trudge along barefoot, five or six together, their boots slung over their shoulders, their shabby bundles under their arms, their sticks, newly cut from some road-side wood, are not eminently prepossessing, but are much less objectionable. There is a tramp-fellowship among them. They pick one another up at resting stations, and go on in companies. They always go at a fast swing—though they generally limp too—and there is invariably one of the company who has much ado to keep up with the rest. They generally talk about horses, and any other means of locomotion than walking; or, one of the company relates some recent experiences of the road—which are always disputes and difficulties. As for example: "So as I'm a standing at the pump in the market, blest if there don't come up a beadle, and he ses, 'Mustn't stand here,' he ses. 'Why not?' I ses. 'No beggars allowed in this town,' he ses. 'Who's a beggar?' I ses.' 'You are,' he ses. 'Who ever see *me* beg? Did *you*?' I ses. 'Then you're a tramp,' he ses. 'I'd rather be that, than a Beadle,' I ses." (The company express great approval.) "'Would you?' he ses to me. 'Yes, I would,' I ses to him. 'Well,' he ses, 'anyhow, get out of this town.' 'Why, blow your little town!' I ses, 'who wants to be in it? Wot does your dirty little town mean by comin' and stickin' itself in the road to anywhere? Why don't you get a shovel and a barrer, and clear your town out o' people's way?'" (The company expressing the highest approval, and laughing aloud, they all go down the hill.)

Then, there are the tramp handicraft men. Are they not all over England, in this Midsummer time? Where does the lark sing, the corn grow, the mill turn, the river run, and they are not among the lights and shadows, tinkering, chair-mending, umbrella-mending, clock-mending, knife-grinding? Surely, a pleasant thing, if we were in that condition of life, to grind our way through Kent, Sussex, and Surrey. For the first six weeks or so, we should see the sparks we ground off, fiery bright against a background of green wheat and green leaves. A little later, and the ripe harvest would pale our sparks from red to yellow, until we got the dark newly-turned land for a back-ground again, and they were red once more. By that time we should have ground our way to the sea cliffs, and the whirr of our wheel wonld be lost in the breaking of the waves. Our next variety in sparks would be derived from contrast with the gorgeous medley of colors in the autumn woods, and, by the time we had ground our way round to the heathy lands between Reigate and Croydon, doing a prosperous stroke of business all along, we should show like a little firework in the light, frosty air, and be the next best thing to the blacksmith's forge. Very agreeable, too, to go on a chair-mending tour. What judges we should be of rushes, and how knowingly, with a sheaf and a bottomless chair at our back, we should lounge on bridges, looking over at osier-beds. Among all the innumerable occupations that cannot possibly be transacted without the assistance of lookers-on, chair-mending may take a station in the first rank. When we sat down with our backs against the barn or the public-house, and began to mend, what a sense of popularity would grow upon us. When all the children came to look at us, and the tailor, and the general dealer, and the farmer who had been giving a small order at the little saddler's, and the groom from the great house, and the publican, and even the two skittle-players (and here note that, howsoever busy all the rest of village human-kind may be, there will always be two people with leisure to play at skittles, wherever village skittles are), what encouragement would be on us to plait and weave! No one looks at us while we plait and weave these words. Clock-mending again. Except for the slight inconvenience of carrying a clock under our arm, and the monotony of making the bell go, whenever we came to a human habitation, with a pleasant privilege to give a voice to the dumb cottage-clock, and set it talking to the cottage family again. Likewise we foresee great interest in going round by the park plantations, under the overhanging boughs, (hares, rabbits, partridges, and pheasants, scudding like mad across and across the checkered ground before us,) and so over the park ladder, and through the wood, until we came to the Keeper's lodge. Then would the Keeper be discoverable at his door, in a deep nest of leaves, smoking his pipe. Then, on our accosting him in the way of our trade, would he call to Mrs. Keeper, respecting "t'ould clock" in the kitchen. Then would Mrs. Keeper ask us into the lodge, and on due examination we should offer to make a good job of it for eighteenpence: which offer, being accepted, would set us tinkling and clinking among the chubby awe-struck little Keepers for an hour and more. So completely to the family's satisfaction should we achieve our work, that the Keeper would mention how that there was something wrong with the bell of the turret stable clock up at the Hall, and that if we thought good of going up to the housekeeper on the chance of that job too, why he would take us. Then should we go, among the branching oaks and the deep fern, by silent ways of mystery known to the Keeper, seeing the herd glancing here and there as we went along, until we came to the old Hall, solemn and grand. Under the Terrace Flower Garden, and round by the stables, would the Keeper take us in, and as we passed we should observe how spacious and stately the stables, and how fine the painting of the horses' names over their stalls, and how solitary all: the family being in London. Then, should we find ourselves presented to the housekeeper, sitting, in hushed state, at needlework, in a bay-window looking out upon a mighty grim red-brick quadrangle, guarded by stone lions disrespectfully throwing somersaults over the escutcheons of the noble family. Then, our services accepted and we insinuated with a candle into the stable turret, we should find it to be a mere question of pendulum, but one that would hold us until dark. Then, should we fall to work, with a general impression of Ghosts being about, and of pictures in-doors that of a certainty came out of their frames and "walked," if the family would only own it. Then, should we work and work, until the day gradually turned to dusk, and even until the dusk gradually turned to dark. Our task at length accomplished, we should be taken into an enormous servants' hall, and there regaled with beef and bread, and powerful ale. Then, paid freely, we should be at liberty to go, and should be told by a pointing helper to keep round over yinder by the blasted ash, and so straight through the woods, till we should see the town-lights right afore us. Then, feeling lonesome, should we desire upon the whole, that the ash had not been blasted, or that the helper had had the manners not to mention it. However, we should keep on, all right, until suddenly the stable bell would strike ten in the dolefullest way, quite chilling our blood, though we had so lately taught him how to acquit himself. Then, as we went on, should we recall old stories, and dimly consider what it would be most advisable to do, in the event of a tall figure, all in white, with saucer eyes, coming up and saying, "I want you to come to a churchyard, and mend a church clock. Follow me!" Then, would we make a burst to get clear of the trees, and should soon find ourselves in the open, with the town-lights bright ahead of us. So should we lie that night at the ancient sign of the Crispin and Crispanus, and rise early in the morning to be betimes on tramp again.

"Bricklayers often tramp, in twos and threes, lying by night at their "lodges" which are scattered all over the country. Bricklaying is another of the occupations that can by no means be transacted in rural parts, without the assistance of spectators—of as many as can be convened. In thinly-peopled spots, I have known bricklayers on tramp, coming up with bricklayers at work, to be so sensible of the indispensability of lookers-on, that they themselves have set up in that capacity, and have been unable to subside into the acceptance of a proffered share in the job, for two or three days together.

Sometimes, the "navvy," on tramp, with an extra pair of half-boots over his shoulder, a bag, a bottle, and a can, will take a similar part in a job of excavation, and will look at it without engaging in it, until all his money is gone. The current of my uncommercial pursuits caused me only last summer to want a little body of workmen for a certain spell of work in a pleasant part of the country; and I was at one time honored with the attendance of as many as seven-and-twenty, who were looking at six.

Who can be familiar with any rustic highway in the summer-time, without storing up knowledge of the many tramps who go from one oasis of town or village to another, to sell a stock in trade, apparently not worth a shilling when sold? Shrimps are a favorite commodity for this kind of speculation, and so are cakes of a soft and spongy character, coupled with Spanish nuts, and brandy balls. The stock is carried on the head in a basket, and, between the head and the basket, are the trestles on which the stock is displayed at trading times. Fleet of foot, but a careworn class of tramp this, mostly; with a certain stiffness of neck, occasioned by much anxious balancing of baskets; and also with a long Chinese sort of eye, which an overweighted forehead would seem to have squeezed into that form.

On the hot dusty roads near seaport towns and great rivers, behold the tramping Soldier. And if you should happen never to have asked yourself whether his uniform is suited to his work, perhaps the poor fellow's appearance as he comes distressfully toward you, with his absurdly tight jacket unbuttoned, his neck-gear in his hand, and his legs well chafed by his trowsers of baize, may suggest the personal inquiry, how you think *you* would like it. Much better the tramping Sailor, although his cloth is somewhat too thick for land service. But why the tramping merchant-mate should put on a black velvet waistcoat, for a chalky country in the dog-days, is one of the great secrets of nature that will never be discovered.

I have my eye upon a piece of Kentish road, bordered on either side by a wood, and having on one hand, between the road-dust and the trees, a skirting patch of grass. Wild flowers grow in abundance, on this spot, and it lies high and airy, with the distant river stealing steadily away to the ocean, like a man's life. To gain the milestone here,—which the moss primroses, violets, blue-bells, and wild roses, would soon render illegible but for peering travelers pushing them aside with their sticks,—you must come up a steep hill, come which way you may. So, all the tramps with carts or caravans—the Gipsy-tramp, the Show-tramp, the Cheap Jack—find it impossible to resist the temptations of the place, and all turn the horse loose when they come to it, and boil the pot. Bless the place, I love the ashes of the vagabond fires that have scorched its grass! What tramp children do I see here, attired in a handful of rags, making a gymnasium of the shafts of the cart, making a feather-bed of the flints and brambles, making a toy of the hobbled old horse who is not much more like a horse than any cheap toy would be! Here, do I encounter the cart of mats and brooms and baskets—with all thoughts of business given to the evening wind—with the stew made and being served out—with Cheap Jack and Dear Jill striking soft music out of the plates that are rattled like warlike symbols when put up for auction at fairs and markets—their minds so influenced, no doubt, by the melody of the nightingales as they begin to sing in the woods behind them, that if I were to propose to deal, they would sell me any thing at cost price. On this hallowed ground, has it been my happy privilege (let me whisper it), to behold the White-haired Lady with the pink eyes, eating meat-pie with the Giant: while, by the hedge-side, on the box of blankets which I knew contained the snakes, were set forth the cups and saucers and the teapot. It was on an evening in August, that I chanced upon this ravishing spectacle, and I noticed that, whereas the Giant reclined half concealed beneath the overhanging boughs and seemed indifferent to Nature, the white hair of the gracious Lady streamed free in the breath of evening, and her pink eyes found pleasure in the landscape. I heard only a single sentence of her uttering, yet it bespoke a talent for modest repartee. The ill-mannered Giant—accursed be his evil race!—had interrupted the Lady in some remark, and, as I passed that enchanted corner of the wood, she gently reproved him, with the words,

"Now, Cobby;" Cobby! so short a name!—"ain't one fool enough to talk at a time?"

Within appropriate distance of this magic ground, though not so near it as that the song trolled from tap or bench at door, can invade its woodland silence, is a little hostelry which no man possessed of a penny was ever known to pass in warm weather. Before its entrance, are certain pleasant trimmed limes: likewise, a cool well, with so musical a bucket-handle that its fall upon the bucket rim will make a horse prick up its ears, and neigh upon the droughty road half a mile off. This is a house of great resort for hay-making tramps and harvest tramps, insomuch that as they sit within, drinking their mugs of beer, their relinquished scythes and reaping-hooks glare out of the open windows, as if the whole establishment were a family war-coach of Ancient Britons. Later in the season, the whole country-side, for miles and miles, will swarm with hopping tramps. They come in families, men, women, and children, every family provided with a bundle of bedding, an iron pot, a number of babies, and too often with some poor sick creature quite unfit for the rough life, for whom they suppose the smell of the fresh hop to be a sovereign remedy. Many of these hoppers are Irish, but many come from London. They crowd all the roads, and camp under all the hedges and on all the scraps of common-land, and live among and upon the hops until they are all picked, and the hop-gardens, so beautiful through the summer, look as if they had been laid waste by an invading army. Then, there is a vast exodus of tramps out of the county; and if you ride or drive round any turn of any road, at more than a foot pace, you will be bewildered to find that you have charged into the bosom of fifty families, and that there are splashing up all around you, in the utmost prodigality of confusion, bundles of bedding, babies, iron pots, and a good-humored multitude of both sexes and all ages, equally divided between perspiration and intoxication.

---

It lately happened that I found myself rambling about the scenes among which my earliest days were passed; scenes from which I departed when I was a child, and which I did not re visit until I was a man. This is no uncommon chance, but one that befalls some of us any day; perhaps it may not be quite uninteresting to compare notes with the reader respecting an experience so familar and a journey so uncommercial.

I will call my boyhood's home (and I feel like a Tenor in an English Opera when I mention it) Dullborough. Most of us come from Dullborough who come from a country town.

As I left Dullborough in the days when there were no railroads in the land, I left it in a stage-coach. Through all the years that have since passed, have I ever lost the smell of the damp straw in which I was packed—like game—and forwarded, carriage paid, to the Cross Keys, Wood-street, Cheapside, London? There was no other inside passenger, and I consumed my sandwiches in solitude and dreariness, and it rained hard all the way, and I thought life sloppier than I had expected to find it.

With this tender remembrance upon me, I was cavalierly shunted back into Dullborough the other day, by train. My ticket had been previously collected, like my taxes, and my shining new portmanteau had had a great plaster stuck upon it, and I had been defied by Act of Parliament to offer an objection to any thing that was done to it, or me, under a penalty of not less than forty shillings, or more than five pounds, compoundable for a term of imprisonment. When I had sent my disfigured property on to the hotel, I began to look about me; and the first discovery I made, was, that the Station had swallowed up the playing-field.

It was gone. The two beautiful hawthorn-trees, the hedge, the turf, and all those buttercups and daisies, had given place to the stoniest of jolting roads; while, beyond the station, an ugly dark monster of a tunnel kept its jaws open, as if it had swallowed them and were ravenous for more destruction. The coach that had carried me away, was melodiously called Timpson's Blue-Eyed Maid, and belonged to Timpson, at the coach-office up-street; the locomotive engine that had brought me back, was called severely No. 97, and belonged to S. E. R., and was spitting ashes and hot water over the blighted ground.

When I had been let out at the platform-door, like a prisoner whom his turnkey grudgingly released, I looked in again over the low wall, at the scene of departed glories. Here, in the hay-making time, had I been delivered from the dungeons of Seringapatam, an immense pile (of haycock), by my countrymen, the victorious British (boy next door and his two cousins), and had been recognized with ecstasy by my affianced one (Miss Green), who had come all the way from England (second house in the terrace) to ransom me, and marry me. Here had I first heard in confidence, from one whose father was greatly connected, being under Government, of the existence of a terrible banditti, called "The Radicals," whose principles were, that the Prince Regent wore stays, and that nobody had a right to any salary, and that the army and navy ought to be put down—horrors at which I trembled in my bed, after supplicating that the Radicals might be speedily taken and hanged. Here, too, had we, the small boys of Boles's, had that cricket match against the small boys of Coles's, when Boles and Coles had actually met upon the ground, and when, instead of instantly hitting out at one another with the utmost fury, as we had all hoped and expected, those sneaks had said respectively, "I hope Mrs. Boles is well," and "I hope Mrs. Coles and the baby are doing charmingly." Could it be that, after all this, and much more, the Playing-field was a Station, and No. 97 expectorated boiling water and red-hot cinders on it, and the whole belonged, by Act of Parliament, to S. E. R.?

As it could be, and was, I left the place with a heavy heart for a walk all over the town. And first of Timpson's, up-street. When I departed from Dullborough in the strawy arms of Timpson's Blue-Eyed Maid, Timpson's was a moderate-sized coach-office (in fact, a little coach-office), with an oval transparency in the window, which looked beautiful by night, representing one of Timpson's coaches in the act of passing a milestone on the London road with great velocity, completely full inside and out, and all the passengers dressed in the first style of fashion, and enjoying themselves tremendously. I found no such place as Timpson's now—no such bricks and rafters, not to mention the name—no such edifice on the teeming earth. Pickford had come and knocked Timpson's down. Pickford had not only knocked Timpson's down, but had knocked two or three houses down on each side of Timpson's, and then had knocked the whole into one great establishment, with a pair of big gates, in and out of which, his (Pickford's) wagons are, in these days, always rattling, with their drivers sitting up so high, that they look in at the second floor windows of the old-fashioned houses in the High-street as they shake the town. I have not the honor of Pickford's acquaintance, but I felt that he had done me an injury, not to say committed an act of boy-slaughter, in running over my childhood in this rough manner; and if ever I meet Pickford driving one of his own monsters, and smoking a pipe the while (which is the custom of his men), he shall know by the expression of my eye, if it catches his, that there is something wrong between us.

Moreover, I felt that Pickford had no right to come rushing into Dullborough and deprive the town of a public picture. He is not Napoleon Bonaparte. When he took down the transparent stage-coach, he ought to have given the town a transparent van. With a gloomy conviction that Pickford is wholly utilitarian and unimaginative, I proceeded on my way.

It is a mercy I have not a red and green lamp and a night-bell at my door, for in my very young days I was taken to so many lyings-in that I wonder I escaped becoming a professional martyr to them in after-life. I suppose I had a very sympathetic nurse, with a large circle of married acquaintance. However that was, as I continued my walk through Dullborough, I found many houses to be solely associated in my mind with this particular interest. At one little green-grocer's shop, down certain steps from the street, I remembered to have waited on a lady who had had four children (I am afraid to write five, though I fully believe it was five) at a birth. This meritorious woman held quite a reception in her room on the morning when I was introduced there, and the sight of the house brought vividly to my mind how the four (five) deceased young people lay, side by side, on a clean cloth, on a chest of drawers: reminding me by a homely association, which I suspect their complexion to have assisted, of pig's feet as they are usually displayed at a neat tripe shop. Hot caudle was handed round on the occasion, and I further remembered as I stood contemplating the green-grocer's, that a subscription was entered into among the company, which became extremely alarming to my consciousness of having pocket-money on my person. This fact being known to my conductress, whoever she was, I was earnestly exhorted to contribute, but resolutely declined: therein disgusting the company, who gave me to understand that I must dismiss all expectations of going to Heaven.

How does it happen that when all else is change wherever one goes, there yet seem, in every place, to be some few people who never alter? As the sight of the green-grocer's house re-called these trivial incidents of long ago, the identical green-grocer appeared on the steps, with his hands in his pockets, and leaning his shoulder against the door-post, as my childish eyes had seen him many a time; indeed, there was his old mark on the door-post yet, as if his shadow had become a fixture there. It was he himself; he might formerly have been an old-looking young man, or he might now be a young-looking old man, but there he was. In walking along the street, I had as yet looked in vain for a familiar face, or even a transmitted face; here was the very green-grocer who had been weighing and handling baskets on the morning of the reception. As he brought with him a dawning remembrance that he had had no proprietary interest in those babies, I crossed the road, and accosted him on the subject. He was not in the least excited or gratified or in any way roused, by the accuracy of my recollection, but said, Yes, summut out of the common—he didn't remember how many it was (as if half a dozen babes either way made no difference)—had happened to a Mrs. What's-her-name, as once lodged there—but he didn't call it to mind, particular. Nettled by this phlegmatic conduct, I informed him that I had left the town when I was a child. He slowly returned, quite unsoftened and not without a sarcastic kind of complacency, *Had* I? Ah! And did I find it had got on tolerable well without me? Such is the difference (I thought, when I had left him a few hundred yards behind, and was by so much in a better temper) between going away from a place and remaining in it. I had no right, I reflected, to be angry with the green-grocer for his want of interest. I was nothing to him: whereas he was the town, the cathedral, the bridge, the river, my childhood, and a large slice of my life, to me.

Of course the town had shrunk fearfully, since I was a child there. I had entertained the impression that the High street was at least as wide as Regent-street, London, or the Italian Boulevard at Paris. I found it little better than a lane. There was a public clock in it, which I had suppose to be the finest clock in the world; whereas it now turned out to be as inexpressive, moon-faced, and weak a clock as ever I saw. It belonged to a Town Hall, where I had seen an Indian (who I now suppose wasn't an Indian) swallow a sword (which I now suppose he didn't). This edifice had appeared to me in those days so glorious a structure, that I had set it up in my mind as the model on which the Genie of the Lamp built the palace for Aladdin. A mean little brick heap, like a demented chapel, with a few yawning persons in leather gaiters, and in the last extremity for something to do, lounging at the door with their hands in their pockets, and calling themselves a Corn Exchange!

The Theatre was in existence, I found, on asking the fishmonger, who had a compact show of stock in his window, consisting of a sole and a quart of shrimps—and I resolved to comfort my mind by going to look at it. Richard the Third, in a very uncomfortable cloak, had first appeared to me there, and had made my heart leap with terror by backing up against the stage-box in which I was posted, while struggling for life against the virtuous Richmond. It was within those walls that I had learned, as from a page of English history, how that wicked king slept in war-time on a sofa much too short for him, and how fearfully his conscience troubled. his boots. There, too, had I first seen the funny countryman, but countryman of noble principles in a flowered waistcoat, crunch up his little hat and throw it on the ground and pull off his coat, saying "Dom thee, squire, coom on with thy fistes then!" At which the lovely young woman who kept company with him (and who went out gleaning, in a narrow white muslin apron with five beautiful bars of five different colored ribbons across it) was so frightened for his sake, that she fainted away. Many wondrous secrets of Nature had I come to the knowledge of in that sanctuary: of which not the least terrific were, that the witches in Macbeth bore an awful resemblance to the Thanes and other proper inhabitants of Scotland; and that the good King Duncan couldn't rest in his grave, but was constantly coming out of it, and calling himself somebody else. To the Theatre, therefore, I repaired for consolation. But I found very little, for it was in a bad and a declining way. A dealer in wine and bottled beer had already squeezed his trade into the box office, and the theatrical money was taken—when it came—in a kind of meat-safe in the passage. The dealer in wine and bottled beer must have insinuated himself under the stage too; for he announced that he had various descriptions of alcoholic drinks "in the wood," and there was no possible stowage for the wood anywhere else. Evidently, he was by degrees eating the establishment away to the core, and would soon have sole possession of it. It was To Let, and hopelessly so, for its old purposes; and there had been no entertainment within its walls for a long time, except a Panorama; and even that had been announced as "pleasingly instructive," and I knew too well the fatal meaning and the leaden import of those terrible expressions. No, there was no comfort in the theatre. It was mysteriously gone, like my own youth. Unlike my own youth, it might be coming back some day; but there was little promise of it.

As the town was placarded with references to the Dullborough Mechanics' Institution, I thought I would go and look at that establishment next. There had been no such thing in the town, in my young day, and it occurred to me that its extensive prosperity might have brought adversity upon the Drama. I found the Institution with some difficulty, and should scarcely have known that I had found it if I had judged from its external appearance only; but this was attributable to its never having been finished, and having no front: consequently, it led a modest and retired existence up a stable-yard. It was—as I learned, on inquiry—a most flourishing Institution, and of the highest benefit to the town: two triumphs which I was glad to understand were not at all impaired by the seeming drawbacks that no mechanics belonged to it, and that it was steeped in debt to the chimney-pots. It had a large room, which was approached by an infirm step-ladder: the builder having declined to construct the intended stair-case, without a present payment in cash, which Dullborough—though so profoundly appreciative of the Institution—seemed unaccountably bashful about subscribing. The large room had cost—or would, when paid for—five hundred pounds; and it had more mortar in it and more echoes, than one might have expected to get for the money. It was fitted up with a platform, and the usual lecturing tools including a large black-board of a menacing appearance. On referring to lists of the courses of lectures that had been given in this thriving Hall, I fancied I detected a shyness in admitting that human nature when at leisure has any desire whatever to be relieved and diverted; and a furtive sliding in of any poor make-weight piece of amusement, shamefacedly and edgewise. Thus, I observed that it was necessary for the members to be knocked on the head with Gas, Air, Water, Food, the Solar System, the Geological periods, Criticism on Milton, the Steam-engine, John Bunyan, and Arrow-Headed Inscriptions, before they might be tickled by those unaccountable choristers, the negro singers in the court costume of the reign of George the Second. Likewise, that they must be stunned by a weighty inquiry whether there was internal evidence in SHAKESPEARE's works, to prove that his uncle by the mother's side lived for some years at Stoke Newington, before they were brought-to by a Miscellaneous Concert. But indeed the masking of entertainment, and pretending it was something else—as people mask bedsteads when they are obliged to have them in sitting-rooms, and make believe that they are book cases, sofas, chests of drawers, any thing rather than bedsteads—was manifest even in the pretense of dreariness that the unfortunate entertainers themselves felt obliged in decency to put forth when they came here. One very agreeable professional singer who traveled with two professional ladies, knew better than to introduce either of those ladies to sing the ballad "Comin' through the Rye," without prefacing it himself, with some general remarks on wheat and clover; and even then, he dared not for his life call the song, a song, but disguised it in the bill as an "Illustration." In the library, also—fitted with shelves for three thousand books, and containing upward of one hundred and seventy (presented copies mostly) seething their edges in damp plaster—there was such a painfully apologetic return of sixty-two offenders who had read Travels, Popular Biography, and mere Fiction descriptive of the aspirations of the hearts and souls of mere human creatures like themselves; and such an elaborate parade of two bright examples who had had down Euclid, after the day's occupation and confinement; and three who had had down Metaphysics after ditto; and one who had had down Theology after ditto; and four who had worried Grammar, Political Economy, Botany, and Logarithms all at once after ditto; that I suspected the boasted class to be one man, who had been hired to do it.

Emerging from the Mechanics' Institution and continuing my walk about the town, I still noticed everywhere the prevalence, to an extraordinary degree, of this custom of putting the natural demand for amusement out of sight, as some untidy housekeepers put dust, and pretending that it was swept away. And yet it was ministered to, in a dull and abortive manner, by all who made this feint. Looking in at what is called in Dullborough "the serious bookseller's," where in my childhood, I had studied the faces of numbers of gentlemen depicted in rostrums with a gas-light on each side of them, and casting my eyes over the open pages of certain printed discourses there, I found a vast deal of aiming at jocosity and dramatic effect, even in them—yes, verily, even on the part of one very wrathful expounder who bitterly anathematized a poor little Circus. Similarly in the reading provided for the young people enrolled in the Lasso of Love, and other excellent unions, I found the writers generally under a distressing sense that they must start (at all events) like story-tellers, and delude the young persons into the belief that they were going to be interesting. As I looked in at this window for twenty minutes by the clock, I am in a position to offer a friendly remonstrance—not bearing on this particular point—to the designers and engravers of the pictures in those publications. Have they considered the awful consequences likely to flow from their representations of Virtue? Have they asked themselves the question, whether the terrific prospect of acquiring that fearful chubbiness of head, unwieldiness of arm, feeble dislocation of leg, crispness of hair, and enormity of shirt-collar, which they represent as inseparable from Goodness, may not tend to confirm sensitive waverers, in

Evil? A most impressive example (if I had believed it) of what a Dustman and a Sailor may come to, when they mend their ways, was presented to me in this same shop-window. When they were leaning (they were intimate friends) against a post, drunk and reckless, with surpassingly bad hats on, and their hair over their foreheads, they were rather picturesque, and looked as if they might be agreeable men if they would not be beasts. But when they had got over their bad propensities, and when, as a consequence, their heads had swelled alarmingly, their hair had got so curly that it lifted their blownout cheeks up, their coat-cuffs were so long that they never could do any work, and their eyes were so wide open that they never could do any sleep, they presented a spectacle calculated to plunge a timid nature into the depths of Infamy.

But, the clock that had so degenerated since I saw it last, admonished me that I had stayed here long enough; and I resumed my walk again.

I had not gone fifty paces along the street when I was suddenly brought up by the sight of a man who got out of a little phaeton at the doctor's door, and went into the doctor's house. Immediately, the air was filled with the scent of trodden grass, and the perspective of years opened, and at the end of it was a little likeness of this man keeping a wicket, and I said, "God bless my soul! Joe Specks!"

Through many changes and much work, I had preserved a tenderness for the memory of Joe, forasmuch as we had made the acquaintance of Roderick Random together, and had believed him to be no ruffian, but an ingenuous and engaging hero. Scorning to ask the boy left in the phaeton whether it was really Joe, and scorning even to read the brass plate on the door—so sure was I—I rang the bell and informed the servant maid that a stranger sought audience with Mr. Specks. Into a room, half surgery, half study, I was shown to await his coming, and I found it, by a series of elaborate accidents, bestrewn with testimonies to Joe. Portrait of Mr. Specks, bust of Mr. Specks, silver cup from grateful patient to Mr. Specks, presentation sermon from local clergyman, dedication poem from local poet, dinner-card from local nobleman, tract on balance of power from local refugee, inscribed *Hommage de l'auteur à Specks.*

When my old school-fellow came in, and I informed him with a smile that I was not a patient, he seemed rather at a loss to perceive any reason for smiling in connection with that fact, and inquired to what was he to attribute the honor? I asked him with another smile, could he remember me at all? He had not (he said) that pleasure. I was beginning to have but a poor opinion of Mr. Specks, when he said, reflectively, "And yet there's a something, too." Upon that, I saw a boyish light in his eyes that looked well, and I asked him if he could inform me, as a stranger who desired to know and had not the means of reference at hand, what the name of the young lady was, who married Mr. Random? Upon that, he said "Narcissa," and, after staring for a moment, called me by my name, shook me by the hand, and melted into a roar of laughter. "Why, of course you'll remember Lucy Green," he said, after we had talked a little. "Of course," said I. "Whom do you think she married?" said he. "You?" I hazarded. "Me," said Specks, "and you shall see her." So I saw her, and she was fat, and if all the hay in the world had been heaped upon her, it could scarcely have altered her face more than Time had altered it from my remembrance of the face that had once looked down upon me into the fragrant dungeons of Seringapatam. But when her youngest child came in after dinner (for I dined with them, and we had no other company than Specks, Junior, Barrister-at-Law, who went away as soon as the cloth was removed, to look after the young lady to whom he was going to be married next week), I saw again, in that little daughter, the little face of the hayfield, unchanged, and it quite touched my heart. We talked immensely, Specks and Mrs. Specks, and I, and we spoke of our old selves as though our old selves were dead and gone, and indeed indeed they were—dead and gone, as the playing-field that had become a wilderness of rusty iron, and the property of S. E. R.

Specks, however, illuminated Dullborough with the rays of interest that I wanted and should otherwise have missed in it, and linked its present to its past, with a highly agreeable chain. And in Speck's society I had new occasion to observe what I had before noticed in similar communications among other men. All the school-fellows and others of old, whom I inquired about, had either done superlatively well or superlatively ill—had either become uncertificated bankrupts, or been felonious and got themselves transported; or had made great hits in life, and done wonders. And this is so commonly the case, that I never can imagine what becomes of all the mediocre people of people's youth—especially, considering that we find no lack of the species in our maturity. But I did not propound this difficulty to Specks, for no pause in the conversation gave me an occasion. Nor could I discover one single flaw in the good doctor—when he reads this, he will receive in a friendly spirit the pleasantly meant record—except that he had forgotten his Roderick Random, and that he confounded Strap with Lieutenant Hatchway; who never knew Random, howsoever intimate with Pickle.

When I went alone to the Railway to catch my train at night (Specks had meant to go with me, but was inopportunely called out) I was in a more charitable mood with Dullborough than I had been all day; and yet in my heart I had loved it all day too. Ah! who was I that I should quarrel with the town for being changed to me, when I myself had come back, so changed, to it? All my early readings and early imaginations dated from this place, and I took them away so full of innocent construction and guileless belief, and I brought them back so worn and torn, so much the wiser and so much the worse!

---

Some years ago, a temporary inability to sleep, referable to a distressing impression, caused me to walk about the streets all night, for a series of several nights. The disorder might have taken a long time to conquer, if it had been faintly experimented on in bed; but it was soon defeated by the brisk treatment of getting up directly after lying down, and going out, and coming home tired at sunrise.

In the course of those nights, I finished my education in a fair amateur experience of houselessness. My principal object being to get through the night, the pursuit of it brought me into sympathetic relations with people who have no other object every night in the year.

The month was March, and the weather damp, cloudy, and cold. The sun not rising before half-past five, the night perspective looked sufficiently long at half-past twelve: which was about my time for confronting it.

The restlessness of a great city, and the way in which it tumbles and tosses before it can get to sleep, formed one of the first entertainments offered to the contemplation of us houseless people. It lasted about two hours. We lost a great deal of companionship when the late public-houses turned their lamps out, and when the potmen thrust the last brawling drunkards into the street; but stray vehicles and stray people going home were left us, after that. If we were very lucky, a policeman's rattle sprang and a fray turned up; but, in general, surprisingly little of this diversion was provided. Except in the Haymarket, which is the worst kept part of London, and about Kent-street in the borough, and along a portion of the line of the Old Kent-road, the peace was seldom violently broken. But it was always the case that London, as if in imitation of individual citizens belonging to it, had expiring fits and starts of restlessness. After all seemed quiet, if one cab rattled by, half a dozen would surely follow; and Houselessness even observed that intoxicated people appeared to be magnetically attracted toward each other, so that we knew when we saw one drunken object staggering against the shutters of a shop, that another drunken object would probably stagger up before five minutes were out, to fraternize or fight with it. When we make a divergence from the regular species of drunkard, the thin-armed puff-faced leaden-lipped gin-drinker, and encountered a rarer specimen of a more decent appearance, fifty to one but that specimen was dressed in soiled mourning. As the street experience in the night, so the street experience in the day; the common folk who come unexpectedly into a little property, come unexpectedly into a deal of liquor.

At length these flickering sparks would die away, worn out—the last veritable sparks of waking life trailed from some late pieman or hot potato man—and London would sink to rest. And then the yearning of the houseless mind would be for any sign of company, any lighted place, any movement, any thing suggestive of any one being up—nay, even so much as awake, for the houseless eye looked out for lights in windows.

Walking the streets under the pattering rain, Houselessness would walk and walk and walk, seeing nothing but the interminable tangle of streets, save at a corner, here and there, two policemen in conversation, or the sergeant or inspector looking after his men. Now and then in the night—but rarely—Houselessness would become aware of a furtive head peering out of a doorway a few yards before him, and, coming up with the head, would find a man standing bolt-upright to keep within the doorway's shadow, and evidently intent upon no particular service to society. Under a kind of fascination, and in a ghostly silence suitable to the time, Houselessness and this gentleman would eye one another from head to foot, and so, without exchange of speech, part, mutually suspicious. Drip, drip, drip, from ledge and coping, splash from pipes and water-spouts, and by-and-by the houseless shadow would fall upon the stones that pave the way to Waterloo-bridge; it being in the houseless mind to have a halfpennyworth of excuse for saying "Good-night" to the toll-keeper, and catching a glimpse of his fire. A good fire and a good great-coat and a good woolen neck-shawl, were comfortable things to see in conjunction with the toll-keeper; also his brisk wakefulness was excellent company when he rattled the change of halfpence down upon that metal table of his, like a man who defied the night, with all its sorrowful thoughts, and didn't care for the coming of dawn. There was need of encouragement on the threshold of the bridge, for the bridge was dreary. The chopped up murdered man, had not been lowered with a rope over the parapet when those nights were; he was alive, and slept then quietly enough most likely, and undisturbed by any dream of where he was to come. But the river had an awful look, the buildings on the banks were muffled in black shrouds, and the reflected lights seemed to originate deep in the water, as if the spectres of suicides were holding them to show where they went down. The wild moon and clouds were as restless as an evil conscience in a tumbled bed, and the very shadow of the immensity of London seemed to lie oppressively upon the river.

Between the bridge and the two great theatres, there was but the distance of a few hundred paces, so the theatres came next. Grim and black within, at night, those great dry Wells, and lonesome to imagine, with the rows of faces faded out, the lights extinguished, and the seats all empty. One would think that nothing in them knew itself at such a time but Yorick's skull. In one of my night walks, as the church steeples were shaking the March wind and rain with the strokes of Four, I passed the outer boundary of one of these great deserts, and entered it. With a dim lantern in my hand, I groped my well-known way to the stage and looked over the orchestra—which was like a great grave dug for a time of pestilence—into the void beyond. A dismal cavern of an immense aspect, with the chandelier gone dead like every thing else, and nothing visible through mist and fog and space, but tiers of winding-sheets. The ground at my feet where, when last there, I had seen the peasantry of Naples dancing among the vines, reckless of the burning mountain which threatened to overwhelm them, was now in possession of a strong serpent of engine-hose, watchfully lying in wait for the serpent Fire, and ready to fly at it if it showed its forked tongue. A ghost of a watchman carrying a faint corpse-candle, haunted the distant upper gallery and flitted away. Retiring within the proscenium, and holding my light above my head toward the rolled-up curtain—green no more, but black as ebony—my sight lost itself in a gloomy vault, showing faint indications in it of a shipwreck of canvas and cordage. Methought I felt much as a diver might, at the bottom of the sea.

In those small hours when there was no movement in the streets, it afforded matter for reflection to take Newgate in the way, and, touching its rough stone, to think of the prisoners in their sleep, and then to glance in at the lodge over the spiked wicket, and see the fire and light of the watching turnkeys, on the white wall. Not an inappropriate time either to linger by that wicked little Debtor's Door—shutting tighter than any other door one ever saw—which has been Death's Door to so many. In the days of the uttering of forged one-pound notes by people tempted up from the country, how many hundreds of wretched creatures of both sexes—many quite innocent—swung out of a pitiless and inconsistent world, with the tower of yonder Christian church of Saint Sepulchre monstrously before their eyes! Is there any haunting of the Bank Parlor by the remorseful souls of old directors, in the nights of these later days, I wonder, or is it as quiet as this degenerate Aceldama of an Old Bailey?

To walk on to the Bank, lamenting the good old times and bemoaning the present evil period, would be an easy next step, so I would take it, and would make my houseless circuit of the Bank, and give a thought to the treasure within; likewise to the guard of soldiers passing the night there, and nodding over the fire. Next I went to Billingsgate, in some hope of market-people, but, it proving as yet too early, crossed London-bridge and got down by the water-side on the Surrey shore among the buildings of the great brewery. There was plenty going on at the brewery; and the reek, and the smell of grains, and the rattling of the plump dray horses at their mangers, were capital company. Quite refreshed by having mingled with this good society, I made a new start with a new heart, setting the old King's Bench prison before me for my next object, and resolving, when I should come to the wall, to think of poor Horace Kinch, and the Dry Rot in men.

A very curious disease the Dry Rot in men, and difficult to detect the beginning of. It had carried Horace Kinch inside the wall of the old King's Bench prison, and it had carried him out with his feet foremost. He was a likely man to look at, in the prime of life, well to do, as clever as he needed to be, and popular among many friends. He was suitably married, and had healthy and pretty children. But, like some fair-looking houses or fair-looking ships, he took the Dry Rot. The first strong external revelation of the Dry Rot in men, is a tendency to lurk and lounge; to be at street corners without intelligible reason; to be going anywhere when met; to be about many places rather than at any; to do nothing tangible, but to have an intention of performing a variety of intangible duties to-morrow or the day after. When this manifestation of the disease is observed, the observer will usually connect it with a vague impression once formed or received, that the patient was living a little too hard. He will scarcely have had leisure to turn it over in his mind and form the terrible suspicion "Dry Rot," when he will notice a change for the worse in the patient's appearance: a certain slovenliness and deterioration, which is not poverty, nor dirt, nor intoxication, nor ill-health, but simply Dry Rot. To this, succeeds a smell as of strong waters, in the morning; to that, a looseness respecting money; to that, a stronger smell as of strong waters, at all times; to that, a looseness respecting every thing; to that, a trembling of the limbs, somnolency, misery, and crumbling to pieces. As it is in wood, so it is in men. Dry Rot advances at a compound usury quite incalculable. A plank is found infected with it, and the whole structure is devoted. Thus it had been with the unhappy Horace Kinch, lately buried by a small subscription. Those who knew him had not nigh done saying, "So well off, so comfortably established, with such hope before him—and yet, it is feared, with a slight touch of Dry Rot!" when lo! the man was all Dry Rot and dust.

From the dead wall associated on those houseless nights with this too common story, I chose next to wander by Bethlehem Hospital; partly because it lay on my road round to Westminster; partly, because I had a night-fancy in my head which could be best pursued within sight of its walls and dome. And the fancy was this: Are not the sane and insane equal at night as the sane lie a dreaming? Are not all of us outside this hospital, who dream, more or less in the condition of those inside it, every night of our lives? Are we not nightly persuaded, as they daily are, that we associate preposterously with kings and queens, emperors and empresses, and notabilities of all sorts? Do we not nightly jumble events and personages and times and places, as these do daily? Are we not sometimes troubled by our own sleeping inconsistencies, and do we not vexedly try to account for them or excuse them, just as these do sometimes in respect of their waking delusions? Said an afflicted man to me, when I was last in a hospital like this, "Sir, I can frequently fly." I was half ashamed to reflect that so could I—by night. Said a woman to me on the same occasion, "Queen Victoria frequently comes to dine with me, and her Majesty and I dine off peaches and macaroni in our night-gowns, and his Royal Highness the Prince Consort does us the honor to make a third on horseback in a Field Marshal's uniform." Could I refrain from reddening with consciousness when I remembered the amazing royal parties I myself had given (at night,) the unaccountable viands I had put on table, and my extraordinary manner of conducting myself on those distinguished occasions? I wonder that the great master who knew every thing, when he called Sleep the death of each day's life, did not call Dreams the insanity of each day's sanity.

By this time I had left the Hospital behind me, and was again setting toward the river; and in a short breathing space I was on Westminster bridge, regaling my houseless eyes with the external walls of the British Parliament—the perfection of a stupendous institution, I know, and the admiration of all surrounding nations and succeeding ages, I do not doubt, but perhaps a little the better now and then for being pricked up to its work. Turning off into Old Palace-yard, the Courts of Law kept me company for a quarter of an hour; hinting in low whispers what numbers of people they were keeping awake, and how intensely wretched and horrible they were rendering the small hours to unfortunate suitors. Westminster Abbey was fine gloomy society for another quarter of an hour; suggesting a wonderful procession of its dead among the dark arches and pillars, each century more amazed by the century following it than by all the centuries going before. And indeed in those houseless night walks—which even included cemeteries where watchmen went round among the graves at stated times, and moved the tell-tale handle of an index which recorded that they had touched it at such an hour—it was a solemn consideration what enormous hosts of dead belong to one old great city, and how, if they were raised while the living slept, there would not be the space of a pin's point in all the streets and ways for the living to come out into. Not only that, but the vast armies of dead would overflow the hills and valleys beyond the city, and would stretch away all round it, God knows how far: seemingly, to the confines of the earth.

When a church clock strikes on houseless ears in the dead of the night, it may be at first mistaken for company and hailed as such. But, as the spreading circles of vibration, which you may perceive at such a time with great clearness, go opening out, forever and ever afterward widening perhaps, as the philosopher has suggested, in eternal space, the mistake is rectified and the sense of loneliness is profounder. Once—it was after leaving the Abbey and turning my face north—I came to the great steps of Saint Martin's church as the clock was striking Three. Suddenly, a thing that in a moment more I should have trodden upon without seeing, rose up at my feet with a cry of loneliness and houselessness, struck out of it by the bell, the like of which I never heard. We then stood face to face looking at one another, frightened by one another. The creature was like a beetle-browed hair-lipped youth of twenty, and it had a loose bundle of rags on, which it held together with one of its hands. It shivered from head to foot, and its teeth chattered, and as it stared at me—persecutor, devil, ghost, whatever it thought me—it made with its whining mouth as if it were snapping at me, like a worried dog. Intending to give this ugly object, money, I put out my hand to stay it—for it recoiled as it whined and snapped—and laid my hand upon its shoulder. Instantly, it twisted out of its garment, like the young man in the New Testament, and left me standing alone with its rags in my hand.

Covent Garden Market, when it was market morning, was wonderful company. The great wagons of cabbages, with growers' men and boys lying asleep under them, and with sharp dogs from market-garden neighborhoods looking after the whole, were as good as a party. But one of the worst night-sights I know in London, is to be found in the children who prowl about this place; who sleep in the baskets, fight for the offal, dart at any object they think they can lay their thieving hands on, dive under the carts and barrows, dodge the constables, and are perpetually making a blunt pattering on the pavement of the Piazza with the rain of their naked feet. A painful and unnatural result comes of the comparison one is forced to institute between the growth of corruption as displayed in the so much improved and cared for fruits of the earth, and the growth of corruption as displayed in these all uncared for—except inasmuch as ever-hunted—savages.

There was early coffee to be got about Covent Garden Market, and that was more company--warm company, too, which was better. Toast of a very substantial quality, was likewise procurable: though the towzled-headed man who made it, in an inner chamber within the coffee room, hadn't got his coat on yet, and was so heavy with sleep that in every interval of toast and coffee he went off anew behind the partition into complicated cross-roads of choke and snore, and lost his way directly. Into one of these establishments (among the earliest) near Bow-street, there came, one morning as I sat over my houseless cup, pondering where to go next, a man in a high and long snuff-colored coat, and shoes, and, to the best of my belief, nothing else but a hat, who took out of his hat a large cold meat pudding; a meat pudding so large that it was a very tight fit, and brought the lining of the hat out with it. This mysterious man was known by his pudding, for, on his entering, the man of sleep brought him a pint of hot tea, a small loaf, and a large knife and fork and plate. Left to himself in his box, he stood the pudding on the bare table, and, instead of cutting it, stabbed it, overhand, with the knife, like a mortal enemy; then took the knife out, wiped it on his sleeve, tore the pudding asunder with his fingers, and ate it all up. The remembrance of this man with the pudding remains with me as the remembrance of the most spectral person my houselessness encountered. Twice only was I in that establishment, and twice I saw him stalk in—as I should say, just out of bed, and presently going back to bed,—take out this pudding, stab his pudding, wipe the dagger, and eat his pudding all up. He was a man whose figure promised cadaverousness, but who had an excessively red face, though shaped like a horse's. On the second occasion of my seeing him, he said, huskily, to the man of sleep, "Am I red to-night?" "You are," he uncompromisingly answered. "My mother," said the spectre, "was a red-faced woman that liked drink, and I looked at her hard when she laid in her coffin, and I took the complexion." Somehow, the pudding seemed an unwholesome pudding after that, and I put myself in its way no more.

When there was no market, or when I wanted variety, a railway terminus with the morning mails coming in, was remunerative company. But like most of the company to be had in this world, it lasted only a very short time. The station lamps would burst out ablaze, the porters would emerge from places of concealment, the cabs and trucks would rattle to their places —the post-office carts were already in theirs,—and, finally, the bell would strike up, and the train would come banging in. But there were few passengers and little luggage, and every thing scuttled away with the greatest expedition. The locomotive post-offices, with their great nets—as if they had been dragging the country for bodies—would fly open as to their doors, and would disgorge a smell of lamp, an exhausted clerk, a guard in a red coat, and their bags of letters; the engine would blow and heave and perspire, like an engine wiping its forehead and saying what a run it had had ; and within ten minutes the lamps were out, and I was houseless and alone again.

But now, there were driven cattle on the high road near, wanting (as cattle always do) to turn into the midst of stone walls, and squeeze themselves through six inches' width of iron railing, and getting their heads down, also as cattle always do, for tossing-purchase at quite imaginary dogs, and giving themselves and every devoted creature associated with them a most extraordinary amount of unnecessary trouble. Now, too, the conscious gas began to grow pale with the knowledge that daylight was coming, and straggling work-people were already in the streets, and, as waking life had become extinguished with the last pieman's sparks, so it began to be rekindled with the fires of the first street-corner breakfast-sellers. And so by faster and faster degrees, until the last degrees were very fast, the day came, and I was tired and could sleep. And it is not, as I used to think, going home at such times, the least wonderful thing in London, that in the real desert region of the night the houseless wanderer is alone there. I knew well enough where to find Vice and Misfortune of all kinds, if I had chosen ; but they were put out of sight, and my houselessness had many miles upon miles of streets in which it could, and did, have its own solitary way.

---

HAVING occasion to transact some business with a solicitor who occupies a highly suicidal set of chambers in Gray's Inn,

I afterward took a turn in the large square of that stronghold of Melancholy, reviewing, with congenial surroundings, my experiences of Chambers.

I began, as was natural, with the Chambers I had just left. They were an upper set on a rotten staircase, with a very mysterious bunk or bulkhead on the landing outside them, of a rather nautical and Screw Collier-like appearance than otherwise, and painted an intense black. Many dusty years have passed, since the appropriation of this Davy Jones's locker to any purpose, and during the whole period within the memory of living man, it has been hasped and padlocked. I cannot quite satisfy my mind whether it was originally meant for the reception of coals, or bodies, or as a place of temporary security for the plunder "looted" by laundresses; but I incline to the last opinion. It is about breast-high, and usually serves as a bulk for defendants in reduced circumstances to lean against and ponder at, when they come on the hopeful errand of trying to make an arrangement without money—under which auspicious circumstances it mostly happens that the legal gentleman they want to see, is much engaged, and they pervade the staircase for a considerable period. Against this opposing bulk, in the absurdest manner, the tomb-like outer door of the solicitor's chambers (which is also of an intense black) stands in dark ambush, half open and half shut, all day. The solicitor's apartments are three in number; consisting of a slice, a cell, and a wedge. The slice is assigned to the two clerks, the cell is occupied by the principal, and the wedge is devoted to stray papers, old game-baskets from the country, a washing-stand, and a model of a patent Ship's Caboose which was exhibited in Chancery at the commencement of the present century on an application for an injunction to restrain infringement. At about half-past nine on every week-day morning, the younger of the two clerks (who, I have reason to believe, leads the fashion at Pentonville in the articles of pipes and shirts) may be found knocking the dust out of his official door-key on the bunk or locker before mentioned; and so exceedingly subject to dust is his key, and so very retentive of that superfluity, that in exceptional summer weather when a ray of sunlight has fallen on the locker in my presence, I have noticed its inexpressive countenance to be deeply marked by a kind of Bramah erysipelas or small-pox.

This set of chambers (as I have gradually discovered, when I have had restless occasion to make inquiries or leave messages, after office hours) is under the charge of a lady, in figure extremely like an old family-umbrella, named Sweeney: whose dwelling confronts a dead wall in a court off Gray's Inn-lane, and who is usually fetched into the passage of that bower, when wanted, from some neighboring home of industry which has the curious property of imparting an inflammatory appearance to her visage. Mrs. Sweeney is one of the race of professed laundresses, and is the compiler of a remarkable manuscript volume, entitled "Mrs. Sweeney's Book," from which much curious statistical information may be gathered respecting the high prices and small uses of soda, soap, sand, firewood, and other such articles. I have created a legend in my mind—and consequently I believe it with the utmost pertinacity—that the late Mr. Sweeney was a ticket-porter under the Honorable Society of Gray's Inn, and that, in consideration of his long and valuable services, Mrs. Sweeney was appointed to her present post. For, though devoid of personal charms, I have observed this lady to exercise a fascination over the elderly ticket-porter mind (particularly under the gateway, and in corners and entries), which I can only refer to her being one of the fraternity, yet not competing with it. All that need be said concerning this set of chambers, is said, when I have added that it is in a large double house in Gray's Inn-square, very much out of repair, and that the outer portal is ornamented in a hideous manner with certain stone remains, which have the appearance of the dismembered bust, torso, and limbs, of a petrified bencher.

Indeed, I look upon Gray's Inn generally as one of the most depressing institutions in brick and mortar, known to the children of men. Can any thing be more dreary than its arid Square, Sahara Desert of the law, with the ugly old tile-topped tenements, the dirty windows, the bills To Let To Let, the door-posts inscribed like gravestones, the crazy gateway giving upon the filthy Lane, the scowling iron-barred prison-like passage into Verulam-buildings, the mouldy red-nosed ticket-porters with little coffin plates and why with aprons, the dry hard atomy-like appearance of the whole dust-heap? When my uncommercial travels tend to this dismal spot, my comfort is, its rickety state. Imagination gloats over the fullness of time, when the staircases shall have quite tumbled down—they are daily wearing into an ill-savored powder, but have not quite tumbled down yet—when the last old prolix bencher all of the olden time, shall have been got out of an upper window by means of a Fire-Ladder, and carried off to the Holborn Union; when the last clerk shall have engrossed the last parchment behind the last splash on the last of the mud-stained windows which, all through the miry year, are pilloried out of recognition in Gray's Inn-lane. Then shall a squalid little trench, with rank grass and a pump in it, lying between the coffee-house and South-square, be wholly given up to cats and rats, and not, as now, have its empire divided between those animals and a few briefless bipeds—surely called to the Bar by the voices of deceiving spirits, seeing that they are wanted there by no mortal—who glance down with eyes better glazed than their casements, from their dreary and lack-lustre rooms. Then shall the way Nor' West-ward, now lying under a short grim colonnade where in summer time pounce flies from law-stationering windows into the eyes of laymen, be choked with rubbish and happily become impassable. Then shall the gardens where turf, trees, and gravel wear a legal livery of black, run rank, and pilgrims go to Gorhambury to see Bacon's effigy as he sat, and not come here (which in truth they seldom do) to see where he walked. Then, in a word, shall the old-established vender of periodicals sit alone in his little crib of a shop behind the Holborn Gate, like that lumbering Marius among the ruins of Carthage, who has sat heavy on a thousand million of similes.

At one period of my uncommercial career, I much frequented another set of chambers in Gray's Inn-square. They were what is familiarly called "a top set," and all the eatables and drinkables introduced into them acquired a flavor of Cockloft. I have known an unopened Strasbourg pâté fresh from Fortnum and Mason's, to draw in this cockloft tone through its crockery dish, and become penetrated with cockloft to the core of its inmost truffle in three-quarters of an hour. This, however, was not the most curious feature of those chambers; that, consisted in the profound conviction entertained by my esteemed friend Parkle (their tenant) that they were clean.

Whether it was an inborn hallucination, or whether it was imparted to him by Mrs. Miggot the laundress, I never could ascertain. But I believe he would have gone to the stake upon the question. Now, they were so dirty that I could take off the distinctest impression of my figure on any article of furniture by merely lounging upon it for a few moments; and it used to be a private amusement of mine to print myself off—if I may use the expression—all over the rooms. It was the first large circulation I had. At other times I have accidentally shaken a window-curtain while in animated conversation with Parkle, and struggling insects which were certainly red, and were certainly not ladybirds, have dropped on the back of my hand. Yet Parkle lived in that top set years, bound body and soul to the superstition that they were clean. He used to say, when congratulated upon them, "Well, they are not like chambers in one respect, you know; they are clean." Concurrently, he had an idea which he could never explain, that Mrs. Miggot was in some way connected with the church. When he was in particularly good spirits, he used to believe that a deceased uncle of her's had been a Dean; when he was poorly and low, he believed that her brother had been a Curate. I and Mrs. Miggot (she was a genteel woman) were on confidential terms, but I never knew her to commit herself to any distinct assertion on the subject; she merely claimed a proprietorship in the church by looking, when it was mentioned, as if the reference awakened the slumbering past, and were personal. It may have been his amiable confidence in Mrs. Miggot's better days that inspired my friend with his delusion respecting the chambers, but he never wavered in his fidelity to it for a moment, though he wallowed in dirt seven years.

Two of the windows of these chambers looked down into the garden; and we have sat up there together, many a summer evening, saying how pleasant it was, and talking of many things. To my intimacy with that top set, I am indebted for three of my liveliest personal impressions of the loneliness of life in chambers. They shall follow here, in order; first, second, and third.

First. My Gray's Inn friend, on a time, hurt one of his legs, and it became seriously inflamed. Not knowing of his indisposition, I was on my way to visit him as usual, one summer evening, when I was much surprised by meeting a lively leech in Field court, Gray's Inn, seemingly on his way to the West End of London. As the leech was alone, and was of course unable to explain his position, even if he had been inclined to do so (which he had not the appearance of being), I passed him and went on. Turning the corner of Gray's Inn-square, I was beyond expression amazed by meeting another leech—also entirely alone, and also proceeding in a westerly direction though with less decision of purpose. Ruminating on this extraordinary circumstance and endeavoring to remember whether I had ever read, in the Philosophical Transactions, or any work on Natural History, of a migration of Leeches, I ascended to the top set, past the dreary series of closed outer doors of offices and an empty set or two, which intervened between that lofty region and the surface. Entering my friend's rooms, I found him stretched upon his back, like Prometheus Bound, with a perfectly demented ticket-porter in attendance on him instead of the vulture: which helpless individual, who was feeble and frightened, had (my friend explained to me in great choler) been endeavoring for some hours to apply leeches to his leg, and as yet had only got on two out of twenty. To this unfortunate's distraction between a damp cloth on which he had placed the leeches to freshen them, and the wrathful adjurations of my friend to "Stick 'em on, sir!" I referred the phenomenon I had encountered: the rather as two fine specimens were at that moment going out at the door, while a general insurrection of the rest was in progress on the table. After a while our united efforts prevailed, and when the leeches came off and had recovered their spirits, we carefully tied them up in a decanter. But I never heard more of them than that they were all gone next morning, and that the out-of-door young man of Bickle Bush and Bodger, on the ground floor, had been bitten and blooded by some creature not identified. They never "took" on Mrs. Miggot, the laundress; but I have always preserved fresh, the belief that she unconsciously carried several about her, until they gradually found openings in life.

Second. On the same staircase with my friend Parkle, and on the same floor, there lived a man of law, who pursued his business elsewhere, and used those chambers as his place of residence. For three or four years, Parkle, rather knew of him than knew him, but after that—for Englishmen—short pause of consideration, they began to speak. Parkle exchanged words with him in his private character only, and knew nothing of his manners, ways, or means. He was a man a good deal about town, but always alone. We used to remark to one another, that although we often encountered him in theatres, concert-rooms, and similar public places, he was always alone. Yet he was not a gloomy man, and was of a decidedly conversational turn; insomuch that he would sometimes of an evening lounge with a cigar in his mouth, half in, half out of Parkle's rooms, and discuss the topics of the day by the hour. He used to hint on these occasions that he had four faults to find with life: firstly that a man was always winding up his watch; secondly, that London was too small; thirdly, that it therefore wanted variety; fourthly, that there was too much dust in it. There was so much dust in his own faded chambers, certainly, that they reminded me of a sepulchre, furnished in prophetic anticipation of the present time, which had newly been brought to light, after having lain buried a few thousand years. One dry, hot autumn evening at twilight, this gentleman, being then five years turned of fifty, looked in upon Parkle in his usual lounging way, with his cigar in his mouth as usual, and said, "I am going out of town." As he never went out of town, Parkle said, "Oh indeed, at last?" "Yes," says he, "at last. For what is a man to do? London is so small! If you go West, you come to Hounslow. If you go East, you come to Bow. If you go South, there's Brixton or Norwood. If you go North, you can't get rid of Barnet. Then the monotony of all the streets, streets, streets—and of all the roads, roads, roads—and the dust,

dust, dust!" When he had said this, he wished Parkle a good evening, but came back again and said, with his watch in his hand, "Oh, I really cannot go on winding up this watch over and over again; I wish you would take care of it." So Parkle laughed, and consented, and he went out of town. He remained out of town so long, that his letter-box became choked, and no more letters could be got into it, and they began to be left at the lodge and to accumulate there. At last the head-porter decided on a conference with the steward to use his master's key and look into the chambers, and give them the benefit of a whiff of air. Then it was found that he had hanged himself to his bedstead, and had left this written memorandum: "I should prefer to be cut down by my neighbor and friend (if he will allow me to call him so), Mr. Parkle." This was the end of Parkle's occupancy of chambers, and he went into lodgings immediately.

Third. While Parkle lived in Gray's Inn, and I myself was uncommercially preparing for the Bar—which is done, as every body knows, by having a frayed old gown put on in a pantry by an old woman in a chronic state of Saint Anthony's fire and dropsy, and so decorated, bolting a bad dinner in a party of four, whereof each individual mistrusts the other three—I say, while these things were, there was a certain elderly gentleman who lived in a court of the Temple, and was a great judge and lover of port wine. Every day he dined at his club and drank his bottle or two of port wine, and every night came home to the Temple and went to bed in his lonely chambers. This had gone on without variation, when one night he had a fit on coming home, and fell and cut his head deep, but partly recovered and groped about in the dark to find the door. When he was afterward discovered, dead, it was clearly established by the marks of his hands about the room that he must have done so. Now, this chanced on the night of Christmas Eve, and over him lived a young fellow who had sisters and young friends, and who gave them a little party that night, in the course of which they played at Blindman's Buff. They played that game, for greater sport, by the light of the fire only, and once when they were all quietly nestling and stealing about, and the blindman was trying to pick out the prettiest sister (for which I am far from blaming him), somebody said, "Hark! The man below must surely be playing Blindman's Buff by himself to-night!" They listened and they heard sounds of some one falling about and stumbling against furniture, and they all laughed at the conceit, and went on with their play more light-hearted and merry than before. Thus those two so different games of life and death were played out together, blindfold, in the two sets of chambers.

These are the occurrences which, coming to my knowledge, imbued me long ago with a strong sense of the loneliness of chambers. There was a fantastic illustration to much the same purpose, implicitly believed by a strange sort of man, now dead, whom I knew when I had not quite arrived at legal years of discretion, though I was already in the uncommercial line.

This was a man who, though not more than thirty, had seen the world in divers irreconcilable capacities—had been an officer in a South American regiment, among other odd things—but had not achieved much in any way of life, and was constitutionally in debt, and hiding. He occupied chambers of the dreariest nature in Lyons Inn; his name, however, was not upon the door, or door-post, but in lieu of it stood the name of a friend who had died in the chambers, and had given him the furniture. The story arose out of the furniture, and was to this effect: Let the former holder of the chambers, whose name was still upon the door and door-post, be Mr. Testator.

Mr. Testator took a set of chambers in Lyons Inn when he had but very scanty furniture for his bedroom, and none for his sitting-room. He had lived some wintry months in this condition, and had found it very bare and cold. One night past midnight, when he sat writing and had still writing to do that must be done before he went to bed, he found himself out of coals. He had coals down stairs, but had never been to the cellar; however, the cellar-key was on his mantel-shelf, and if he went down and opened the cellar it fitted, he might fairly assume the coals in that cellar to be his. As to his laundress, she lived among the coal-wagons and Thames watermen—for there were Thames watermen at that time—in some unknown rat-hole by the river, down lanes and alleys on the other side of the Strand. As to any other person to meet him or obstruct him, Lyons Inn was dreaming, drunk, maudlin, moody, betting, brooding over bill-discounting or renewing: asleep or awake, minding its own affairs. Mr. Testator took his coalscuttle in one hand, his candle and key in the other, and descended to the dismallest dens of Lyons Inn, where the late vehicles in the streets became thunderous, and all the water-pipes in the neighborhood seemed to have Macbeth's Amen sticking in their throats, and to be trying to get it out. After groping here and there among low doors to no purpose, Mr. Testator at length came to a door with a rusty padlock, which his key fitted. Getting the door open with much trouble, and looking in, he found, no coals, but a confused pile of furniture. Alarmed by this intrusion on another man's property, he locked the door again, found his own cellar, filled his scuttle, and returned up-stairs.

But the furniture he had seen ran on castors across and across Mr. Testator's mind incessantly, when, in the chill hour of five in the morning he got to bed. He particularly wanted a table to write at, and a table expressly made to be written at, had been the piece of furniture in the foreground of the heap. When the laundress emerged from her burrow in the morning to make his kettle boil, he artfully led up to the subject of cellars and furniture; but the two ideas had evidently no connection in her mind. When she left him, and he sat at his breakfast, thinking about the furniture, he recalled the rusty state of the padlock, and inferred that the furniture must have been stored in the cellars for a long time—was perhaps forgotten—owner dead, perhaps? After thinking it over a few days, in the course of which he could pump nothing out of Lyons Inn about the furniture, he became desperate, and resolved to borrow that table. He did so that night. He had not had the table long, when he determined to borrow an easy-chair; he had not had that long, when he made up his mind to borrow a bookcase; then a couch; then a carpet and rug. By that time, he felt he was "in furniture stepped in so far," as that it could be no worse to borrow it all. Consequently he borrowed it all, and locked up the cellar for good

He had always locked it, after every visit. He had carried up every separate article in the dead of the night, and, at the best, had felt like a Resurrection Man. Every article was blue and furry when brought into his rooms, and he had had, in a murderous and wicked sort of way, to polish it up while London slept.

Mr. Testator lived in his furnished chambers two or three years, or more, and gradually lulled himself into the opinion that the furniture was his. This was his convenient state of mind when, late one night, a step came up the stairs, and a hand passed over his door feeling for his knocker, and then one deep and solemn rap was rapped that might have been a spring in Mr. Testator's easy-chair to shoot him out of it: so promptly was it attended with that effect.

With a candle in his hand, Mr. Testator went to the door, and found there a very pale and very tall man; a man who stooped; a man with very high shoulders, a very narrow chest, and a very red ones; the shabby genteel man was wrapped in a long threadbare black coat, fastened up the front with more pins than buttons, and under his arm he squeezed an umbrella without a handle, as if he was playing bagpipes. He said, "I ask your pardon, sir, but can you tell me——" and stopped; his eye resting on some object within the chambers.

"Can I tell you what?" asked Mr. Testator, noting this stoppage with quick alarm.

"I ask your pardon," said the stranger, "but—this is not the inquiry I was going to make—DO I see in there any small article of property belonging to *me*?"

Mr. Testator was beginning to stammer that he was not aware—when the visitor slipped past him, into the chambers. There, in a goblin way that froze Mr. Testator to the marrow, he examined, first, the writing-table, and said, "Mine;" then, the easy-chair, and said, "Mine;" then, the bookcase, and said, "Mine;" then turned up a corner of the carpet, and said, "Mine;" in a word, inspected every item of furniture from the cellar, in succession, and said, "Mine!" Toward the end of this investigation, Mr. Testator perceived that he was sodden with liquor, and that the liquor was gin. He was not unsteady with gin, either in his speech or carriage ; but he was stiff with gin in both respects.

Mr. Testator was in a dreadful state, for (according to his making out of the story) the possible consequences of what he had done in recklessness and hardihood flashed upon him in their fullness for the first time. When they had stood gazing at one another for a little while, he tremulously began :

"Sir, I am conscious that the fullest explanation, compensation, and restitution, are your due. They shall be yours. Allow me to entreat that without temper, without even natural irritation on your part, we may have a little——"

"Drop of something to drink," interposed the stranger. "I am agreeable."

Mr. Testator had intended to say, "a little quiet conversation," but with great relief of mind adopted the amendment. He produced a decanter of gin, and was bustling about for hot water and sugar, when he found that his visitor had already drunk half of the decanter's contents. With hot water and sugar the visitor drank the remainder before he had been an hour in the chambers by the chimes of the church of Saint Mary in the Strand, and during the process he frequently repeated to himself, "Mine !"

The gin gone, the visitor rose and said, with increased stiffness, "At what hour of the morning sir, will it be convenient ?" Mr. Testator hazarded, "At ten ?" "Sir," said the visitor, "at ten, to the moment, I shall be here." He then contemplated Mr. Testator somewhat at leisure, and said, "God bless you ! How is your wife ?" Mr. Testator, who never had a wife, replied, "Deeply anxious, poor soul, but otherwise well." The visitor thereupon turned and went away, and fell twice in going down stairs. From that hour he was never heard of. Whether he was a ghost, or a spectral illusion, or a drunken man who had no business there, or the drunken rightful owner of the furniture, who had that business there; whether he got safe home, or had no home to get to ; whether he died of liquor on the way, or lived in liquor ever afterward; he never was heard of more. This was the story received with the furniture, held to be as substantial, by its second possessor in an upper set of chambers in grim Lyons Inn.

It is to be remarked of chambers in general, that they must have been built for chambers, to have the right kind of loneliness. You may make a great dwelling-house very lonely by isolating suites of rooms and calling them chambers, but you cannot make the true kind of loneliness. In dwelling-houses there have been family festivals; children have grown in them, girls have bloomed into women in them, courtships and marriages have taken place in them. True chambers never were young, childish, maidenly; never had dolls in them, or rocking-horses, or christenings, or betrothals, or little coffins. Let Gray's Inn identify the child who first touched hands and hearts with Robinson Crusoe, in any one of its many "sets," and that child's little statue, in white marble, shall be at its service, at my cost and charge, as a drinking fountain for the spirit, to freshen its dry square. Let Lincoln's produce from all its houses a twentieth of the possession derivable from any dwelling-house, or twentieth of its age, of fair young brides who married for love and hope, not settlements, and all the Vice-Chancellors shall thenceforward be kept in nosegays for nothing, on application at this office. It is not denied that on the terrace of the Adelphi, or in any of the streets of that subterranean-stable-haunted spot, or about Bedford-row, or James-street of that ilk (a grewsome place,) or anywhere among the neighborhoods that have done flowering and have run to seed. You may find Chambers replete with the accommodations of Solitude, Closeness, and Darkness, where you may be as low spirited as in the genuine article, and might be as easily murdered, with the placid reputation of having gone down to the sea-side. But the many waters of life did run musical in those dry channels once;—among the Inns, never. The only popular legend known in relation to any one of the dull family of Inns, is a dark Old Bailey whisper concerning Clement's, and imparting how the black creature who holds the sun dial there, was a negro who slew his master and built the dismal pile out of the contents of his strong-box—for which offense alone he ought to have been condemned to live in it. But what populace would waste a fancy upon such a place, or on New Inn, Staple Inn, Barnard's Inn, or any of the shabby crew?

The genuine laundress, too, is an institution not to be had in its entirety out of and away from the genuine Chambers. Again, it is not denied that you may be robbed elsewhere. Elsewhere you may have—for money—dishonesty, drunkenness, dirt, laziness, and profound incapacity. But the veritable shining-red-faced, shameless laundress; the true Mrs. Sweeney, in figure, color, texture, and smell, like the old damp family umbrella; the tiptop complicated abomination of straggling heels and hair, stockings, spirits, bonnet, limpness, looseness, and larceny, is only to be drawn at the fountain-head. Mrs. Sweeney is beyond the reach of individual art. It requires the united efforts of several men to insure that great result, and it is only developed in perfection under an Honorable Society in an Inn of Court.

---

THERE are not many places that I find it more agreeable to revisit when I am in an idle mood, than some places to which I have never been. For, my acquaintance with those spots is of such long standing, and has ripened into an intimacy of so affectionate a nature, that I take a particular interest in assuring myself that they are unchanged.

I never was in Robinson Crusoe's Island, yet I frequently return there. The colony he established on it soon faded away, and it is uninhabited by any descendants of the grave and courteous Spaniards, or of Will Atkins and the other mutineers, and has relapsed into its original condition. Not a twig of its wicker houses remains, its goats have long run wild again, its screaming parrots would darken the sun with a cloud of many flaming colors if a gun were fired there, no face is ever reflected in the waters of the little creek which Friday swam across when pursued by his two brother cannibals with sharpened stomachs. After comparing notes with other travelers who have similarly visited the Island and conscientiously inspected it, I have satisfied myself that it contains no vestige of Mr. Atkins's domesticity or theology, though his track on the memorable evening of his landing to set his captain ashore, when he was decoyed about and round about until it was dark, and his boat was stove, and his strength and spirits ailed him, is yet plainly to be traced. So is the hill-top on which Robinson was struck dumb with joy when the reinstated captain pointed to the ship, riding within half a mile of the shore, that was to bear him away, in the nine-and-twentieth year of his seclusion in that lonely place. So is the sandy beach on which the memorable footstep was impressed, and where the savages hauled up their canoes when they came ashore for those dreadful public dinners, which led to a dancing worse than speech-making. So is the cave where the flaring eyes of the old goat made such a goblin appearance in the dark. So is the site of the hut where Robinson lived with the dog and the parrot and the cat, and where he endured those first agonies of solitude, which—strange to say—never involved any ghostly fancies; a circumstance so very remarkable, that perhaps he left out something in writing his record? Round hundreds of such objects, hidden in the dense tropical foliage, the tropical sea breaks evermore; and over them the tropical sky, saving in the short rainy season, shine bright and cloudless.

Neither, was I ever belated among wolves, on the borders of France and Spain; nor, did I ever, when night was closing in and the ground was covered with snow, draw up my little company among some felled trees which served as a breastwork, and there fire a train of gunpowder so dexterously that suddenly we had three or four score blazing wolves illuminating the darkness around us. Nevertheless, I occasionally go back to that dismal region and perform the feat again; when indeed to smell the singeing and the frying of the wolves afire, and to see them setting one another alight as they rush and tumble, and to behold them rolling in the snow vainly attempting to put themselves out, and to hear their howlings taken up by all the echoes as well as by all the unseen wolves within the woods, makes me tremble.

I was never in the robbers' cave, where Gil Blas lived, but I often go back there and find the trap-door just as heavy to raise as it used to be, while that wicked old disabled Black lies everlastingly cursing in bed. I was never in Don Quixote's study where he read his books of chivalry until he rose and hacked at imaginary giants, and then refreshed himself with great draughts of water, yet you couldn't move a book in it without my knowledge, or with my consent. I was never, thank Heaven, in company with the little old woman who hobbled out of the chest and told the merchant Abudah to go in search of the Talisman of Oromanes, yet I make it my business to know that she is well preserved and as intolerable as ever. I was never at the school where the boy Horatio Nelson got out of bed to steal the pears: not because he wanted any, but because every other boy was afraid: yet I have several times been back to this Academy, to see him let down out of window with a sheet. So with Damascus, and Bagdad, and Brobdingnag, which has the curious fate of being usually misspelt when written, and Lilliput, and Laputa, and the Nile, and Abyssinia, and the Ganges, and the North Pole, and many hundreds of places—I was never at them, yet it is an affair of my life to keep them intact, and I am always going back to them.

But when I was in Dullborough one day, revisiting the associations of my childhood as recorded in previous pages of these notes, my experience in this wise was made quite inconsiderable and of no account, by the quantity of places and people—utterly impossible places and people, but none the less alarmingly real—that I found I had been introduced to by my nurse before I was six years old, and used to be forced to go back to at night without at all wanting to go. If we all knew our own minds (in a more enlarged sense than the popular acceptation of that phrase), I suspect we should find our nurses responsible for most of the dark corners we are forced to go back to, against our wills.

The first diabolical character that intruded himself on my peaceful youth (as I called to mind that day at Dullborough), was a certain Captain Murderer. This wretch must have been an offshoot of the Blue Beard family, but I had no suspicion of the consanguinity in those times. His warning name would seem to have awakened no general prejudice against him, for he was admitted into the best society and possessed immense wealth. Captain Murderer's mission was matrimony, and the gratification of a cannibal appetite with tender brides. On his marriage morning, he always caused both sides of the way to church to be planted with curious flowers; and when his bride said, "Dear Captain Murderer, I never saw flowers like these before: what are they called?" he answered, "They are called Garnish for house-lamb," and laughed at his ferocious practical joke in a horrid manner, disquieting the minds of the noble bridal company, with a very sharp show of teeth, then displayed for the first time. He made love in a coach and six, and married in a coach and twelve, and all his horses were milk-white horses with one red spot on the back which he caused to be hidden by the harness. For, the spot *would* come there, though every horse was milk-white when Captain Murderer bought him. And the spot was young bride's blood. (To this terrific point I am indebted for my first personal experience of a shudder and cold beads on the forehead.) When Captain Murderer had made an end of feasting and revelry, and had dismissed the noble guests, and was alone with his wife on the day month after their marriage, it was his whimsical custom to produce a golden rolling-pin and a silver pie-board. Now, there was this special feature in the Captain's courtships, that he always asked if the young lady could make pie-crust; and if she couldn't by nature or education, she was taught. Well. When the bride saw Captain Murderer produce the golden rolling-pin and silver pie-board, she remembered this, and turned up her laced-silk sleeves to make a pie. The Captain brought out a silver pie-dish of immense capacity, and the Captain brought out flour and butter and eggs and all things needful, except the inside of the pie; of materials for the staple of the pie itself, the Captain brought out none. Then said the lovely bride, "Dear Captain Murderer, what pie is this to be?" He replied, "A meat pie." Then said the lovely bride, "Dear Captain Murderer, I see no meat." The Captain humorously retorted, "Look in the glass." She looked in the glass, but still she saw no meat, and then the Captain roared with laughter, and, suddenly frowning and drawing his sword, bade her roll out the crust. So she rolled out the crust, dropping large tears upon it all the time because he was so cross, and when she had lined the dish with crust and had cut the crust all ready to fit the top, the Captain called out, "*I* see the meat in the glass!" And the bride looked up at the glass, just in time to see the Captain cutting her head off; and he chopped her in pieces, and peppered her, and salted her, and put her in the pie, and sent to the baker's, and ate it all, and picked the bones.

Captain Murderer went on in this way, prospering exceedingly, until he came to choose a bride from two twin sisters, and at first didn't know which to choose. For though one was fair and the other dark, they were both equally beautiful. But the fair twin loved him, and the dark twin hated him, so he chose the fair one. The dark twin would have prevented the marriage if she could, but she couldn't; however, on the night before it, much suspecting Captain Murderer, she stole out and climbed his garden wall, and looked in at his window through a chink in the shutter, and saw him having his teeth filed sharp. Next day she listened all day, and heard him make his joke about the house-lamb. And that day month, he had the paste rolled out, and cut the fair twin's head off, and chopped her in pieces, and peppered her, and salted her, and put her in the pie, and sent it to the baker's, and ate it all, and picked the bones.

Now, the dark twin had had her suspicions much increased by the filing of the Captain's teeth, and again by the house-lamb joke. Putting all things together when he gave out that her sister was dead, she divined the truth, and determined to be revenged. So she went up to Captain Murderer's house, and knocked at the knocker and pulled at the bell, and when the Captain came to the door, said: "Dear Captain Murderer, marry me next, for I always loved you and was jealous of my sister." The Captain took it as a compliment, and made a polite answer, and the marriage was quickly arranged. On the night before it, the bride again climbed to his window, and again saw him having his teeth filed sharp. At this sight, she laughed such a terrible laugh, at the chink in the shutter, that the Captain's blood curdled, and he said: "I hope nothing has disagreed with me!" At that she laughed again, a still more terrible laugh, and the shutter was opened and search made, but she was nimbly gone and there was no one. Next day they went to church in the coach and twelve, and were married. And that day month, she rolled the pie-crust out, and Captain Murderer cut her head off, and chopped her in pieces, and peppered her, and salted her, and put her in the pie, and sent it to the baker's, and ate it all, and picked the bones.

But before she began to roll out the paste she had taken a deadly poison of a most awful character, distilled from toads' eyes and spiders' knees; and Captain Murderer had hardly picked her last bone, when he began to swell, and to turn blue, and to be all over spots, and to scream. And he went on swelling and turning bluer and being more all over spots and screaming, until he reached from floor to ceiling and from wall to wall; and then, at one o'clock in the morning, he blew up with a loud explosion. At the sound of it, all the milk-white horses in the stables broke their halters and went mad, and then they galloped over every body in Captain Murderer's house (beginning with the family blacksmith who had filed his teeth) until the whole were dead, and then they galloped away.

Hundreds of times did I hear this legend of Captain Murderer, in my early youth, and added hundreds of times was there a mental compulsion upon me in bed, to peep in at his window as the dark twin peeped, and to revisit his horrible house, and look at him in his blue and spotty and screaming stage, as he reached from floor to ceiling and from wall to wall. The young woman who brought me acquainted with Captain Murderer, had a fiendish enjoyment of my terrors, and used to begin, I remember—as a sort of introductory overture—by clawing the air with both hands, and uttering a long low hollow groan. So acutely did I suffer from this ceremony in combination with this infernal Captain, that I sometimes used to plead I thought I was hardly strong enough and old enough to hear the story again just yet. But she never spared me one word of it, and indeed commended the awful chalice to my lips as the only preservative known to science against "The Black Cat"—a weird and glaring-eyed supernatural Tom, who was reputed to prowl about the world by night, sucking the breath of infancy, and who was endowed with a special thirst (as I was given to understand) for mine.

This female bard—may she have been repaid my debt of obligation to her in the matter of nightmares and perspirations!—reappears in my memory as the daughter of a shipwright. Her name was Mercy, though she had none on me. There was something of a shipbuilding flavor in the following story. As it always recurs to me in a vague association with calomel pills, I believe it to have been reserved for dull nights when I was low with medicine.

There was once a shipwright, and he wrought in a Government Yard, and his name was Chips. And his father's name before him was Chips, and *his* father's name before *him* was Chips, and they were all Chipses. And Chips the father had sold himself to the Devil for an iron pot and a bushel of tenpenny nails and a half a ton of copper and a rat that could speak; and Chips the grandfather had sold himself to the Devil for an iron pot and a bushel of tenpenny nails and half a ton of copper and a rat that could speak; and Chips the great-grandfather had disposed of himself in the same direction on the same terms; and the bargain had run in the family for a long long time. So one day when young Chips was at work in the Dock Slip all alone, down in the dark hold of an old Seventy-four that was hauled up for repairs, the Devil presented himself and remarked:

"A Lemon has pips,
And a Yard has ships,
And *I'll* have Chips!"

(I don't know why, but this fact of the Devil's expressing himself in rhyme was peculiarly trying to me.) Chips looked up when he heard the words, and there he saw the Devil with saucer eyes that squinted on a terrible great scale, and that struck out sparks of blue fire continually. And whenever he winked his eyes, showers of blue sparks came out, and his eyelashes made a clattering like flints and steels striking lights. And hanging over one of his arms by the handle was an iron pot, and under that arm was a bushel of tenpenny nails, and under his other arm was half a ton of copper, and sitting on one of his shoulders was a rat that could speak. So the Devil said again:

"A Lemon has pips,
And a Yard has ships,
And *I'll* have Chips!"

(The invariable effect of this alarming tautology on the part of the Evil Spirit was to deprive me of my senses for some moments.) So Chips answered never a word, but went on with his work. "What are you doing, Chips?" said the rat that could speak. "I am putting in new planks where you and your gang have eaten the old ones away," said Chips. "But we'll eat them too," said the rat that could speak; "and we'll let in the water, and we'll drown the crew, and we'll eat them too." Chips, being only a shipwright, and not a Man-of-war's man, said, "You are welcome to it." But he couldn't keep his eyes off the half a ton of copper, or the bushel of tenpenny nails; for nails and copper are a shipwright's sweethearts, and shipwrights will run away with them whenever they can. So the Devil said, "I see what you are looking at, Chips. You had better strike the bargain. You know the terms. Your father before you was well acquainted with them, and so were your grandfather and your great-grandfather before him." Says Chips, "I like the copper, and I like the nails, and I don't mind the pot, but I don't like the rat." Says the Devil, fiercely, "You can't have the metal without him—and *he's* a curiosity. I'm going." Chips, afraid of losing the half a ton of copper and the bushel of nails, then said, "Give us hold!" So he got the copper and the nails and the pot and the rat that could speak, and the Devil vanished.

Chips sold the copper, and he sold the nails, and he would have sold the pot; but whenever he offered it for sale, the rat was in it, and the dealers dropped it, and would have nothing to say to the bargain. So Chips resolved to kill the rat, and, being at work in the Yard one day with a great kettle of hot pitch on one side of him and the iron pot with the rat in it on the other, he turned the scalding pitch into the pot, and filled it full. Then he kept his eye upon it till it cooled and hardened, and then he let it stand for twenty days, and then he heated the pitch again and turned it back into the kettle, and then he sank the pot in water for twenty days more, and then he got the smelters to put it in the furnace for twenty days more, and then they gave it him out, red hot, and looking like red-hot glass instead of iron—yet there was the rat in it, just the same as ever! And the moment it caught his eye, it said with a jeer:

"A Lemon has pips,
And a Yard has ships,
And *I'll* have Chips!"

(For this Refrain I had waited since its last appearance, with inexpressible horror, which now culminated.) Chips now felt certain in his own mind that the rat would stick to him; the rat, answering his thought, said, "I will—like pitch!"

Now, as the rat leaped out of the pot when it had spoken, and made off, Chips began to hope that it wouldn't keep its word. But a terrible thing happened next day. For, when dinner time came and the Dock-bell rang to strike work, he put his rule into the long pocket at the side of his trowsers, and there he found a rat—not that rat, but another rat. And in his hat, he found another; and in his pocket handkerchief, another; and in the sleeves of his coat, when he pulled it on to go to dinner, two more. And from that time he found himself so frightfully intimate with all the rats in the Yard, that they climbed up his legs when he was at work, and sat on his tools while he used them. And they could all speak to one another, and he understood what they said. And they got into his lodging, and into his bed, and into his teapot, and into his beer, and into his boots. And he was going to be married to a corn-chandler's daughter; and when he gave her a workbox he had himself made for her, a rat jumped out of it; and when he put his arm round her waist, a rat clung about her; so the marriage was broken off, though the bans were already twice put up—which the parish clerk well remembers, for, as he handed the book to the clergyman for the second time of asking, a large fat rat ran over the leaf. (By this time a special cascade of rats was rolling down my back, and the whole of my small listening person was overrun with them. At intervals ever since, I have been morbidly afraid of my own pocket, lest my exploring hand should find a specimen or two of those vermin in it.)

You may believe that all this was very terrible to Chips; but even all this was not the worst. He knew besides, what the rats were doing, wherever they were. So sometimes he would cry aloud, when he was at his club at night, "Oh! Keep the rats out of the convicts' burying-ground! Don't let them do that!" Or, "There's one of them at the cheese down stairs!" Or, "There's two of smelling them at the baby in the garret!" Or other things of that sort. At last he was voted mad, and lost his work in the Yard, and could get no other work. But King George wanted men, so before very long he got pressed for a sailor. And so he was taken off in a boat one evening to his ship, lying at Spithead, ready to sail. And so the first thing he made out in her as he got near her, was the figure-head of the old Seventy-four, where he had seen the Devil. She was called the Argonaut, and they rowed right under the bowsprit where the figure-head of the Argonaut, with a sheepskin in his hand and a blue gown on, was looking out to sea; and sitting staring on his forehead was the rat who could speak, and his exact words were these: "Chips ahoy! Old boy! We've pretty well eat them too, and we'll drown the crew, and will eat them too!" (Here I always became exceedingly faint, and would have asked for water, but that I was speechless.)

The ship was bound for the Indies; and if you don't know where that is, you ought to and angels will never love you. (Here I felt myself an outcast from a future state.) The ship set sail that very night, and she sailed, and sailed, and sailed. Chips's feelings were dreadful. Nothing ever equaled his terrors. No wonder. At last, one day he asked leave to speak to the Admiral. The Admiral giv' leave. Chips went down on his knees in the Great State Cabin. "Your Honor, unless your Honor, without a moment's loss of time makes sail for the nearest shore, this is a doomed ship, and her name is the coffin!" "Young man, your words are a madman's words." "Your Honor, no; they are nibbling us away," "They?" "Your Honor, them dreadful rats. Dust and hollowness where solid oak ought to be! Rats nibbling a grave for every man on board! Oh! Does your Honor love your Lady and your pretty children?" "Yes, my man, to be sure." "Then, for God's sake make for the nearest shore, for at this present moment the rats are all stopping in their work, and are all looking straight toward you with bare teeth, and are all saying to one another that you shall never, never, never, never, see your Lady and your children more." "My poor fellow you are a case for the doctor. Sentry, take care of this man!"

So he was bled and he was blistered, and he was this and

that, for six whole days and nights. So then he again asked leave to speak to the Admiral. The Admiral giv' leave. He went down on his knees in the Great State Cabin. "Now, Admiral, you must die! You took no warning; you must die! The rats are never wrong in their calculations, and they make out that they'll be through at twelve to-night. So, you must die!—With me and all the rest!" And so at twelve o'clock there was a great leak reported in the ship, and a torrent of water rushed in and nothing could stop it, and they all went down, every living soul. And what the rats—being water-rats—left of Chips, at last floated to shore, and sitting on him was an immense overgrown rat, laughing, that dived when the corpse touched the beach and never came up. And there was a deal of seaweed on the remains. And if you get thirteen bits of seaweed, and dry them and burn them in the fire, they will go—off—like in these thirteen words as plain as plain can be ·

"A Lemon has pips,
And a Yard has ships,
And *I*'ve got Chips!"

The same female bard—descended, possibly, from those terrible old Scalds who seem to have existed for the express purpose of addling the brains of mankind when they begin to investigate languages—made a standing pretense which greatly assisted in forcing me back to a number of hideous places that I would by all means have avoided. This pretense was, that all her ghost stories had occurred to her own relations. Politeness toward a meritorious family, therefore forbade my doubting them, and they acquired an air of authentication that impaired my digestive powers for life. There was a narrative concerning an unearthly animal foreboding death, which appeared in the open street to a parlor-maid who "went to fetch the beer" for supper: first (as I now recall it) assuming the likeness of a black dog, and gradually rising on its hind-legs and swelling into the semblance of some quadruped greatly surpassing a hippopotamus: which apparition—not because I deemed it in the least improbable, but because I felt it to be really too large to bear—I feebly endeavored to explain away. But on Mercy's retorting with wounded dignity that the parlor-maid was her own sister-in-law, I perceived there was no hope, and resigned myself to this zoological phenomenon as one of my many pursuers. There was another narrative describing the apparition of a young woman who came out of a glass-case and haunted another young woman until the other young woman questioned it and elicited that its bones (Lord! To think of its being so particular about its bones!) were buried under the glass-case, whereas she required them to be interred, with every Undertaking solemnity up to twenty-four pound ten, in another particular place. This narrative I considered I had a personal interest in disproving, because we had glass-cases at home, and how, otherwise, was I to be guaranteed from the intrusion of young women requiring *me* to bury them up to twenty-four pound ten, when I had only twopence a week? But my remorseless nurse cut the ground from under my tender feet, by informing me that She was the other young woman; and I couldn't say "I don't believe you;" it was not possible.

Such are a few of the uncommercial journeys that I was forced to make, against my will, when I was very young and unreasoning. And really, as to the latter part of them, it is not so very long ago—now I come to think of it—that I was asked to undertake them once again, with a steady countenance.

---

Being in a humor for complete solitude and uninterrupted meditation this autumn, I have taken a lodging for six weeks in the most unfrequented part of England—in a word, in London.

The retreat into which I have withdrawn myself, is Bond street. From this lonely spot I make pilgrimages into the surrounding wilderness, and traverse extensive tracts of the Great Desert. The first solemn feeling of isolation overcome, the first oppressive consciousness of profound retirement conquered, I enjoy that sense of freedom, and feel reviving within me that latent wildness of the original savage which has been (upon the whole somewhat frequently) noticed by Travelers.

My lodgings are at a hatter's—my own hatter's. After exhibiting no articles in his window for some weeks, but sea-side wide-awakes, shooting-caps, and a choice of rough water-proof head-gear for the moors and mountains, he has put upon the heads of his family as much of this stock as they could carry, and has taken them off to the Isle of Thanet. His young man alone remains—and remains alone—in the shop. The young man has let out the fire at which the irons are heated, and, saving his strong sense of duty, I see no reason why he should take the shutters down.

Happily for himself and for his country, the young man is a Volunteer; most happily for himself, or I think he would become the prey of a settled melancholy. For, to live surrounded by human hats, and alienated from human heads to fit them on, is surely a great endurance. But the young man, sustained by practicing his exercise, and by constantly furbishing up his regulation plume (it is unnecessary to observe that, as a hatter, he is in a cock's-feather corps), is resigned, and uncomplaining. On a Saturday, when he closes early and gets his knickerbockers on, he is even cheerful. I am gratefully particular in this reference to him, because he is my companion through many peaceful hours. My hatter has a desk up certain steps behind his counter, inclosed like the clerk's desk at Church. I shut myself into this place of seclusion, after breakfast and meditate. At such times, I observe the young man loading an imaginary rifle with the greatest precision, and maintaining a most galling and destructive fire upon the national enemy. I thank him publicly for his companionship and his patriotism.

The simple character of my life, and the calm nature of the scenery by which I am surrounded, occasion me to rise early. I go forth in my slippers, and promenade the pavement. It is pastoral to feel the freshness of the air in the uninhabited town, and to appreciate the shepherdess character of the few milk-women who purvey so little milk that it would be worth nobody's while to adulterate it, if any body were left to undertake the task. On the crowded sea-shore, the great demand for milk, combined with the strong local temptation of chalk, would betray itself in the lowered quality of the article. In Arcadian London, I derive it from the cow.

The Arcadian simplicity of the metropolis altogether, and

the primitive ways into which it has fallen in this autumnal Golden Age, make it entirely new to me. Within a few hundred yards of my retreat, is the house of a friend who maintains a most sumptuous butler. I never, until yesterday, saw that butler out of superfine black broad cloth. Until yesterday, I never saw him off duty, never saw him (he is the best of butlers) with the appearance of having any mind for any thing but the glory of his master and his master's friends. Yesterday morning, walking in my slippers near the house of which he is the prop and ornament—a house now a waste of shutters—I encountered that butler, also in his slippers, and in a shooting suit of one color, and in a low-crowned straw hat, smoking an early cigar. He felt that we had formerly met in another state of existence, and that we were translated into a new sphere. Wisely and well, he passed me without recognition. Under his arm he carried the morning paper, and shortly afterward I saw him sitting on a rail in the pleasant open landscape of Regent-street, perusing it at his ease under the ripening sun.

My landlord having taken his whole establishment to be salted down, I am waited on by an elderly woman laboring under a chronic sniff, who, at the shadowy hour of half-past nine o'clock of every evening, gives admittance at the street door to a meagre and mouldy old man whom I have never yet seen detached from a flat pint of beer in a pewter pot. The meagre and mouldy old man is her husband, and the pair have a dejected consciousness that they are not justified in appearing on the surface of the earth. They come out of some hole when London empties itself, and go in again when it fills. I saw them arrive on the evening when I myself took possession, and they arrived with the flat pint of beer, and their bed in a bundle. The old man is a weak old man, and appeared to me to get the bed down the kitchen stairs by tumbling down with and upon it. They make their bed in the lowest and remotest corner of the basement, and they smell of bed, and have no possession but bed; unless it be (which I rather infer from an under-current of flavor in them) cheese. I know their name, through the chance of having called the wife's attention, at half-past nine on the second evening of our acquaintance, to the circumstance of there being some one at the house door; when she apologetically explained, "It's on'y Mister Klem." What becomes of Mr. Klem all day, or when he goes out, or why, is a mystery I cannot penetrate; but at half-past nine he never fails to turn up on the door-step with the flat pint of beer. And the pint of beer, flat as it is, is so much more important than himself, that it always seems to my fancy as if it had found him driveling in the street and had humanely brought him home. In making his way below, Mr. Klem never goes down the middle of the passage, like another Christian, but shuffles against the wall as if entreating me to take notice that he is occupying as little space as possible in the house; and whenever I come upon him face to face, he backs from me in fascinated confusion. The most extraordinary circumstance I have traced in connection with this aged couple, is, that there is a Miss Klem, their daughter, apparently ten years older than either of them, who has also a bed and smells of it, and carries it about the earth at dusk and hides it in deserted houses. I came into this piece of knowledge through Mrs. Klem's beseeching me to sanction the sheltering of Miss Klem under that roof for a single night, "between her takin' care of the upper part of a 'ouse in Pall Mall which the family of his back, and another 'ouse in Serjameses-street, which the family of leaves towng termorrer." I gave my gracious consent (having nothing that I know of to do with it), and in the shadowy hours Miss Klem became perceptible on the door-step, wrestling with a bed in a bundle. Where she made it up for the night I cannot positively state, but, I think, in a sink. I know that with the instinct of a reptile or an insect, she stowed it and herself away in deep obscurity. In the Klem family, I have noticed another remarkable gift of nature, and that is a power they possess of converting every thing into flue. Such broken victuals as they take by stealth, appear (whatever the nature of the viands) invariably to generate flue; and even the nightly pint of beer, instead of assimilating naturally, strikes me as breaking out in that form, equally on the shabby gown of Mrs. Klem, and the threadbare coat of her husband.

Mrs. Klem has no idea of my name—as to Mr. Klem, he has no idea of any thing—and only knows me as her good gentleman Thus, if doubtful whether I am in my room or no,

Mrs. Klems taps at the door and says, "Is my good gentleman here?" Or, if a messenger desiring to see me were consistent with my solitude, she would show him in with "Here is my good gentleman." I find this to be a generic custom. For, I meant to have observed before now, that in its Arcadian time all my part of London is indistinctly pervaded by the Klem species. They creep about with beds, and go to bed in miles of deserted houses. They hold no companionship, except that sometimes, after dark, two of them will emerge from opposite houses, and meet in the middle of the road as on neutral ground, or will peep from adjoining houses over an interposing barrier of area railings, and compare a few reserved mistrustful notes respecting their good ladies or good gentlemen. This I have discovered in the course of various solitary rambles I have taken northward from my retirement, along the awful perspectives of Wimpole-street, Harley-street, and similar frowning regions. Their effect would be scarcely distinguishable from that of the primeval forests, but for the Klem stragglers; these may be dimly observed, when the heavy shadows fall, flitting to and fro, putting up the door-chain, taking in the pint of beer, lowering like phantoms at the dark parlor windows, or secretly consorting underground with the dust-bin and the water cistern.

In the Burlington Arcade, I observe, with peculiar pleasure, a primitive state of manners to have superseded the baneful influences of ultra civilization. Nothing can surpass the innocence of the ladies' shoe-shops, the artificial flower repositories, and the head-dress depots. They are in strange hands at this time of year—hands of unaccustomed persons, who are imperfectly acquainted with the prices of the goods, and contemplate them with unsophisticated delight and wonder. The children of these virtuous people exchange familiarities in the Arcade, and temper the asperity of the two tall beadles. Their youthful prattle blends in an unwonted manner with the harmonious shade of the scene, and the general effect is, as of the voices of birds in a grove. In this happy restoration of the golden time, it has been my privilege even to see the bigger beadle's wife. She brought him his dinner in a basin, and he ate it in his arm-chair, and afterward fell asleep like a satiated child. At

Mr Truefitt's, the excellent hairdresser's, they are learning French to beguile the time ; and even the few solitaries left on guard at Mr. Atkinson's, the perfumer's round the corner (generally the most inexorable gentlemen in London, and the most scornful of three-and-six-pence), condescend a little as they drowsily bide or recall their turn for chasing the ebbing Neptune on the ribbed sea-sand. From Messrs. Hunt & Roskell's, the jewelers, all things are absent but the precious stones, and the gold and silver, and the soldierly pensioner at the door with his decorated breast. I might stand night and day for a month to come, in Saville-row, with my tongue out, yet not find a doctor to look at it for love or money. The dentists' instruments are rusting in their drawers, and their horrible cool parlors, where people pretend to read the Every-Day Book and not to be afraid, are doing penance for their grimness in white sheets. The light-weight of shrewd appearance, with one eye always shut up, as if he were eating a sharp gooseberry in all seasons, who usually stands at the gateway of the livery stables on very little legs under a very large waistcoat, has gone to Doncaster. Of such undesigning aspect is his guileless Yard now, with its gravel and scarlet beans, and the yellow Break housed under a glass roof in a corner, that I almost believe I could not be taken in there, if I tried. In the places of business of the great tailors, the cheval-glasses are dim and dusty for lack of being looked into. Ranges of brown paper coat and waistcoat bodies look as funereal as if they were the hatchments of the customers with whose names they are inscribed ; the measuring tapes hang idle on the wall ; the order-taker, left on the hopeless chance of some one looking in, yawns in the last extremity over the books of patterns, as if he were trying to read that entertaining library. The hotels in Brook street have no one in them, and the staffs of servants stare disconsolately for next season out of all the windows. The very man who goes about like an erect Turtle, between two boards recommendatory of the Sixteen Shilling Trowsers, is aware of himself as a hollow mockery, and eats filberts while he leans his hinder shell against a wall.

Among these tranquilizing objects, it is my delight to walk and meditate. Soothed by the repose around me, I wander insensibly to considerable distances, and guide myself back by the stars. Thus, I enjoy the contrast of a few still partially inhabited and busy spots where all the lights are not fled, where all the garlands are not dead, whence all but I have not departed. Then, does it appear to me that in this age three things are clamorously required of Man in the miscellaneous thoroughfares of the metropolis: Firstly, that he have his boots cleaned. Secondly, that he eat a penny ice. Thirdly, that he get himself photographed. Then do I speculate, What have these seam-worn artists been who stand at the photograph doors in Greek caps, sample in hand, and mysteriously salute the public—the female public with a pressing tenderness—to come in and be "took"? What did they do with their greasy blandishments before the era of cheap photography? Of what class were their previous victims, and how victimized? And how did they get, and how did they pay for, that large collection of likenesses, all purporting to have been taken inside, with the taking of none of which had that establishment any more to do than with the taking of Delhi?

But these are small oases, and I am soon back again in metropolitan Arcadia. It is my impression that much of its serene and peaceful character is attributable to the absence of customary Talk. How do I know but there may be subtle influences in Talk, to vex the souls of men who don't hear it? How do I know but that Talk, five, ten, or twenty miles off, may get into the air and disagree with me? If I get up, vaguely troubled and wearied and sick of my life in the session of Parliament, who shall say that my noble friend, my right reverend friend, my right honorable friend, my honorable friend, my honorable and learned friend, or my honorable and gallant friend, may not be responsible for that effect upon my nervous system? Too much Ozone in the air, I am informed and fully believe,—though I have no idea what it is,—would affect me in a remarkably disagreeable way; why may not too much Talk? I don't see or hear the Ozone; I don't see or hear the Talk. And there is so much Talk; so much too much; such loud cry, and such scant supply of wool; such a deal of fleecing, and so little fleece! Hence, in the Arcadian season, I find it a delicious triumph to walk down to deserted Westminster, and see the Courts shut up; to walk a little further and see the Two Houses shut up; to stand in the Abbey Yard, like the New Zealander of the grand English History (concerning which unfortunate man a rookery of mare's nests is generally being discovered), and gloat upon the ruins of Talk. Returning to my primitive solitude and lying down to sleep, my grateful heart expands with the consciousness that there is no adjourned Debate, no ministerial explanation, nobody to give notice of intention to ask the noble Lord at the head of her Majesty's Government five-and-twenty bootless questions in one, no term time with legal argument, no Nisi Prius with eloquent appeal to British Jury, that the air will to-morrow, and to-morrow, and to-morrow, remain untroubled by this superabundant generating of Talk. In a minor degree it is a delicious triumph to me to go into the club, and see the carpets up, and the Bores and the other dust dispersed to the four winds. Again, New Zealander-like, I stand on the cold hearth, and say in the solitude, "Here I watched Bore A 1, with voice always mysteriously low and head always mysteriously drooped, whispering political secrets into the ears of Adam's confiding children. Accursed be his memory forever and a day!"

But I have all this time been coming to the point, that the happy nature of my retirement is most sweetly expressed in its being the abode of Love. It is, as it were, an inexpensive Agapemone: nobody's speculation: every body's profit. The one great result of the resumption of primitive habits, and (convertible terms) the not having much to do, is, the abounding of Love.

The Klem species are incapable of the softer emotions; probably, in that low nomadic race, the softer emotions have all degenerated into flue. But with this exception, all the sharers of my retreat make love.

I have mentioned Saville-row. We all know the Doctor's servant. We all know what a respectable man he is, what a hard dry man, what a firm man, what a confidential man; how he lets us into the waiting-room, like a man who knows minutely what is the matter with us, but from whom the rack should not wring the secret. In the prosaic "season," he has distinctly the appearance of a man conscious of money in the savings bank, and taking his stand on his respectability with both feet. At that time it is as impossible to associate him with relaxation, or any human weakness, as it is to meet his eye without feeling guilty of indisposition. In the blest Arcadian time, how changed! I have seen him in a pepper-and-salt jacket—jacket—and drab trowsers, with his arm round the waist of a bootmaker's housemaid, smiling in open day. I have seen him at the pump by the Albany, unsolicitedly pumping for two fair young creatures, whose figures as they bent over their cans, were—if I may be allowed an original expression—a model for the sculptor. I have seen him trying the piano in the doctor's drawing-room with his forefinger, and have heard him humming tunes in praise of lovely woman. I have seen him seated on a fire engine, and going (obviously in search of excitement) to a fire. I saw him one moonlight evening when the peace and purity of our Arcadian west were at their height, polk with the lovely daughter of a cleaner of gloves, from the door-steps of his own residence, across Saville-row, round by Clifford-street and Old Burlington-street, back to Burlington-gardens. In this the Golden Age revived, or Iron London?

The Dentist's servant. Is that man no mystery to us, no type of invisible power? The tremendous individual knows (who else does?) what is done wiih the extracted teeth: he knows what goes on in the little room where something is always being washed or filed; he knows what warm spicy infusion is put into the comfortable tumbler from which we rinse our wounded mouth, with a gap in it that feels a foot wide; he knows whether the thing we spit into is a fixture communicating with the Thames, or could be cleared away for a dance; he sees the horrible parlor when there are no patients in it, and he could reveal, if he would, what becomes of the Every-Day Book then. The conviction of my coward conscience when I see that man in a professional light, is, that he knows all the statistics of my teeth and gums, my double teeth, my single teeth, my stopped teeth, and my sound. In this Arcadian rest, I am fearless of him as of a harmless powerless creature in a Scotch cap, who adores a young lady in a voluminous crinoline, at a neighboring billiard-room, and whose passion would be uninfluenced if every one of her teeth were false. They may be. He takes them all on trust.

In secluded corners of the place of my seclusion, there are little shops withdrawn from public curiosity, and never two together, where servants' perquisites are bought. The cook may dispose of grease at these modest and convenient marts; the butler, of bottles; the valet and lady's maid, of clothes; most servants, indeed, of most things they may happen to lay hold of. I have been told that in sterner times, loving correspondence otherwise interdicted may be maintained by letter through the agency of some of these useful establishments. In the Arcadian autumn, no such device is necessary. Every body loves, and openly and blamelessly loves. My landlord's young man loves the whole of one side of the way of Old Bond-street, and is beloved several doors up New Bond-street besides. I never look out of window but I see kissing of hands going on all around me. It is the morning custom to glide from shop to shop and exchange tender sentiments; it is the evening custom for couples to stand hand in hand at house doors, or roam, linked in that flowery manner, through the unpeopled streets. There is nothing else to do but love; and what there is to do, is done.

In unison with this pursuit, a chaste simplicity obtains in the domestic habits of Arcadia. Its few scattered people dine early, live moderately, sup socially, and sleep soundly. It is rumored that the Beadles of the Arcade, from being the mortal enemies of boys, have signed with tears an address to Lord Shaftsbury, and subscribed to a ragged school. No wonder! For they might turn their heavy maces into crooks and tend sheep in the Arcade, to the purling of the water-carts as they give the thirsty streets much more to drink than they can carry.

A happy Golden Age, and a serene tranquillity. Charming picture, but it will fade. The iron age will return, London will come back to town, if I show my tongue then in Saville-row for half a minute I shall be prescribed for, the Doctor's man and the Dentist's man will then pretend that these days of unprofessional innocence never existed. Where Mr. and Mrs. Klem and their bed will be, at that time, passes human knowledge; but my hatter hermitage will then know them no more, nor will it then know me. The desk at which I have written these meditations will retributively assist at the making out of my account, and the wheels of gorgeous carriages and the hoofs of high-stepping horses will crush the silence out of Bond-street —will grind Arcadia away, and give it to the elements in granite powder.

---

THE rising of the Italian people from under their unutterable wrongs, and the tardy burst of day upon them after the long long night of oppression that has darkened their beautiful country, has naturally caused my mind to dwell often of late on my own small wanderings in Italy. Connected with them, is a curious little drama, in which the character I myself sustained was so very subordinate, that I may relate its story without any fear of being suspected of self-display. It is strictly a true story.

I am newly arrived one summer evening, in a certain small town on the Mediterranean. I have had my dinner at the inn, and I and the musquitoes are coming out into the streets together. It is far from Naples; but a bright brown plump little woman-servant at the inn, is a Neapolitan, and is so vivaciously expert in pantomimic action, that in the single moment of answering my request to have a pair of shoes cleaned which I left up-stairs, she plies imaginary brushes, and goes completely through the motions of polishing the shoes up, and laying them at my feet. I smile at the brisk little women in perfect satisfaction with her briskness; and the brisk little woman, amiably pleased with me because I am pleased with her, claps her hands and laughs delightfully. We are in the inn yard. As the little woman's bright eyes sparkle on the cigarette I am smoking, I make bold to offer her one; she accepts it none the less merrily, because I touch a most charming little dimple in her fat cheek, with its light paper end. Glancing up at the many green lattices to assure herself that the mistress is not looking on, the little woman then puts her two little dimpled arms a-kimbo, and stands on tiptoe to light her cigarette at mine. "And now, dear little sir," says she, puffing out smoke in a most innocent and Cherubic manner, " keep quite straight on, take the first to the right, and probably you will see him standing at his door."

I have a commission to "him," and I have been inquiring

about him. I have carried the commission about Italy, several months. Before I left England, there came to me one night a certain generous and gentle English nobleman—he is dead in these days when I relate the story, and exiles have lost their best British friend,—with this request: "Whenever you come to such a town, will you seek out one Giovanni Carlavero, who keeps a little wine-shop there, mention my name to him suddenly, and observe how it affects him?" I accepted the trust, and am on my way to discharge it.

The sirocco has been blowing all day, and it is a hot unwholesome evening with no cool sea-breeze. Musquitoes and fire-flies are lively enough, but most other creatures are faint. The coquettish airs of pretty young women in the tiniest and wickedest of dolls' straw hats, who lean out at opened lattice blinds, are almost the only airs stirring. Very ugly and haggard old women with distaffs, and with a gray tow upon them that looks as if they were spinning ou their own hair (It suppose they were once pretty, too, but it is very difficult to believe so), sit on the footway leaning against house walls. Every body who has come for water to the fountain, stays there, and seems incapable of any such energetic idea as going home. Vespers are over, though not so long but that I can smell the heavy resinous incense as I pass the church. No man seems to be at work, save the coppersmith. In an Italian town he is always at work, and always thumping in the deadliest manner.

I keep straight on, and come in due time to the first on the right: a narrow dull street, where I see a well-favored man of good stature and military bearing, in a great cloak, standing at a door. Drawing nearer to this threshold, I see it is the threshold of a small wine-shop; and I can just make out, in the dim light, the inscription that it is kept by Giovanni Carlavero.

I touch my hat to the figure in the cloak, and pass in, and draw a stool to a little table. The lamp (just such another as they dig out of Pompeii) is lighted, but the place is empty. The figure in the cloak has followed me in, and stands before me.

"The master?"

"At your service, sir."

"Please to give me a glass of the wine of the country."

He turns to a little counter, to get it. As his striking face is pale, and his action is evidently that of an enfeebled man, I remark that I fear he has been ill. It is not much, he courteously and gravely answers, though bad while it lasts: the fever.

As he sets the wine on the little table, to his manifest surprise I lay my hand on the back of his, look him in the face, and say in a low voice: "I am an Englishman, and you are acquainted with a friend of mine. Do you recollect —— ?" and I mention the name of my generous countryman.

Instantly, he utters a loud cry, bursts into tears, and falls on his knees at my feet, clasping my legs in both his arms and bowing his head to the ground.

Some years ago, this man at my feet, whose overfraught heart is heaving as if it would burst from his breast, and whose tears are wet upon the dress I wear, was a galley-slave in the North of Italy. He was a political offender, having been concerned in the then last rising, and was sentenced to imprisonment for life. That he would have died in his chains, is certain, but for the circumstance that the Englishman happened to visit his prison.

It was one of the vile old prisons of Italy, and a part of it was below the waters of the harbor. The place of his confinement was an arched underground and under-water gallery, with a grill-gate at the entrance, through which it received such light and air as it got. Its condition was insufferably foul, and a stranger could hardly breathe in it, or see in it with the aid of a torch. At the upper end of this dungeon, and consequently in the worst position, as being the furthest removed from light and air, the Englishman first beheld him, sitting on an iron bedstead to which he was chained by a heavy chain. His countenance impressed the Englishman as having nothing in common with the faces of the malefactors with whom he was associated, and he talked with him, and learned how he came to be there.

When the Englishman emerged from the dreadful den into the light of day, he asked his conductor, the governor of the jail, why Giovanni Carlavero was put into the worst place?

"Because he is particularly recommended," was the stringent answer.

"Recommended, that is to say, for death?"

"Excuse me; particularly recommended," was again the answer.

"He has a bad tumor in his neck, no doubt occasioned by the hardship of his miserable life. If it continues to be neglected, and he remains where he is, it will kill him."

"Excuse me, I can do nothing. He is particularly recommended."

The Englishman was staying in that town, and he went to his home there; but the figure of this man chained to the bedstead made it no home, and destroyed his rest and peace. He was an Englishman of an extraordinarily tender heart, and he could not bear the picture. He went back to the prison gate: went back again and again, and talked to the man and cheered him. He used his utmost influence to get the man unchained from the bedstead, were it only for ever so short a time in the day, and permitted to come to the grate. It took a long time, but the Englishman's station, personal character, and steadiness of purpose, wore out opposition so far, and that grace was at last accorded. Through the bars, when he could thus get light upon the tumor, the Englishman lanced it, and it did well, and healed. His strong interest in the prisoner had greatly increased by this time, and he formed the desperate resolution that he would exert his utmost self-devotion and use his utmost efforts, to get Carlavero pardoned.

If the prisoner had been a brigand and a murderer, if he had committed every non-political crime in the Newgate Calendar and out of it, nothing would have been easier than for a man of any court or priestly influence to obtain his release. As it was, nothing could have been more difficult. Italian authorities, and English authorities who had interest with them, alike assured the Englishman that his object was hopeless. He met with nothing but evasion, refusal, and ridicule. His political prisoner became a joke in the place. It was especially observable that English Circumlocution, and English Society on its travels, were as humorous on the subject as Circumlocution and Society may be on any subject without loss of caste. But, the Englishman possessed (and proved it well in his life) a courage very uncommon among us: he had not the least fear of being considered a bore, in a good, humane cause. So he went on persistently trying, and trying, and trying, to get Giovanni Carlavero out. That prisoner had been rigorously rechained, after the tumor operation, and it was not likely that his miserable life could last very long.

One day, when all the town knew about the Englishman and his political prisoner, there came to the Englishman, a certain sprightly Italian Advocate of whom he had some knowledge; and he made this strange proposal: "Give me a hundred pounds to obtain Carlavero's release. I think I can get him a pardon, with that money. But I cannot tell you what I am going to do with the money, nor must you ever ask me the question if I succeed, nor must you ever ask me for an account of the money if I fail." The Englishman decided to hazard the hundred pounds. He did so, and heard not another word of the matter. For half a year and more, the Advocate made no sign, and never once "took on" in any way, to have the subject on his mind. The Englishman was then obliged to change his residence to another and more famous town in the North of Italy. He parted from the poor prisoner with a sorrowful heart, as from a doomed man for whom there was no release but Death.

The Englishman lived in his new place of abode another half-year or more, and had no tidings of the wretched prisoner. At length, one day, he received from the Advocate a cool, concise, mysterious note, to this effect. "If you still wish to bestow that benefit upon the man in whom you were once interested, send me fifty pounds more, and I think it can be insured." Now, the Englishman had long settled in his mind that the Advocate was a heartless sharper, who had preyed upon his credulity and his interest in an unfortunate sufferer. So, he sat down and wrote a dry answer, giving the Advocate to understand that he was wiser now than he had been formerly, and that no more money was extractable from his pocket.

He lived outside the city gates, some mile or two from the post-office, and was accustomed to walk into the city with his letters and post them himself. On a lovely spring day, when the sky was exquisitely blue, and the sea Divinely beautiful, he took his usual walk, carrying this letter to the Advocate in his pocket. As he went along, his gentle heart was much moved by the loveliness of the prospect, and by the thought of the slowly-dying prisoner chained to the bedstead, for whom the universe had no delights. As he drew nearer and nearer to the city where he was to post the letter, he became very uneasy in his mind. He debated with himself, was it remotely possible, after all, that this sum of fifty pounds could restore the fellow-creature whom he pitied so much, and for whom he had striven so hard, to liberty? He was not a conventionally rich Englishman—very far from that—but he had a spare fifty pounds at the banker's. He resolved to risk it. Without doubt, GOD has recompensed him for the resolution.

He went to the banker's, and got a bill for the amount, and inclosed it in a letter to the Advocate that I wish I could have seen. He simply told the Advocate that he was quite a poor man, and that he was sensible it might be a great weakness in him to part with so much money on the faith of so vague a communication; but that there it was, and that he prayed the Advocate to make a good use of it. If he did otherwise no good could ever come of it, and it would lie heavy on his soul one day.

Within a week, the Englishman was sitting at his breakfast, when he heard some suppressed sounds of agitation on the staircase, and Giovanni Carlavero leaped into his room and fell upon his breast, a free man!

Conscious of having wronged the Advocate in his own thoughts, the Englishman wrote him an earnest and grateful letter, avowing the fact, and entreating him to confide by what means and through what agency he had succeeded so well. The Advocate returned for answer through the post.

"There are many thing, as you know, in this Italy of ours, that are safest and best not even spoken of—far less written of. We may meet some day, and then I may tell you what you want to know; not here, and now." But, the two never did meet again. The Advocate was dead when the Englishman gave me my trust; and how the man had been set free, remained as great a mystery to the Englishman, and to the man himself, as it was to me.

But, I knew this:—here was the man, this sultry night, on his knees at my feet, because I was the Englishman's friend; here were his tears upon my dress; here were his sobs choking his utterance; here were his kisses on my hands, because they had touched the hands that had worked out his release. He had no need to tell me it would be happiness to him to die for his benefactor; I doubt if I ever saw real, sterling, fervent gratitude of soul, before or since.

He was much watched and suspected, he said, and had had enough to do to keep himself out of trouble. This, and his not having prospered in his worldly affairs, had led to his having failed in his usual communications to the Englishman for—as I now remember the period—some two or three years. But, his prospects were brighter, and his wife who had been very ill had recovered, and his fever had left him, and he had bought a little vineyard, and would I carry to his benefactor the first of its wine? Ay, that I would (I told him with enthusiasm), and not a drop, of it should be spilled or lost!

He had cautiously closed the door before speaking of himself, and had talked with such excess of emotion, and in a provincial Italian so difficult to understand, that I had more than once been obliged to stop him, and beg him to have compassion on me and be slower and calmer. By degrees he became so, and tranquilly walked back with me to the hotel. There, I sat down before I went to bed and wrote a faithful account of him to the Englishman: which I concluded by saying that I would bring the wine home, against any difficulties, every drop.

Early next morning when I came out at the hotel door to pursue my journey, I found my friend waiting with one of those immense bottles in which the Italian peasants store their wine—a bottle holding some half-dozen gallons—bound round with basket-work for greater safety on the journey. I see him now, in the bright sunlight, tears of gratitude in his eyes, proudly inviting my attention to this corpulent bottle. (At the street corner hard by, two high-flavored, able-bodied monks—pretending to talk together, but keeping their four evil eyes upon us.)

How the bottle had been got there, did not appear; but the

difficulty of getting it into the ramshackle vetturino carriage in which I was departing, was so great, and it took up so much room when it was got in, that I elected to sit outside. The last I saw of Giovanni Carlavero was his running through the town by the side of the jingling wheels, clasping my hand as I stretched it down from the box, charging me with a thousand last loving and dutiful messages to his dear patron, and finally looking in at the bottle as it reposed inside, with an admiration of its honorable way of traveling that was beyond measure delightful.

And now, what disquiet of mind this dearly-beloved and highly-treasured Bottle began to cost me, no man knows. It was my precious charge through a long tour, and, for hundreds of miles, I never had it off my mind by day or by night. Over bad roads—and they were many—I clung to it with affectionate desperation. Up mountains, I looked in at it and saw it helplessly tilting over on its back, with terror. At innumerable inn doors when the weather was bad, I was obliged to be put into my vehicle before the Bottle could be got in, and was obliged to have the Bottle lifted out before human aid could come near me. The Imp of the same name, except that his associations were all evil and these associations were all good, would have been a less troublesome traveling companion. I might have served Mr. Cruikshank as a subject for a new illustration of the miseries of the Bottle. The National Temperance Society might have made a powerful Tract of me.

The suspicions that attached to this innocent Bottle, greatly aggravated my difficulties. It was like the apple-pie in the child's book. Parma pouted at it, Modena mocked it, Tuscany tackled it, Naples nibbled it, Rome refused it, Austria accused it, Soldiers suspected it, Jesuits jobbed it. I composed a neat Oration, developing my inoffensive intentions in connection with this Bottle, and delivered it in an infinity of guard-houses, at a multitude of town gates, and on every draw-bridge, angle, and rampart, of a complete system of fortifications. Fifty times a day, I got down to harangue an infuriated soldiery about the Bottle. Through the filthy degradation of the abject and vile Roman states, I had as much difficulty in working my way with the Bottle, as if it had bottled up a complete system of heretical theology. In the Neapolitan country, where every body was a spy, a soldier, a priest or a lazarone, the shameless beggars of all four denominations incessantly pounced on the Bottle and made it a pretext for extorting money from me. Quires —quires do I say? Reams—of forms illegibly printed on whity-brown paper were filled up about the Bottle, and it was the subject of more stamping and sanding than I had ever seen before. In consequence of which haze of sand, perhaps, it was always irregular, and always latent with dismal penalties of going back, or not going forward, which were only to be abated by the silver crossing of a base hand, poked shirtless out of a ragged uniform sleeve. Under all discouragements, however, I stuck to my Bottle, and held firm to my resolution that every drop of its contents should reach the Bottle's destination.

The latter refinement cost me a separate heap of troubles on its own separate account. What corkscrews did I see the military power bring out against that Bottle: what gimlets, spikes, divining rods, gauges, and unknown tests and instruments! At some places they persisted in declaring that the wine must not be passed, without being opened and tasted; I, pleading to the contrary, used then to argue the question seated on the Bottle lest they should open it in spite of me. In the southern parts of Italy, more violent shrieking, face-making, and gesticulating, greater vehemence of speech and countenance and action, went on about that Bottle than would attend fifty murders in a northern latitude. It raised important functionaries out of their beds, in the dead of night. I have known half a dozen military lanterns to disperse themselves at all points of a great sleeping Piazza, each lantern summoning some official creature to get up, put on his cocked hat instantly, and come and stop the Bottle. It was characteristic that while this innocent Bottle had such immense difficulty in getting from little town to town, Signor Mazzini and the fiery cross were traversing Italy from end to end.

Still, I stuck to my Bottle, like any fine old English gentleman all of the olden time. The more the Bottle was interfered with, the stauncher I became (if possible) in my first determination that my countryman should have it delivered to him intact, as the man whom he had so nobly restored to life and liberty had delivered it to me. If ever I have been obstinate in my days—and I may have been, say, once or twice—I was obstinate about the Bottle. But I made it a rule always to keep a pocket full of small coin at its service, and never to be out of temper in its cause. Thus I and the Bottle made our way. Once, we had a break-down; rather a bad break-down, on a steep high place with the sea below us, on a tempestuous evening when it blew great guns. We were driving four wild horses abreast, Southern fashion, and there was some little difficulty in stopping them. I was outside, and not thrown off; but no words can describe my feelings when I saw the Bottle—traveling inside, as usual—burst the door open, and roll obesely out into the road. A blessed Bottle with a charmed existence, he took no hurt, and we repaired damage, and went on triumphant.

A thousand representations were made to me that the Bottle must be left at this place, or that, and called for again. I never yielded to one of them, and never parted from the Bottle, on any pretense, consideration, th[illegible]eaty. I had no faith in any official receipt for the Bottle, and nothing would induce me to accept one. These unmanageable politics at last brought me and the Bottle, still triumphant, to Genoa. There, I took a tender and reluctant leave of him for a few weeks, and consigned him to a trusty English captain, to be conveyed to the Port of London by sea.

While the Bottle was on his voyage to England I read the Shipping Intelligence as anxiously as if I had been an underwriter. There was some stormy weather after I myself had got to England by way of Switzerland and France, and my mind greatly misgave me that the Bottle might be wrecked. At last to my great joy, I received notice of his safe arrival, and immediately went down to Saint Katharine's Docks, and found him in a state of honorable captivity in the Custom House.

The wine was mere vinegar when I set it down before the generous Englishman—probably it had been something like vinegar when I took it up from Giovanni Carlavero—but not a drop of it was spilled or gone. And the Englishman told me, with much emotion in his face and voice, that he had never tasted wine that seemed to him so sweet and sound. And long afterward, the Bottle graced his table. And the last time I saw him in this world that misses him, he took me aside in a crowd, to say, with his amiable smile: "We were talking of you only to-day at dinner, and I wished you had been there, for I had some claret up in Carlavero's Bottle."

THE END.

www.ingramcontent.com/pod-product-compliance
Lightning Source LLC
LaVergne TN
LVHW021121110826
845150LV00005B/905

* 9 7 8 1 4 2 5 5 5 1 6 0 5 *